# WORDS FOR WORSHIP

*Compiled and Edited by*
CHRISTOPHER CAMPLING
and MICHAEL DAVIS

Edward Arnold

First published in 1969
by Edward Arnold (Publishers) Ltd.
41 Bedford Square, London WC1B 3DQ

Reprinted 1970, 1972, 1974
Reprinted as a paperback 1977
Reprinted 1979, 1982

ISBN: 07131 0148 2

For Margaret, Anne, Robert, Penelope
Angela and Peter



Printed in Great Britain by
WESTERN PRINTING SERVICES LTD
BRISTOL

# WORDS FOR WORSHIP

# Preface

We hope that this book will be useful to men and women of all denominations who arrange school assemblies and religious services for boys and girls of secondary school age. Our aim has been to provide plenty of varied material for large congregations as at a full school assembly, and small groups as at house prayers. We have had particularly in mind the planning of short week-day services, but the material in this book would be equally suitable for longer services, such as those held on Sundays at boarding schools.

The editors wish to thank all the many kind people who have helped them to compile this book, in particular the Rev. Peter Allen, the Rev. Edward Bailey, Ian Birnie, the Rev. R. J. Bowyer, Juliet Campling, Brother Cassian, P. A. Coggin, Mrs. Joyce Cooper, John Dancy, Ian Davie, Elaine Davis, the Rev. F. Deacon, Laurence Ellis, the Rev. Peter Hancock, the Rev. Peter Hardman, Nicholas Milner-Gulland, the Rev. Guy Mindelsohn, Rachel Philips, Dennis Silk and John Thompson.

# Contents

Preface *page* v

Introduction *page* xi

BIBLE READINGS Items 1–106

THE CHRISTIAN LIFE Items 1–38

The Beatitudes 1–9. The Bible 10. A Christian Community 11. Christian Living 12. Compassion 13. Detachment 14. Eternal Life 15. The Eucharist 16–17. The House of God 18. Faith 19. Laws and Commandments 20–21. Martyrdom 22. Membership: Baptism and Confirmation 23. Men for God 24. Missionaries 25. The Ten Commandments 26–36. Vocation 37–38.

THE CHURCH'S YEAR Items 39–85

Advent to Trinity 39–63. Saints' Days 64–84. Harvest Thanksgiving 85.

THE SCHOOL YEAR Items 86–88

The Beginning of Term 86. An Important School Occasion 87. The End of Term 88.

FROM THE OLD TESTAMENT Items 89–96

The Journey to the Promised Land 89. The People's Reluctance to Enter the Promised Land 90. Lessons from the Book of Daniel 91–95. The Book of Jonah (The Reluctant Missionary) 96.

JESUS CHRIST Items 97–101

The Good Shepherd 97. What Jesus Does for Men 98–99. Opposition to Jesus 100–101.

THE TEACHING OF JESUS Items 102–106

The Sermon on the Mount 102. Parables of Jesus 103–106.

PRAYERS Items 107–604

GENERAL PRAYERS OF INVOCATION Items 107–237

Opening Prayers 107–115. Prayers of Praise 116–133. Prayers of Thanksgiving 134–158. Prayers of Confession and Forgiveness 159–188. Prayers of Self-Dedication 189–204. Morning Prayers 205–221. Evening Prayers 222–237.

PRAYERS FOR LIFE AND LIVING Items 238–443

In Activities and Work 238–251. Attitude to and Relationship with Other People 252–281. The Church's Year (Advent to Trinity) 282–315. Saints' Days 316–346. Church and State Occasions 347–357. School Term 358–365. Feelings, Senses, Faculties 366–378. Concerning Virtues, Vices and Values 379–443.

RELATIONSHIP WITH GOD Items 444–487

Come Close, O God 444–448. Grace to know and do the Will of God 449–460. Spiritual Gifts 461–474. Jesus Christ 475–481. True Response to God 482–487.

PRAYERS FOR THE WORLD, NATIONS, INSTITUTIONS, PEOPLE Items 488–560

All Sorts and Conditions of Men and Creatures 488–536. The Church 537–547. The School and its Members Past and Present 548–560.

LITANIES AND ACTS OF WORSHIP REQUIRING A SPOKEN RESPONSE Items 561–574

EXTENDED PRAYERS AND MEDITATIONS Items 575–588

Meditations by Michel Quoist 580–588.

CLOSING PRAYERS Items 589–604

After Other Prayers 589–591. After Worship 592–604.

READINGS Items 605–825

THE LIFE, DEATH AND RESURRECTION OF JESUS CHRIST Items 605–618

THE CHRISTIAN CHURCH AND CHRISTIAN ACTIVITY AND WORSHIP Items 619–629

GOD AND NATURE Items 630–642

GOD AND MANKIND Items 643–652

ATTITUDES TO GOD, TO LIFE AND TO OURSELVES Items 653–680

THE BODY Items 681–687

CHALLENGE AND ACTION Items 688–696

FREEDOM AND LOVE Items 697–702

ATTITUDES TO OTHER PEOPLE Items 703–714

HELPING OTHER PEOPLE Items 715–720
DISCIPLES, SAINTS AND CRUSADERS Items 721–725
PEOPLE AND SOCIETY Items 726–739
WEALTH Items 740–741
SUFFERING Items 742–751
DEATH AND ETERNITY Items 752–760
FABLES AND LEGENDS Items 761–772
SHORT READINGS Items 773–825

INDEXES
BIBLE READINGS with cross references to Prayers and Readings *page* 439
PRAYERS with cross references to Bible Readings and Readings *page* 447
READINGS with cross references to Bible Readings and Prayers *page* 454

ACKNOWLEDGEMENTS *page* 461

# Introduction

## CHOOSING MATERIAL FOR SERVICES

Teachers and other adults responsible for planning assemblies and services are usually very busy people. They can seldom find much time for digging out from the Bible, from books of prayers and from secular writings, material precisely suited to their needs. We hope that we have done much of the necessary spade-work for them, by digging out a wide selection of material, and that we have presented it to them in a way which makes their final choice easy and swift. This final choice must be left to the individual, because he knows his particular congregation and the precise circumstances in which the service will be held. We have not produced a book of rigid, prefabricated services, but a do-it-yourself kit so that each user of the book can make up the services he or she needs, can choose a Bible reading or a secular reading or both, one prayer or two or three or none, a litany, a meditation or a period of silence. The order of the material, too, remains for the service-builder to decide.

## HOW TO USE THE INDEXES

Because some further help may be welcome, however, we have suggested, in the indexes which follow the material for services, various combinations of items.

There are three indexes, one each for *Bible Readings*, *Prayers*, and *Readings*. These indexes enable the user to start from any item in any of the three sections and from there to compile a complete service with a common theme. Most entries in each section offer a number of alternatives, thus allowing the compiler great scope in varying the content and length of any service.

A diagram on the opposite page shows how the *Readings* index works. The other two indexes follow this principle but in a different order. In all indexes the type conventions are the same.

Ribbon markers have been provided so that the service-builder does not lose track of material that he is considering.

## BIBLE READINGS

Our selection of readings from the Old Testament, New Testament and Apocrypha provides for a wide variety of approaches.

Groups of readings, which we have based roughly on the plan of services being built up a week at a time, can be cut, combined or augmented at the reader's discretion. Many individual readings can be lengthened or shortened. For example, in 7 (e) we have left it to the service-planner to decide whether verses 15–24 and 29–33 are to be added. Brief headings and a few explanations have been provided, and some congregations may benefit by hearing them read aloud or by seeing them written on a notice-board.

Which translation to use is also something for the service-planner to decide. Probably the best modern translations of the Old Testament are the Revised Standard Version and the Jerusalem Bible, and of the New Testament the best translations are probably those two and J. B. Phillips's and the New English Bible. We have suggested particular translations of a few readings, for instance when the Authorised Version is difficult to understand. Because most Bibles do not include the Apocrypha, we have said which readings come from it: the clearest translation of them is the Jerusalem Bible, which we recommend.

## PRAYERS

The prayers suggested in the indexes are, for any one service, often very different in age, style and length. We expect that some service-builders will want consistency and others will want variety, their preference being influenced partly by their congregation and partly by the time and place of the service.

To address God both as 'thou' and 'you' in one service does seem incongruous. However, although 'you' is now appropriate, old prayers cannot be modernized without losing their harmony of tone. New prayers which call God 'thou' usually sound synthetic. Schoolchildren, who sometimes welcome the chance to write prayers for their services, often succeed when they are encouraged to use natural modern rhythms and to call God 'you'.

We think that good prayers of different ages generally go well together: but when consistency is needed, we hope that users of the indexes will find that we have recommended enough prayers for them to choose from.

## LITANIES

We have included litanies in the belief that they can help some congregations to pray in a more active, participating manner.

It is true that litanies are more open to abuse than ordinary prayers, but rightly used they can give a strong sense of corporate worship. We have adapted them in order to make the congregation's cues as obvious as possible. If each member of the congregation can be given a typed copy, the responses will probably gain vigour and crispness.

## MEDITATIONS

We have included some meditations which, if well read, can be extremely effective, especially for smaller and more mature groups. Although the indexes suggest combining Michel Quoist's meditations with other material, a service might consist only of one meditation, some music, and a blessing or grace.

Most of the readings, prayers and litanies in this book can well be given to boys and girls to speak aloud at services and assemblies, provided that adults supervise rehearsals and insist on a high standard: but when Michel Quoist's meditations are read aloud, the best reader is probably a man.

## READINGS

This anthology includes more readings on some themes than on others. For example, there are many pieces about mountains but very few on flight, many about colour prejudice but few about old people. We have tried to provide a large number of readings on a few subjects, and a few readings on each of a wide range of subjects. We know that we have far from exhausted the possible readings even on those subjects which we have covered most fully.

A service-builder who wants fuller treatment of a subject may feel encouraged to find more readings about it, perhaps asking his pupils to dig out suitable pieces of material from books that he suggests. He may consider, too, asking boys and girls to pick out from newspapers very short passages that can be used to reveal topical attitudes towards chosen themes: for instance, number 788 on possessions and number 814 on race.

We have shortened many of the pieces for reading aloud. A few unnecessary phrases can seriously weaken a reading. Some users of this book may wish to make further cuts to suit their congregations. When we have taken many extracts from one book (such as Children of the Sun) we have tried to make each extract as self-sufficient as possible, even though we hope that the extracts will be read in consecutive services, as a serial.

Like Michel Quoist's meditations, some of the readings may need little other material in a service: perhaps a hymn, a short period of silence and a grace or a blessing; maybe even less.

Most of the prose is straightforward and it can, if the service-builder wishes, be read aloud effectively by an articulate boy or girl after some rehearsal. Extracts arranged as a serial gain an air of continuity if one person reads them all. However, if each extract is entrusted to a different reader, variety and a sense of wider participation can be achieved and may appeal to a young congregation.

Poetry should only be entrusted to a talented reader who can be relied on to speak it properly. When well spoken by a skilful reader who has given time to preparation with a tape-recorder and to rehearsal with a live critic, poetry can be superbly effective. Complex poems are not the only ones that need care: even the simplest verse demands it.

## MUSIC

We have included a few folk hymns and their music (for instance, items 610 and 614) because these may be particularly acceptable now when many children play guitars. We regret that we lack room to include more, and that we cannot extend the scope of this already large book to include suggestions for hymns and for recorded music, sacred and secular. We know that listening to music is being increasingly accepted as a valuable part of services for young people, and we hope that our themes and readings may stimulate school musicians to match them with suitable music, whether recorded or performed.

## SILENCE

Periods of silence are sometimes appreciated by congregations of boys and girls. The silence may be used for private prayer, for personal thought, or for considering some earlier part of the service.

The length of the silence must be controlled by the person taking the service who must be sensitive to the feelings of the congregation. The silence should end before the shuffling starts, and the ending should be firmly announced with words or music. We find that for young congregations several short periods of silence (for example, between the words 'let us pray for . . .' and the actual prayer) are better than pre-announced long periods. Silence should be seen as an essential part of corporate worship, not as an extra item occasionally added to it. Silence may be the most demanding part of worship, but often it is the most rewarding.

## THEMES

We have grouped Bible readings and readings together under 'themes' partly because the subjects are too big for a single reading and partly because it is good that daily worship should be seen as part of a pattern. There are certainly many other themes which could be traced from the readings in different parts of this book. For example, readings could be linked to develop such themes as 'What is Man?', 'Ambition', 'The Generations', 'Violence' and 'Personal Relations'.

Some schools like to have a pattern of worship that repeats itself each week, for example 'Praise and Thanksgiving' on Monday, 'My Neighbour' on Tuesday, 'The School' on Wednesday, 'Service' on Thursday, and 'Penitence' on Friday. From this book, readings and prayers can be chosen for each theme of the day.

## PARTICIPATION BY CHILDREN

As the responsibility for building services is generally taken by adults, we have thought of this book being used by them rather than by the boys and girls themselves. But in many schools, pupils are playing an increasing part in devising and conducting services. The results are often lively, relevant and fresh. When it is generally known in a school that a teacher and pupils have jointly created a service, the atmosphere in which it is held can gain vitality and harmony. We hope that this book will be useful in such joint planning by adults and children, and also suitable for lending to boys and girls when they take over the planning of a service, for instance in those schools where services are made the responsibility of different forms in turn.

## RESOURCES

Many services, in which we hope that this book will be used, will be enriched by groups of musicians, choirs and organs. Other such services will perhaps be illustrated by paintings or photographs projected onto a screen, or by slides, short films or film-strips. Some service-builders will use panel-discussions, short plays, mimes and dances, tape-recordings of voices and natural sounds as well as of music. A wealth of techniques awaits people who are willing to experiment. To fully explore the possibilities of sound, sight and movement in worship should be an exciting development in school assemblies and services for young people.

## CONCLUSION

Throughout this book we have tried to keep in mind the main object of worship which is to perceive God in the whole of life, and to offer the whole of life to God: so that religion becomes life-centred, and life becomes God-centred. We hope that the words we offer in this book will help to achieve that purpose and will be found useful and acceptable for worship.

# The Christian Life

## 1 THE BEATITUDES 1

'Blessed are the poor in spirit: for theirs is the Kingdom of Heaven.' (Matthew 5.3 AV)

*'Poor in spirit' does not mean 'weak in spirit': it means 'willingness to be poor'.*

'How blest are those who know that they are poor; the kingdom of Heaven is theirs.' (Matthew 5.3 NEB)

(a) LUKE 2.1–7 Jesus himself, the King of Kings, is born in a common stable.
(b) LUKE 14.16–24 Jesus tells a parable about people who are too busy with their affairs to accept an invitation to a feast.
(c) ACTS 4.31–37 The first Christians shared their possessions; and Barnabas gave up everything to join them.
(d) 2 CORINTHIANS 6.1, 3–10 Paul speaks of the contrast between earthly suffering and poverty on the one hand, and the rich blessing of the Christian life, on the other.
(e) 1 TIMOTHY 6.7–11 (AV) Strong words against greed.

## 2 THE BEATITUDES 2

'Blessed are they that mourn: for they shall be comforted.' (Matthew 5.4 AV)
'How blest are the sorrowful; they shall find consolation.' (Matthew 5.4 NEB)

(a) 2 SAMUEL 1.17–27 David mourns over the death of Saul and Jonathan.
(b) 2 SAMUEL 12.1–23 (this could be split at verse 14) King David has murdered Uriah in order to marry his wife, Bathsheba, with whom he has committed adultery. He is punished, and mourns for his sin and for his punishment. But when it is over he goes on living.
(c) 2 SAMUEL 18.19–33 King David's favourite son, Absalom, has led a rebellion against him and has been killed. This is the story of the news of the battle and of Absalom's death being brought to David. David weeps because of his love for Absalom.
(d) LUKE 13.31–34; 19.41–44 Jesus mourns over the fate of Jerusalem.
(e) JOHN 11.30–46 Moved by Mary's grief, Jesus mourns because

his friend Lazarus is dead. He gives life to Lazarus, and we are told later that this action is the immediate cause of his own death.

## 3 THE BEATITUDES 3

'Blessed are the meek: for they shall inherit the earth.' (Matthew 5.5 AV)

*'Meekness' means 'humility', the opposite to 'arrogance'. We are not asked to pretend that we have no goodness in us, or to be hypocritical or cowardly. We* are *asked to recognize that we have nothing of ourselves, that we are in all things dependent upon God and other people, and that others are dependent upon us. A humble man, therefore, acknowledges his gifts, is open to listen and to receive, and is ready to serve others.*

'How blest are those of gentle spirit; they shall have the earth for their possession.' (Matthew 5.5 NEB)

(a) GENESIS 3.1–6, 22–24 Human pride makes man disobedient and causes him to fall from God.
(b) GENESIS 11.1–9 This story of the Tower of Babel is a myth told to provide an explanation for the origin of different languages, which in Old Testament times were regarded as a sign of the disunity of mankind. Today we regard the diversities of language and culture as something which enriches rather than divides the human race. Nevertheless, the moral of the story stands: that human pride has caused the disaster of human disunity.
(c) I SAMUEL 17.38–50 A man who trusts God overcomes a boaster who glories in his own human strength.
(d) MARK 10.35–45 A lesson in humility.
(e) JOHN 13.1–17 Jesus gives a practical example of humble service.
(f) PHILIPPIANS 2.3–11 Paul speaks of the humility of Christ.
(g) PSALM 37.1–11

## 4 THE BEATITUDES 4

'Blessed are they which do hunger and thirst after righteousness: for they shall be filled.' (Matthew 5.6 AV)

*'To hunger and thirst after righteousness' means 'to want passionately the right—justice, truth, goodness—to prevail'.*

'How blest are those who hunger and thirst to see right prevail; they shall be satisfied.' (Matthew 5.6 NEB)

(a) AMOS 5.(11–13) 14–15 (16–20) 21–24 Amos rebukes the people for their vicious ways, in particular for the insincerity of their religion, and from verse 21 onwards ('I hate, I despise your feast days . . .') he imagines the utterance of God. 'In the gate' is equivalent to 'in the law-court'.

(b) ISAIAH 5.8–12, 20–24 A generation after Amos, the Prophet Isaiah preaches the same message of righteousness.

(c) I KINGS 3.16–28 King Solomon, who prayed for the gift of wisdom, exercises it when called upon to give righteous judgement.

(d) APOCRYPHA: WISDOM OF SOLOMON 3.1–8 The rewards of righteousness.

(e) PROVERBS 10.5–14 or 12.1–8 or 13.1–9 Righteousness is commended.

(f) MARK 11.15–19 Jesus shows righteous anger in clearing the Temple Court for prayer.

(g) MATTHEW 7.15–29 Righteousness means *doing* the word of God.

## 5 THE BEATITUDES 5 (i)

'Blessed are the merciful: for they shall obtain mercy.' (Matthew 5.7 AV)

*'The merciful' can mean 'those who forgive' and also 'those who help people in need'. This series of readings is concerned with the mercy of forgiveness.*

'How blest are those who show mercy; mercy shall be shown to them.' (Matthew 5.7 NEB)

(a) MARK 2.1–12 Jesus brings forgiveness and healing to a paralysed man.

(b) LUKE 23.33–34 Jesus prays for the forgiveness of those who crucify him.

(c) MATTHEW 18.21–35 The duty and logic of Christian forgiveness.

(d) I PETER 2.21–24 The example of Christ himself.

(e) ACTS 7.54–60 Stephen follows Jesus' example and prays for the forgiveness of the people who kill him.

## 6 THE BEATITUDES 5 (ii)

'Blessed are the merciful: for they shall obtain mercy.' (Matthew 5.7 AV)

*This series of readings is concerned with deeds of mercy. 'The merciful' are those who not only forgive but also help other people.*

'How blest are those who show mercy; mercy shall be shown to them.' (Matthew 5.7 NEB)

(a) MARK 1.40–45 Jesus shows mercy by touching the 'untouchable' leper and healing him.
(b) JOHN 4.46–54 Jesus heals the nobleman's son.
(c) LUKE 10.25–37 The Parable of the Good Samaritan.
(d) MATTHEW 25.31–46 In the Parable of the Last Judgement Jesus demonstrates the essence of Christian commitment.
(e) JAMES 2.13–20 James' very stern warning that Christian 'faith' without 'good works' is dead.

## 7 THE BEATITUDES 6

'Blessed are the pure in heart: for they shall see God.' (Matthew 5.8 AV)

*'Purity of heart' means 'single-mindedness' and implies 'complete sincerity'.*

'How blest are those whose hearts are pure; they shall see God.' (Matthew 5.8 NEB)

(a) I KINGS 18.17–21 Elijah tells the people that they must make up their minds and choose between God and Baal.
(b) MATTHEW 16.19–24 Jesus tells the disciples to be single-minded in their loyalty to God.
(c) LUKE 9.57–62 Jesus warns his would-be disciples that to follow him means 'all-or-nothing'.
(d) MATTHEW 6.1–6, 16–18 Christians must do what they should do *for God,* and not to be seen by men.
(e) MATTHEW 23.13–14 (15–24) 25–28 (29–33) Jesus speaks fiercely to the scribes and pharisees for their insincerity and hypocrisy.
(f) MARK 7.14–23 It is the attitude of a person's mind that determines his behaviour.

## 8 THE BEATITUDES 7

'Blessed are the peacemakers: for they shall be called the children of God.' (Matthew 5.9 AV)

*'Peacemakers' are those who seek to heal the divisions between other people and so to create unity, love, harmony. They are called the 'children of God' because they are carrying on his work.*

'How blest are the peacemakers; God shall call them his sons.' (Matthew 5.9 NEB)

(a) JEREMIAH 31.1–9 Jeremiah foresees the peaceful restoration of Israel.

(b) MARK 4.35–41 Jesus brings 'the peace of God' to the storm-tossed disciples. This story was told in the early Church to encourage the Christians who were undergoing the 'storms' of persecution.

(c) JOHN 14.25–31 Jesus promises peace to his disciples.

(d) PHILEMON VERSES 8–19 Paul makes peace between Philemon and his runaway slave, Onesimus.

(e) EPHESIANS 4.25–32 Paul tells the Ephesians to live peacefully among themselves.

(f) COLOSSIANS 3.(15–17) 18–4.1 Paul gives specific instructions to Christian husbands, wives, fathers, children, masters, servants, to live at peace with one another.

## 9 THE BEATITUDES 8

'Blessed are they which are persecuted for righteousness' sake: for theirs is the Kingdom of Heaven. . . . Rejoice and be exceeding glad: for great is your reward in heaven: for so persecuted they the prophets which were before you.' (Matthew 5.10–12 AV)

*It is not difficult to understand that Christians should expect to suffer for their faith as indeed Jesus suffered. It is more difficult to understand why they should rejoice in their suffering; and yet we find that this is what they did.*

'How blest are those who have suffered persecution for the cause of right; the kingdom of Heaven is theirs.' (Matthew 5.10 NEB)

(a) MARK 8.27–38 Jesus speaks of the suffering that he and his disciples are to endure.

(b) LUKE 6.22, 23, 26 Luke's forceful version of Jesus' words about the suffering of disciples and the easy popularity of false prophets.

(c) ACTS 5.(24–32) 33–42 The Apostles are arrested for preaching about the Resurrection of Jesus. They would have lost their lives but for the intervention of Gamaliel. They are beaten instead—but go on their way rejoicing.

(d) ACTS 16.19–34 Despite their suffering, Paul and Silas rejoice and triumph.

(e) HEBREWS 11.32–12.2 The suffering of martyrs and the suffering of Jesus.

(f) ROMANS 8.35–39 No suffering can separate us from the love of God which comes to us through Jesus Christ.

## 10 THE BIBLE

The Bible is a library of books all connected directly or indirectly with the demonstration of God's love towards the world through the life of Jesus Christ. The process of selecting some books and rejecting others was a very long one; and even now there is disagreement about the books in the 'apocrypha': but a list like our present list (including the apocrypha) was published at a Council in Rome in 382 A.D.

(a) MATTHEW 5.17–20 Jesus claims that far from destroying the scriptures, his life and teaching fulfil them.

(b) JOHN 5.39–47 Jesus tells the Jews bluntly that if they really understood the Old Testament they would believe in him. In this passage 'Moses' stands for the law books of the Old Testament.

(c) LUKE 24.13–27 Jesus explains to two disciples how the scriptures refer to himself.

(d) LUKE 1.1–4 and JOHN 21.24–25 The writers of the third and fourth Gospels claim to be using eye-witness accounts.

## 11 A CHRISTIAN COMMUNITY

(a series of readings particularly suitable for the beginning of a school term)

(a) ROMANS 12.1–8 Paul tells the Christians of Rome to offer themselves individually to God and to live together in harmony and cooperation.

(b) ROMANS 12.9–13 The members of the Christian body are held together by love: this involves us all in the practical duty of helping one another.

(c) ROMANS 13.1–7 Human authority must be respected as something created by God for the benefit of society.

(d) ROMANS 13.8–14 Paul speaks of the urgent necessity of turning away from evil to the life of love, the love that comes from Jesus Christ.

## 12 CHRISTIAN LIVING

Jesus did not give his followers a set of commandments to obey. He gave them his love, and sometimes he told them what it is like to live by love.

(a) MATTHEW 5.1–16 Jesus speaks of the kind of people whose behaviour brings upon themselves the blessing of God.

(b) MATTHEW 6.19 (or 24)–34 The first principle of Christian living is to put God first and to trust in his goodness.
(c) JOHN 15.1–11 (12, 13) Christian living is sharing the life and the love and the joy of Jesus.
(d) ACTS 2. (37–8) 41–47 Luke describes the first joyful days of the Christian Church.
(e) PHILIPPIANS 4.4–8 Christian goodness.

## 13 COMPASSION

The word 'compassion' means 'suffering alongside someone else': hence doing all that is possible to alleviate his suffering. Jesus came alongside men in order to share human suffering and, in the power of God's love, to alleviate it.

(a) MARK 1.40–42 and 3.1–6 Two examples of Jesus' compassion. In each he defies human prejudice and gives help to a person in need.
(b) LUKE 19.1–10 Jesus shows compassion to an unpopular person. Tax-gatherers were outcasts from society.
(c) LUKE 10.25–37 The Parable of the Good Samaritan.
(d) MATTHEW 25.31–46 'Loving God' is inseparable from 'loving one's neighbour'.
(e) LUKE 23.29–43 and JOHN 19.25–27 Even on the Cross, Jesus shows care for other people.

## 14 DETACHMENT

Jesus did not despise the good things of life. He used them and appreciated them. But he warned his followers that riches can usurp the place of God and spoil human relationships.

(a) JOB 1 This story shows that a man can be good when he has great possessions—and that he can continue to be good when they are taken away from him.
(b) MATTHEW 11.18–19 and MATTHEW 8.18–20 Unlike John the Baptist, Jesus had the reputation of enjoying the pleasures of life: yet he had no permanent home of his own, nowhere 'to lay his head'.
(c) MARK 10.17–22; 10.23–31 The man who finds it difficult to be detached from his riches. Jesus warns his disciples about the difficulties created by riches. He assures Peter that giving up things to serve him unhindered is very much worth while.
(d) MATTHEW 6.19–34 Set your mind on the Kingdom of God before everything else.

(e) LUKE 12.13–21 Jesus warns people against being covetous, and illustrates his point with the Parable of the Rich Fool.

(f) LUKE 16.(14–15) 19–31 The man who by his covetousness made a barrier between himself and his neighbour, found that the barrier was an eternal one.

## 15 ETERNAL LIFE

In the Bible, 'life' means more than 'existence here on earth'; and 'death' is not just 'the end of existence here on earth'. 'Life' means the full, rich quality of life that comes from God, enhances the value of everything here and now and overflows into all eternity. 'Death' is what limits life now and makes everything cramped and selfish and petty. 'Life' is positive—the goodness of God. 'Death' is negative, the spoiling of things.

(a) EZEKIEL 37.1–14 The Prophet is told that the people of Israel will be restored from their 'dead' life in exile to a new good life in their own land.

(b) JOHN 1.1–5 At the very beginning of his gospel John shows that the 'Word', which 'became Flesh' in the human life of Jesus, is the source of all life.

(c) JOHN 3.16–17; 5.24–9 Jesus brings the life of God to those who accept him.

(d) JOHN 11.1–46 (this passage can be split 1–16; 17–46) The Raising of Lazarus. This is the 'sign' in John's Gospel that Jesus is the Source of Life.

(e) JOHN 10.7–11 and 11.47–53 Jesus brings life at the cost of his own life. After he has given life to Lazarus, the authorities decide to put him to death.

(f) ROMANS 6.19–23 Paul associates 'sin' with 'death' and speaks of Christ bringing the gift of eternal life.

## 16 THE EUCHARIST 1

'Eucharist' comes from the Greek word (still used) meaning 'thanksgiving'. It is the earliest name in general use for the service of the Lord's Supper, the Holy Communion. By associating it with some important events from the Old Testament and above all with his own life, death and resurrection, Jesus gave it to the Church as the supreme token of God's gift to man and man's offering to God.

(a) EXODUS 24.2–8 The old 'Covenant' is sealed by the blood of the animal which is sacrificed. It is important to remember that 'blood' stands for 'life'; and a 'sacrifice' was an 'offering of life through death'.

(b) MATTHEW 26.26–9 Jesus' 'New Covenant' is sealed by the shedding of his 'blood', symbol of his life which is shared by Christians in the Holy Communion.
(c) EXODUS 12.21–27 The Passover is instituted to commemorate the deliverance of the Israelites out of Egypt.
(d) MATTHEW 26.17–19 The Last Supper was thought of as the Old Passover made new; to commemorate the deliverance of the world from evil.
(e) JOHN 6.51–56 Jesus says what will result from receiving his Body and Blood in Communion.

## 17 THE EUCHARIST 2

The Observance of the Eucharist in the first days of the Church. When Jesus kept the Last Supper with his disciples, he 'Took bread, blessed it, broke it and gave it'. He had done the same at the Feeding of the Five Thousand. Hence the expression 'Breaking of Bread' for this action—whenever it was repeated.

(a) LUKE 24.28–35 Jesus, after his resurrection, makes himself known to two disciples in the 'breaking of the bread'.
(b) ACTS 2.41–47 The first Christians continue together in the 'breaking of bread'.
(c) ACTS 20.1–7 Paul and the first Christians in Macedonia meet on 'the first day of the week' in order 'to break bread' in the Eucharist together.
(d) I CORINTHIANS 11.19–24 (NEB) Paul in a letter rebukes the Corinthians for spoiling the sacrament of the Lord's Supper.
(e) I CORINTHIANS 11.25–30 (NEB) Paul explains the purpose of the Eucharist and emphasizes the importance of preparing for it properly.

## 18 THE HOUSE OF GOD

God is Spirit and needs no 'house' to dwell in. But we are 'human' beings and it often helps us to think of him dwelling *close* to us in his 'house'; protecting us and inspiring us with a sense of his beauty and majesty.

(a) GENESIS 6.13–22 God promises to save Noah and his family from destruction in the 'Ark'. The community of all Christian people (The Church) is sometimes called 'The Ark of God'.
(b) EXODUS 25.1–11, 21–22 After making their agreement with God on the basis of the Ten Commandments, the people are told to

construct a beautiful tent ('tabernacle') in which to worship him, and an 'ark' (in the shape of a box) to symbolize his presence, with a 'mercy seat' on top to show that he is always there to help them when they come to him.

(c) JOHN 2.13–22 Jesus is angry with the Jews for misusing the Temple and making it impossible for ordinary people to worship God in it. Jesus' remarks are interpreted as forecasting his resurrection.

(d) EPHESIANS 2.18–22 (NEB) Paul tells the Christians that *they* are now God's dwelling place.

## 19 FAITH

Christian faith is not an attitude of blind wishful thinking. It is trust in a person, Jesus. In terms of practical behaviour it consists of *doing* things that make one *receptive* to God's love.

(a) MARK 10.46–52 In spite of everybody, blind Bartimaeus insists on coming to Jesus.

(b) MARK 2.1–12 The positive action of four men enables Jesus to forgive and heal their friend.

(c) MARK 6.1–6 Over familiarity prevents Jesus' own people from trusting him as they should, with the result that his effectiveness is impaired.

(d) LUKE 7.36–50 In contrast to the stuffy self-righteousness of Simon the Pharisee, a woman shows love, penitence (or 'sorrow for sin') and great generosity.

(e) MARK 9.14–29 To do the work of God requires faith in God; and Jesus shows a power that only comes through prayer. We note the importance of the faith of the boy's father.

(f) GALATIANS 3.1–9 (Modern Translation recommended) Paul argues that Christian salvation does not come to those who 'keep the law' but to those who have 'faith' in Christ.

## 20 LAWS AND COMMANDMENTS: OLD TESTAMENT

God gave the people laws and commandments not in order to spoil life but to improve it. Laws showed them how to live the best kind of life together.

(a) EXODUS 19.1–9 Soon after the escape from Egypt, God tells Moses that he will continue to care for the Israelites and will make them his special people, as long as they are faithful to him and keep his commandments.

(b) EXODUS 20.1–17 The Ten Commandments.

(c) DEUTERONOMY 22.1–4, 6–9 Some kind and sensible laws.

(d) EXODUS 21.23–25, 33–36 The primitive law that only allowed restricted revenge (a law that was later challenged by Jesus). Some regulations about the responsibility for animals.

(e) ISAIAH 5.1–7 Isaiah tells the parable of the vineyard that will be destroyed, in order to warn the people what will happen to them if they do not live by the laws of righteousness that they have been given.

(f) JEREMIAH 31.31–34 Through the prophet Jeremiah, God promises to make a new deal with his people based not on the outward observance of laws, but on the inward principles of loyalty and love.

## 21 LAWS AND COMMANDMENTS: NEW TESTAMENT

(a) MATTHEW 5.1–12 This passage is often known as 'The Beatitudes' and is thought to be Jesus' way of matching the Commandments that came through Moses on Mount Sinai. But instead of 'commanding', Jesus commends ways of behaving that result in happiness.

(b) MATTHEW 5.17–26 Jesus says that his way of living does not destroy the old law, but makes it harder and completes it. He gives an example concerned with murder and hatred and quarrelling.

(c) MATTHEW 5.38–48 More examples of 'completing' the old law. Instead of 'limited revenge' there must be 'no revenge at all': instead of loving only our friends, we must love and be good to our enemies as well.

(d) MATTHEW 5.33–37 Another example of Jesus 'completing and making harder' the old Jewish law. Jesus tells the people that they should no longer use oaths to guarantee their word; for their word should always be the truth.

(e) MARK 2.23–28 Jesus shows his attitude to the regulations concerning the Sabbath. Rules are meant to help, not to hinder: in an emergency they can be broken.

(f) MARK 3.1–6 The laws of the Sabbath are not meant to prevent good deeds but to promote them.

(g) MARK 7.1–13 Jesus is angry with the Pharisees for spoiling the law of God by their 'traditions'. He gives an example of a way in which they are using a religious rule (that of not giving away money that had been dedicated to God) to save them from a moral obligation (that of looking after their old parents).

(h) MARK 7.14–23 Jesus has rebuked the Pharisees for spoiling the law of God by man-made traditions. Now he tells them that true goodness in a man depends upon his inner attitudes.

(i) MARK 12.28–34 Asked to give his opinion about the controversial matter of 'Which is the most important of all the commandments?' Jesus very firmly brings together two passages from the Old Testament about loving God and loving one's neighbour.

(j) ROMANS 13.7–10 Paul underlines Jesus' teaching that 'love' is the fulfilment of the law.

(k) I CORINTHIANS 13 Paul praises love.

(N.B. The AV uses the word 'charity' throughout this passage. RV, RSV and NEB have 'love'.)

## 22 MARTYRDOM

'Martyr' comes from a Greek word meaning 'witness', and was used by Christians to mean a person who had the courage to say what he knew to be true about God and Christ. As such people often died for their faith, the word 'martyrdom' came to mean 'the act of giving up one's life for one's faith'.

(a) MARK 8.31–38 Jesus speaks of his own sufferings that are to come. He tells people that if they are to follow him they must be prepared to give up their lives for his sake.

(b) MARK 10.32–45 James and John ask for privilege. The real question is, Are they prepared to suffer? Both did in fact suffer along with other disciples, and James was the first Apostle to be killed for his faith.

(c) ACTS 6.8–7.2a; 7.51–8.1 Stephen becomes the first Christian martyr.

(d) HEBREWS 11.32–12.2 The faith of the martyrs.

## 23 MEMBERSHIP: BAPTISM AND CONFIRMATION

It is clear from the New Testament that the sacrament of Baptism was regarded as the usual means by which a person joined the community of the Christian Church to begin his new Christ-centred life. The gift of the Holy Spirit (by the laying-on of hands) seems sometimes to have been part of this, sometimes extra to it.

(a) ACTS 2.37–38, 41 (42–47) New Christians are baptized after Peter's speech at the Feast of Pentecost.
(b) ACTS 8.27–40 Philip teaches and baptizes an Ethiopian.
(c) ACTS 8.5–6, (7–11) 12, (13) 14–17 The Apostles go to Samaria to give the Holy Spirit to those who have already been baptized.
(d) ROMANS 6.3–11 Paul explains that as people 'join the Body of Christ' and become Christians, they accept his victory over sin, and the gift of his life.

## 24 MEN FOR GOD

(a) JUDGES 7.1–8 (16–18) 19–23 Gideon and the chosen Three Hundred rout the Midianites.
(b) I SAMUEL 17.4–19
(c) I SAMUEL 17.20–31
(d) I SAMUEL 17.(32–37) 38–54
} The story of David and Goliath.
(e) APOCRYPHA: I MACCABEES 2.1–2a, 6–22 In the year 16 B.C., Mattathias began the revolt against Antiochus Epiphanes who was attempting to stamp out the Jewish religion. This was the beginning of the Maccabean Wars which ended with the liberation of the Jewish people.
(f) DANIEL 6.10–23 Daniel in the lion's den. This story was written to encourage the Jews, who were being persecuted, to be courageous and loyal in their religion.

## 25 MISSIONARIES

The work of the Church is to carry on the work of Christ: so in a sense all Christians are 'missionaries', that is, people who are 'sent' to do God's work.

(a) MATTHEW 10.1, 7–15 Jesus' instructions to the first 'missionaries'.
(b) MATTHEW 10.16–33
(c) MATTHEW 28.16–20 or ACTS 1.4–9 (NEB) Jesus' final instructions to his disciples.
(d) 2 CORINTHIANS 4.5–10 Paul speaks of the committed Christian life.
(e) 2 CORINTHIANS 5.17–21 Paul sums up the truth of Christianity and the object of the Christian life.

## 26 THE TEN COMMANDMENTS 1 and 2: WORSHIP

'Thou shalt have no other gods before me.'
'Thou shalt not make unto thee any graven image. . . .' (Exodus 20.3–4)

The first principle of Christian living is that God, who is the creator of all things and whose goodness therefore embraces all things, must be the centre of life, the object of all living.

(a) EXODUS 20.1–6 No substitute for the one living God can be allowed or created. To turn from him to worship other things is to incur disaster for ourselves and others. But God rewards his faithful worshippers.

(b) EXODUS 32.1–6 In their impatience at the apparent inactivity of God and his prophet, Moses, the people persuade Aaron to make them a new god.

(c) EXODUS 32.15–24 Moses catches them in the act of worshipping the Golden Calf and Aaron makes his poor excuse.

(d) EXODUS 32.30–35 They are punished for their sin.
(N.B. A sterner and more blood-thirsty punishment is described in Exodus 32.25–29.)

(e) ISAIAH 44.9–20 The prophet in Babylon scorns the idolatry of the Babylonians and ridicules people who 'create' their own gods and then bow down and worship them.

(f) MATTHEW 6.24–33 Jesus tells his followers to be single-minded: to seek *first* the kingdom of God.

## 27 THE TEN COMMANDMENTS 3: GOD'S NAME

'Thou shalt not take the name of the Lord thy God in vain: for the Lord will not hold him guiltless that taketh his name in vain.' (Exodus 20.7)

*A name stands for the person known by that name. The Jews knew God by the name Yahweh; but they never dared utter this name, so they called him 'The Lord' instead.*

(a) EXODUS 3.(11–12), 13–15 (16–18) In order to satisfy the Israelites, Moses needed to know God's name. The name Yahweh, translated 'I AM THAT I AM', suggests the Creator God who would gradually reveal himself to his people.

(b) LUKE 1.26–31 Mary is told that her son will be called 'Jesus', which means 'God saves his people'.

(c) MATTHEW 28.16–20 The disciples are instructed to baptize people 'in the name' of the Trinity.

(d) ACTS 3.1–8 Peter heals a lame man 'in the name' of Jesus.

(e) ACTS 19.13–20 Jewish exorcists are punished for presuming to use the name of Jesus.
(f) Philippians 2.5–11 Paul speaks of the honour due to the holy name of Jesus.

## 28 THE TEN COMMANDMENTS 4: THE SABBATH (i)

'Remember the sabbath day, to keep it holy. . . .' (Exodus 20.9–11)

No one knows the origin of the Sabbath, but from earliest times the Jews insisted on making this a day of rest and worship.

(a) EXODUS 16.22–26 The daily routine of gathering manna in the wilderness is interrupted because of the need to rest on the sabbath day. This is the earliest mention of the Sabbath in the Old Testament.
(b) JEREMIAH 17.19–27 The Prophet Jeremiah insists on the observance of the Sabbath.
(c) NEHEMIAH 13.15–19 Shortly after the return from exile in Babylon, the Jewish leader Nehemiah insists on the proper observance of the Sabbath.
(d) GENESIS 2.1–3 One of the latest writers in the Old Testament gives extra authority to the Sabbath laws by claiming that God himself 'rested' from the act of creation on the seventh day.

## 29 THE TEN COMMANDMENTS 4: THE SABBATH (ii)

Jesus' attitude to the Sabbath.

(a) MATTHEW 12.1–8 Jesus shows that in an emergency rules can be broken and that he, the Son of Man, has authority over the Sabbath.
(b) MATTHEW 12.9–14 Jesus shows that it is right to do good on the Sabbath; and the authorities determine on his death.
(c) JOHN 5.10–18 After healing the paralysed man at the Pool of Bethesda, Jesus is in trouble with the Jews about the Sabbath. He tells them clearly that God's good work must go on all the time.
(d) LUKE 13.11–17 Jesus again heals on the Sabbath, to the fury of the authorities and the joy of ordinary people.

## 30 THE TEN COMMANDMENTS 4: THE SABBATH (iii)

The observance of the Sabbath in the New Testament.

(a) LUKE 4.14–22 (23–32) It was Jesus' custom to 'go to synagogue' on the Sabbath.

(b) JOHN 20.1–10 The 'first day of the week' was the 'day of the Lord's resurrection'.

(c) ACTS 20.6–8 (9–12) Luke describes the Church at Troas coming together for 'the breaking of bread' on the Sabbath.

(d) I CORINTHIANS 16.1–3 Paul tells the Christians at Corinth that they should set aside money regularly on the first day of the week, so that it could be collected together and given to the poverty-stricken Christians in Judaea.

## 31 THE TEN COMMANDMENTS 5: HONOURING PARENTS

'Honour thy father and thy mother: that thy days may be long upon the land which the Lord thy God giveth thee.' (Exodus 20.12)

(a) LUKE 2.40–52 The boy Jesus acts independently of his parents, but nevertheless grows up in obedience to them.

(b) MATTHEW 15.1–9 Jesus rebukes the scribes and pharisees for using their own law about money offered in the Temple as a means of evading God's law that men should honour, by providing for, their parents.

(c) LUKE 15.11–32 Jesus' story of the lost son who sought and found forgiveness from his father.

(d) EPHESIANS 6.1–4 Paul, who has been writing about Christian unity, applies this teaching to family life and mentions here the duty of parents and children towards one another.

## 32 THE TEN COMMANDMENTS 6: MURDER

'Thou shalt not kill.' (Exodus 20.13)

(a) GENESIS 4.1–15 The story of Cain and Abel.

(b) MATTHEW 5.21–26 Jesus tells his followers that it is not enough to avoid murder: they must avoid hatred and quarrelling.

(c) MATTHEW 5.38–48 Jesus tells his followers that for revenge and hatred they must substitute generosity and love.

(d) MATTHEW 21.33–46 In his parable of the vineyard, Jesus exposes the murderous attitude of the Jewish authorities.

(e) JOHN 3.16–17 and 10.7–18 All evil is 'death'. Jesus came to banish it with his gift of 'life'.

(f) I JOHN 3.14–18 John underlines Jesus' teaching that hatred and death go together. 'Love' brings 'life'.

## 33 THE TEN COMMANDMENTS 7: ADULTERY

'Thou shalt not commit adultery.' (Exodus 20.14)

(a) 2 SAMUEL 11.2–17 The story of David's adultery with Bathsheba, and the murder of Uriah the Hittite.

*It may be explained that although David's sins were certainly very bad ones, the fact that he employed such a subterfuge and then accepted Nathan's sentence shows that unlike other kings of that time David realized that he was 'under the law' and answerable to God for his actions.*

(b) 2 SAMUEL 11.18–27 David gets his way.

(c) 2 SAMUEL 12.1–14 The Prophet Nathan comes to tell David his punishment.

(d) 2 SAMUEL 12.15–24 David accepts his punishment. Life goes on.

(e) MATTHEW 5.27–32 Jesus says that his followers must be pure in intention, and advises them to avoid causes of temptation.

## 34 THE TEN COMMANDMENTS 8: STEALING

'Thou shalt not steal.' (Exodus 20.15)

(a) LEVITICUS 6.1–7 The Old Testament law insisted that people who stole should make restitution and an offering to God.

(b) EPHESIANS 4.28 People who have stolen should now work hard and be generous to others.

(c) ROMANS 13.8–14 Honesty, like other good qualities, is a form of love.

## 35 THE TEN COMMANDMENTS 9: TRUTH

'Thou shalt not bear false witness against thy neighbour.' (Exodus 20.16)

(a) MATTHEW 5.33–37 The old law was that a man should not strengthen a lie by falsely swearing it to be true: Jesus says that a man should never have to strengthen his word by swearing, for he should always tell the truth.

(b) MARK 3.22–30 For saying that Jesus has done a good deed through the power of evil, the scribes are accused of 'blasphemy against the Holy Spirit': that is, the sin against truth, the sin of calling good evil and evil good. This sin by its nature excludes the possibility of forgiveness.

(c) MATTHEW 7.15–23 Goodness and truth go together. Insincerity, falseness, hypocrisy can be detected by their 'fruits', the deeds that grow out of them.

(d) ACTS 5.1–11 Truth and the fulness of life go together. This first lie in the Christian Church was a sin against the Spirit of Life: it was an act of death.
(e) MARK 14.53–59 False witnesses are brought against Jesus.
(f) LUKE 22.54–62 Peter is afraid to give true witness to Jesus.
(g) ACTS 4.13–23 After receiving the Holy Spirit, and having been arrested for working in the name of Jesus, Peter now has the courage to speak the truth boldly for God's sake.

## 36 THE TEN COMMANDMENTS 10: COVETOUSNESS

'Thou shalt not covet. . . .' (Exodus 20.17)
Covetousness, the desire for other peoples' things, can lead to envy and hatred.
(a) I SAMUEL 18.5–16 Saul's jealousy of David.
(b) I KINGS 21.1–14 The desire for a vineyard leads to murder.
(c) I KINGS 21.15–29 Ahab's punishment.
(d) LUKE 12.13–21 Some teaching and a parable about covetousness.

## 37 VOCATION: GOD CALLS PEOPLE TO HIS SERVICE 1

God does not work in the world *despite* people, but *through* them. Therefore he always needs people and waits for them to be responsive to his call. When God calls people, it is not for privilege but for responsibility.
(a) I SAMUEL 3.1–10 The child Samuel finds that the words he supposed came from his master, Eli, have in fact come to him from the Lord God.
(b) EXODUS 3.1–7, 9–12 and 4.10–12 Moses is called to be God's instrument in delivering the Israelites out of Egypt.
(c) I SAMUEL 16.6–13 David the shepherd boy is chosen from among his older brothers.
(d) ISAIAH 6.1–8 In the course of a service in the Temple, Isaiah sees God: after he has been forgiven, he hears and accepts his commission.
(e) JEREMIAH 1.7–10 The call of Jeremiah.
(f) EZEKIEL 1.1 and 2.1–3.4 After a strange vision, Ezekiel is told to 'inwardly digest' God's word, which will be both bitter and sweet, and to proclaim it courageously to the people.

## 38 VOCATION: GOD CALLS PEOPLE TO HIS SERVICE 2

(a) LUKE 5.1–11 Two pairs of brothers are shown that they must become 'Fishers of Men'.
(b) MARK 2.13–17 Jesus calls Levi from a dishonest profession and shows that his first care is for people who are sinners. *Publicans were the men who made themselves rich in the process of collecting taxes for the occupying power of Rome. In Matthew's version of this story, 'Levi' is called 'Matthew'.*
(c) MARK 10.17–22 A young man finds it too difficult to give up his possessions and obey Jesus' call to follow him.
(d) ACTS 9.1–9 (10–22) Saul, who has seen Stephen die and is on his way to Damascus to carry out more persecutions, is himself called to follow Christ.
(e) 1 CORINTHIANS 1.18–31 *Modern translation recommended.* The humility of a man, Paul, who was called to serve God.

# The Church's Year

## 39 ADVENT: THE COMING OF CHRIST (i)

Advent is the season in which Christians prepare themselves for the coming of Christ at Christmas. They also think of his final coming to judge the world.

(a) ISAIAH 35.1–10 A vision of the coming reign of God on earth.
(b) ISAIAH 1.4–6, 16–20 The need for repentance and the hope of forgiveness.
(c) ISAIAH 40.1–9 Behold your God.
(d) ISAIAH 11.1–9 The rule of the Messiah who is to come.

## 40 ADVENT: THE COMING OF CHRIST (ii)

(a) LUKE 3.(1–3) 7–14, 18 John the Baptist makes it clear that repentance is an essential part of a person's preparation for the coming of Christ.
(b) LUKE 1.26–38 Luke tells us how Mary was prepared for the birth of Jesus.
(c) MATTHEW 1.18–25 Matthew tells the story, through the experiences of Joseph, of the events leading up to the birth of Jesus.

(d) REVELATION 3.20 Jesus will not force his way in, but comes to those who ask him.

## 41 AN ADVENT CAROL SERVICE

(a) ISAIAH 40.1–8 The Prophet proclaims good news to a people in distress.
(b) ISAIAH 11.1–9 The Prophet proclaims the coming of the King.
(c) ISAIAH 35.1–6, 8a, 10 The Prophet tells of the glory and goodness of the Kingdom of God.
(d) MALACHI 3.1–5; 4.1–2a The Prophet warns that the King will come to judge as well as to heal his people.
(e) LUKE 1.26–35, 38 The Angel Gabriel tells Mary that she is to be the mother of Jesus.
(f) MATTHEW 1.18–23 Joseph is told of the coming birth of Jesus.

## 42 A CHRISTMAS CAROL SERVICE

(a) GENESIS 3.8–15 The old legend describes how evil first came into the world as a result of man's disobedience to God's command.
(b) GENESIS 22.15–18 God prepares to rescue man from the consequences of his sin, and promises Abraham that he will be the father of a great nation through whom the divine plan will be carried out.
(c) ISAIAH 9.2, 6, 7 The Prophet Isaiah looks forward to a time when a wise and just ruler will arise among the people and deliver them from war and oppression.
(d) MICAH 5.2–4 The Prophet Micah foresees the glory of Bethlehem.
(e) LUKE 1.26–35 and 38 The Angel Gabriel is sent to Nazareth to tell Mary that she will be the mother of Jesus.
(f) MATTHEW 1.18–23 Matthew tells the story of the birth of Jesus at Bethlehem.
(g) LUKE 2.8–16 Luke tells of the shepherds who leave their flocks and hasten to Bethlehem to see the holy child.
(h) MATTHEW 2.1–12 Matthew tells the story of the wise men of the East who came to acknowledge the infant Christ as King of all the nations.
(i) JOHN 1.1–14 John unfolds the mystery of the incarnation.

## 43 CHRISTMAS

(a) ISAIAH 9.2–7 Isaiah speaks of a 'birth' that will bring about a New Age.

(b) LUKE 2.1–20 Luke's story of the birth of Jesus.
(c) MATTHEW 1.18–25 Matthew's story of the birth of Jesus.
(d) HEBREWS 1.1–12 *The Epistle for Christmas Day.* The life of Christ is God's new and best way of 'speaking' to the world.
(e) JOHN 1.1–14 *The Gospel for Christmas Day.* John unfolds the mystery of the Incarnation.
(Or, John tells his readers that the life, the light, the goodness and the truth of God are summed up and brought to the world through the human life of Christ.)
(f) PHILIPPIANS 2.1–11 The humility of Christ and the honour due to him.

## 44 EPIPHANY: THE SHINING LIGHT

'Epiphany' means 'shining out'. The word has been used for the many occasions in which the glory of Jesus 'shone out' and was seen by men: but it is generally used for the story told by Matthew of the star of Bethlehem 'shining out' and guiding to Christ a group of men who were Gentiles, not Jews.

(a) ISAIAH 60.1–7 The Third Isaiah's vision of Gentiles in their darkness seeing the 'light' of the Lord. It may be that the tradition (not in the Bible) that the 'wise men' were 'kings' (and that they came on camels) arose when the early Christians linked this passage with Matthew's story.
(b) MATTHEW 2.1–15
(c) MATTHEW 2.16–23
Matthew's story of the wise men of the East who 'saw the light' and came to worship Jesus. Matthew, a Jew, was particularly anxious to show his Jewish readers that everything about Jesus' birth was in fulfilment of the scriptures: not least that his life was to be for all men and not just the Jews.
(d) ROMANS 15.8–21 Paul explains that his particular mission in life was to take the Gospel of Christ to the Gentiles, rather than to the Jews.
(e) JOHN 2.1–11 Another story of the glory of Christ 'shining out' to men.
(f) MATTHEW 5.15–16 Jesus tells his followers that their lives must now 'shine out' with the light of God.

## 45 SEPTUAGESIMA: CREATION

This Sunday begins the season when we start to 'look forward' to Easter. There are about seventy days to go. The traditional theme for this time is that of 'creation'. There is no scientific account of physical creation in the Bible, but there are stories told to illustrate what kind of world it is that we live in.

(a) GENESIS 2.4–14 This is the beginning of the earliest 'creation story' in the Bible. It originates from Babylon. There is no time-scheme in this story: but man is created first and a very pleasant world is built around him.

(b) GENESIS 2.15–25 This passage continues the earliest creation story in the Bible. 'Adam' (the Hebrew word for 'mankind') is allowed to give things names, and thus has a special power over them. Woman is then created and man and woman are shown living happily together without fear or shame.

(c) GENESIS 1.1–13 Although it appears first in the Bible, this is a much later story of creation and was probably written after the Jews had returned from Exile in Babylon. It may have been recited by priest and people in the course of worship. Its purpose is to proclaim that everything comes from God; everything fits together: everything is *good*.

(d) GENESIS 1.14–25 The order of events in this creation story is not what we scientifically know to be true: but the story goes on asserting the harmony and goodness of things. It may be that the people used to join in the 'choruses', the repeated phrases such as 'And God saw that it was good'.

(e) GENESIS 1.26–2.3 Whereas in the earlier story man's importance was emphasized by the fact that he was created first, in this account it is emphasized by his coming last, as the crowning glory of creation. Man and woman are made together; they are given power over the rest of creation; and they are made 'in the image of God': that is, in a special relationship with him. The writer adds that God rested on the seventh day, in order to give extra authority to the laws about the Sabbath.

## 46 SEXAGESIMA: THE FALL

The traditional theme for this week is that of the 'Fall'; the belief that the good world is no longer good, but is evil, spoilt, 'fallen' from perfection.

(a) GENESIS 3.1–13 and (b) GENESIS 3.14–24 The stories of the 'good' creation are followed by this story of the 'Fall' into evil. Remember that 'Adam' means 'mankind'; 'the Garden of Eden' represents the good world in which God and man are close to one another. The forbidden tree represents the possibility of evil; the serpent represents the power of temptation within man arising from his possession of free-will. The result of man's disobedience is that he is separated from God, and his troubles begin.

(c) GENESIS 4.1–15 After the 'Fall', comes the first murder.

(d) ROMANS 7.7–25 Paul describes the vicious grip which 'sin' (made worse by rules and regulations) had over him until he was delivered by Jesus Christ.

(e) I CORINTHIANS 15.20–22 Paul explains that just as all men share the condition of 'Adam', the fallen human race, so all now can share the condition of Christ who by his death and resurrection has restored the human race.

## 47 QUINQUAGESIMA: CHRISTIAN LOVE

The theme for this week is 'Christian love'. Christianity is different from all other religions in that it believes that God is not only supremely great but is also supremely loving, a fact that he has expressed through the perfect life of Jesus Christ, the 'Love of God in action'.

(a) I John 4.7–21 John speaks of the love of God which Christians must share and live by.

(b) EPHESIANS 3.14–21 Paul prays that his readers will be filled with the love of Christ.

(c) LUKE 7.36–50 This story shows the contrast between two people in their attitude to Jesus. One is hard, self-righteous and critical of other people: the other is sorry for her sins, loving, and extremely generous.

(d) I CORINTHIANS 12.12–27 Paul describes the unity of the Body of Christ.

(e) I CORINTHIANS 12.27–13.13 Paul describes Christian love, the gift of the Holy Spirit which unifies the Body of Christ.

## 48 LENT 1

Jesus' First Temptation: (1) to use his divine power to save himself from human pain and hardship.

(a) LUKE 2.1–7 Jesus is born in an uncomfortable stable.

(b) MATTHEW 8.18–20 Jesus, the 'Son of Man', has not as much as a bed of his own; and he can promise his followers no easy time.

(c) MATTHEW 4.1–4 Jesus is tempted to put an end to his own hunger.

(d) MATTHEW 26.47–56 Jesus refuses to use force against those who arrest him.

(e) MATTHEW 27.39–43 The people who mocked Jesus on the cross truly said that he, who came in the power of the love of God to save all others, was not able to save himself. In his love he died *for them.*

## 49 LENT 2

Jesus' First Temptation: (2) 'man shall not live by bread alone.'

(a) EXODUS 16.1–3, 9–18 Manna is provided in the wilderness.
(b) JOHN 6.1–14 Jesus provides bread in the wilderness.
(c) MATTHEW 4.1–4 Man shall not live by bread alone.
(d) JOHN 6.27–35 Jesus brings spiritual bread from heaven.
(e) JOHN 6.51–58 The 'Bread of Heaven' is connected with the sacrament of the Body and Blood of Christ.

## 50 LENT 3

Jesus' Second Temptation: to do 'signs' in order to reassure himself and to win popularity by self-display.

(a) MATTHEW 4.5–7 'Tempt' means 'put to the test': Jesus was being tempted to ask for signs in order to convince himself; *and* to convince other people.

(b) MATTHEW 12.38–41 Jesus refuses to give the Pharisees a 'sign' to satisfy their curiosity; except (he adds) the 'sign of Jonah' which refers to Jesus' resurrection and the immediate effect of his preaching.

(c) MATTHEW 13.10–17 Jesus explains that he teaches in parables so that only those who wish to understand may do so.

(d) LUKE 23.3–12 Jesus at his trial refuses to 'perform' in front of Herod.

(e) JOHN 20.24–29 Jesus does eventually show himself to Thomas; and commends those who believe without demanding a 'sign' first.

(f) I CORINTHIANS 1.18–24 The death of Christ seems foolish to many, but it shows the power and the wisdom of God.

## 51 LENT 4

Jesus' Third Temptation: (1) to give in to the Devil by worshipping him.

(a) MATTHEW 4.8–11 The Devil tempts Jesus with a false bargain.
(b) EXODUS 32.1–6 Aaron persuades the people to worship the golden calf.
(c) EXODUS 32.15–24, 30, 31 and 35 Moses catches them in the act; Aaron makes a feeble excuse; and God punishes them.
(d) DANIEL 3.1–12 Shadrac, Meshach and Abednego refuse to worship Nebuchadnezzar's 'Golden Image'. This story was written in the Book of Daniel to encourage the Jews not to worship the idols that they were being commanded to worship.
(e) DANIEL 3.(13–18) 19–30 Many Jews, encouraged by this story, did in fact resist the Greek king's command to commit idolatry; and in spite of much bloodshed, the Jewish religion lived on.

## 52 LENT 5

Jesus' Third Temptation: (2) to bow down and accept the offer of an earthly kingdom.

(a) MATTHEW 4.8–11 'The kingdoms of the earth, and the glory of them' suggested the possibility of earthly power and authority.
(b) JOHN 6.11–16 Men misunderstand the miracle of the Feeding of the Five Thousand and wish to make Jesus king: but he eludes them.
(c) MARK 10.35–45 James and John misunderstand the nature of Jesus' work and their part in it. He tells them that what matters is not their glory and their earthly authority, but their readiness to suffer with him.
(d) MATTHEW 26.62–65 'Christ' means 'King'. Before the High Priest at the first part of his trial, Jesus admits that he is the 'Christ' in the religious sense of the word; and so he is condemned for the religious crime of 'blasphemy'.
(e) JOHN 19.8–16 Before the Roman Governor at the second part of his trial, Jesus is accused of being 'Christ', 'king' in a political sense. For this he is condemned to death.
(f) JOHN 19.19–22 Ironically, Jesus is condemned for being what he in fact is: King of the Jews. Pilate knows that the word 'king' is misleading, but, in spite of the Jews' request, he refuses to change it.

## 53 PALM SUNDAY AND HOLY WEEK

(a) ZECHARIAH 9.9, 16–17a It is prophesied that the Christ will come to his people in humility and peace and with power to save.

(b) ISAIAH 53 The Prophet in exile sees that God's work of restoring mankind is done at the cost of personal suffering.

(c) EXODUS 13.5–7, 14–16 The Passover Feast is to be kept as a memorial of God's action of delivering his people from Egypt.

(d) EXODUS 24.3–8, 12–14 A covenant is made between God and people on the basis of the commandments, sealed by the 'life-blood' of the sacrifice.

(e) GENESIS 22.1–18 Abraham's faith is so great that he is even prepared to sacrifice his son. However, he learns that this is not necessary: God will provide the sacrifice.

## 54 PALM SUNDAY

On this day Jesus the King rode in triumph into Jerusalem, his capital city. People welcomed him by strewing the way with their garments, waving branches of palm trees in the air and shouting: 'Hosanna to the Son of David: Blessed is he that cometh in the name of the Lord; Hosanna in the Highest.'

The Christian Church welcomes the King of Kings into its midst today, remembering the suffering that he is to endure and the victory he is to achieve. From ancient custom, many Christians receive palm crosses on Palm Sunday; 'palm' for the welcome we give to Jesus, 'crosses' to symbolize his Passion and Resurrection. In doing this we feel ourselves involved in the events of the week; sin, sorrow, death, victory.

(a) MATTHEW 21.1–11 In fulfilment of the scriptures, Jesus the King enters his capital city in peace and humility.

or, (b) JOHN 12.12–16 The people of Jerusalem welcome their King with shouts of praise and branches of palm.

## 55 THE EVENTS OF HOLY WEEK

*Monday*

(a) MARK 11.15–19: *The Cleansing of the Temple.* Jesus makes the outer court of the Temple fit for its proper purpose, the worship of God by the Gentiles.
(Do we act in a way which prevents other people from worshipping him?)

*Tuesday*

(b) MARK 11.27–33, 12.13–17 (18–27) 28–34: *The Day of Questions.* These questions were put to Jesus in the hope of discrediting him with the people. Each of his 'answers' was intended to make his questioner think more deeply about the question. (It is good to ask questions about God. When we do so, do we listen honestly to the answers?)

Or, (c) MARK 12.1–12: *The Parable of the Vineyard.* After the cleansing of the Temple, it was this parable that made the authorities determine on Jesus' death.
(History is full of people who have opposed God. Are we the same today? If so, what are our motives?)

*Wednesday*

(d) JOHN 12.1–9: *The Feast at Bethany.*
(Do we love Jesus enough to make great sacrifices for him? Do we sneer at other people's love for him? If so, what are our motives?)

(e) MARK 14.10–11: *The Betrayal.*
(Would we sell Jesus for money, comfort, self-justification, popularity?)

## 56 MAUNDY THURSDAY

'Maundy' is derived from the Latin word 'mandatum' (command) and refers to the new commandment to love one another which Jesus gave to the apostles at the Last Supper on this, the night before his death (John 13.34).

On this day Jesus returned to Jerusalem to keep the Last Supper with his disciples. After his prayer and agony in the Garden of Gethsemane he is betrayed by Judas. He is arrested and tried by the Jewish Council. Peter denies that he knows him.

(a) 1 CORINTHIANS 11.(17–22) 23–25 (26–34) Paul, in telling the Corinthians how they should behave at the Lord's Supper, describes how Jesus himself started it on the night before he died. This is the earliest account in the Bible of the Lord's Supper.

(b) JOHN 13.1–14 Jesus washes his disciples' feet.
(Are we humble enough to allow Jesus to cleanse us? Are we humble enough to serve one another?)

(c) JOHN 18.1–27 Jesus suffers agony in the Garden of Gethsemane. He is arrested and his trial begins. Peter denies that he ever knew him.
(How would we have helped Jesus? How might we have hurt him? Are we as brave as we think we are?)

## 57 GOOD FRIDAY AND HOLY SATURDAY

*Good Friday*

Jesus was crucified on this day.

(a) LUKE 23.1–26 Jesus is tried by the Roman Governor for crimes against the State. Pontius Pilate yields to pressure from the Jewish authorities and condemns him to death.

(b) LUKE 23.27–56 The remainder of the Passion according to Luke.

*Holy Saturday*

Jesus' body lies in the tomb. With him lies 'dead' the power of sin.

(c) MATTHEW 27.62–66 The tomb is guarded.

## 58 EASTER 1

On this day Jesus rose from the dead.

The Resurrection of Jesus means the victory of love over hatred, goodness over evil, life over death. Christian people share in that victory in the sacrament of Holy Communion and in their acceptance of the Christian life.

Every Sunday is kept as a day of rejoicing for the Resurrection of Jesus.

(a) MARK 16.1–8 The earliest account in the Bible of the finding of the empty tomb.

(b) JOHN 20.1–18 John's account of the empty tomb and Jesus' appearance to Mary Magdalen.

(c) LUKE 24.13–35 Two disciples meet Jesus on the road to Emmaus. Jesus makes himself known to them in the breaking of the bread.

(d) JOHN 20.19–29 Jesus appears to the disciples, but at first Thomas cannot believe it.

(e) JOHN 21.1–14 Jesus appears to his disciples on the Lake of Galilee.

(f) JOHN 21.15–25 Jesus' commission to Peter.

(g) MATTHEW 28.9–20 Matthew, seeming to continue the story where Mark broke off, tells of Jesus' appearance at Galilee and his final charge to the disciples.

## 59 EASTER 2

(a) ACTS 2.22–24 (25–31) 32–36 This, according to Luke, was the first time that the news of the Resurrection was proclaimed to the people of Jerusalem.

(b) ACTS 4.1–10 Peter tells the rulers that it was through the power of the risen Christ that the crippled man had been healed.
(c) ACTS 17.18–34 Paul causes a stir amongst the people of Athens by preaching about the one God and the Resurrection of Jesus.
(d) I CORINTHIANS 15.1–11 Paul reminds the Corinthians that their faith rests on the truth of the Resurrection of Jesus; and that at the time of writing there were many eye-witnesses of the Resurrection still alive.
(e) I CORINTHIANS 15.13–22 Belief in 'eternal life' and belief in the Resurrection of Christ are inseparable.
(f) REVELATION 1.4–8 (9–17) 18–19 (20) John writes to the churches about his vision of the eternal, living Christ.

## 60 THE ASCENSION

The Ascension marks the end of the period of time in which it is said that Jesus appeared to people in the flesh. From now onwards he was to be thought of as being 'with' men through the presence of the Holy Spirit.

(a) LUKE 24.44–53 Luke's first account of the Ascension. It is only Luke who relates the story of the physical 'going-up' of Jesus. (*Mark 16.19–20 is one of the endings added later to Mark's Gospel.*)
(b) MATTHEW 28.16–20 Matthew's account of Jesus' last appearance to his disciples, his instructions to them, and his promise to be with them always.
(c) ACTS 1.1–11 Luke's fuller account of the story of the Ascension which begins his second book, The Acts of the Apostles.
(d) ROMANS 8.33–39 Paul sees that the truth of the Ascension guarantees the ultimate triumph of Christ's love. There is nothing now that can defeat or keep us from this love.
(e) I Peter 3.18–22 Peter says that Christ's work is effective for the past generations of mankind as well as present and future ones. (This is the meaning in the clause of the Creed, 'He descended into Hell'; 'Hell' meaning the 'state of all the departed'.)

## 61 WHITSUN 1

Whitsun is the festival of the Holy Spirit. The Holy Spirit is God everywhere, living in the hearts of all people. By their sin men and women have separated themselves from God. By this new coming of the Holy Spirit, made possible through the life of Christ, God's presence is renewed in the lives of all people.

(a) ACTS 2.1–13 Luke tells the dramatic story of 'The Feast of Pentecost', the Jewish 'Harvest Festival'. Fire and wind symbolize the strength, the energy, the power to cleanse and the power to spread, of the Spirit of God.

(b) ACTS 2.14–21, 37–47 Part of Peter's speech at Pentecost and its immediate result.

(c) I CORINTHIANS 12.1–13 Paul writes about the different gifts which the Holy Spirit gives to individual Christians; and explains that these gifts should not divide Christians but unite them.

(d) I CORINTHIANS 12.27–13.13 The greatest gift, for it unifies all the others, is the gift of love (or, 'charity', as in the AV).

(e) GALATIANS 5.22–6.8 It is often said in the Bible that men and women can be likened to 'fruit trees' which bring forth 'fruit', good, bad or indifferent. Paul here speaks of the 'good fruit' brought forth from a life nourished by the Holy Spirit of God.

## 62 WHITSUN 2

(a) ISAIAH 11.1–9 Isaiah's prophecy of the Man of the Spirit who would start the New Age.

(b) EZEKIEL 37.1–14 In the Bible 'spirit', 'breath' and 'wind' are the same, and indicate the 'life' of God dwelling in men. In their state of exile in Babylon it seems as if God's life-Spirit has gone out of the Jewish people. Ezekiel prophesies that it will be given back to them; they will return to Jerusalem and 'live' again.

(c) APOCRYPHA: WISDOM 1.1–7 The Spirit of God is the source of all wisdom.

(d) APOCRYPHA: WISDOM 9.1–4, 9–11 The wise man's prayer for the Spirit of God.

(e) JOEL 2.28–32 Joel's prophecy of the new outpouring of God's Spirit upon men.

## 63 TRINITY

At this festival of the Holy Trinity we think of the greatness of God and his love towards mankind.

(a) ISAIAH 6.1–8 During a service in the Temple, Isaiah glimpses something of the glory of God and answers a call to serve him.

(b) REVELATION 4.1–11 John sees a vision of the glory of God.

(c) MARK 1.1–13 Jesus is baptized. This story shows the unity of God in Heaven with Jesus Christ, the focus of God's own love on earth.

(d) 1 JOHN 4.7–21 God is love.

# Saints Days

## 64 ST. ANDREW (NOVEMBER 30th)

Andrew was the Apostle who brought his brother Peter to Jesus. Once, when many were hungry and there was nothing to eat except five barley loaves and two small fishes, it was Andrew who brought the boy along to offer these to Jesus; and it was Andrew who helped to distribute the bread to the crowds.

On St. Andrew's day we pray particularly for Christian missionaries. These are the men and women who devote their lives to bringing other people to Jesus and sharing his love, compassion and creative goodness with those who need him.

(a) MATTHEW 4.18–22 Andrew is called with his brother and friends to follow Jesus.

(b) JOHN 1.35–42 John the Baptist points the way to Jesus. Andrew finds Jesus and then brings his brother, Simon, to meet him.

(c) JOHN 6.1 (or 5)–14 Andrew helps in the Feeding of the Five Thousand.

(d) JOHN 12.20–26 Andrew and Philip bring Greeks to Jesus. Jesus knows that it is only through suffering that the Gospel will spread.

## 65 ST. THOMAS (DECEMBER 21st)

Thomas is called 'Doubting Thomas' because he doubted the story of Jesus' resurrection. But then he experienced for himself the living Jesus, and worshipped him as his Lord and his God.

(a) JOHN 20.24–19 (30–31)

(b) JOB 23.1–9 Job, who has suffered exceedingly, longs for a direct confrontation with God.

(c) JOB 38.1–7 God appears to Job.

(d) JOB 40.1–14 Job is humble and worships God, who lifts him up and restores his confidence.

(e) APOCRYPHA: ECCLESIASTICUS 2.1–11 The certainty of testing: the necessity of faith.
(f) APOCRYPHA: ECCLESIASTICUS 2.12–18 The reward of faith.
(g) I PETER 1.3–9 Peter writes a letter of encouragement to Christians who are facing persecution.

## 66 THE CONVERSION OF ST. PAUL (JANUARY 25th) 1

Saul of Tarsus, Jewish Pharisee and Roman Citizen, an upright man of great learning and strict discipline, becomes Paul the Apostle, the friend of Gentiles, the servant of Jesus Christ.

(a) ACTS 7.54–60 Saul (later to become Paul) shares in the Jews' fury against Stephen and takes part in his death.
(b) ACTS 9.1–9 The conversion of Saul.
(c) ACTS 9.10–18 Saul is received into the Church.
(d) ACTS 13.44–52 At Pisidion Antioch, Paul turns from the Jews to preach to the Gentiles.
(e) 2 TIMOTHY 4.1–8 Paul's final charge to Timothy.

## 67 THE CONVERSION OF ST. PAUL 2

Some extracts from the Letters of Paul.

Paul wrote letters to the Christian churches, some of which he had founded himself, in order to encourage them in matters of belief and behaviour. Sometimes he expressed himself in language that is so clear and inspired that his words have been taken out of their context and read aloud (as his letters originally were) to all generations of Christians.

(a) ROMANS 7.14–25 Paul says that he cannot do what he knows to be right except through the grace of Jesus Christ.
(b) ROMANS 8.31–39 The assurance of Christian hope.
(c) I CORINTHIANS 13 Love (or, charity) is the supreme Christian virtue.
(d) ROMANS 12 (or stop at v. 9, or 18, or 21) The life of a Christian community.
(e) 2 Corinthians 6.1–10 The shame and the glory of being an apostle.
(f) PHILIPPIANS 2.1–11 Christ's humility in entering upon a human life.
(g) PHILIPPIANS 4.4–8 Farewell and encouragement.

## 68 THE PRESENTATION OF CHRIST IN THE TEMPLE, or, THE PURIFICATION OF ST. MARY THE VIRGIN (FEBRUARY 2nd)

Doing her duty as a Jewish mother, Mary dedicates her first-born son to God. She is thus offering to God that which she has received from him, and for all time gives the perfect example of Christian dedication.

(a) LUKE 2.22–33 (34–40) Jesus is offered to God in accordance with Jewish law; and Simeon (in the words that we now know as the Nunc Dimittis) claims that at last he has seen 'God's salvation' in this infant Saviour.

(b) I SAMUEL 1.19–28 Hannah offers her son Samuel to serve the Lord.

(c) ROMANS 11.33–12.2 Christians are told to offer their lives to God.

(d) HEBREWS 10.1–10 The offering of Jesus Christ supersedes all the sacrifices of the Old Testament.

## 69 ST. MATTHIAS (FEBRUARY 24th)

Matthias was the man who took the place of the traitor, Judas.

All through the history of the Church there have been Judases, and faithful Matthiases to take their place. That is why despite much disloyalty the work of Christ has been carried on.

(a) I SAMUEL 2.27–35 The Lord prepares to replace the sons of Eli with a priest who will serve him faithfully.

(b) I SAMUEL 16.1–13 The Lord calls David, the son of Jesse, to replace King Saul.

(c) MATTHEW 7.15–27 Jesus' teaching about false and true prophets.

(d) Acts 1.15–17 (18–20) 21–26 The election of Matthias.

## 70 THE ANNUNCIATION OF THE BLESSED VIRGIN MARY (MARCH 25th)

Mary is told beforehand of the birth of Jesus. She is afraid, but accepts the responsibility that is being laid upon her.

(a) ISAIAH 52.7–10 This prophecy was made when the Jews were in exile in Babylon. Its note of joy and sense of the great things that were going to happen suits this occasion very well.

(b) ISAIAH 7.10–16 This prophecy was made by the First Isaiah when the kingdom was in danger from foreign invasion. Within nine months, he was saying, the danger would pass and God would be known to be 'with them' again. When the scriptures were translated into Greek the idea of 'virgin' was introduced. With it or without it, the words perfectly suit the occasion on which Mary was told that her baby would be 'God With Us', Jesus, the Saviour of the world.

(c) I SAMUEL 2.1–10 Hannah's song of thanksgiving for the birth of Samuel. This is very like the Magnificat which Luke attributes to Mary.

(d) LUKE 1.26–38 The story of the Annunciation.

(e) LUKE 1.39–56 Mary shares the news with her cousin Elizabeth.

## 71 ST. GEORGE (APRIL 23rd)

George, the patron saint of England, was the soldier who fought and died for his faith in the early years of the fourth century. Stories and legends grew around his name, including the one that he had slain the 'dragon'—a monster of evil.

He became a favourite saint with the English (and especially King Richard I) in the time of the crusades: but it was not until the reign of Edward III that he was adopted the patron saint of England. This king founded St. George's Chapel at Windsor in 1348; and the story goes that when Edward was fighting the French at Calais in 1349 he suddenly drew his sword and rushed forward shouting, 'Ha! St. Edward, Ha! St. George'; and routed the French.

The idea of the Christian life being the life of a 'soldier' fighting against 'evil' is common in the Bible and in Christian literature and hymns.

(a) EPHESIANS 6.10–18 Paul speaks of the spiritual weapons with which Christians must fight against evil.

## 72 ST. MARK (APRIL 25th)

John Mark is the author of the earliest Gospel. There are many theories about his writing of it, the first being that he wrote down what Peter told him of the events of Jesus' life without trying to put them into chronological order. Many think that it is a carefully constructed book written to encourage the Christians who were being persecuted in Rome in the years 64 to 68 A.D.

Whatever the truth, this Gospel is clearly of the greatest importance not only because it gives us the earliest written accounts of some of the episodes in Jesus' life, but also because Matthew and Luke made wide use of this Gospel when writing their own.

John Mark lived in Jerusalem, possibly in the house where Jesus held his Last Supper with the disciples. He started out on Paul's first missionary journey, but to Paul's disgust turned back when they reached Perga in Pamphylia.

(a) ACTS 12.11–19 An incident at John Mark's home after Peter's escape.
(b) ACTS 12.24–35; 13.4–13 The beginning of the missionary journey from which John Mark turned back.
(c) ACTS 15.36–41 Paul refuses to take John Mark with him a second time: but Barnabas takes him to Cyprus instead, so the missionary work continues.
(d) MARK 14.46–52 A young man escapes when Jesus is arrested. Many people have guessed that this man was John Mark himself.

## 73 ST. PHILIP AND ST. JAMES (MAY 1st)

Both Philip and James were amongst the Twelve Apostles, and not very much more than that is known about them. This is not the James, son of Zebedee, who was the brother of John; but it is just possible that he was the same person as 'the brother of the Lord' mentioned in the Acts of the Apostles. If he was, he may also have been the author of the Epistle of St. James, in the New Testament.

(a) JOHN 1.43–51 Philip is called, and brings along a friend.
(b) JOHN 6.1–14 Philip is at the Feeding of the Five Thousand.
(c) JAMES 1.1–12 The importance of having strong faith.
(d) JAMES 1.13–27 The first truth of religion is that all goodness, and only goodness, comes from God. The first demand is that we live in this goodness by *doing* what is right.
(e) JAMES 2.1–8 It is wrong to favour the rich and despise the poor.
(f) JAMES 2.14–26 'Faith' in this passage means believing in God and being receptive to his goodness. 'Works' means *doing things* that are according to the goodness of God. James is saying that 'faith' is not genuine unless it results in 'works'.
(g) JAMES 3.1–10 (11–18) Guard your tongue! (or, the power for good and the power for evil of what we *say*).
(h) JAMES 4.1–17 Stern words against sin. In this passage 'the world' means 'the world in so far as it is opposed to God'.
(i) JAMES 5.1–6 Harsh words against the rich.

(j) JAMES 5.7–11 (12) Patience is rewarded.
(k) JAMES 5.13–18 (19–20) The importance of prayer and repentance.

## 74 ST. BARNABAS (JUNE 11th)

The story of Barnabas—the rich man who sold his possessions, gave them to the Church and followed Jesus as a missionary, preacher and martyr—nicely matches the story of the other rich young man whom Jesus loved but who was unable at the time to follow him because of his many possessions. Possessions need not be a hindrance to a life of sacrifice and adventure; but some people certainly do better without them.

(a) ACTS 4.33–37
(b) ACTS 9.22–28 Barnabas has the courage to accept the newly converted Saul of Tarsus and present him to the other Apostles.
(c) ACTS 11.22–30 Barnabas plays an important part in the affairs of the early Church.
(d) ACTS 12.24–13.13 Barnabas goes off with Paul on their first missionary journey.
(e) ACTS 14.8–18 To their embarrassment, Paul and Barnabas are taken for gods.
(f) ACTS 14.19–28 The absurd flattery by the men of Lystra quickly turns to vicious opposition. Paul and Barnabas survive and courageously return to Antioch by their former route.
(g) ACTS 15.35–41 Paul and Barnabas part company after a disagreement. But the work of spreading the Gospel continues.

## 75 THE NATIVITY OF ST. JOHN THE BAPTIST (JUNE 24th)

In his way of life and the sternness of his teaching, John the Baptist is like the prophets of the Old Testament. Indeed there was a tradition that he was actually the Prophet Elijah coming back to earth to complete his work. Certainly he did complete the work of the old prophets by preparing the people for the coming of Christ.

(a) Malachi 4.1–3, 5–6 The beginning of the tradition that Elijah would return to prepare people for the 'day of the Lord'.
(b) LUKE 1.5–25 Zacharias is told of John's birth.
(c) LUKE 1.57–80 The naming of John.
(d) MATTHEW 3.1–17 The ministry of John and the Baptism of Jesus.

(e) JOHN 1.19–34 Another account of John meeting Jesus in the wilderness.

(f) MATTHEW 11.1–15 (16–19) John wonders whether Jesus really is the Messiah. Jesus convinces him by referring to Isaiah's words about the healing work of the Messiah. (Jesus goes on to praise John for his great courage and strength.)

(g) ACTS 19.1–7 Paul meets some men who had been converted by John the Baptist but who had not heard of Jesus or received the Holy Spirit.

## 76 ST. PETER (JUNE 29th)

Peter is the Apostle who was changed: from the brash, self-confident, weak man who asserted his loyalty but then denied his Lord, to the first hero of the Christian Church who preached the Gospel and gave his life for his faith.

(a) LUKE 5.1–11 Peter obeys a strange command and finds himself called to be a 'Fisher of Men'.

(b) MATTHEW 14.22–33 Peter shows faith—and fear—on the sea of Galilee.

(c) MATTHEW 16.13–23 Peter makes a statement of faith and is given special responsibility by Jesus; but he shows that there are still things about The Christ that he does not yet understand.

(d) MATTHEW 17.1–8 The Transfiguration of Jesus in the presence of Peter, James and John.

(e) MARK 10.28–31 Peter is told of the rewards—in this life and eternally—of following Jesus.

(f) JOHN 13.6–10 Jesus washes his disciples' feet and overcomes Peter's reluctance.

(g) LUKE 22.31–34 Jesus says that Peter will deny him.

(h) LUKE 22.54–62 Peter denies Jesus three times, and weeps bitterly.

(i) JOHN 20.1–10 Although outrun by John, Peter is the first to enter the empty tomb.

(j) JOHN 21.1–14 Peter with the other disciples meets the risen Lord by the Lake of Galilee.

(k) JOHN 21.15–25 The risen Lord asks Peter to look after his Church; and speaks to him about his death.

(l) ACTS 2.14–23, 32, and 36–40 (this gives the gist of Peter's speech at Pentecost and its immediate sequel: it would be possible to omit also verses 17, 19 and 20) Peter takes the lead at the Feast of Pentecost.

(m) ACTS 3.1–11 (12–20) Peter, with John, heals the cripple at the gate of the Temple, and explains his actions.

(n) ACTS 4.1–22 After a night in prison, Peter explains his actions to the authorities. He and the disciples are threatened and released.
(o) ACTS 8.14–25 Peter and John go to Samaria to confer the gift of the Holy Spirit on those who have been baptized. Peter rebukes Simon the sorcerer for wanting to 'buy' his powers.
(p) ACTS 9.32–43 Peter at Lydda and Joppa.
(q) ACTS 11.1–18 Peter explains his new Christian attitude towards the Gentiles.
(r) ACTS 12.1–19 Peter is arrested by King Herod but escapes and rejoins the Church. Apart from his words at the Council of Jerusalem, this is the last we hear of Peter in the Acts. Tradition has it that he was killed (crucified upside down) in Rome in Nero's persecution, probably in A.D. 64.

## 77 ST. MARY MAGDALEN (JULY 22nd)

Luke tells us that Mary Magdalen had been mentally and spiritually healed by Jesus. She was near him at his crucifixion and, according to John, was the first to see and greet him after his resurrection.

(a) LUKE 8.1–3
(b) JOHN 20.11–18
(c) ZEPHANIAH 3.14–20 The joy of one who has been forgiven and healed.
(d) 2 CORINTHIANS 5.14–17 The joy of knowing Christ.

## 78 ST. JAMES THE APOSTLE (JULY 25th)

James the brother of John was one of the first of the Apostles to be called by Jesus to follow him; and he was the first to be martyred.

(a) MARK 1.14–20 James and his brother and their friends give up their fishing business and follow Jesus.
(b) MARK 10.35–45 James and John ask for a privilege, but are told that they must learn to suffer.
(c) MATTHEW 26.36–46 In the Garden of Gethsemane, Peter, James and John sleep while Jesus suffers.
(d) ACTS 12.1–6 James is martyred and Peter is imprisoned.

## 79 ST. MATTHEW (SEPTEMBER 21st)

We know little of the authorship of Matthew's Gospel, but a tradition which dates from the end of the first century attributes it to Matthew the tax-collector, the disciple of Jesus.

(It is certain that the Gospel was written particularly for Jewish readers by one who understood their point of view. The author is proud of the Jewish heritage; but he shows a sad anger with the Jewish authorities for the way they failed to recognize—and then crucified—their Christ.)

(a) MATTHEW 9.9–13 The call of Matthew.
('Publicans' were the people who collected tax for the Romans: they were hated and despised.)

(b) 2 CORINTHIANS 4.1–6 Paul speaks of the responsibility of those who have been saved from evil ways to spread the good news of Christ.

For selections from Matthew's Gospel see Nos. 5(c), 13(d), 40(c), 44(b) (c), 58(g), 76(b), 106(c)

## 80 ST. MICHAEL AND ALL ANGELS (SEPTEMBER 29th)

In the Bible 'angels' are beings that represent the presence of God when he wishes to make some direct communication to a human being. Michael is considered to be the first of the angels; and he is the chief contender in the 'war against evil'.

(It is sometimes helpful for us to be reminded that (1) God's presence with us is personal; (2) we are all involved in the struggle between the great forces of good and evil.)

(a) REVELATION 12.7–12 The war between good and evil.
(b) DANIEL 12.1–4 A vision of the victory of the good.

## 81 ST. LUKE (OCTOBER 18th) 1

Luke, an educated man, a gentile, a doctor, a companion of Paul on many of his missionary journeys, was the writer of the Third Gospel and the Acts of the Apostles. His books show us both the sternness and the tender compassion of Jesus' character; and the joy and the demands of Christianity.

(a) APOCRYPHA: ECCLESIASTICUS 38.1–4, 12–14 In praise of doctors.
(b) COLOSSIANS 4.14–18 Paul in prison sends Luke's greetings to the Colossians.
(c) 2 TIMOTHY 4.5–18 In his final charge to Timothy, Paul mentions the faithfulness of Luke.
(d) ACTS 28.1–14 Luke gives an eye-witness account of the events at Malta (after the ship-wreck) on the way to Rome.

## 82 ST. LUKE 2

Some passages that only come in Luke's Gospel.

(a) LUKE 3.10–14 The practical advice of John the Baptist.

(b) LUKE 6.17–26 The beginning of Luke's version of 'The Sermon on the Plain', equivalent to Matthew's 'Sermon on the Mount'. Luke's version is sterner and more concerned with the present.

(c) LUKE 7.36–50 Jesus' care for a woman who was sorry.

(d) LUKE 10.1–11 Luke alone records the 'mission of the seventy', symbolizing, it is generally supposed, the ministry to the Gentiles.

(e) LUKE 10.25–37 A parable about neighbourliness.

(f) LUKE 10.38–42 Immediately following the parable about neighbourliness, Luke reminds his readers that they must not be so busy that they have no time for Jesus himself.

(g) LUKE 15.(1–10) 11–31 Three parables (or, a parable) about the joy of forgiveness.

See also Nos. 1(a), 5(b), 7(c)

## 83 ST. SIMON AND ST. JUDE (OCTOBER 28th)

Very little is known about Simon and Jude individually, except that they were Apostles and (according to tradition) martyrs.

(a) LUKE 6.12–19 Luke's version of the choosing of the Twelve.

(b) John 15.17–27 Part of Jesus' instructions to his disciples.

(c) MATTHEW 28.16–20 Jesus' final instructions to the Eleven.

(d) ACTS 1.12–14 After the Ascension they await the coming of the Holy Spirit.

(e) EPHESIANS 2.11–22 Paul describes the unity of the Christian Church in terms of a building, 'built on the foundation of the apostles and prophets'. (*These words come in the Collect for the day.*)

## 84 ALL SAINTS' DAY (NOVEMBER 1st)

Originally the word 'saint' was applied to all Christian people and meant 'someone who is being made holy by the Holy Spirit'. Later it came to be used of very eminent Christians.

Some Christians also recognize All Souls' Day on November 2nd, when they pray especially for those whom they have personally known and loved and who are now dead.

(a) APOCRYPHA: 2 ESDRAS 2.42–48 A vision of the saints.

(b) APOCRYPHA: WISDOM 3.1–9 The immortality of the saints.

(c) APOCRYPHA: ECCLESIASTICUS 44.1–15 In praise of great men.

(d) REVELATION 7.2–4 (5–8) 9–12 A New Testament vision of the saints. The 'Lamb' is a symbol for Christ.

(e) MATTHEW 5.1–12 Jesus speaks of the qualities of a saintly life.

(f) JOHN 11.21–27 Jesus assures Martha about eternal life.

(g) MATTHEW 22.23–33 Questioned about the after-life, Jesus shows that you cannot speak about heavenly things in earthly terms. He then quotes from the Old Testament to show that as God is the God of Abraham, Abraham must in a sense be 'living'.

(h) I CORINTHIANS 15.12–22 Paul's certainty of the after-life rests on his certainty of the Resurrection of Jesus.

(i) I CORINTHIANS 15.35–58 Paul says that in the after-life people retain their individuality and distinctiveness, but live in a 'body' which does not have the physical limitations of our present bodies. He explains that the relationship between our present lives and our lives in heaven is like the relationship between a seed and the flower it grows to be.

## 85 HARVEST THANKSGIVING

(a) DEUTERONOMY 8.7–20 The Jews are reminded of their obligation to thank God for all his gifts.

or

(b) DEUTERONOMY 26.1–11 Offerings are to be made in a spirit of thanksgiving.

or

(c) DEUTERONOMY 28.1–14 Some of the blessings that God gives to his people.

(d) MATTHEW 13.1–9 (10–13, 18–23) The parable of the sower.

(e) 2 CORINTHIANS 9.6–15 Paul begs the Corinthians to be generous in their offerings, as they have received so much from God. (At this time there was a famine and great poverty amongst the Christians in Judea and Paul is asking the Corinthians to give them all the help they can.)

# The School Year

## 86 THE BEGINNING OF TERM

(a) JOSHUA 1.1–9 God gives encouragement to Joshua who is about to lead the Israelites into the land of Palestine.

(b) GALATIANS 6.2–10 Living and working together.
or
(c) EPHESIANS 4.1–7 Community life.
See also 35(c).
For a series, see 11, 12, 20, 21, 24, 37, 38, 47, 61, 89, 90, 91–5

## 87 AN IMPORTANT SCHOOL OCCASION

(a) I KINGS 3.5–15 King Solomon chooses the gift of wisdom.
or
(b) JOB 28.12–28 In praise of wisdom.
or
(c) PROVERBS 4.1–13 In praise of wisdom.
or
(d) APOCRYPHA: WISDOM 7.22–30 In praise of wisdom.
or
(e) APOCRYPHA: ECCLESIASTICUS 44.1–15 In praise of great men.
(f) I CORINTHIANS 2.1–9 The wisdom that comes from God.
(g) EPHESIANS 6.10–18 The armour of God.
See also 25(f), 26(f), 27(f), 35(c), 63(a), 67(b) (c)

## 88 THE END OF TERM

(a) PHILIPPIANS 4.4–8 (9) In this passage the original word for 'rejoice' is the same as the word for 'farewell'.
(b) I THESSALONIANS 5.14–23 (24–28).
See also 21(j) (k), 31(d), 44(f), 76(e), 83(c), 89(e)

# From The Old Testament

## 89 THE JOURNEY TO THE PROMISED LAND: MANY DIFFICULTIES ARE OVERCOME

Jews and Christians tell these stories to remind themselves that God is always present to help, lead and provide for his people.

(a) EXODUS 14.5–18, 21–25 The Israelites are caught between the enemy and the sea: but God makes a way through for them.
(b) EXODUS 16.1–3, 11–15 The people are hungry, and God sends food.

(c) EXODUS 17.1–7 The people are thirsty, and God sends water.
(d) EXODUS 17.8–16 An enemy bars the way: Moses prays, the men fight, and the enemy is routed.
(e) EXODUS 19.1–6 God encourages the people.

## 90 THE PEOPLE'S RELUCTANCE TO ENTER THE PROMISED LAND

From the writer of the Epistle to the Hebrews onwards, Christians have interpreted this story as illustrating people's reluctance to go forward to a new stage in the Christian life.

(a) NUMBERS 13.1–3, 17–20 Spies are sent to look at the land.
(b) NUMBERS 13.25–33 The spies come back with a glowing report: but all except Caleb say that the difficulties would be too great for the Israelites to overcome, and they had better not attempt the journey.
(c) NUMBERS 14.1–10a Terrified by the spies' report, the people decide to go back to Egypt again, forgetting that it was through God's help, not their own strength, that they had been able to come so far.
(d) NUMBERS 14.10b–19 God is angry with the people for their faithlessness; but Moses pleads for them.
(e) NUMBERS 14.20–25, 39–45 God tells the people that they must stay in the Wilderness, but that their children will go up into the Promised Land. The people try to go in their own strength, but are defeated.
(f) JOSHUA 1.1–2 (3–5) 6–10 The Lord tells Joshua to lead the new generation into the Promised Land.

## 91 LESSONS FROM THE BOOK OF DANIEL 1: DISCIPLINE

The Book of Daniel was written between the years 168 and 165 B.C. at the time when the Jews were resisting what seemed like an attempt to stamp out their religion. The Greek king Antiochus Epiphanes had not only ordered the scriptures to be burnt and the Jewish laws to be ignored, but he had also desecrated the Temple by taking all the money from the treasury and erecting a statue of Zeus (carved to resemble himself) in the Holy of Holies. Many Jews gave in to him; but many resisted, at first passively, then by taking up arms. In the end they were successful.

This book was written to encourage the heroes of the day by stories of heroism rewarded by God. The stories are put in an historical setting, but the characters and circumstances are only a thin disguise for the affairs of the writer's own day: and the lessons of the stories are true for all time.

Since the time of Alexander peaceful efforts had been made to hellenize Palestine and allure the Jews from their religious customs and allegiance. The writer thought discipline in these matters to be essential; and this first story shows Daniel and three other men of God being rewarded for faithfully doing what they knew to be right, in spite of the powerful temptation to do what was easy and (to them) wrong. This was in the matter of what they should eat and drink.

(a) DANIEL 1.1–8.
(b) DANIEL 1.9–21.

## 92 LESSONS FROM THE BOOK OF DANIEL 2: LOYALTY TO GOD

This is a story about the temptation to commit idolatry, that is, to worship a man-made idol, instead of the living God. In his attempt to destroy their religion, Antiochus had ordered the Jews to worship images and idols in the Temple and synagogues throughout the land. Indeed this was the crux of the matter, for the rebellion against Antiochus began when an aged priest called Mattathias refused to obey the king's officer when ordered to sacrifice to an idol, and then in his rage slew a Jew who did so.

(The question, 'Whom or what shall I worship?'—that is: 'Who or what is worthy of my complete devotion?'—is the most important question of life. There are many pressures upon us all to devote our lives to worthless substitutes for God.)

(a) DANIEL 3.1–13.
(b) DANIEL 3.14–25.
(c) DANIEL 3.26–30.

## 93 LESSONS FROM THE BOOK OF DANIEL 3: REVERENCE

This is a story about an act of blasphemy.

The particular blasphemy the writer had in mind was the looting of the temple by Antiochus and the placing of the pagan statue of Zeus in the Holy of Holies.

Antiochus did not meet the sudden dramatic death which the story seems to expect; but his policies were defeated and the Jews won their independence.

(Blasphemy is the act of mocking God, cursing God, and yet—strangely—treating him as if he does not exist. The beginning of blasphemy is to mock and despise what is good and to behave as if there is no difference between good and evil.)

(a) DANIEL 5.1–8.
(b) DANIEL 5.9–16.
(c) DANIEL 5.17–31.

## 94 LESSONS FROM THE BOOK OF DANIEL 4: FAITH

This is a story of courage and personal faith.

In spite of the pressures against him, Daniel refused to give up the practice of praying faithfully to the Lord, his God.

When the book of Daniel was being written, there were thousands of Jews who had given in to the pressures of persuasion to give up worshipping the Lord God; but the nation was saved by the few who had the courage to be loyal.

(It is those who give up being faithful who not only lose their faith but spread faithlessness. Being faithful requires courage, but it wins in the end.)

(a) DANIEL 6.1–17.
(b) DANIEL 6.18–23 (24–28).

## 95 LESSONS FROM THE BOOK OF DANIEL 5: PENITENCE AND HOPE

(a) DANIEL 9.3–6, 9–10, 16–19 Daniel's act of repentance on behalf of his people.
(b) DANIEL 10.10–19 (20–21) Daniel's assurance of forgiveness and new strength.
(c) DANIEL 12.1–4 (5–13) Daniel is given a glimpse of the future glory which helps to make sense of the present strife. (This is the first time that teaching about judgement and the resurrection of the righteous comes in the Bible.)

## 96 THE BOOK OF JONAH (THE RELUCTANT MISSIONARY)

The Book of Jonah was written towards the end of the Jews' exile in Babylon. It is about a reluctant missionary, and was written to teach the Jews that God, the creator of ALL men, cares for other people just as much as he cares for the Jews. Even if the Jews do not want to, they ought to be ready to share the knowledge of his goodness with others.

(a) JONAH 1.1–17 Jonah is sent by God to the foreign city, Nineveh. He tries to escape, but finds that God is always with him.

(b) JONAH 2.1–10 Jonah's prayer. He shows that he has learnt his lesson that one cannot escape from the presence of God.

(c) JONAH (2.1 and 10 *if (b) has not been read*) 3.1–10 This time Jonah obeys, and his mission is successful.

(d) JONAH 4.1–11 Jonah dislikes the Ninevites so much that he is angry that they have been forgiven and saved. God shows that it is natural for the creator of the world to love and wish to preserve *all* his creatures.

# Jesus Christ

## 97 THE GOOD SHEPHERD

In biblical times the 'shepherd' was no sentimental figure. He was a man of authority, ability, courage and strength. Rulers (good and bad) were often spoken of as 'shepherds'; and the Christian Church preserves this metaphor by its word 'pastor' (the Latin for 'shepherd') and the shepherd's crook carried by a bishop.

(a) EZEKIEL 34.1–12, 16 and 30 In this passage the rulers of Israel are spoken of as 'shepherds' of the people. They are denounced as bad shepherds who care more for themselves than they do for the sheep: The Lord promises that one day he will come himself to be the true 'shepherd' of his people.

(b) PSALM 23 The Lord is the 'shepherd' who guides and protects his people.

or

(c) PSALM 80 (This is not so well known and the metaphor changes to that of the vinedresser.)

(d) JOHN 10.7–18 Jesus speaks of himself first as the 'door' by which people enter the 'fold' of eternal life; then as the Good Shepherd who knows his sheep individually, cares for them and is ready to die for them.

(e) 1 PETER 5.1–4 Peter speaks of the 'elders' of the Church as 'shepherds' and tells them how they should behave.

## 98 SOME STORIES WHICH ILLUSTRATE WHAT JESUS DOES FOR MEN 1 (from MARK)

(a) MARK 1.21–45 Jesus shows his compassion for men and his power over every kind of human sickness: spiritual, mental, moral and physical.
(b) MARK 2.1–17 Jesus shows that he is concerned to make people *completely* whole; and this may involve forgiving them their sins.
(c) MARK 4.35–41 To the Jews the sea was a symbol of chaos and evil, a storm at sea particularly so. The early Christians suffering persecution were reminded by this story that Jesus brings 'the peace of God which passes all understanding' to those who are being 'tossed in the storms of life'.
(d) MARK 7.31–37 The ears of a deaf man are 'opened' by the love of Jesus.
(e) MARK 8.22–26 A man who is blind is made able (by degrees) to 'see the light'.

## 99 SOME STORIES WHICH ILLUSTRATE WHAT JESUS DOES FOR MEN 2 (from JOHN)

(a) JOHN 2.1–11 Jesus saves a situation by transforming water into wine.
(There are good reasons for thinking that this was a parable recounted here as an event, one being the enormous quantity of wine.)
(b) JOHN 2.12–22 The stern side of Jesus' transforming power. The old Jewish Temple must be transformed—at the cost of Jesus' death and resurrection—into the 'temple' of his new 'body', the Christian Church.
(c) JOHN 4.5–14 Jesus offers the 'water of life'.
(d) JOHN 6.1–14, 35, 47–51 Jesus offers the 'bread of life'.
(e) JOHN 6.15–21 Jesus is the 'way of life'. He joins disciples who are struggling across the lake and brings them to their destination.

## 100 OPPOSITION TO JESUS 1

(a) MARK 2.1–17 People resent the fact that Jesus forgives sins. They disapprove of the company he keeps, but he says that he has come to serve the 'bad' as well as the so-called 'good'.

(b) MARK 2.18–28; 3.1–8 People disapprove because Jesus does not 'keep the rules'. He shows that rules cannot contain the power of his goodness. So, the outraged authorities plot to put him to death.

(c) MARK 3.22–30 We are told elsewhere (Matthew 12.22) that Jesus has cast an unclean spirit out of a man who was blind and dumb. The authorities cannot deny that he has done this, so they ascribe his action to the power of evil. Jesus tells them that to call 'good evil, and evil good' is to put yourself beyond the power of forgiveness.

(d) MARK 6.1–6 Jesus is rejected in his own neighbourhood.

## 101 OPPOSITION TO JESUS 2

(a) MARK 7.1–13 The authorities try to catch Jesus with one of their own regulations, and are told that they use their regulations to harm the true law of God. ('Corban' means 'something dedicated to God'. The rule was that money made 'corban' in the Temple could not be given away. The Pharisees were using this rule to enable them to escape the obligation of giving money to their parents.)

(b) MARK 11.15–19 Jesus restores the Temple to its proper use; but the authorities resent this exercise of his authority.

(c) MARK 12.1–12 Jesus tells the authorities that they are as bad as —and worse than—their forefathers.

(d) MARK 14.55–64 The authorities accuse Jesus of religious crimes, but fail to prove them. He admits to being the 'Christ' —the 'King'—in the religious sense of the word.

(e) LUKE 23.1–5 (6–12), 13–25 Before the civil governor, Jesus is accused of civil crimes. He is found innocent, but condemned to death all the same.

# The Teaching of Jesus

## 102 THE SERMON ON THE MOUNT
(Matthew, chapters 5–7)

For Beatitudes (Matthew 5.1–12) see 21(a)

(a) MATTHEW 5.13–16 Christian 'light' must 'shine' and be seen.
For Matthew 5.17–26 see 21(b)

For Matthew 5.27–32 see 33(e)
For Matthew 5.33–37 see 21(d)
For Matthew 5.38–48 see 21(c)

(b) MATTHEW 6.1–4, 16–18 Acts of charity and acts of self-discipline must be for God, not for one's own reputation.

(c) MATTHEW 6.5–15 Lessons on prayer. It must be God-centred and trusting, and made in a spirit of humility and love.

For Matthew 6.19–34 see 14(d)

(d) MATTHEW 7.1–5 Christians are forbidden to judge other people.

(e) MATTHEW 7.7–12 Christians are told to go on asking and seeking.

(f) MATTHEW 7.13–23 The difficulty of the Christian way. Ultimately it all depends on what we *do*.

(g) MATTHEW 7.24–29 The strong life—and the weak.

## 103 PARABLES OF JESUS 1: THE KINGDOM

Jesus used parables partly to make his meaning more clear, but also to ensure that only those who really wanted to consider his teaching faithfully and sincerely would be able to understand it. The truth cannot be forced on people. They must choose to receive it.

(a) MARK 4.1–20 Different people respond to the word of God in different ways: but in spite of much waste the Kingdom of God grows.

(b) MARK 4.24–29 The more generously a person listens to the word of God, the more generously will he be rewarded. But results come slowly, not dramatically.

(c) MARK 4.30–32 In individual people and in the world as a whole, the Kingdom of God grows from something very small to something very large.

(d) MATTHEW 13.44–46 It is worth giving up everything for the Kingdom of Heaven.

## 104 PARABLES OF JESUS 2: PRAYER AND FORGIVENESS

(a) LUKE 18.1–8 The importance of persistence in prayer.

(b) LUKE 18.9–14 The importance of humility in prayer.

(c) MATTHEW 18.21–35 The importance of forgiving other people.

(d) LUKE 15.1–3, (4–7), (8–10), 11–32 God loves to forgive.

## 105 PARABLES OF JESUS 3: HOW TO TREAT OTHER PEOPLE

(a) LUKE 10.25–37 The good neighbour.
(b) LUKE 16.19–31 The bad neighbour.
(c) MATTHEW 25.31–46 Your neighbour is Christ.

## 106 PARABLES OF JESUS 4: RESPONSE TO GOD AND USE OF HIS GIFTS

(a) LUKE 14.12–24 It is those who know their own need who are ready to accept the Kingdom of God.
(b) MATTHEW 25.14–30 Gifts and responsibilities.
(c) MATTHEW 25.1–13 Efficiency.
(d) LUKE 13.6–9 Judgement is by results.
(e) MATTHEW (19.27–30) 20.1–16 We cannot bargain with God.

# Prayers

## General Prayers of Invocation

### OPENING PRAYERS

107 Almighty God, unto whom all hearts be open, all desires known, and from whom no secrets are hid; cleanse the thoughts of our hearts by the inspiration of thy Holy Spirit, that we may perfectly love thee, and worthily magnify thy holy name; through Jesus Christ our Lord.

*Book of Common Prayer*

108 Almighty God, you are ready at all times to hear the prayers of those who call upon you: open our hearts and lips to bless and glorify your name; through Jesus Christ our Lord.

Uppingham School (adapted)

109 Cleanse our hearts, we beseech thee, O God, that we may worship thee in spirit and in truth; through Jesus Christ our Lord.

*Prayer Book, 1549*

110 Loving Lord God, fill us with a sense of your life-giving, joy-giving, peace-giving presence; that we may praise you now with our lips and all the day long with our lives: through Jesus Christ our Lord.

C.R.C.

111 O God, our Father, for this short time of worship direct and control our thoughts that we may think only of you.
Grant us
Reverence as we remember your glory;
Penitence as we remember your holiness;
Gratitude as we remember your love:
So that we may rise from our worship
With knowledge deepened;
With love kindled;
With strength to live more nearly as we ought:
Through Jesus Christ our Lord.

*Epilogues and Prayers* (adapted)

112 O God, who art Spirit, and willest to be worshipped in spirit and in truth: grant to us that, loving thee in all things and above all things, we may please thee by our prayers and by our lives; through Jesus Christ our Lord.

William Bright, 1824–1901

113 O God, you are present with us all the time, but we forget you as we go about our daily lives. Help us now to realize your presence, respond to your love, and give you worship that is true and sincere; through Jesus Christ our Lord.

C.R.C.

114 This day (or, night), O God, we bring to you
Our sorrow for our wrong-doing;
Our gratitude for your gifts;
Our requests for our needs;
Our remembrance of others,
In the certainty that you will hear them all;
Through Jesus Christ our Lord.

*Epilogues and Prayers*

115 We are told that you see us here, Lord, and that you know our hearts; so we do not need to hide our reluctance and faithlessness, our anger and rebelliousness, our sin and unworthiness. Please accept whatever prayers we can offer, and answer them by giving us the courage in all things and at all times to do what is right: through Jesus Christ our Lord.

C.R.C.

## PRAYERS OF PRAISE

116 Almighty, all-loving Father, as we think of the wonder of this world which you created, and of the wonders which are being discovered every day, we humbly bow our heads and say:
We praise and adore you.
We acknowledge you to be the Lord.
We love you, and long to serve you; through Jesus Christ our Lord.

L. Maude Spedding

117 Blessed be the God of Heaven and Earth for the glory of nature. We offer you praise, Heavenly Father, for the growth of seed, the blossom and fruit, the cleansing frosts of winter, for the earth's rebirth in spring, and the harvest of your gifts. All the earth worships its Creator: your law and power are everywhere. Praised be your name.

A. G. Bullivant

118 Great, O Lord, is thy kingdom, thy power, and thy glory; great are thy works, thy wonders, and thy praises; great also is thy wisdom, thy goodness, thy justice, thy mercy; and for all these we do bless thee, and will magnify thy holy name for ever and ever.

George Wither, 1588–1667

119 Let us praise God and honour his name in everything that we do.
Let us pray that he will help us to serve him faithfully.
Let us praise God in his holiness, and love him wholeheartedly.
Let us praise him for his loving care and thank him for showing himself to us.
May our lives, our thoughts, our actions and our prayers be to the honour of God, now and evermore.

A. G. Bullivant

120 Most high, omnipotent, good Lord.
Thine be the praise, the glory, the honour, and all benediction.
To thee alone, Most High, they are due,
and no man is worthy to mention thee.

Be thou praised, my Lord, with all thy creatures,
above all Brother Sun,
who gives the day and lightens us therewith.

And he is beautiful and radiant with great splendour,
of thee, Most High, he bears similitude.

Be thou praised, my Lord, of Sister Moon and the stars,
in the heaven hast thou formed them, clear and precious
and comely . . .

Be thou praised, my Lord, of Sister Water,
which is much useful and humble and precious and pure.

Be thou praised, my Lord, of Brother Fire,
by which thou hast lightened the night,
and he is beautiful and joyful and robust and strong.

Be thou praised, my Lord, of our Sister Mother Earth,
which sustains and hath us in rule,
and produces divers fruits with coloured flowers and herbs. . . .

Praise ye and bless my Lord, and give him thanks,
and serve him with great humility.

*The Mirror of Perfection*
Franciscan—Translated by Robert Steele (adapted)

121 O Lord our God, glorious in majesty, infinite in mercy, we praise and magnify thy holy name, and offer unto thee, Father, Son and Holy Spirit, the worship of our hearts; through Jesus Christ our Lord.

Scotch College, Melbourne

122 O most high, almighty, good Lord God: to thee belong praise, glory, honour and all blessing!
Praised be my Lord by all those who pardon one another for thy love's sake, and who endure weakness and tribulation.
Blessed are they who peaceably shall endure, for thou, O Most Highest, shall give them a crown.
Praise ye and bless ye the Lord, and give thanks unto him, and serve him with great humility.

Franciscan (from *Cantico delle Creature*)

123 Thou art my Life; if thou but turn away,
My life's a thousand deaths: thou art my Way;
Without thee, Lord, I travel not, but stray.

My light thou art; without thy glorious sight
My eyes are darkened with perpetual night:
My God, thou art my Way, my Life, my Light.

Francis Quarles, 1592–1644

124 We praise thee, O God, for thy glory displayed in all the creatures of the earth,
In the snow, in the rain, in the wind, in the storm; in all of thy creatures, both the hunters and the hunted.
They affirm thee in living; all things affirm thee in living; the bird in the air, both the hawk and the finch; the beast on the earth, both the wolf and the lamb; the worm in the soil and the worm in the belly.
Therefore, man, whom thou hast made to be conscious of thee, must consciously praise thee, in thought and in word and in deed.
Even with the hand to the broom, the back bent in laying the fire, the knee bent in cleaning the hearth,
The back bent under toil, the knee bent under sin, the hands to the face under fear, the head bent under grief,
Even in us the voices of seasons, the snuffle of winter, the song of spring, the drone of summer, the voices of beasts and of birds, praise thee.

T. S. Eliot, 1888–1965
*Murder in the Cathedral* (adapted)

*From the Psalms*

125 I will sing unto the Lord as long as I live: I will praise my God while I have my being. And so shall my words please him: my joy shall be in the Lord.

Psalm 104.33–4

126 Kings of the earth and all people: princes and all judges of the world; young men and maidens, old men and children, praise the name of the Lord: for his name only is excellent, and his praise above heaven and earth.

Psalm 148.11–2

127 O praise the Lord, for it is a good thing to sing praises unto our God: yea, a joyful and pleasant thing it is to be thankful.

Psalm 147.1

128 O praise the Lord with me,
and let us magnify his name together.
I will sing unto the Lord as long as I live,

I will praise my God while I have my being.
O give thanks unto the Lord, for he is gracious;
and his mercy endureth for ever.

Psalms 34, 104, 107
*Daily Prayer*

129 Praise the Lord, O my soul; and all that is within me praise his holy name. Praise the Lord, O my soul; and forget not all his benefits.

Psalm 103.1–2

*Man the Viceroy of God*

130 How great is your name, O Lord our God,
through all the earth!

Your majesty is praised above the heavens;
on the lips of children and of babes
you have found praise to foil your enemy,
to silence the foe and the rebel.

When I see the heavens, the work of your hands,
the moon and the stars which you arranged,
what is man that you should keep him in mind,
mortal man that you care for him?

Yet you have made him little less than a god;
with glory and honour you crowned him,
gave him power over the works of your hand,
put all things under his feet.

All of them, sheep and cattle,
yes, even the savage beasts,
birds of the air, and fish
that make their way through the waters.

How great is your name, O Lord our God,
through all the earth.

Psalm 8
*The Psalms: A New Translation*

### *Harvest Song*

131

O God, be gracious and bless us
and let your face shed its light upon us.
So will your ways be known upon earth
and all nations learn your saving help.

*Let the peoples praise you, O God;
let all the peoples praise you.

Let the nations be glad and exult
for you rule the world with justice.
With fairness you rule the peoples,
you guide the nations on earth.

*Let the peoples praise you, O God;
let all the peoples praise you.

The earth has yielded its fruit
for God, our God has blessed us.
May God still give us his blessing
till the ends of the earth revere him.

*Let the peoples praise you, O God;
let all the peoples praise you.

* This refrain (or just its second line) can be said by the congregation.

Psalm 66
*The Psalms: A New Translation*

### *God's Boundless Care for his Creation*

132

Bless the Lord, my soul!
Lord God, how great you are,
clothed in majesty and glory,
wrapped in light as in a robe!

How many are your works, O Lord!
In wisdom you have made them all.
The earth is full of your riches. . . .

You stretch out the heavens like a tent.
Above the rains you build your dwelling.
You make the clouds your chariot,
you walk on the wings of the wind,
you make the winds your messengers
and flashing fire your servants.

From your dwelling you water the hills;
earth drinks its fill of your gift.
You make the grass grow for the cattle
and the plants to serve man's needs,
that he may bring forth bread from the earth
and wine, to cheer man's heart;
oil, to make his face shine
and bread to strengthen man's heart.

You made the moon to mark the months;
the sun knows the time for its setting.
When you spread the darkness it is night
and all the beasts of the forest creep forth.
The young lions roar for their prey
and ask their food from God.

All these look to you
to give them their food in due season.
You give it, they gather it up:
you open your hand, they have their fill.

I will sing to the Lord all my life,
make music to my God while I live.

Bless the Lord, my soul.

From Psalm 103
*The Psalms: A New Translation*

*Summons to Praise*

133 Alleluia!

Praise God in his holy place,
praise him in his mighty heavens.

Praise him for his powerful deeds,
praise his surpassing greatness.

O praise him with sound of trumpet,
praise him with lute and harp.
Praise him with timbrel and dance,
praise him with strings and pipes.

O praise him with resounding cymbals,
praise him with clashing of cymbals.
Let everything that lives and that breathes
give praise to the Lord. Alleluia!

Psalm 150
*The Psalms: A New Translation*

## PRAYERS OF THANKSGIVING

### *For the Life and Teaching of Christ*

134 O God, we thank thee for the life and teaching of Jesus; for the new ideals and new hope that he has given to mankind; for his inspiration to the struggling, his comfort to the fallen; for all the strength and vision which he gives to those who try to spread his spirit on earth. Help us to be more truly thankful for all that his life has meant; and grant that we may thus more worthily strive to follow him and make his love known among men; through the same Jesus Christ our Lord.

Westminster School

### *For Food: Graces*

135 For food to eat, and those who prepare it,
For health to enjoy it, and friends to share it,
We thank Thee, O Lord.

Charles Shepherd, *Benedictus, Benedicatur*

136 For life and love and home and food,
For all You give us for our good,
We thank You, Heavenly Father.

Charles Shepherd, *Benedictus, Benedicatur* (adapted)

137 For these and all His blessings, God's Holy Name be praised, through Jesus Christ our Lord.

Charles Shepherd, *Benedictus, Benedicatur*

138 For what we are about to receive, thank God.

Charles Shepherd, *Benedictus, Benedicatur*

139 O Lord, give us grateful hearts
For the food now set before us,
And supply the wants of others
For Christ's sake.

Charles Shepherd, *Benedictus, Benedicatur*

*For Friendship*

140 Thanksgiving and praise be to our God for his gift of friends: for the comfort of knowing that we can trust them; for the joy of sharing our time, our work, amusements, sports, hobbies and everything we do with them. May he teach us to be true friends to others, and guard us from letting them down or doing them harm in any way. Above all else, let us thank God for the friendship of Jesus, who laid down his life to save us, his friends and his servants.

A. G. Bullivant

*General Thanksgiving*

141 Almighty God, Father of all mercies, we thine unworthy servants do give thee most humble and hearty thanks for all thy goodness and loving-kindness to us and to all men; we bless thee for our creation, preservation, and all the blessings of this life; but above all for thine inestimable love in the redemption of the world by our Lord Jesus Christ; for the means of grace, and for the hope of glory. And we beseech thee, give us that due sense of all thy mercies, that our hearts may be unfeignedly thankful, and that we show forth thy praise, not only with our lips, but in our lives; by giving up ourselves to thy service, and by walking before thee in holiness and righteousness all our days; through Jesus Christ our Lord, to whom with thee and the Holy Ghost be all honour and glory, world without end.

*Book of Common Prayer*

142 Mighty God,
we lift up our hearts to you
in gratitude for your love to us.
Take our lives—
our work and leisure,
the ordinary things of life and the special things,
the sadness and joy we know and have known.
Accept our praise and thanksgiving
as we offer ourselves to you
in worship and adoration.
Through Jesus Christ our Lord.

*Contemporary Prayers for Public Worship* (adapted)

143 O God our Father, from whom all good things do come:

We give our deep and humble thanks for all your goodness and kindness to us, and to all mankind.

We thank you for making us and giving us life, for keeping us in health, for preserving us in safety, and for all the blessings of this life.

But above all we thank you for your measureless love in sending our Lord Jesus Christ, to bring us back to you, for the joy of grace, and for the hope of glory.

And we ask that we may show our gratitude not only in what we say, but in what we do, by giving up ourselves to be your servants, and by walking before you in the right way, all the days of our life.

Through Jesus Christ our Lord.

*Prayers for Every Day* (adapted)

144 O God, whose love we cannot measure, whose blessings we cannot number; we thank you for all your goodness to us. In our weakness, you are our strength; in our darkness, you give us light; in our sorrows, you bring comfort and peace; and always you are our God, Father, Son and Holy Spirit, world without end.

*Daily Prayer* (adapted)

### *For the Goodness of Other People*

145 Let us thank God for those who have endured that we might enjoy; who have suffered that we might survive; for doctors and

scientists; for those statesmen and reformers who against ignorance and prejudice have upheld a good cause; for artists, poets and musicians; for the perseverance of all those whose work is dangerous or tedious; for the courage of all good men and for the dauntless patience of our Lord himself who endured to the end and was crucified for our sakes. Let us show our gratitude in the prayers we offer and in the lives we lead, trying humbly to follow our Master, Jesus Christ.

Brentwood School

146 For fellowship and all things good,
We praise Thy Name, O Lord.

Charles Shepherd, *Benedictus, Benedicatur*

*For Homes*

147 O God, we thank thee for our homes and the loving influence of our parents, for our brothers and sisters, our relations and our friends, and for all who by their life and example have helped us to know more of thee. Grant us to show forth our gratitude in love and joy and service, through the love of Jesus Christ our Lord.

W. L. Anderson,
in *A Book of Prayers for Schools* (adapted)

148 We thank you, God our father, for the homes you have given to us:
for the love of our parents when things go well and when things go badly;
for the care which our parents take of us and for the food, clothes and comforts which they buy for us;
for the security we find in their affection, and for their reliability, their warmth and their strength.

We thank you, God our father, for our brothers, our sisters, our relations and our friends:
for the fellowship and enrichment they bring to us in happy times and in sad times;
for the pleasures we enjoy together;

for merriment and laughter, and for consolation shared in time of sorrow.

Finally, for the opportunities you give us to show our love for our parents, our relations and our friends,

we thank you, God our father, through your son who lived with his family in a home on earth and knew, like us, its joys and sorrows,

Jesus Christ our Lord.

Marlborough College

*For Life and the Gifts of Life*

149 Let us praise and thank God for all great and simple joys;

For the gift of wonder and the joy of discovery; for the everlasting freshness of experience;

For all that comes to us through sympathy and through sorrow, and for the joy of work attempted and achieved;

For musicians, poets and craftsmen, and for all who work in form and colour to increase the beauty of life;

For the likeness of Christ in ordinary people, their forbearance, courage and kindness, and for all obscure and humble lives of service;

Glory be to the Father and to the Son and to the Holy Spirit ever world without end.

*The Kingdom, the Power and the Glory* (adapted)

150 O God, our Father, we would thank thee for all the bright things of life. Help us to see them, and to count them, and to remember them, that our lives may flow in ceaseless praise: for the sake of Jesus Christ our Lord.

J. H. Jowett, 1864–1923

151 Thanks be to God for the air we breathe, for the life we live, for the strength of our bodies, and for the thoughts of our minds. We thank You for the happiness which brightens life and for the love which brings happiness. We thank You above all for the life of Jesus, who teaches us the true way to live. We pray to be reminded every day of the many blessings which come to us through You; our Saviour and God for ever and ever.

A. G. Bullivant (adapted)

152 Thanks be to you, O Lord our God, for all the gifts you have given mankind to enjoy: for mind, body, and soul, through which we can worship you; for the heavens and the earth, which declare your majesty. More than everything else, we thank you for the life of Jesus: for his example, his courage, his kindness, his death on the cross, his resurrection, and his Church.

A. G. Bullivant

153 We thank you, O Father, for the beauty of earth and sea and sky; for peaceful homes and healthful days; for all the powers of mind and body; for the joy of loving and being loved. Give us grace to show our praise not only with our lips but in our lives; through Jesus Christ our Lord.

*Prayers for Dragons* (adapted)

154 We thank you, O God, for all the interesting things in life.

For music and for rhythm;
For pictures and for plays;
For wireless and for television;
For the things which make us laugh;
For the things which command our interest;
For the things which widen our knowledge;
We thank you, O God.

For our work and for our study;
And for the real satisfaction of a difficult task mastered, completed and done:
We thank you, O God: through Jesus Christ our Lord.

*Epilogues and Prayers*

*Personal Thanksgiving and Penitence*

155 I thank thee, my Creator and Lord, that thou hast given me these joys in thy creation, this ecstasy over the works of thy hands. I have made known the glory of thy works to men as far as my finite spirit was able to comprehend thy infinity. If I have said anything wholly unworthy of thee, or have aspired after my own glory, graciously forgive me.

Johann Kepler, Astronomer, 1571–1630

(His hands were crippled and his eyesight permanently impaired by smallpox at the age of four. He may be called the founder of physical astronomy.)

*For the Saints*

156 We thank you, O Father, for the example of the saints of old, for their words and deeds and lives of love; and we ask for the courage to serve you as they served you on earth; through Jesus Christ our Lord.

C.R.C.

*Thanksgiving for the School*

157 There are many things, O God our father, that we have to thank you for, and yet we often forget, our hearts are cold, our gratitude weak. We should thank you particularly for this school; for the life we have together; the help, friendship and teaching we receive from each other; all the opportunities for service, responsibility, fulfilment and happiness that come to us; and the knowledge, strength and skill that we are acquiring. We thank you for the generosity of those who started this school, and for the loyalty of those who have served it and serve it now. Help us to enjoy to the full all that we receive here and to express our thanks by living lives that give happiness to others; through the love of your son, Jesus Christ our Lord.

C.R.C.

158 We humbly thank thee, O almighty God, for the blessings which thou hast bestowed upon us in this school. Help us to use these in thy service and teach us to serve thee not only in word and prayer, but in everything that we do; and this we ask for Jesus Christ's sake, our blessed Lord and Saviour.

Uppingham School

## PRAYERS OF CONFESSION AND FORGIVENESS

*Absolution*

159 Almighty God have mercy upon you,
Pardon and deliver you from all your sins,

Confirm and strengthen you in all goodness,
And keep you in life eternal;
Through Jesus Christ our Lord.

*An Order for Holy Communion* (S.P.C.K.)

160 Almighty God, our heavenly father, who of his great mercy has promised forgiveness of sins to all who forgive their brethren and with hearty repentance and true faith turn unto him; pardon and deliver you from all your sins; confirm and strengthen you in all goodness; and bring you to eternal life; through Jesus Christ our Lord.

*Book of Common Worship*, Church of South India

161 The almighty and merciful Lord grant unto you pardon and remission of all your sins, time for amendment of life, and the grace and comfort of the Holy Spirit.

Compline

*Assurance of Forgiveness*

162 God so loved the world, that he gave his only begotten son, that whosoever believeth in him should not perish, but have everlasting life.

John 3.16

163 'Here are words you may trust,
words that merit full acceptance:
"Christ Jesus came into the world to save sinners".'

To all who confess their sins
and resolve to lead a new life
he says:
'Your sins are forgiven',
and he also says,
'Follow me'.

'Now to the King of all worlds,
immortal, invisible, the only wise God,
be honour and glory for ever and ever. Amen.'

(The first and last quotations are from 1 Timothy 1.15 NEB.)

164 Jesus said, 'I am come that they may have life, and have it more abundantly.'

John 10.10

*As We Forgive Them*

165 O Lord Jesus, we confess how quickly we see other people's faults, and how slow we are to recognize our own. Forgive us, and make us more forgiving; through Jesus Christ our Lord.

Beryl Bye, *Prayers at Breakfast*

*Prayers of Confession*

166

Almighty God, our heavenly Father,
we have sinned against thee,
through our own fault,
in thought, and word, and deed,
and in what we have left undone.

For thy Son our Lord Jesus Christ's sake,
forgive us all that is past;
and grant that we may serve thee,
in newness of life,
to the glory of thy name.

*An Order for Holy Communion* (S.P.C.K.)

167 Father, we have sinned, and are no more worthy to be called thy sons.

Luke 15.21 (adapted)

168 God:

Take fire and burn our guilt and our lying hypocrisies.

Take water and wash away our brothers' blood which we have caused to be shed.

Take hot sunlight and dry the tears of those we have hurt, and heal their wounded souls, minds, and bodies.

Take love and root it in our hearts, so that brotherhood may grow, transforming the dry desert of our prejudices and hatreds.

Take our imperfect prayers and purify them, so that we mean what we pray and are prepared to give ourselves to you along with our words, through Jesus Christ, who did not disdain to take our humanness upon him and live among us, sharing our life, our joys, and our pains.

Malcolm Boyd, *Are you running with me, Jesus?*

169 Heavenly Father, we admit the mistakes of our life which we cannot undo. Help us to accept their consequences without bitterness, and within their limits to see our immediate obedience, and to act upon it with joy: through Jesus Christ our Lord.

*Contemporary Prayers for Public Worship*

170 Lord we confess:
That by silence and the ill-considered word
  We have built up the walls of prejudice.
That by selfishness and lack of sympathy
  We have stifled generosity.
That in thinking of our safety and reputation
  We have passed by on the other side.
That by obsession with our own affairs
  We have had no time for others.
For all our failures
  Lord, forgive us.
And in your mercy
  Accept us, good Lord.

*Outreach, an Act of Worhsip* (adapted)

171 Most gracious God,
full of loving-kindness and longsuffering:

We confess unto thee
our neglect and forgetfulness of thy commandments,
our wrong doing, speaking and thinking,
the hurt we have done to others,
and the good we have left undone:

O Lord, blot out
the transgressions that are against us,
for thy goodness and thy glory,
and for the sake of thy Son our Saviour, Jesus Christ.

*Daily Prayer*

172 O God our Father,
we have sinned against you
in thought, word and deed:
we have not loved you with all our heart;
we have not loved our neighbours as ourselves.
Have mercy on us;
strip us of all that is un-Christian;
and help us to live up to our calling;
through Jesus Christ our Lord.

*Contemporary Prayers for Public Worship*
(adapted)

173 O God, our sins are many; strip us of them like a garment.

Sumerian poet, about 2000 B.C.

174 We confess to God Almighty, the Father, the Son, and the Holy Ghost (before the whole company of Heaven), that we have sinned in thought, word and deed through our own fault. Therefore, we pray God to have mercy upon us.

Almighty God have mercy upon us, forgive us all our sins, and bring us to everlasting life: through Jesus Christ our Lord.

Compline (adapted)

### *By the Cross*

175 Forgive us daily, Lord, the sins which crucify you anew.

Forgive the hatred of the crowd which chose Barabbas; and the hate so often lying in our hearts.

Forgive the selfishness and ambition of Caiaphas, and the pride and vanity of all men.

Forgive the weakness of Pilate, and our inability to resist temptation.

Forgive the brutality of the soldiers, and the cruelties of our world.

Forgive the hard-heartedness and sneers of those who passed by, and forgive us when we sneer at holy things, or pass by suffering, or ignore unhappiness.

Take all these sins from the world, crucified Saviour; bear

them away in your dying body, let evil die and be conquered for ever, cast out by your undying love.

A. G. Bullivant

*For Forgiveness*

176 Grant, we beseech thee, merciful Lord, to thy faithful people pardon and peace, that they may be cleansed from all their sins and serve thee with a quiet mind, through Jesus Christ our Lord.

*Book of Common Prayer*

177 Lord, for thy tender mercy's sake, lay not our sins to our charge, but forgive that is past and give us grace to amend our lives; to decline from sin and incline to virtue, that we may walk with a perfect heart before thee, now and evermore.

Bishop Ridley, *Prayers, 1500–1555*

178 May the almighty and merciful Lord grant unto us pardon and remission of all our sins, time for amendment of life, and the grace and comfort of the Holy Spirit.

Compline (adapted)

179 O thou who wast strong enough to bear all our sins: impart to us thy strength that we may sin no more; for thy tender mercy's sake.

*Daily Prayer*

180 Praise and thanksgiving be given to our God for his free forgiveness to all who sin against him. May he enable us to forgive others their sins against us, and to recognise faults in ourselves, through Jesus Christ our Lord.

A. G. Bullivant

*Prayer of Repentance and Trust*

181 Out of the depths I cry to you, O Lord,
Lord, hear my voice!
O let your ears be attentive
to the voice of my pleading.

If you, O Lord, should mark our guilt,
Lord, who would survive?
But with you is found forgiveness:
for this we revere you.

My soul is waiting for the Lord,
I count on his word.
My soul is longing for the Lord
more than watchmen for daybreak.

Because with the Lord there is mercy
and fullness of redemption,
his people indeed he will redeem
from all their iniquity.

Psalm 130 (adapted)
*The Psalms: A New Translation*

*Sins*

182 Forgive me my sins, O Lord—the sins of my present and the sins of my past, the sins of my soul and the sins of my body, the sins which I have done to please myself and the sins which I have done to please others. Forgive me my casual sins and my deliberate sins and those which I have laboured so to hide that I have hidden them even from myself. Forgive me them, O Lord, forgive them all; for Jesus Christ's sake.

Thomas Wilson, 1663–1755

*Besetting Sins*

183 O God, very often we fail to learn from our mistakes and continue to repeat them. Give us your grace to conquer our besetting sins; through Jesus Christ our Lord.

Beryl Bye, *Prayers at Breakfast* (adapted)

*Thanksgiving for Forgiveness*

184 My soul, give thanks to the Lord,
all my being bless his holy name.

My soul give thanks to the Lord
and never forget all his blessings.

It is he who forgives all your guilt,
who heals every one of your ills,
who redeems your life from the grave,
who crowns you with love and compassion,
who fills your life with good things,
renewing your youth like an eagle's.

The Lord is compassion and love,
slow to anger and rich in mercy.
His wrath will come to an end;
he will not be angry for ever.
He does not treat us according to our sins
nor repay us according to our faults.

For as the heavens are high above the earth
so strong is his love for those who fear him.
As far as the east is from the west
so far does he remove our sins.

As a father has compassion on his sons,
the Lord has pity on those who fear him;
for he remembers of what we are made,
he remembers that we are dust.

Give thanks to the Lord, all his hosts,
his servants who do his will.
Give thanks to the Lord all his works,
in every place where he rules.
My soul, give thanks to the Lord!

From Psalm 102 (adapted)
*The Psalms: A New Translation*

*Time Wasted*

185 O Lord in whose hands are life and death, by whose power we are sustained, forgive us that we have suffered the days and hours, of which we must give account, to pass away without any

endeavour to accomplish thy will. Make us to remember, O God, that every day is thy gift and ought to be used according to thy command. Grant us therefore so to repent of our negligence that we may pass the time which thou shalt yet allow us in diligent service; through Jesus Christ.

Samuel Johnson, 1709–1784

*Unkindness*

186 O Lord Jesus Christ, who showed patience and generosity in your judgment of the people round you, forgive us our careless criticisms and unkind words which cause suffering to others; help us not to indulge in cruel gossip, but to seek the best that lies in everyone and use it to the glory of your name; through yourself our Lord and Saviour.

*An Anthology of Prayers* (adapted)

187 O Lord Jesus, we confess that we are sometimes deliberately unkind to other people. Forgive us and help us to show them your love; through Jesus Christ our Lord.

Beryl Bye, *Prayers at Breakfast*

188 When we hear, O God, of man's unspeakable inhumanity to man, we are appalled. In comparison, our own mean actions—when we torment other people or hurt them by our coldness or by our hostility—these actions seem trivial. But they are not. The monstrous cruelties of the world grow out of small, mean cruelties. We ask you to forgive us for having been cold and unfriendly, and to give us the strength to be kind to those people whom we don't much like; in the name of Jesus Christ our Lord.

Marlborough College

## PRAYERS OF SELF-DEDICATION

189 Almighty God,
we offer thee our souls and bodies,
to be a living sacrifice,

through Jesus Christ our Lord.
Send us out into the world
in the power of thy Spirit,
to live and work
to thy praise and glory.

*An Order of Holy Communion* (S.P.C.K.)

190 Blessed Saviour, receive what I have, strengthen my body and uplift my mind; let my heart be cleansed from any base feeling, let it become the temple of the Holy Ghost; and let me speak and act and think and live under his inspiration for thy Name's sake.

Reed's School

191 Grant, O God, that at all times and in all places, in all things great and small, we may do thy most perfect will; through Jesus Christ our Lord.

Community of the Servants of the Will of God

192 Lord, make us instruments of thy peace.
Where there is hatred, let us sow love;
where there is injury, pardon;
where there is discord, union;
where there is doubt, faith;
where there is despair, hope;
where there is darkness, light;
where there is sadness, joy;
O Divine Master, grant that we may not so much seek to be consoled as to console; to be understood as to understand; to be loved, as to love; through the love of thy Son who died for us, Jesus Christ our Lord.

St. Francis of Assisi, 1181–1266

193 Lord, please show us some practical way in which we can serve you today.

Beryl Bye, *Prayers at Breakfast*

194 Loving Father, Creator of all things, Author of all goodness, Source of all unifying love, make us aware at this moment of your

love for us. Bless our world, our country, our friends, ourselves. Enrich our leisure (holidays), enhance our work, make noble our love for others; and grant that at all times and in all places in all things great and small we may do thy perfect will: through Jesus Christ our Lord.

C.R.C.

195 O God, from whom every good and perfect gift doth come, give us grace to consecrate to thy service the talents which thou hast committed to our charge, that, whether as teachers or learners, we may do all things as in thy sight and to thy glory; through Jesus Christ our Lord.

Source unknown

196 O Lord God, take our lives today and use them for good here in this school. Help us at work and play to be honest and truthful; guide us to help those who need what we can give; through Jesus Christ our Lord.

Brentwood School

197 O Lord God, we acknowledge thee as our Father,
ourselves as thy children,
and our neighbours as our brothers.
We dedicate to thy obedience and to their service,
our hearts and minds, our wills and works:
resolved to stand forth in thy faith,
to seek the help of thy Holy Spirit,
And to do battle for thy kingdom,
in the name of Jesus Christ our Lord.

Warwick School

198 O Lord Jesus Christ,
Take our hands, and work with them;
Take our lips, and speak through them;
Take our minds, and think with them;
Take our hearts, and set them on fire
With love for thee and for all mankind:
For thy sake.

Warwick School

199 Remember, O Lord, what thou hast wrought in us, and not what we deserve, and as thou hast called us to thy service, make us worthy of our calling, through Jesus Christ our Lord.

*Book of Common Prayer*

200 Teach us, good Lord, to serve thee as thou deservest; to give and not to count the cost, to fight and not to heed the wounds, to toil and not to seek for rest, to labour and not to ask for any reward, save that of knowing that we do thy will; through Jesus Christ our Lord.

Ignatius Loyola, 1491–1556

201 Take our lives and consecrate them to your service, dear Lord, so that we may not hanker after merely worldly things, but fill our days with the search for the heavenly treasure of your Son Jesus; for his name's sake.

A. G. Bullivant

202

Teach me, my God and King
In all things thee to see;
And what I do in anything
To do it as for thee.

George Herbert, 1593–1632

*Possessions*

203 Dear Father God, help us to look on our possessions as gifts from you, and not as symbols of our own importance.

Beryl Bye, *Prayers at Breakfast*

204 O God, we dedicate to you all the money and personal property of those in this school, and pray that perfect honesty and generosity may be found among us. Grant that we never sacrifice spiritual things for mere gain, but lay up for ourselves treasures of the spirit: through Jesus Christ our Lord.

*Prayer Book for Catholic Seafarers,*
*Apostleship of the Sea* (adapted)

## MORNING PRAYERS

*Collect for Grace*

205 O Lord, our heavenly Father, almighty and everlasting God, who hast safely brought us to the beginning of this day; defend us in the same with thy mighty power, and grant that this day we fall into no sin, neither run into any kind of danger; but that all our doings may be ordered by thy governance, to do always that is righteous in thy sight; through Jesus Christ our Lord.

*Book of Common Prayer*

*Collect for Peace*

206 O God, who are the author of peace and lover of concord, in knowledge of whom standeth our eternal life, whose service is perfect freedom: defend us thy humble servants in all assaults of our enemies; that we, surely trusting in thy defence, may not fear the power of any adversaries; through the might of Jesus Christ our Lord.

*Book of Common Prayer*

*God's Gift*

207 Make us remember, O God, that every day is thy gift, and ought to be used according to thy command: through Jesus Christ our Lord.

Samuel Johnson, 1709–1784

*God's Presence and Guidance throughout the Day*

208 Christ, protect me this day.
Christ be with me, Christ before me,
Christ behind me, Christ within me,
Christ beneath me, Christ above me,
Christ at my right, Christ at my left.
Christ in the heart of every man who thinks of me;
Christ in the mouth of every man who speaks to me;
Christ in every eye that sees me;

Christ in every ear that hears me.
May thy Salvation, Lord, be ever with me!

*Prayer Book for Catholic Seafarers,*
*Apostleship of the Sea*

209 Fill us with thy mercy, O Lord, at this morning hour; that we may go on our way rejoicing, and live to thy glory all the day long; through Jesus Christ our Lord.

Prime (adapted)

210 Give us this day, O Father,
Reverence,
to realise your presence;
Humility,
to know our own need;
Trust,
to ask your help;
Obedience,
to accept whatever you say to us:
through Jesus Christ Our Lord.

*Epilogues and Prayers* (adapted)

211 Grant, O Lord God, that in all the rush and bustle of this day (or life), we may not be too busy to hear your voice; through Jesus Christ Our Lord.

Stowe School

212 Into thy hands, O God, we commend ourselves this day; let thy presence be with us to its close; enable us to feel that in doing our work we are doing thy will, and that in serving others we are serving thee, through Jesus Christ our Lord.

Uppingham School

213 Lord, thou knowest how busy we must be this day. If we forget thee, do not thou forget us.

Sir J. Astley, before the Battle of
Edgehill, 1642

214 O loving Father, our eternal friend, may we never forget or dishonour thee this day; but in all things and in all occupations

remember thy presence and cherish thy love; for Jesus Christ's sake.

Dean Vaughan, 1816–1897

215 O God,
Give us light this day
  that we may see clearly what we should do:
Give us strength
  that we may have the courage and power to do it:
Give us love
  that in all things and with all people
  we may be patient and forgiving and trusting:
And so fill our lives with joy:
through Jesus Christ our Lord.

C.R.C.

216 Thou knowest, O Lord, the duties that lie before us this day, and the sins that so easily beset us. Guide us, strengthen us, and protect us, O Lord our strength and our Redeemer.

Mabel Dearmer in *A Book of Prayers for Schools*

*A Good Deed*

217 O God, show us this day a good deed or a generous gift that we can do or give for you, and help us to keep it secret from everyone else.

Beryl Bye, *Prayers at Breakfast*

*Thanksgiving and Dedication*

218 We thank thee for all thy mercies to our souls and bodies this night, and all our days and nights: for our rest and safety, and this morning's light. Cause us to spend this day in thy fear and faithful service. Preserve our souls from sin, and our bodies from all dangers or hurt which would hinder us from thy service. Cause us to live as in thy presence, and let us do all to please thee, and to thy glory, and to the good of our own souls and of one another: and let thy love, and praise, and service, be our

continual delight; for Jesus Christ's sake, our Saviour and Intercessor at thy right hand.

Richard Baxter, 1615–1691

219 O God, we thank thee:
For the clear morning light;
For the simple blessings of neat clothes, and good food;
For the certainty of work to do, and a place that is ours,
For the chance and challenge of this fresh, unspoiled day.

Father at the beginning of this day, we would quietly recollect in thy presence our aims and purposes:
We wish to get on, to be a success.
We wish to be well thought of, to earn the good esteem of others.

In these our desires, O God, may we never seek easy unworthy short-cuts to success or personal popularity. Help us to stand firmly by our principles, and avoid riding roughshod over the rights and feelings of others. Give us grace to deal courteously with difficult people. Help us to withstand all temptation to scorn or irritation when people disagree with us, or point out our weaknesses. Help us to admit sensibly and swiftly when we are wrong; through the grace of Jesus Christ our Lord.

Cleveland Grammar School

*On Waking*

220 O God, chase from our hearts all gloomy thoughts and make us glad with the brightness of hope; through Jesus Christ our Lord.

Bishop Brent, 1862–1929

*Blessing on Work*

221 We humbly implore thy blessing, O Lord God, upon the work of this day, that we may do it heartily as unto thee; and that both in school and out we may seek each other's good, and rejoice in each other's happiness; through Jesus Christ our Lord.

Dean Vaughan, 1816–1897

222 Abide with us, eternal Father, for the darkness is no darkness with thee, but the night is as clear as the day. Renew our hearts with thy forgiveness, and our bodies with untroubled sleep, that we may wake to use more faithfully thy gift of life; through Jesus Christ our Lord.

Source unknown

223 Be present, O merciful God, and protect us through the silent hours of this night, so that we, who are wearied by the changes and chances of this fleeting world, may repose upon thy eternal changelessness; through the everlasting Jesus Christ our Lord.

Compline

224 Lighten our darkness, we beseech thee, O Lord, and by thy great mercy defend us from all perils and dangers of this night; for the love of thy only Son, our Saviour, Jesus Christ.

*Book of Common Prayer*

225 Look down, O Lord, from thy heavenly throne; illuminate the darkness of this night with thy celestial brightness, and from the sons of light banish the deeds of darkness; through Jesus Christ our Lord.

Compline

226 Lord Jesus, Light of the World, give us your light tonight;
Light to help us to see the truth;
Light to help us to see the way we ought to go;
Light to see ourselves as we are;
Light to see you in all your majesty and your love.
This we ask for thy name's sake.

*Epilogues and Prayers* (adapted)

227 O God, from whom all holy desires, all good counsels, and all just works do proceed: give unto thy servants that peace which the world cannot give; that both our hearts may be set to obey thy commandments, and also that by thee we being defended from

the fear of our enemies may pass our time in rest and quietness; through the merits of Jesus Christ our Saviour.

*Book of Common Prayer*

228 O God, who by making the evening to succeed the day hast bestowed the gift of sleep on human weakness, grant, we beseech thee, that while we enjoy the continuing blessings we may acknowledge him from whom they come, through Jesus Christ our Lord.

*Mozarabic Sacramentary, c. 600*

229 O Lord, support us all the day long of this troublous life, until the shades lengthen and the evening comes, the busy world is hushed, the fever of life over, and our work done; then Lord in thy mercy grant us safe lodging, a holy rest and peace at the last; through Jesus Christ our Lord.

Cardinal Newman, 1801–1890

230 Save us, O Lord, while waking, and guard us while sleeping, that awake we may watch with Christ, and asleep we may rest in peace.

Compline

231 Take us, we pray thee, O Lord of life, into thy keeping this night and ever. O thou Light of lights, keep us from inward darkness; grant us so to sleep in peace, that we may arise to work according to thy will: through Jesus Christ our Lord.

Bishop Lancelot Andrews, 1555–1626

232

The night is come like to the day,
Depart not thou great God away.
Let not my sinnes, blacke as the night,
Eclipse the lustre of thy light.
Keepe still in my horizon, for to me
The sunne makes not the day, but thee.
Thou whose nature cannot sleepe,
On my temples centry keepe;
Guard me 'gainst those watchfull foes,

Whose eyes are open while mine close.
Let no dreames my head infest,
But such as Jacob's temples blest.
While I doe rest, my soule advance,
Make my sleepe a holy trance;
That I may, my rest being wrought,
Awake into some holy thought;
And with as active vigour runne
My course, as doth the nimble sunne.
Sleepe is a death, O make me trie
By sleeping what it is to die.
Howe're I rest, great God, let me,
Awake againe at laste with thee.

Sir Thomas Browne, 1605–1682

(From *Religio Medici*, written at the age of thirty. Thomas Browne entitles it 'An Evening Colloquy with God', introducing it as 'the dormitive I take to bedward'.)

233 Thine is the day, O Lord, and thine is the night. Grant that the Sun of Righteousness may abide in our hearts to drive away the darkness of evil thoughts; through Jesus Christ our Lord.

Source unknown

234 This night, O God, we bring to you
Our sorrow for our wrong-doing;
Our gratitude for your gifts;
Our requests for our needs;
Our remembrance of others,
in the certainty that you will hear them all;
through Jesus Christ our Lord.

*Epilogues and Prayers*

235 Visit, we beseech thee, O Lord, this dwelling and drive far from it all snares of the enemy. Let thy holy angels dwell herein to preserve us in peace, and may thy blessing be upon us evermore; through Jesus Christ our Lord.

Compline

236 Watch thou, dear Lord, with those who wake, or watch, or weep tonight, and give thine angels charge over those who sleep.

Tend the sick, O Lord Christ;
rest the weary; bless the dying;
sooth the suffering; shield the joyous;
and all for thy love's sake.

St. Augustine of Hippo, 354–430

237 We will lay us down in peace
and take our rest:
for it is thou, Lord, only
that makest us dwell in safety.
Into thy hands, O Lord,
we commend our spirits,
for thou hast redeemed us,
O Lord, thou God of truth.

Psalms 4 and 31, *Daily Prayer* (adapted)

# Prayers for Life and Living

## IN ACTIVITIES AND WORK

### *Daily Life*

238 Help us, O Lord, to use our minds and bodies in your service. No part of our daily life is too small or too great for you to enter, inspire and share, if we will let you. Show us how to welcome you, and give us the will to make our minds and bodies worthy of your vital presence, through the example of your son, our inspiration, Jesus Christ.

Marlborough College

### *For God's Grace and Help*

239 Go before us, O Lord, in all our doings with thy most gracious favour, and further us with thy continual help; that in all our works begun, continued and ended in thee, we may glorify thy

holy name, and finally by thy mercy obtain everlasting life; through Jesus Christ our Lord.

*Book of Common Prayer* (adapted)

240 Help us, O God, at all times to do the things we ought to do.
To that end give us,
Clear sight,
that we may know what to do;
Courage,
to embark upon it;
Skill,
to find a way through all its problems;
Perseverance,
to bring it to its appointed end;
Strength
to resist all the temptations which would lure us aside.
So help us to begin, to continue and to end all things in you; through Jesus Christ our Lord.

*Epilogues and Prayers* (adapted)

### *Work*

241 Heavenly Father, show us that good work, well done, is praise in itself, because it honours you.

Beryl Bye, *Prayers at Breakfast*

242 O God, who hast ordained that whatever is to be desired should be sought by labour, and who, by thy blessing, bringest honest labour to good effect: look with mercy upon our studies and endeavours. Grant us, O Lord, to design only what is lawful and right, and afford us calmness of mind and steadiness of purpose, that we may so do thy will in this short life as to obtain happiness in the world to come.

Samuel Johnson, 1709–1784

243 We praise you, Lord, for the hard work and difficult tasks we must undertake, which bring out the best in us. Inspire us at all

times to persevere with them, and not to be discouraged, so that we may fulfil your will, to the glory of our leader, Jesus Christ our Lord.

A. G. Bullivant

*Work as Prayer*

244 We have heard it said, Lord God, that 'to work is to pray'. We would like this to be true with us. So please help us, you who worked as a carpenter at Nazareth, to worship you through the work we do; to praise you with our hands, to glorify you with our minds, to make, to paint, to study, to play, to do all we have to do for your glory and honour; so that as we are praying now about our work, our work may become prayer in your sight; through Jesus Christ our Lord.

C.R.C.

*Perseverance*

245 Lord, it is a blessed thing to work hard at whatever you have given us to do. When, Lord, we undertake anything for you, let us keep at it until it is completed. Keep us aware of your will, and teach us that everything a Christian does is for his Lord and Saviour, Jesus Christ.

A. G. Bullivant

246 O Lord God, when thou givest to thy servant to endeavour any great matter, grant us also to know that it is not the beginning, but the continuing of the same unto the end, until it be thoroughly finished, which yieldeth the true glory; through him who for the finishing of thy work laid down his life, our Redeemer, Jesus Christ.

Based on this sentence by Sir Francis Drake, 1540–1596:

There must be a beginning of any great matter, but the continuing unto the end until it be thoroughly finished yields the true glory.

247 When a job is hard, Lord, help us to persevere until it is completed. When the competition is stiff, encourage us not to give up halfway. Teach us, in everything, to live our lives for Him who persevered until the end, and won our salvation, Jesus Christ, our Lord.

A. G. Bullivant

*Sense of Responsibility*

248 God of heaven and earth, creator of man, and guide of his endeavours, give us a sense of our responsibility. Take away from us all laziness, pride, vainglory and selfishness, and show us clearly where our duty lies. Then, Lord God, in your mercy, bind us to our tasks, and fill us with a desire to fulfil our responsibilities without shirking, whether at home, in school, or out in the world, for Jesus' sake.

A. G. Bullivant

*In Studies and Enquiries*

249 Almighty God, in whose hands are all the powers of man, who givest understanding, and takest it away: who, as it seemeth good unto thee, lightenest the thoughts of the simple, and darkenest the meditations of the wise, be present with us in our studies and enquiries.

Grant, O Lord, that we may not lavish away the life which thou hast given us on useless trifles, nor waste it in vain searches after things which thou hast hidden from us.

Enable us, by the Holy Spirit, so to shun sloth and negligence, that every day may discharge part of the task which thou hast allotted us; and so further with thy help that labour which, without thy help, must be ineffectual, that we may obtain, in all our undertakings, such success as will most promote thy glory, and the salvation of our own souls, for the sake of Jesus Christ.

Samuel Johnson, 1709–1781 (adapted)

*The Use of Talents*

250 Save us, Lord, from the sin of wasting or hiding our talents. Draw out of each of us the capabilities which you have planted

there, and help us to use them all to your glory and the welfare of our fellow-men, for Jesus' sake.

A. G. Bullivant

251 O God, Who hast commanded that no man should be idle, give us grace to employ all our talents and faculties in the service appointed for us; that, whatsoever our hand findeth to do, we may do it with our might; through Jesus Christ our Lord.

James Martineau, 1806–1900

## ATTITUDE TO AND RELATIONSHIP WITH OTHER PEOPLE

*Against Barriers of Class, Race and Colour*

252 O Lord God, give your strength and courage to all who try to break down barriers of class, colour and nationality. Show us our own prejudice and narrow-mindedness; and help us to foster in our lives the true brotherhood of all mankind; through Jesus Christ our Lord.

Marlborough College

*I see white and black, Lord*

253 I see white teeth in a black face.
I see black eyes in a white face.
Help us to see *persons*, Jesus—not a black person or a white person, a red person or a yellow person, but human persons.

Malcolm Boyd, *Are you running with me, Jesus?*

*Caring for Old People*

254 Give us a love for old people, Lord, and make us quick to see their needs and ever ready to help them.

Beryl Bye, *Prayers at Breakfast*

### *Caring about People*

255 O God, help us to care about other people, whether we like them or not. The unpopular, the stupid and the weak need our special concern: help us to befriend them unselfishly and graciously. In these and in all human relationships give us the love of thy Son, who cared for all men and died for our salvation, Jesus Christ, our Lord.

Marlborough College

### *Against Condemning Others*

256 We confess to you, our heavenly Father, that we are too eager to condemn other people when they disagree with us. Help us to value what other people say, and to be fair to them; in the spirit of Jesus Christ our Lord.

A. G. Bullivant

### *For Courtesy*

257 O God, teach us to show consideration to others by being courteous in our manner, thoughtful in our ways, generous in our spirit: and so to follow the example of our Lord, Jesus Christ.

Clarendon Secondary Modern Girls' School

### *Against Envy and Hatred*

258 May it be thy will, O Lord, that no man foster hatred against us in his heart, and that we foster no hatred in our hearts against any man; that no man foster envy of us in his heart, and that we foster no envy in our hearts of any man.

*The Talmud*

### *In Family Life*

259 Lord Jesus, help us to find true joy in serving our families and our friends, because we know that in serving them we are serving You.

Beryl Bye, *Prayers at Breakfast*

260 O God, we pray that you will help us in our homes. Make us value the love that we receive from our families. When we feel like grumbling and criticizing, help us to be thankful. When we are lazy and selfish, make us active for others. Give us the will and the power to play a full and happy part in family life. So not only shall we repay the care, love and effort that our families spend on us, but we shall also serve you, our heavenly Father.

Marlborough College

261 Our heavenly Father, help us to give our earthly parents our respect and love and to be observant of their needs.

Beryl Bye, *Prayers at Breakfast*

*Friendships*

262 O eternal God, grant that the friendships formed between us here may not be broken by sin or forgetfulness. May we be bound together by thy Holy Spirit and so drawn nearer to thee and to each other; through Jesus Christ our Lord.

Source unknown

*For Generosity*

263 Help us, O God, to follow the example of your son in giving all we can to other people. He gave his care, his time, his gifts as a doctor and a teacher. He held back nothing. Strengthen us to give, without reserve, whatever care and time and gifts we can where they are most needed. Through the inspiration of him who gave even his life, Jesus Christ our Lord.

Marlborough College

*Human Understanding*

264 Give us, O God, thoughtfulness, imagination and patience to discover why other people feel and think and behave as they do, so that our understanding may grow and our sympathy may deepen. Show us how to use our insight to help our friends, our companions and our enemies, in the spirit of him whose knowledge of humanity was as deep as life itself, Jesus Christ our Lord.

Marlborough College

265 Break through, break through, blessed Lord Christ,
Break through the narrowness of our love.
Make us to love the Russians.
Make us to love the Chinese.
Make us to be generous in economics.
Make us to be imaginative in politics.
Give us vision.
Give us patience.
Give us reconciliation.
For your world's sake.

A prayer spoken at the launching of the
Polaris submarine, 25th February 1967

266 Help us, Lord, to work together for the good of mankind. Teach us to live at peace with one another, and to love even those who seem to be our enemies. May truth and justice rule our homes, our country, and our world. We ask this in Jesus' name.

A. G. Bullivant

267 Teach us, O Lord, to consider international affairs in the light of our creed; to check in ourselves every impulse which makes for war, all ungenerous judgments, all self-assertion, all presumptuous claims. Help us to recognise the needs and aspirations of other nations, and to honour all men, through Jesus Christ our Lord.

Bishop Westcott, 1825–1901 (adapted)

*We can't make it alone, Lord*

268 God knows, we've tried, and we've even reached the point where we could blow up everybody, including ourselves. Teach us how to listen carefully and patiently to other people. Teach us how to say what we have to say clearly, simply, and openly. Teach us what responsibility toward you and others really means.

Cut through all our egoism and self-interest, Jesus. Make us understand what patriotism must mean in one world of conflicting nationalisms. Educate us to support the United Nations and other international organizations which bring people together in a shared sense of human concern. Work with us, Lord, to bridge gulfs and divisions between nations and persons.

Malcolm Boyd, *Are you running with me, Jesus?*

*Kindness*

269 Lord, we want to feel and to show kindness. Don't let us be held back from warm-heartedness by apathy, by embarrassment, by fear of public opinion, or by laziness. The power to give genuine sympathy, courtesy and warmth of heart is what we ask for, in the name of Jesus Christ our Lord.

Marlborough College

*Love of Enemies*

270 Dear Father God, help us to love and not to hate. Help us to bless and not to curse. Help us to pray for, and do good to those who give us cause to dislike them.

Beryl Bye, *Prayers at Breakfast*

271 O Lord, who taught us to love our fellow men, to forgive those who do wrong to us, to be generous to those who are our enemies, help us day by day to be kind and generous, loving and forgiving.

Help us to be patient no matter how much we are provoked.

Help us to keep things in proportion no matter how unreasonable other people may be.

Help us, O Lord, to be like you and to forgive those who do us wrong.

This we ask for your love's sake.

Wheatley Hills High School for Boys, Doncaster

*Love of People*

272 O God of Love, who hast given us a commandment that we should love one another, even as thou didst love us and give thy beloved Son for our life and salvation; we pray thee to give to us thy servants, in all times of our life on the earth, a mind forgetful

of past ill-will and a heart to love our brethren; for the sake of Jesus Christ, our Lord and only Saviour.

Coptic Liturgy of St. Cyril, fifth century

273 Give us, O God, at all times love for others,

So that we may never refuse an appeal for help; never do anything which would injure or hurt anyone else in body or in mind.

May we find our joy in service and not in selfishness; in giving and not in getting; in sharing and not in keeping.

*Epilogues and Prayers* (adapted)

274 O Lord, the Author and Persuader of peace, love and goodwill: soften our hard and steely hearts, warm our frozen and icy hearts, that we may wish well to one another, and may be the true disciples of Jesus Christ. And give us grace even now to begin to show forth that heavenly life, wherein there is no hatred, but peace and love on all hands, one toward another; through the love of Jesus Christ our Lord.

Ludovicus Vives, 1492–1540

### *For Loyalty*

275 Grant us, O God, loyalty of heart, that as we demand that others should be faithful to us, so we may also be faithful to them; for Jesus Christ's sake.

*Daily Prayer*

276 Almighty God, grant us your gift of loyalty. For our homes give us love and obedience: for our country sacrifice and service: for our Church reverence and devotion: and in everything make us true to you, through your Son our Saviour Jesus Christ.

*Book of Common Prayer*, U.S. Episcopal Church

### *Peace in Community*

277 Help us, O Lord, not only to pray for the peace of the world, but to seek it in our lives here. Give us the will and the strength to control ourselves and deny ourselves, for the good of our

friends and companions; so that we may act in harmony, live at peace and unite to serve you, through Jesus Christ our Lord.

Marlborough College

*Responsibility*

278 Lord God, my Father, help me to live as your son should, and help me to do no harm to any of your other children, be they boys or girls, men or women. Do not let me make it easier for any of my companions to do wrong, especially if they are younger than I am. Help me to please you by helping them, and by honestly keeping them out of trouble: through the grace of Jesus Christ our Lord.

*Prayer Book for Catholic Seafarers, Apostleship of the Sea*

*Sensitivity to Other People*

279 O Lord, the Creator of all things, open our eyes so that we may see the good that exists in all the people about us, not only in those whom we like or love, but in those to whom we feel indifferent, cold or hostile, for such insight will bring us to the heart of your creation and to you, through Jesus Christ our Lord.

Marlborough College

*Towards Those Who Serve Us*

280 O Lord God, help us, whether at school or at home, to bear in mind the needs of all who serve us, and to try to enter into the lives of those on whom we depend for our daily comfort. Teach us to be considerate in our demands, courteous in our speech, and generous in our gratitude; always showing to all men and women the honour that is their due; through Jesus Christ our Lord.

M. L. Jacks in *A Book of Prayers for Schools*

281 Lord help us to enlarge our sympathy and understanding
to include the old,
the lonely,

those with physical and mental handicaps,
  those of other races
    and other cultural backgrounds,
those who have become outcasts in society,
  who are friendless and rootless.

Help us to turn our sympathy and understanding
  where possible
    into action.
Help us to be channels of your Love.

Christian Education Movement and Christian Aid,
*World of Strange Contrasts*

## THE CHURCH'S YEAR

### *Advent*

282 Almighty God, give us grace that we may cast away the works of darkness, and put upon us the armour of light, now in the time of this mortal life, in which thy Son Jesus Christ came to visit us in great humility; that in the last day when he shall come again in his glorious majesty to judge both the quick and the dead, we may rise to the life immortal, through him who liveth and reigneth with thee and the Holy Ghost, now and ever.

*Book of Common Prayer*

283 O Father, who hast declared thy love to men by the birth of the Holy Child at Bethlehem: help us to welcome him with gladness and to make room for him in our daily life; so that we may live at peace with one another and in goodwill with all thy family; through thy Son, Jesus Christ our Lord.

*A Devotional Diary*

284 O Lord, raise up (we pray thee) thy power, and come among us, and with great might succour us; that whereas, through our sins and wickedness, we are sore let and hindered in running the race that is set before us, thy bountiful grace and mercy may

speedily help and deliver us; through the satisfaction of thy Son our Lord, to whom with thee and the Holy Ghost be honour and glory, world without end.

*Book of Common Prayer*

285 When Jesus comes at Christmas, O God, it will be very tempting for us to find no room for him whilst we enjoy ourselves with pleasures. Help us to be generous towards him and allow him to be born again in the stable of our hearts; that our lives may be transformed by his light, his warmth, his love; who lives and reigns with you and the Holy Spirit, one God, world without end.

C.R.C.

286 We greet your coming, God, with wonder:
You come to be with us; yet you remain far greater than we can imagine.
You are near; yet your wisdom sets you apart from us.
You appear among us; yet we cannot describe your glory.

We greet your coming, God, with repentance:
We are satisfied with ourselves; but your presence exposes our sin and failure.
We are self-confident; but you challenge confidence in ourselves.
We are proud of our understanding; but you show us that we do not know everything.

We greet your coming, God, with joy:
We had no true idea of what you are like; but you have shown us yourself in Jesus Christ.
We felt our human life could be of no importance to you; but you have shown its value by appearing among us as a man.
We are aware of the gulf between us and you; but you have bridged it with love.

God, we greet your coming in Jesus Christ our Lord!

*Contemporary Prayers for Public Worship*

*Christmas*

287 Almighty God, who didst wonderfully create man in thine own image, and didst yet more wonderfully restore him: grant, we

beseech thee, that as thy Son our Lord Jesus Christ was made in the likeness of men, so we may be made partakers of the divine nature; through the same thy Son, who with thee and the Holy Ghost liveth and reigneth, one God, world without end.

*Prayer Book, 1928*

288 Almighty God, who hast given us thy only-begotten Son to take our nature upon him, and as at this time to be born of a pure Virgin: grant that we being regenerate, and made thy children by adoption and grace, may daily be renewed by thy Holy Spirit; through our Lord Jesus Christ, who liveth and reigneth with thee and the Holy Spirit, ever one God, world without end.

*Book of Common Prayer* (adapted)

289 Lord Jesus, Lord Christ; we thank you for showing us the power of God in the weakness of a baby, the beauty of God in the squalor of a stable, the love of God in those humble swaddling clothes as you lie there in the manger. Please come into us so that we too can serve people with the power of humility, the beauty of holiness, and selfless love. This is what you did, Lord Jesus; and again we thank you for it and humbly offer ourselves for your service; for your name's sake.

C.R.C.

*Epiphany*

290 O God, who by the leading of a star didst manifest thy only-begotten Son to the Gentiles: mercifully grant, that we, which know thee now by faith, may after this life have the fruition of life eternal; through Jesus Christ our Lord.

*Book of Common Prayer* (adapted)

291 We have read, O Lord, about the wise men of the East who were guided to you by a star and who brought generous gifts of gold, frankincense and myrrh; give us the wisdom to seek you, light to guide us to you, courage to search until we find you, graciousness to worship you and generosity to lay great gifts before you, who are our King and our God for ever and ever.

C.R.C.

### *Septuagesima*

292 O Lord, we beseech thee favourably to hear the prayers of thy people; that we, who are justly punished for our offences, may be mercifully delivered by thy goodness, for the glory of thy name; through Jesus Christ our Saviour, who liveth and reigneth with thee and the Holy Ghost, ever one God, world without end.

*Book of Common Prayer*

### *Sexagesima*

293 O Lord God, who seest that we put not our trust in any thing that we do: mercifully grant that by thy power we may be defended against all adversity; through Jesus Christ our Lord.

*Book of Common Prayer*

### *Quinquagesima*

294 O Lord, who hast taught us that all our doings without charity are nothing worth; send thy Holy Ghost, and pour into our hearts that most excellent gift of charity, the very bond of peace and of all virtues, without which whosoever liveth is counted dead before thee: grant this for thine only Son Jesus Christ's sake.

*Book of Common Prayer*

### *Ash Wednesday and Lent*

295 Almighty and everlasting God, who hatest nothing that thou hast made, and dost forgive the sins of all them that are penitent: create and make in us new and contrite hearts, that we worthily lamenting our sins, and acknowledging our wretchedness, may obtain of thee, the God of all mercy, perfect remission and forgiveness; through Jesus Christ our Lord.

*Book of Common Prayer*

296 O Lord Jesus Christ, you taught your disciples to pray, to do good deeds and to fast cheerfully, without hypocrisy or ostentation; help us to* [use this season of Lent sincerely for your service,

* The words in brackets may be omitted if the prayer is used outside the season of Lent.

so that we may] pray more, do more and discipline ourselves cheerfully for your sake; for you died for us but now you live, for ever and ever, world without end.

C.R.C.

*Palm Sunday and Holy Week*

297 Almighty and everlasting God, who, of thy tender love towards mankind, hast sent thy Son, our Saviour Jesus Christ, to take upon him our flesh, and to suffer death upon the cross, that all mankind should follow the example of his great humility: mercifully grant, that we may both follow the example of his patience, and also be made partakers of his resurrection; through Jesus Christ our Lord.

*Book of Common Prayer*

298 O Jesus, King of the Jews, King of Heaven, King of love; you rode meekly upon an ass, you were crowned with a crown of thorns, you received your title on the executioner's cross and were acclaimed by a dying thief; help us to bear with you the suffering and humiliation of this week and receive from you the joy and the victory of your resurrection; and may you be King in our hearts for ever and ever.

C.R.C.

*Good Friday*

299 Almighty God, we beseech thee graciously to behold this thy family, for which our Lord Jesus Christ was contented to be betrayed, and given up into the hands of wicked men, and to suffer death upon the cross, who now liveth and reigneth with thee and the Holy Ghost, ever one God, world without end.

*Book of Common Prayer*

300 Almighty God, whose Son, our Saviour Jesus Christ, was received and honoured as a king by those who soon were to ask for his death; grant that we may never seek the praise nor fear the blame of men, but may always have the courage to do what we know to be right; through Jesus Christ our Lord.

W. E. Scudamore in *A Book of Prayers for Schools* (adapted)

301 Blessed Lord, you bore on the shameful cross an undeserved punishment, and forgave even those who nailed you there. You spoke comfort to those who were dying beside you, even during your own agony. Teach us your love and compassion. We can only hope to follow your example if you guide us every step of the way.

A. G. Bullivant

*Easter*

302 Almighty God, who through thine only-begotten Son Jesus Christ hast overcome death, and opened unto us the gate of everlasting life: we humbly beseech thee, that as thy special grace goes before us and puts into our minds good desires, so by thy continual help we may bring these to good effect; through Jesus Christ our Lord, who liveth and reigneth with thee and the Holy Ghost, ever one God, world without end.

*Book of Common Prayer* (adapted)

303 The Lord is risen!
He is risen indeed!
Alleluia!

Lord Jesus, we greet you, risen from the dead.

We thought your way of love was a dead end, leading only to the cross: now we see that it is the way to life.
We thought that your whole life was wasted: now we know that it was gloriously worthwhile.
We thought that your suffering was pointless: now we can see God's purpose in it.
We thought that death was the end of you: now we know that your life was too great to be ended by death.

Lord Jesus, we greet you, risen from the dead.

*Contemporary Prayers for Public Worship*

304 We are bound to praise thee, Almighty God, for the glorious resurrection of thy Son Jesus Christ our Lord: for he is the very Passover Lamb, which was offered for us, and hath taken away

the sin of the world. By his death he hath destroyed death, and by his rising to life again hath restored to us everlasting life. Therefore with angels and archangels and all the company of heaven, we laud and magnify thy glorious name; evermore praising thee and saying, Holy, holy, holy, Lord God of hosts, heaven and earth are full of thy glory. Glory be to thee, O Lord most high.

*Book of Common Prayer* (adapted)

*Ascension Day*

305 Ascended Lord Jesus, pioneer of our salvation, we adore you.

You have found a way through life's maze and won through to the centre of things.
You have blazed a trail through all the confusing tangles of life and opened up a path for us.
You were the first to struggle through to perfection.

Lead us along the path to God
and bring us through all our struggles to the perfection you have achieved.

Ascended Lord Jesus, pioneer of our salvation, we adore you!

*Contemporary Prayers for Public Worship* (adapted)

306 Ascended Lord Jesus, we adore you!
Once you lived a human life subject to the limitations of time:
now you are the same yesterday, today and for ever.
Once you were limited to one particular place:
now you are present wherever men turn to you.
Once only those who met you face to face knew you:
now your divine love extends through all the world.

Jesus, ascended Lord of time and space,
love as wide as life, we adore you.

*Contemporary Prayers for Public Worship*

307 Grant, we beseech thee, Almighty God, that like as we do believe thy only-begotten Son our Lord Jesus Christ to have ascended into the heavens; so we may also in heart and mind thither ascend, and with him continually dwell, who liveth and

reigneth with thee and the Holy Ghost, one God, world without end.

*Book of Common Prayer*

308 O God, the King of glory, who hast exalted thine only Son Jesus Christ with great triumph unto thy kingdom in heaven; we beseech thee, leave us not comfortless; but send to us thine Holy Spirit to comfort us, and exalt us unto the same place whither our Saviour Christ is gone before, who liveth and reigneth with thee and the Holy Spirit, one God, world without end.

*Book of Common Prayer*

## *Whitsunday*

309 God, who as at this time didst teach the hearts of thy faithful people, by the sending to them the light of thy Holy Spirit: grant us by the same Spirit to have a right judgment in all things, and evermore to rejoice in his holy comfort; through the merits of Jesus Christ our Saviour, who liveth and reigneth with thee, in the unity of the same Spirit, one God, world without end.

*Book of Common Prayer*

310 O God, who in the burning fire of thy love wast pleased to pour out the Holy Spirit on thy disciples: grant us by the same Spirit to be lit with heavenly desires and with the power to fulfil them; through Jesus Christ our Lord.

*Book of Common Prayer*

311 May our lives be filled with the spirit of God, so that inspired by his power we can serve him with full energy and love, in the name of Jesus Christ our Lord.

Marlborough College

312 O Lord, Spirit of beauty and of holiness, dwell within our hearts: that as the disciples at this time were made brave and faithful by thy presence, so we may be filled with the same courage and devotion, and may set ourselves with all thy servants to win the world for Christ; for his name's sake.

M. L. Jacks in *A Book of Prayers for Schools*

313 Strengthen us, we beseech thee, O Lord, with the Holy Spirit, the Comforter, and daily increase in us thy manifold gifts of grace; the spirit of wisdom and understanding; the spirit of counsel and inner strength; the spirit of knowledge and true godliness; and fill us, O Lord, with the spirit of thy holy fear, now and for ever.

*Book of Common Prayer* (adapted)

## *Trinity*

314 Almighty and everlasting God, who hast given unto us thy servants grace by the confession of a true faith to acknowledge the glory of the eternal Trinity, and in the Divine Majesty to worship the unity: we beseech thee, that thou wouldest keep us steadfast in this faith, and evermore defend us from all adversities, who livest and reignest, one God, world without end.

*Book of Common Prayer*

315 We praise and adore you, God our Father.
You are the maker of everything,
and because of your will
things came to be and continue in being.

We praise and adore you, Jesus Christ.
You are the Word made flesh,
and because of your life
we both know the Father and trust in his love.

We praise and adore you, Holy Spirit.
You are the Father's gift to men,
and because of your ceaseless activity
nothing is cut off from God.

With the whole Church on earth and in heaven we praise and adore you, most holy, blessed and glorious Trinity, world without end.

*Contemporary Prayers for Public Worship* (adapted)

## SAINTS' DAYS

(only those that occur in term time are included)

### *St. Andrew* (November 30th)

316 Almighty God, who did give such grace unto thy holy Apostle Saint Andrew, that he readily obeyed the calling of thy Son Jesus Christ, and followed him without delay: grant unto us all, that we, being called by thy holy Word, may forthwith give up ourselves obediently to fulfil thy holy commandments; through the same Jesus Christ our Lord.

*Book of Common Prayer*

317 O God, your servant Andrew showed himself ready to share your love and friendship with other people: help us both to receive and to share those things that you have given us through the goodness of your Son Jesus Christ our Lord.

C.R.C.

### *St. Thomas* (December 21st)

318 Almighty and everliving God, who for the strengthening of the faith didst allow thy holy Apostle Thomas to be doubtful of thy Son's resurrection: grant us so perfectly, and without all doubt, to believe in thy Son Jesus Christ, that our faith in thy sight may never be reproved. Hear us, O Lord, through the same Jesus Christ, to whom with thee, and the Holy Ghost, be all honour and glory, now and for evermore.

*Book of Common Prayer* (adapted)

319 Lord Christ, it is difficult for us to be certain that you are here, as you give us no visible sign of your presence. If you are with us now, please understand our doubts and forgive them. Strengthen our hold on what we inwardly know to be good and true so that in these we may find the reality of your love and be able to acknowledge you, as St. Thomas did, to be our Lord and our God. We ask this humbly for your name's sake.

C.R.C.

*The Conversion of St. Paul* (January 25th)

320 O God, who, through the teaching of the blessed Apostle Saint Paul, hast caused the light of the Gospel to shine throughout the world: grant, we beseech thee, that we, having his wonderful conversion in remembrance, may show forth our thankfulness unto thee for the same, by following the holy doctrine which he taught; through Jesus Christ our Lord.

*Book of Common Prayer*

*The Presentation of Christ in the Temple* (February 2nd)
(*The Purification of St. Mary the Virgin*)

321 Almighty and everlasting God, we humbly beseech thy Majesty, that as thy only-begotten Son was this day presented in the temple as a truly human baby, so we may be presented unto thee with pure and clean hearts, by the same thy Son Jesus Christ our Lord.

*Book of Common Prayer* (adapted)

*St. Matthias* (February 24th)

322 O almighty God, who into the place of the traitor Judas didst choose thy faithful servant Matthias to be of the number of the twelve Apostles: grant that thy Church, being always preserved from false Apostles, may be ordered and guided by faithful and true pastors; through Jesus Christ our Lord.

*Book of Common Prayer*

*The Annunciation of the Blessed Virgin Mary* (March 25th)

323 We beseech thee, O Lord, pour thy grace into our hearts; that, as we have known the incarnation of thy Son Jesus Christ by the message of an angel, so by his cross and passion we may be brought unto the glory of his resurrection; through the same Jesus Christ our Lord.

*Book of Common Prayer*

*St. George* (April 23rd)

324 Almighty God, who hast made us heirs of all the victories of faith: arm us like St. George, with such trust in the truth, that we may seek no rest from its demands, and have no fear in its

service; through the same Jesus Christ our Lord, who liveth and reigneth with thee and the Holy Ghost, ever one God, world without end.

*Cambridge Bede Book* (adapted)

### *St. Mark* (April 25th)

325 O almighty God, who hast instructed thy holy Church with the heavenly teaching of thy Evangelist Saint Mark: give us grace, that, being not like children carried away with every blast of vain doctrine, we may be established in the truth of thy holy Gospel; through Jesus Christ our Lord.

*Book of Common Prayer* (adapted)

### *St. Philip and St. James* (May 1st)

326 O almighty God, whom truly to know is everlasting life: grant us perfectly to know thy Son Jesus Christ to be the way, the truth, and the life; that following the steps of thy holy Apostles, Saint Philip and Saint James, we may steadfastly walk in the way that leadeth to eternal life; through the same thy Son Jesus Christ our Lord.

*Book of Common Prayer*

### *St. Barnabas* (June 11th)

327 O Lord God almighty, who didst endue thy holy Apostle Barnabas with singular gifts of the Holy Ghost: leave us not, we beseech thee, destitute of thy manifold gifts, nor yet of grace to use them alway to thy honour and glory; through Jesus Christ our Lord.

*Book of Common Prayer*

328 We have read about St. Barnabas, Lord; his complete generosity and his zest in serving the Church and telling other people about you: give us a bold and daring faith so that we can serve you and other people without caring too much about ourselves; for the sake of thy Son Jesus Christ our Lord.

C.R.C.

### *St. John Baptist* (June 24th)

329 Almighty God, by whose providence thy servant John the Baptist was wonderfully born, and sent to prepare the way of thy Son our Saviour, by preaching repentance: make us to follow his teaching and holy life, that we may truly repent according to his preaching; and following his example may constantly speak the truth, boldly rebuke wickedness, and patiently suffer for the truth's sake; through Jesus Christ our Lord.

*Book of Common Prayer*

### *St. Peter* (June 29th)

330 O almighty God, who by thy Son Jesus Christ didst give to thy Apostle Saint Peter many excellent gifts, and commandedst him earnestly to feed thy flock: make, we beseech thee, all Bishops and Pastors diligently to preach thy Holy Word, and the people obediently to follow the same, that they may receive the crown of everlasting glory; through Jesus Christ our Lord.

*Book of Common Prayer*

331 Dear God, we find that we are often ready to start something and then do not want to finish it; to jump in and then regret it; to give other people the impression that we are brave, and then act in a way that is cowardly. Please help us as you helped St. Peter, and through the Holy Spirit make us strong, resolute and brave; so that we may be loyal and effective servants of your Son Jesus Christ our Lord.

C.R.C.

### *St. Mary Magdalen* (July 22nd)

332 O almighty God, whose blessed Son did call and sanctify Mary Magdalen to be a witness to his resurrection: mercifully grant that by thy grace we may be healed of all our weaknesses, and serve thee in the power of his endless life, who with thee and the Holy Ghost liveth and reigneth, one God, world without end.

*Prayer Book, 1928*

*St. James the Apostle* (July 25th)

333 Grant, O merciful God, that as thine holy Apostle Saint James, leaving his father and all that he had, was instantly obedient to the calling of thy Son Jesus Christ, and followed him; so we may be ready to forsake all false worldly ties and follow thy holy commandments; through Jesus Christ our Lord.

*Book of Common Praver* (adapted)

*St. Matthew* (September 21st)

334 O almighty God, who by thy blessed Son didst call Matthew from the receipt of custom to be an Apostle and Evangelist: grant us grace to forsake all greedy desires and too much love of riches, and to follow the same thy Son Jesus Christ, who liveth and reigneth with thee and the Holy Ghost, one God, world without end.

*Book of Common Prayer* (adapted)

*St. Michael and All Angels* (September 29th)

335 O everlasting God, who hast ordained and constituted the services of Angels and men in a wonderful order: mercifully grant, that as thy holy Angels alway do thee service in Heaven, so by thy appointment they may succour and defend us on earth; through Jesus Christ our Lord.

*Book of Common Prayer*

*St. Luke* (October 18th)

336 Almighty God, who calledst Luke the Physician, whose praise is in the Gospel, to be an Evangelist, and Physician of the soul: may it please thee, that by the wholesome medicines of the teaching delivered by him, all the diseases of our soul may be healed; through the merits of thy Son Jesus Christ our Lord.

*Book of Common Prayer* (adapted)

*St. Simon and St. Jude* (October 28th)

337 O almighty God, who hast built thy Church upon the foundation of the Apostles and Prophets, Jesus Christ himself being the chief

corner-stone: grant us so to be joined together in unity of spirit by their teaching, that we may be made an holy temple acceptable unto thee; through Jesus Christ our Lord.

*Book of Common Prayer* (adapted)

*All Saints' Day* (November 1st)

338 Almighty and everlasting God, who dost enkindle the flame of thy love in the hearts of the saints: grant to our minds the same faith and power of love; that as we rejoice in their triumphs, we may profit by their examples; through Jesus Christ our Lord.

*Gothic Missal, 1680*

339 O almighty God, who hast knit together thine elect in one communion and fellowship, in the mystical body of thy Son Christ our Lord: grant us grace so to follow thy blessed Saints in all virtuous and godly living, that we may come to those unspeakable joys, which thou hast prepared for them that truly love thee; through Jesus Christ our Lord.

*Book of Common Prayer* (adapted)

*All Souls' Day* (November 2nd)

340 O Lord, the maker and redeemer of all believers: grant to the faithful departed all the unsearchable benefits of thy Son's passion; that in the day of his appearing they may be shown as thy true children; through the same thy Son Jesus Christ our Lord.

*Prayer Book, 1928* (adapted)

*Saints, Martyrs and Missionaries of the Church of England*
(November 8th)

341 We beseech thee, O Lord, to multiply thy grace upon us who commemorate the saints of our nation; that, as we rejoice to be their fellow-citizens on earth, so we may have fellowship also with them in heaven; through Jesus Christ our Lord.

*Prayer Book, 1928*

*A Martyr*

342 Almighty God, by whose grace and power thy holy Martyr . . . triumphed over suffering and death: give us the courage to endure hardship and to fight for what is right, that with the noble army of martyrs we may receive the crown of everlasting life; through Jesus Christ our Lord.

*Prayer Book, 1928* (adapted)

*A Bishop*

343 O God, the light of the faithful, and shepherd of souls, who didst set blessed . . . to be a Bishop in the Church, that he might feed thy sheep by his word and guide them by his example: grant us, we pray thee, to keep the faith which he taught, and to follow in his footsteps; through Jesus Christ our Lord.

*Prayer Book, 1928*

*A Christian Teacher*

344 O God, who hast enlightened thy Church by the teaching of thy servant . . . : enrich it evermore, we beseech thee, with thy heavenly grace, and raise up faithful witnesses, who by their life and teaching may set forth to all men the truth of thy salvation; through Jesus Christ our Lord.

*Prayer Book, 1928* (adapted)

345 O God, by whose grace . . . , enkindled with the fire of thy love, became a burning and a shining light in thy Church: grant that we may be enflamed with the same spirit of discipline and love, and ever walk before thee as children of light; through Jesus Christ our Lord.

*Prayer Book, 1928*

*A Missionary*

346 O Lord Jesus Christ, we thank thee for calling thy servant . . . to preach thy Gospel to the nations; and we humbly pray thee to raise up among us those who shall be heralds and evangelists of

thy kingdom, and shall build up thy Church in every land; who livest and reignest with the Father and the Holy Spirit, one God, world without end.

*Prayer Book, 1928* (adapted)

## CHURCH AND STATE OCCASIONS

### *Before a Confirmation*

347 A soldier is seeking active enlistment in your army, Jesus. A pilgrim is asking for a passport which is not of this earth, although it will involve deep and possibly very costly service for you on this earth.

Someone wants to share in the sacrament of your body and blood, Lord. Someone seeks to be crucified and risen to new life with you.

Thanks for being with us here, Jesus, and sharing your vision of the Kingdom of God with us.

Malcolm Boyd, *Are you running with me, Jesus?*

348 O God, who through the teaching of thy Son Jesus Christ didst prepare the disciples for the coming of the Comforter: make ready, we beseech thee, the hearts and minds of thy servants who at this time are seeking the gift of the Holy Spirit through the laying on of hands, that drawing near with penitent and faithful hearts, they may be filled with the power of his divine indwelling; through the same Jesus Christ our Lord.

*Prayer Book, 1928*

### *Approach to the Eucharist*

349 Grant, we pray thee, O Father, that all those that meet tomorrow at thy table may come with true repentance, steadfast purpose, living faith, and a thankful remembrance of the death and resurrection of thy dear Son; so that their bodies and souls may be preserved unto everlasting life, and that they may feed on him in their hearts by faith with thanksgiving.

Lionel James in *A Book of Prayers for Schools* (adapted)

350 Jesus, we're here again. What are we doing here? I mean, how is communion with you possible? You're holy, and we're very human. Yet I remember that you also became human.

I wonder how we can honestly be nourished and cleansed by your body and blood. Yet I realize communion is an outward and visible sign of an inward and spiritual grace. I accept this mystery.

We are grateful for this intimacy with you, Jesus. We thank you for letting us share this corporate action as we offer to God all of creation including our own lives. Give us faith to understand what it means to be thankful.

Malcolm Boyd, *Are you running with me, Jesus?*

351 O Christ of the Eucharist, make thyself known to us in the breaking of the Bread, that by faith we may clearly see thy form and humbly adore thy presence, who art God for ever and ever.

Bishop Brent, 1862–1929

352 O God our Father, you gave us our lives and made them good: help us to prepare for your Son Jesus Christ who is coming in the sacrament of Holy Communion to restore them. There is much that we have enjoyed and we offer it to him in thanks. There is much that we find difficult and we ask now for his help. Much has gone wrong and needs to be put right. In particular there are our friendships, responsibilities and difficulties with other people; and for these we ask the blessing of his love. O Father, we bring ourselves to him: may he come to us and touch us and make us more like himself; to your honour and glory for ever and ever.

C.R.C.

353 We do not presume to come to this thy table, O merciful Lord,
trusting in our own righteousness,
but in thy manifold and great mercies.
We are not worthy so much as to gather up the crumbs under thy table.
But thou art the same Lord,
whose nature it is always to have mercy.
Grant us therefore, gracious Lord,
so to eat the flesh of thy dear Son Jesus Christ,

And to drink his blood,
that we may evermore dwell in him, and he in us.

*An Order of Holy Communion* (S.P.C.K.)

*Before a General Election*

354 O Lord Jesus Christ who came to build the Kingdom of God on earth; please bless our country at this time of General Election. Bless the candidates, the parties, the voters. Help us all to judge the issues by the standards of truth, justice and goodness; that thy will may be done, thy Kingdom come on earth as it is in Heaven—for thine is the Kingdom, the power and the glory for ever and ever.

C.R.C.

*Remembrance Day*

355 Blessed Saviour, murdered by man's sinfulness, forgive mankind for the unholy slaughter of war. Forgive us, for we know how deeply we sin against your love in murdering our brothers of other nations. Save us, Good Lord, from a repetition of this blasphemy: save us we pray, and teach us to bear suffering rather than to inflict it on others. Give us the long-suffering and forbearance which you showed in your agony on the cross.

A. G. Bullivant

*At the Laying of a Wreath on Remembrance Sunday*

356 To the glory of God;
In honour of those who have died;
In dedication of ourselves;
We lay this wreath:
In the name of the Father and the Son and the Holy Spirit.

C.R.C.

*Before the Study of Scripture*

357 Blessed Lord, who hast caused all holy Scriptures to be written for our learning; grant that we may in such wise hear them, read,

mark, learn, and inwardly digest them, that by patience, and comfort of thy holy word, we may embrace, and ever hold fast the blessed hope of everlasting life, which thou hast given us in our Saviour Jesus Christ.

*Book of Common Prayer*

## SCHOOL TERM

### *At the Beginning of Term*

358 Lord God, and Heavenly Father, look in love upon us, now once more gathered into the family of this school.

Grant that, refreshed and renewed by the happiness and freedom of our holidays, we may take up our daily tasks with energy and joy, and grow in knowledge and wisdom and in love of you; through Jesus Christ our Lord.

*Prayers for Every Day*

359 O God our heavenly Father, as we gather together on the first day of a new term we thank you for the holidays which have just ended. We thank you for the love of our homes, for our friends, for recreation, for the beauties of nature, for the many pleasures we have experienced and for your constant presence and care. We thank you for our health and strength and our ability to enjoy your many gifts to each one of us. We pray that we may show our gratitude in the lives that we shall live this term. May they always be acceptable in your sight through the grace of Jesus Christ our Lord.

Kingswood School, Bath

360 With grateful hearts we thank thee, merciful Father, for the rest and enjoyment of our holidays; for sunshine and freedom and pleasant places; for the happiness of our homes, and the love of those about us. We pray thee that we may come back to our daily tasks at school refreshed and invigorated, and set about them with cheerfulness and goodwill, resolved to use the opportunities of the term to the best of our strength and ability; we ask this in the name and for the love of Jesus Christ our Lord.

Lionel James in *A Book of Prayers for Schools*

*At the End of Term*

361 Go forth into the world in peace; be of good courage; hold fast that which is good; render to no man evil for evil; strengthen the faint-hearted; support the weak; help the afflicted; honour all men; love and serve the Lord, rejoicing in the power of the Holy Spirit.

And the blessing of God Almighty, the Father, the Son and the Holy Ghost be upon you and remain with you for ever.

*Prayer Book, 1928*

*At the End of a Term (or Week)*

362 We thank thee, O God, for the term/week that is past, for all the opportunities it has given us for progress and happiness, for any success we have achieved, for any good we have done; forgive what has been imperfect, and help us to strive after what is true, honest and of real value, that we may serve thee better, and love thee more; through Jesus Christ our Lord.

Stowe School

*On Founder's Day*

363 O God of our Fathers, our Father, our Lord; we thank you for the rich inheritance that we enjoy in this place; for the life and vision and courage of . . . our Founder; and for the loyalty and generosity of all who have dedicated their service and their lives to this school. May we in our generation have the grace to use to the utmost all that we receive here; so that by the way we live, by the way we work, by the way we pray, and by the way we serve you and one another, we may enrich this school for the benefit of others, the fulfilment of ourselves, and the honour and glory of your son, Jesus Christ our Lord.

C.R.C.

*After a Short Holiday*

364 Thank you, Lord, for these days of happiness and refreshment. Thank you for our families and friends, our health and our pleasures. Through Jesus Christ our Lord.

Marlborough College

*For the Remainder of the Term*

365 Whatever you give us to do during the remainder of this term, let it be done, O Lord, not casually, grudgingly or cynically, but with a vigorous and willing spirit; through your son, Jesus Christ our Lord.

Marlborough College

## FEELINGS, SENSES, FACULTIES

*Sorrow*

366 Crucified Lord of Sorrow, save us, we pray, from grief and sickness of body, mind and spirit. In distress, teach us to turn to you for comfort, and to know that you are always more ready to help us than we can imagine. We ask this for your name's sake.

A. G. Bullivant

*Success*

367 O Lord God, you created all things good and have given us life to live and enjoy. We thank you particularly for . . .

Help us not to spoil this occasion in any way at all (or, by selfishness, or, by boasting) but to enjoy it fully together and give thanks to you, through the love of your son, Jesus Christ our Lord.

C.R.C.

*Suffering*

368 Bestow, O God, this grace on us, that in the school of suffering we should learn self-conquest, and through sorrow, even if it be against our will, learn self-control.

Aeschylus, 525–456 B.C.

*Tragedy and Bereavement*

369 Almighty God, help us to trust in thy love and mercy when those things occur which we neither welcome nor understand. Give us grace to feel for the sorrows of others. Strengthen all who mourn

and comfort those who are bereaved. We ask this through him who knew loneliness, sorrow and death, Jesus Christ our Lord.

Truro School

*Hearing*

370 Blessed Lord, we thank you for the gift of hearing. Grant that our ears may ever be open to all loveliness: to music, and the laughter of friends; to running water; to the wind in the trees, to the call of birds and beasts—and to all the multitude of voices in your strange creation.

Grant that we may ever hear in them the music of your love and goodness and power; through Jesus Christ our Lord.

*Prayers for Every Day*

371 (Let us be very still for a moment and think about the wonder of being able to hear. If we could not hear, the world would be a dull and silent place. Thanks be to God our Father for giving us the sense of hearing.)

Teach us, good Lord, to use our ears to hear good things: help us to enjoy music, laughter, people talking, the wind blowing, the birds and animals calling, and all the good things given to us so freely in this lovely world; through Jesus Christ our Lord.

A. G. Bullivant

*Hunger and Food*

372 Help us, O God, to care about the needs of the hungry. Give us self-control to overcome our greed. Help us not to grumble about our food, and not to waste it; but make us thankful that we are fed at all, when men, women and children in other parts of the world are weak with hunger. Move us to contribute to their relief, and let them be fed. Through Jesus Christ our Lord.

Marlborough College

*Sight*

373 (Let us think for a moment about the wonder of being able to see. Without sight we should find it hard to learn anything at all,

and the world would be a sad, dark place. Thanks be to God our Father for the gift of sight.)

Thank you, God, for giving us eyes to see the world that you have made, and to learn about it by looking and reading. May we always see pure and good things and use our eyesight to your glory, and in the service of our fellow-men; through Jesus Christ our Lord.

A. G. Bullivant

*Speech*

374 Guard our speech, Lord, and prevent us from saying anything to hurt anyone else. Help us to keep our tongues from lies, foul language, dirtiness, unfriendly or hateful words, and all the sinful things which hurt you. Let our guide to a right use of speech be your son Jesus Christ.

A. G. Bullivant

375 God grant that when the chance to say something helpful comes our way, we shall be brave enough to say it.

Beryl Bye, *Prayers at Breakfast*

*Words*

376 Gracious Lord, help us to refrain from speaking unkind words, so that our tongue may be known for its kindness.

Beryl Bye, *Prayers at Breakfast*

377 O God, who has given us the amazing gift of words—which we use and abuse for many purposes: to express friendship and love; to tell lies; to praise, slander, curse, persuade, amuse; to spread scandal, wisdom, faith or corruption—help us to think before we speak; to keep silent when mercy and discretion demand it; to say what is kind, true, brave, clean and sincere; and always to speak what would be acceptable to your son, Jesus Christ our Lord.

Marlborough College

378 O God, grant that no word may fall from us, against our will, unfit for the present need.

Pericles, 495–429 B.C.

## CONCERNING VIRTUES, VICES AND VALUES

### *Boldness*

379 O God our father, help us to meet the challenges of life with a bold and daring spirit. Give us courage to overcome our fears, doubts and hesitations. Inspire us with bravery so that we can develop and use in your service all the powers which you have given us. We ask for this boldness in the name of Jesus Christ our Lord.

Marlborough College

### *Cheer*

380 Give us cheerful faces, Lord, cheerful thoughts, and happy words to pass on our joy to others; for Christ's sake.

A. G. Bullivant

### *Courage*

381 Jesus, even if I am laughed at or mocked for trying to please you, let me never give in. Let me never laugh at others for trying to do right. Grant this for thy name's sake.

*Prayer Book for Catholic Seafarers, Apostleship of the Sea*

382 Let us not pray to be sheltered from dangers, but to be fearless in facing them.

Let us not beg for the stilling of pain, but for the heart to conquer it.

Let us not look for allies in life's battlefield, but to our own strength.

Let us not crave in anxious fear to be saved, but hope for the patience to win freedom.

Grant that we may not be cowards, O Lord, feeling your mercy in our success alone; but let us find the grasp of your hand in our failures.

Rabindranath Tagore, 1861–1941
*Fruit Gathering* (adapted)

383 Lord, give us courage to do what is right even when we feel afraid of doing it, or find that a good life is tedious, or when it means sacrificing something we like, for thy name's sake.

*Prayer Book for Catholic Seafarers,*
*Apostleship of the Sea* (adapted)

384 O God our heavenly Father, we pray for the gift of courage. If we find our work in school difficult, help us to face our difficulties with a determination which will enable us to overcome them; if in our games we sometimes give in through a lack of physical courage, give us that strength which will enable us to overcome fear; if in our relationships with others we are tempted to lower our own standards and to follow an influence we know to be wrong, give us strength to resist and to stand for all that is right; and if in our personal lives we have some weakness or some temptation which we find hard to overcome, grant us the great gift of moral courage to live and act according to our highest ideals. In all times of our weakness, be our strength, through Jesus Christ our Lord.

Kingswood School, Bath

385 O Lord, give us the insight to see what we should do, the courage to act upon it whatever our friends and enemies may say, and the determination to persevere to the end as did your son, our pattern, Jesus Christ.

Marlborough College

### *Detachment*

386 O God, who in thy love has given us gifts that our fathers never knew or dreamed of, mercifully grant that we do not become so occupied with material things that we forget the things which are spiritual, lest having gained the whole world, we lose our souls.

Clarendon Secondary Modern Girls' School

### *Freedom*

387 Help us, O God, to understand what true freedom means: give us the will to seek it, persistence to find it and strength to use it

for the good of other people, in the name of Jesus Christ our Lord.

Marlborough College

*Generosity*

388 Dear God, give us an honest mind,
A responsive heart,
And a generous hand,
Through Jesus Christ our Lord.

Stowe School

389 Give us generous hearts, O God, to give back to you something of what you have given us; through Jesus Christ our Lord.

Beryl Bye, *Prayers at Breakfast*

390 O God, who has given us more than we would have dared to ask, make us generous with everything that we have, for we know that we have it only in trust for you; through Christ our Lord.

Beryl Bye, *Prayers at Breakfast*

*Gladness*

391 Hear us, O Lord, we beseech thee, and in our times of unhappiness pity us; grant unto us gladness of spirit, and give us thine everlasting peace; through Jesus Christ our Lord.

Source unknown

*Gratitude*

392 Lord, change our hearts from hearts of stone to hearts of flesh, and let us give thanks to you for all of life.

Malcolm Boyd, *Are you running with me, Jesus?*

393 O Lord, that lends us life,
Lend us a heart replete with thankfulness.

William Shakespeare, *2 Henry VI*

394 Thou who hast given so much to me,
Give one thing more, a grateful heart.

George Herbert, 1593–1633

*High Purpose and Lofty Aspiration*

395 Give us, Lord, lofty ambition such as will be satisfied with nothing less than the best and nothing short of the goal of final reality, that we may come to know the truth and that the truth may make us free; through him who is the Way, the Truth, and the Life, Jesus Christ.

Bishop Brent, 1862–1929

*Honesty*

396 Teach us, good Lord, the value of honesty. Make us straightforward and devoted to truth. When we are in a tight corner, teach us to be ashamed of telling lies to make things easy for ourselves. May all our service in your name be honestly and sincerely performed, to the honour of Jesus our Saviour.

A. G. Bullivant

397 When we do wrong, O God, make us honest and brave to acknowledge that we are responsible. Save us from those lies, half-lies, near-truths and excuses that spring to our lips because we are afraid. Give us courage to follow your son, who never spared himself in his fearless love of truth, Jesus Christ our Lord.

Marlborough College

*Humility*

398 O Father, give us the humility which
Realises its ignorance,
Admits its mistakes,
Recognises its need,
Welcomes advice,
Accepts rebuke.
Help us always
To praise rather than to criticise,
To sympathise rather than to condemn.
To encourage rather than to discourage,
To build rather than to destroy,
And to think of people at their best rather than at their worst.
This we ask for thy name's sake.

William Barclay

399 O Jesus, take from us the arrogance by which we deceive ourselves and hurt other people. Make us gentle and strong as you were; for your name's sake.

C.R.C.

400 O Lord Jesus Christ, who didst humble thyself to become man, and to be born into the world for our salvation: teach us the grace of humility, root out of our hearts all pride and haughtiness, and so fashion us after thy holy likeness in this world, that in the world to come we may be made like unto thee, our Saviour Jesus Christ.

W. W. How, 1823–1897 (adapted)

401 Take from us, O God,
All pride and vanity,
All boasting and forwardness;
And give us the true courage that shows itself by gentleness,
The true wisdom that shows itself by simplicity,
And the true power that shows itself by modesty; through Jesus Christ our Lord.

Charles Kingsley, 1819–1875

*Sense of Humour*

402 Give us a sense of humour, Lord, and also things to laugh about. Give us the grace to take a joke against ourselves, and see the funny side of the things we do. Save us from annoyance, bad temper, resentfulness against our friends. Help us to laugh even in the face of trouble. Fill our minds with the love of Jesus; for his name's sake.

A. G. Bullivant

*Hypocrisy*

403 Save us, good Lord, from the sin of hypocrisy. Save us from pretending to be better than other people. Save us from deceiving

ourselves into thinking that we are virtuous and good, when we fall short of the standard of your son Jesus.

A. G. Bullivant

### *Idle Pleasures*

404 Preserve us, O Lord, from idle pleasures which profit nothing; and more especially from those which leave behind nothing but shame and bitterness: for thy mercy's sake.

*A Book of School Worship*

### *Independence*

405 Give us courage, O God, to think for ourselves and to rely on our own judgement, not to thoughtlessly follow the crowd; but save us from arrogance, in the name of Jesus Christ our Lord.

Marlborough College

### *Jealousy*

406 Father God, thank you for making ourselves ourselves. Help us to enjoy life so much that we never want to be other people or be jealous of their abilities or possessions; through the love of thy Son Jesus Christ our Lord.

C.R.C.

407 O God, we ask you to free us from the sin of jealousy which so often leads us to hate and disunity. For the sake of Jesus Christ, our King of Love, we ask it.

Beryl Bye, *Prayers at Breakfast*

408 O Lord God, help us to share in other people's successes and not to be jealous when their work gains more praise than our own; through Jesus Christ our Lord.

Beryl Bye, *Prayers at Breakfast*

### *Knowledge*

409 O God, who has given us inquisitive and teachable minds, stir us out of our mental laziness and inspire us to seek the truth. Increase our desire for knowledge. Draw our minds actively

towards the light, which is yourself, so that we may become wiser, humbler and truer in your service; through the love of you and of your son, Jesus Christ.

Marlborough College

*Love of Life*

410 Lord, may we love all your creation, all the earth and every grain of sand in it. May we love every leaf, every ray of your light.

May we love the animals: you have given them the rudiments of thought and joy untroubled. Let us not trouble it; let us not harass them, let us not deprive them of their happiness, let us not work against your intent.

For we acknowledge unto you that all is like an ocean, all is flowing and blending, and that to withhold any measure of love from anything in your universe is to withhold that same measure from you.

Feodor Dostoevsky, 1821–1881
*The Brothers Karamazov* (adapted)

*Attitude to Money*

411 Protect us, O God, from excessive desire for money and possessions, and help us to use rightly whatever you give into our keeping. Through Jesus Christ our Lord.

Marlborough College

412 Whatever we have is yours, God of our world, so help us to use it rightly. When we have money, teach us how to spend it wisely. When we have none, show us how to manage without it. Forgive us when we grumble about money, or envy those who have more than us. Guide us in our search for the true riches of heaven, the love, faith, and hope which are the gifts of the Spirit of Jesus Christ.

A. G. Bullivant

*Open-mindedness*

413 O God, help us not to despise or oppose what we do not understand; through Jesus Christ our Lord.

William Penn, 1644–1718

*For Patience*

414 O Lord God, sometimes you know we are unjustly judged for something that is not our fault. Help us to take it patiently for your sake.

Beryl Bye, *Prayers at Breakfast*

*For Peace*

415 O Jesus, in your life you gave peace to those who were in the anguish of sin and fear and disease, and by your death you gave men the gift of peace with God and with one another. Please make all this real for us in our lives now, so that we in turn can become peace-makers fit to be called the sons of our heavenly father; for your name's sake.

C.R.C.

*Against Pride*

416 Help us, O God, to overcome our pride, our vanity and our boastfulness. Whatever talents we possess we owe to you: make us thankful for them and modest in all that we do and in all that we say, through Jesus Christ our Lord.

Marlborough College

*For Purity*

417 Lord Jesus, we see in you unselfish purity and strength. Help us to be rid of the weakness and selfishness which spoil our characters, so that we may live pure and integrated lives in worship of you, love of other people, and fulfilment of ourselves, for your name's sake.

C.R.C.

418 *Faith in the Right*

Lord, give us faith that right makes might.

Abraham Lincoln, 1809–1865

*Against Selfishness*

419 Help us, O God, to leave the prison of our selfishness. Give us greatness of spirit to break the bars, follow your son and live for others, abandoning our mean self-love for your noble service, in the name of Jesus Christ our Lord.

Marlborough College

420 Lord, help us to remember that the worst form of selfishness is to withhold ourselves, the worst ignorance is not to act, the worst lie is to steal away. Help us in the name of Jesus Christ.

Marlborough College

*Mastery of Self*

421 O Lord help us to be masters of ourselves that we may be the servants of others.

Sir Alec Paterson, 1884–1947

*For True Self-esteem*

422 Eternal and most glorious God, who hast stamped the soul of man with thine Image, received it into thy Revenue, and made it a part of thy Treasure; suffer us not so to undervalue ourselves, nay, so to impoverish thee, as to give away these souls for nothing, and all the world is nothing if the soul must be given for it. Do this, O God, for his sake who knows our natural infirmities, for he had them, and knows the weight of our sins, for he paid a dear price for them, thy Son, our Saviour Jesus Christ.

John Donne, 1572–1631

423 Give us, O God, at all times respect for ourselves,
So that we may never do work of which we would be ashamed;
So that we may never stoop to that which is mean and low;
So that we may never do in the present that which in the future we would have cause to regret: through Jesus Christ our Lord.

*Epilogues and Prayers*

*A Sense of Proportion*

424 Help us, O Lord, to distinguish what is important, to care about vital matters and not to be upset by trivialities. In the name of your son, who always saw life clearly, Jesus Christ our Lord.

Marlborough College

*For Sensitivity to Goodness*

425 O Lord, keep me sensitive to the grace that is round about me. May the familiar not become the neglected. May I see thy goodness in my daily bread, and may the comfort of my home take my thoughts to the mercy-seat of God; through the grace of Jesus Christ our Lord.

J. H. Jowett, 1864–1923

*For Serenity*

426 Take from us now, O God, all tediousness of spirit, all impatience and unquietness. Let us possess ourselves in patience, and resign our souls and bodies into thy hands, through Jesus Christ our Lord.

Jeremy Taylor, 1613–1667

*Single-mindedness*

427 Give us, O Lord, a steadfast heart, which no unworthy affection may drag downwards; give us an unconquered heart, which no tribulation can wear out; give us an upright heart, which no unworthy purpose may tempt aside. Bestow upon us also, O Lord our God, understanding to know thee, diligence to seek thee, wisdom to find thee, and a faithfulness that may finally embrace thee; through Jesus Christ our Lord.

Thomas Aquinas, 1225–1274

428 Lord God, our father, help us to aim at achievements that are worth pursuing. Give us single-mindedness, energy and devotion. Whatever worthy activity we undertake, help us in our efforts always to rise above a slovenly acceptance of the second-best. May we find inspiration in the single-mindedness of your son, Jesus Christ our Lord.

Marlborough College

*That We May Help the Deaf*

429 O God, the Father of our Lord Jesus Christ, who opened the ears of the deaf and made the dumb speak, teach us, after his example, to give help and understanding to those who are deaf, and to be patient with them, through Jesus Christ our Lord.

The Church of England Council for the Deaf (adapted)

*Strength in Weakness*

430 O God, who hast proclaimed the victorious destiny of man by thyself achieving it in human form, give us strength in weakness, quiet in turbulence and triumph in failure; through Jesus Christ our Lord.

Bishop Brent, 1862–1929

*Tact*

431 Teach us, O Lord, the value of tact and discretion; may we know when silence is better than speech, and when withdrawal is better than interference. Give us a sympathetic ear and make us sensitive to the needs and problems of others; through Jesus Christ our Lord.

Stowe School

*Trust*

432 Help us, O Lord, to trust one another, and to be worthy of mutual trust. Make us see that hypocrisy, malice, scandal and lies corrupt and weaken the person who indulges in them. Strengthen us all against those evils, and give us the power to face ourselves and one another with honesty and courage, so that we can grow to full stature in your service; through Jesus Christ our Lord.

Marlborough College

*Truth*

433 O God, give us courage
to accept what is true,

to speak what is true,
to do what is true.
Through Jesus Christ our Lord.

Marlborough College

434 O God, help us to guard our words, to keep our promises and to speak the truth; through Jesus Christ our Lord.

Source unknown

435 Where there are lies, Lord, bring truth.

Where there is deceit, make everything clear, and shame the deceiver.

Where there is error, guide our faltering footsteps by the Spirit of Truth who was in Christ Jesus.

A. G. Bullivant

*Unselfishness*

436 Break through, break through, Lord Jesus; break through the hardness, the ignorance, the stuffy selfishness of our hearts. Come in with your love and help us to venture outside ourselves, beyond the restrictions of our interests and prejudices; that we may find the truth and goodness of life with you in other people; for your name's sake.

C.R.C.

437 O Lord, help us to put aside our own trials and difficulties, so that we may be a help to others; for your name's sake.

Beryl Bye, *Prayers at Breakfast*

*A Sense of Values*

438 Give to us, O Lord, a sense of values, and an awareness of true priorities, that we may offer to all their due: to our parents, gratitude and affection, to our friends, loyalty and comradeship, to ourselves, the determination to produce the best of which we are capable, and to thee sincere worship and unceasing service, through Jesus Christ our Lord.

Stowe School

439 Grant us, O Lord, to know that which is worth knowing, to love that which is worth loving, to praise that which can bear with praise, to hate what in thy sight is unworthy, to prize what to thee is precious, and, above all, to search out and to do what is well-pleasing unto thee; through Jesus Christ our Lord.

Thomas à Kempis, 1380–1471

*Technology*

440 Radios, gramophones, television sets, tape recorders, telephones: these we take for granted as we do water from a tap and electric light from a wire. Give us gratitude and humility, O God, to thank you for the astonishing inspiration, care and skill that have made these devices. And give us good sense enough to use them well. Through Jesus Christ our Lord.

Marlborough College

*The World*

441 O God, help us to value this world only because it is yours. We brought nothing into it: we can take nothing out of it. The world does not belong to us. We are here to make it a better place by serving you and by helping other people. Guide us so that we not only understand this truth with our minds, but live it every day of our lives, with the help of your son, our friend and teacher, Jesus Christ.

Marlborough College

*Worry*

442 O Lord, we know we very often worry about things that may never happen. Help us to live one day at a time, and to live it for you; for your name's sake.

Beryl Bye, *Prayers at Breakfast*

*Zeal*

443 Deliver me, O God, from a slothful mind, from all lukewarmness, and all dejection of spirit. I know these can only deaden my love to thee; mercifully free my heart from them, and give me a lively, zealous, active, and cheerful spirit; that I may vigorously perform

whatever thou commandest, thankfully suffer whatever thou choosest for me, and be ever ardent to obey in all things thy holy love.

John Wesley, 1703–1791 (adapted)

# Relationship with God

## COME CLOSE, O GOD

444 Christ be with me, Christ within me,
Christ behind me, Christ before me,
Christ beside me, Christ to win me,
Christ to comfort and restore me.
Christ beneath me, Christ above me,
Christ in quiet, Christ in danger,
Christ in heart of all that love me,
Christ in mouth of friend and stranger.

St. Patrick, 389–461

445 Eternal Light, shine into our hearts,
Eternal Goodness, deliver our thoughts from evil,
Eternal Power, support our prayer,
Eternal Wisdom, enlighten the darkness of our ignorance,
Eternal Pity, have mercy upon us;
that with all our heart and mind and soul and strength we may seek thy face, and be brought by thine infinite mercy to thy holy presence; through Jesus Christ our Lord.

Alcuin, 735–804

446 God be in my head, and in my understanding;
God be in my eyes, and in my looking;
God be in my mouth, and in my speaking;
God be in my heart, and in my thinking;
God be at mine end, and at my departing.

*The Sarum Primer Prayer*

447 O Holy Spirit, the Comforter, come and dwell in our souls; make our bodies thy temple. Fill our minds with thy light, and our

hearts with thy love, that over our whole character thy power may be seen in the beauties of holiness. May we live as something sacred to thee as well as perfected by thee. Come in all thy sevenfold energy, and replenish us with thy illuminating, comforting, sanctifying influence. Baptize us with celestial fire, and give us in thine abundant grace the earnest of glory everlasting.

John Angell James, 1785–1859

448 When the heart is hard and parched up, come upon me with a shower of mercy.

When grace is lost from life, come with a burst of song.

When tumultuous work raises its din on all sides, shutting me out from beyond, come to me, my Lord of silence, with thy peace and rest.

When my beggarly heart sits crouched, shut up in a corner, break open the door, my king, and come with the ceremony of a king.

When desire blinds the mind with delusion and dust, O thou holy one, thou wakeful, come with thy light and with thy thunder.

Rabindranath Tagore, 1861–1941, *Gitanjali*

## GRACE TO KNOW AND DO THE WILL OF GOD

449 Almighty and everlasting God, with whom nothing is obscure, nothing dark, send forth thy light into our hearts that we may perceive the brightness of thy Law, and walking in thy holy way may fall into no sin, through thy beloved Son and our beloved example, Jesus Christ.

St. Gregory, 550–604

450 Almighty God, enlighten our understandings with knowledge of right that no deceit may mislead us, and govern our wills by thy laws that no temptation corrupt us; so may we always endeavour to do good and hinder evil. Amidst all the hopes and fears of this world, take not thy Holy Spirit from us, in the name of Christ our Lord.

Samuel Johnson, 1709–1784

451 God of all goodness, grant us to desire ardently, to seek wisely, to know surely, and to accomplish perfectly thy holy will, for the glory of thy name.

St. Thomas Aquinas, 1226–1274

452 God of Heaven and Earth, to whom the universe gives homage, and whose laws all creatures obey, we too wish to be under your perfect rule, and not under the power of our sins or the greed and hate of men. Adopt us, we pray, as sons and daughters, use us as servants, rule us as your subjects. May your kingdom of love be built in our world as surely as it is in your heavenly home. May your will be done willingly by all humanity, now and ever, through Jesus Christ our Lord.

A. G. Bullivant

453 Grant to us, Lord, we beseech thee, the spirit to think and do always such things as be rightful; that we, who cannot do anything that is good without thee, may by thee be enabled to live according to thy will; through Jesus Christ our Lord.

*Book of Common Prayer*

454 Lord, let thy glory be my end, thy word my rule, and then thy will be done.

King Charles I, 1600–1649

455 Lord, we pray, have mercy on us, and help us always to obey your laws of love, even when it is difficult, and when we are weary of trying. Give us strength to obey your will, and a clear mind to find out what it is. We pray to be made obedient, and so to copy the example of your Son, Jesus Christ our Lord.

A. G. Bullivant

456 My God, you created me, and all my body and mind belong to you. O God, all-wise, put right thoughts in my head. O God, all-powerful, keep my will strong. O God, my loving Father, help me when I specially need you and am tempted to forget you. Through Jesus Christ our Lord.

*Prayer Book for Catholic Seafarers,*
*Apostleship of the Sea*

457 O Almighty God, who alone canst order the unruly wills and affections of sinful men; grant unto thy people, that they may love the thing which thou commandest, and desire that which thou dost promise; that so, among the sundry and manifold changes of the world, our hearts may surely there be fixed, where true joys are to be found; through Jesus Christ our Lord.

*Book of Common Prayer*

458 O God, forasmuch as without thee we are not able to please thee; mercifully grant that thy Holy Spirit may in all things direct and rule our hearts; through Jesus Christ our Lord.

*Book of Common Prayer*

459 O Holy Spirit, giver of light and life,
Impart to us thoughts higher than our own thoughts,
and prayers better than our own prayers,
and powers beyond our own powers,
that we may spend and be spent
in the ways of love and goodness,
after the perfect image,
of our Lord and Saviour Jesus Christ.

*Daily Prayer*

460 Vouchsafe, we beseech thee, O God, to direct, sanctify, and govern both our hearts and bodies in the ways of thy laws and in the works of thy commandments; that through thy most mighty protection both here and ever, we may be preserved in body and soul; through our Lord and Saviour Jesus Christ.

*Book of Common Prayer*

## SPIRITUAL GIFTS

### *Increase of Faith*

461 Almighty and everlasting God, give us the increase of faith, hope, and charity; and that we may obtain that which thou dost promise, make us to love that which thou dost command; through Jesus Christ our Lord.

*Book of Common Prayer*

*Good Works*

462 Stir up, we beseech thee, O Lord, the wills of thy faithful people; that they, plenteously bringing forth the fruit of good works, may by thee be plenteously rewarded; through Jesus Christ our Lord.

*Book of Common Prayer*

*Grace*

463 Defend, O Lord, us thy children with thy heavenly grace, that we may continue thine for ever, and daily increase in thy Holy Spirit more and more, until we come to thy everlasting Kingdom.

*The Second Prayer Book of Edward VI, 1552*

(Words like these are used by a Bishop in the act of confirming.)

464 Lord, we beseech thee, grant thy people grace to withstand the temptations of the world, the flesh, and the devil, and with pure hearts and minds to follow thee the only God; through Jesus Christ our Lord.

*Book of Common Prayer*

465 O thou, from whom to be turned is to fall,
to whom to be turned is to rise,
and in whom to stand is to abide for ever;
Grant us in all our duties thy help,
in all our perplexities thy guidance,
in all our dangers thy protection,
and in all our sorrows thy peace;
through Jesus Christ our Lord.

St. Augustine, 354–430

*The Light of Christ*

466 O Jesus Christ, your life focuses the light of God upon us: it stabs the darkness of untruth and shows up in clear simplicity the sin, squalor and drabness which we have allowed to sully the world. Do not let us dim your light by ignorance or scorn of what you did on earth, but make our lives shine with your light and brighten the world we live in, to the glory of our heavenly father; for your name's sake.

C.R.C.

467 O everlasting God, who created the morning of life, and sent light from your Son to shine upon our boyhood; enlighten us with the knowledge of your Love, so that in the brightness of Christ we may see the vision of our true manhood; and after our days on earth come to the light of true glory; through the same Jesus Christ our Lord.

Epsom College (adapted)

*The Love of God*

468 O God, who hast prepared for them that love thee such good things as pass man's understanding, pour into our hearts such love towards thee, that we, loving thee above all things, may obtain thy promises, which exceed all that we can desire; through Jesus Christ our Lord.

*Book of Common Prayer*

*Mercy*

469 O God, the protector of all that trust in thee, without whom nothing is strong, nothing is holy; increase and multiply upon us thy mercy, that thou being our ruler and guide, we may so pass through things temporal, that we finally lose not the things eternal; grant this, O heavenly Father, for Jesus Christ's sake our Lord.

*Book of Common Prayer*

*Protection*

470 Almighty God, who seest that we have no power of ourselves to help ourselves; keep us both outwardly in our bodies, and inwardly in our souls; that we may be defended from all adversities which may happen to the body, and from all evil thoughts which may assault and hurt the soul; through Jesus Christ our Lord.

*Book of Common Prayer*

*Revelation*

471 Blessed Lord, you speak to us in so many different ways: teach us to recognize your voice at all times.

Beryl Bye, *Prayers at Breakfast*

### *Strength*

472 May the strength of God pilot us.
May the power of God preserve us.
May the wisdom of God instruct us.
May the hand of God protect us.
May the way of God direct us.
May the shield of God defend us.
May the host of God guard us against the snares of evil and the temptations of the world.
May Christ be with us, Christ before us, Christ in us, Christ over us.
May thy salvation, O Lord, be always ours this day and for evermore.

St. Patrick, 389–461

### *True Religion*

473 Lord of all power and might, who art the author and giver of all good things: graft in our hearts the love of thy name, increase in us true religion, nourish us with all goodness, and of thy great mercy keep us in the same; through Jesus Christ our Lord.

*Book of Common Prayer*

### *Trust*

474 O God our Father, when things seem at their worst, and there appears to be no way out of a difficulty, teach us then to trust in you; through Jesus Christ our Lord.

Beryl Bye, *Prayers at Breakfast*

## JESUS CHRIST

### *Why is reality about you so shocking to us, Lord?*

475 They've made the cross you hung on so pretty, Jesus.

I know the real cross wasn't pretty at all, but I guess I understand why they want to make copies of it out of fine woods and even semiprecious stones because *you* hung on it.

Yet doesn't this romanticize your death, Lord, and give it a kind of gloss it didn't have? Your death was bloody and dirty and very real. Can't we face it that way, Jesus? And can't we face the fact that you were a real man, living a human life, as well as God?

Malcolm Boyd, *Are you running with me, Jesus?*

*You're hanging on a cross again, Jesus*

476 The symbol is so familiar to us that maybe we don't think about the reality any more. Wasn't it simply the means of your execution, something like an electric chair or hangman's noose would be today?

In churches the cross always seems to be everywhere, over altars and in stained-glass windows and even hanging in clergymen's offices. I know it represents the act of redemption, but your whole life seems to do this much more significantly.

Is your death more important to us than your life, Lord? Is your death more central than your resurrection? Help us to keep these things in balance so that we don't lose sight of you among all the religious symbols we put up in your honour.

Malcolm Boyd, *Are you running with me, Jesus?*

*Friendship and Discipleship*

477 O heavenly Father, send into our hearts and into the hearts of all men everywhere the spirit of our Lord Jesus Christ.

John Oxenham

478 Jesus, true friend of men, teach us to value your friendship. Daily increase our understanding of your love, and help us to pass on your friendship to others. May our lives, as your disciples, show the joy and contentment that comes from serving you.

A. G. Bullivant

479 Thanks be to thee, my Lord Jesus Christ,
for all the benefits which thou hast given me,
for all the pains and insults which thou hast borne for me:

O most merciful Redeemer, Friend and Brother;
may I know thee more clearly,
love thee more dearly,
follow thee more nearly,
day by day.

St. Richard of Chichester, 1197–1253

480 When we are following in your footsteps, Lord Jesus, trying to be your faithful disciples, help us to overcome the discouragements and discomforts of the way. If people scoff at our ideas, teach us patience. If they ridicule our faith, help us to persevere. When they tempt us to do what we know is wrong, help us to remain steadfast; for thy name's sake.

A. G. Bullivant

*The Service of Christ*

481 Christ has many services to be done: some are easy, others are difficult; some bring honour, others bring reproach; some are suitable to our natural inclinations and interests, others are contrary to both. In some we may please Christ and please ourselves, in others we cannot please Christ except by denying ourselves. Give us the power to do all these things, O Spirit of God, in the strength of Christ our Lord.

Methodist Covenant Service

## TRUE RESPONSE TO GOD

482 Lord God, Light of the minds that know thee, Life of the souls that love thee, and Strength of the thoughts that seek thee; help us so to know thee that we may truly love thee, and so to love thee that we may fully serve thee, whose service is perfect freedom; through Jesus Christ our Lord.

*Gelasian Sacramentary*

483 O God,
You are King; help us to come to you in loyal allegiance;
You are Judge; help us to come to you in heartfelt sorrow for the wrong that we have done;

You are Father; help us to come to you in confident and loving trust;
You are God; help us to come to you in humble reverence and adoration.
Hear these our prayers: through Jesus Christ our Lord.

*Epilogues and Prayers*

484 O gracious and holy Father,
Give us wisdom to perceive thee,
intelligence to understand thee,
diligence to seek thee,
patience to wait for thee,
eyes to behold thee,
a heart to meditate upon thee,
and a life to proclaim thee;
through the power of the Spirit of Jesus Christ our Lord.

St. Benedict, 480–543

485 O Lord our God, grant us grace to desire thee with a whole heart, that so desiring thee we may seek and find thee, and so finding thee may love thee, and loving thee, may hate those sins which separate us from thee, for the sake of Jesus Christ.

St. Anselm, 1033–1109

486 O Lord Jesus Christ, who art the Way, the Truth, and the Life, we pray thee suffer us not to stray from thee, who art the Way, nor to distrust thee, who art the Truth, nor to rest in any other thing than thee, who art the Life. Teach us by the Holy Spirit what to believe, what to do, and wherein to take our rest.

Desiderius Erasmus, 1466–1536

487 To different people, O God, you reveal yourself in different ways: grant to us all such open and generous minds that we may respond to you, however you come to us, with all the warmth and vigour that the highest love demands, through Jesus Christ our Lord.

Marlborough College

# Prayers for the World, Nations, Institutions, People

## ALL SORTS AND CONDITIONS OF MEN AND CREATURES

488 O God, the Creator and Preserver of all mankind, we humbly beseech thee for all sorts and conditions of men; that thou wouldest be pleased to make thy ways known unto them, thy saving health unto all nations. More especially we pray for the good estate of the Catholick Church; that it may be so guided and governed by thy good Spirit, that all who profess and call themselves Christians may be led into the way of truth, and hold the faith in unity of spirit, in the bond of peace, and in righteousness of life. Finally, we commend to thy fatherly goodness all those, who are any ways afflicted, or distressed, in mind, body, or estate; that it may please thee to comfort and relieve them, according to their several necessities, giving them patience under their sufferings, and a happy issue out of all their afflictions. And this we beg for Jesus Christ his sake.

*Book of Common Prayer*

### *Animals and Pets*

489 Hear our humble prayer, O God, for our friends the animals, especially for animals who are suffering;

for all that are overworked and underfed and cruelly treated;

for all wistful creatures in captivity that beat against their bars;

for any that are hunted or lost or deserted or frightened or hungry;

for all that are in pain or dying;

for all that must be put to death.

We entreat for them all thy mercy and pity, and for those who deal with them we ask a heart of compassion and gentle hands and kindly words. Make us ourselves to be true friends to animals, and so to share the blessing of the merciful, for the sake of thy Son the tenderhearted, Jesus Christ, our Lord.

Russian Prayer
*Book of School Worship*

*Atomic Power*

490 God of the Universe, we see your majesty and power in the mighty energy of the atom, locked away in the perfect pattern of your creation. Give to us, we pray, a true sense of awe and of humility. Prevent us from damaging your world and harming mankind by the senseless explosion of atomic energy in bombs which can only destroy. Teach us, rather, to use atomic power for peaceful ends, in the service of industry and medicine, and so to build a new and better world for everyone. In this way alone shall we be fit to enter the Kingdom of the King of Peace, Jesus Christ.

A. G. Bullivant

*Birds*

491 Lord, creator of the eagle and the sparrow, the dove and the humming bird, we praise and thank you for the varied beauty of birds, their songs and their flight. Help us to care for this marvellous part of your creation; for your name's sake.

Marlborough College

*Children*

492 Look with favour, Heavenly Father, on little children everywhere. Defend them from the unkindness of men and all evil influences; through Jesus Christ our Lord.

Bishop Brent, 1862–1929

*Children Who are Deaf*

493 O Lord Jesus Christ, we pray for children who have never been able to hear. Help them to persevere in learning to speak, and in gaining knowledge. And to their teachers give great patience. We ask this for your name's sake.

The Church of England Council for the Deaf (adapted)

*Children Who are Destitute*

494 O God, our heavenly Father, we remember before you all destitute and sorrowful children: those whose homes have been destroyed by war: those living in camps for whom family life has had little meaning: those without knowledge of their parents: those who have suffered years of terror and persecution: all who are sick with loneliness or suffering from bodily disease. Make our hearts burn within us for the children of the dark places of the world. Lead us to pray for them and give for them, and inspire the efforts of all who are striving to help them: through Jesus Christ our Lord.

Epsom College

*Children in Other Countries*

495 Dear Father, we pray that you will help those children in other countries who do not have the opportunities we have. We ask you to give them the skill to read and write, and the spirit to use their skill for the good of mankind; through Jesus Christ thy Son our Lord.

Clarendon Secondary Modern Girls' School

*Christian Aid*

496 O Lord God, in our affluence we remember before you those in all corners of the world who are starving and homeless. Look in mercy upon all who lack security and live amid disease and squalor. And as you have assured those who do good to others, that, in as much as they do it to your brethren, they do it unto you, let your tender compassion move men to house the homeless, feed the hungry and lighten the burdens of the needy. Guide those also who govern the nations that their actions may set free those who are living in want and fear: so that all the families of the earth may be blessed; for Jesus Christ's sake.

Epsom College

*For the Dead*

497 May the souls of the faithful, through the mercy of God, rest in peace.

Compline

498 O Father of all, we pray to thee for those whom we love, but see no longer. Grant them thy peace; let light perpetual shine upon them; and in thy loving wisdom and almighty power work in them the good purpose of thy perfect will; through Jesus Christ our Lord.

*Prayer Book, 1928*

*Schools for the Deaf*

499 Almighty God, who, in the earthly life of Christ our Saviour, has revealed to us your boundless compassion; we pray that you will bless the work of the schools for your deaf children. Give love and patience to those who teach, courage and perseverance to those who learn; make your presence felt and known among them, and lead them in the gladness of fellowship with one another and with you; through Jesus Christ our Lord.

The Church of England Council for the Deaf (adapted)

*For Disarmament*

500

Lord, here is your cross,<br>
You must bear it alone.<br>
It is too hard for us,<br>
We need other defences.<br>
It is too simple,<br>
We must have our strategists.<br>
We know all the arguments,<br>
We have never heard yours.<br>
Lord, argue with us,<br>
Show us new ways,<br>
Get us out of the situation<br>
We landed ourselves in.<br>
For your world's sake.

A prayer spoken at the launching of the Polaris submarine on 25th February, 1967

*Government*

501 O Holy Spirit of God, guide, we pray thee, all those to whom thou hast committed the responsibility of government at this time.

Give them wisdom and understanding, discernment and self-control, that they may uphold what is right and perform what is just, so that in all things thy will may be done; through Jesus Christ our Lord.

Uppingham School

*Local Government*

502 Grant, O God, that Christian people may undertake the work of local government as a vocation and ministry; that they may bring to their work brains that think, and hearts that feel; that they may have ideals, imagination, wisdom and courage; that they may never be enslaved by routine and convention and popular opinion, but always be upheld by your free spirit, through the grace of our Lord Jesus Christ.

G. C. Binyon, *Prayers for the City of God*

*Great Men and Women*

503 God, whose almighty Spirit has guided men and women throughout history and everywhere in the world, send your call today to the great people of our time. Inspire them with wisdom, courage, and love of truth. Make their work effective for good in your world, so that your kingdom may advance and all men praise the name of the greatest of all, Jesus Our Lord.

A. G. Bullivant

504 O God, almighty Father, King of kings and Lord of all our rulers, grant that the hearts and minds of all who go out as leaders before us, the statesmen, the judges, the men of learning and the men of wealth, may be so filled with the love of thy laws and of that which is righteous and life-giving, that they may serve as a wholesome salt unto the earth, and be worthy stewards of thy good and perfect gifts, through Jesus Christ our Lord.

Order of the Knights of the Garter,
fourteenth century

*The Handicapped*

505 Our Lord showed a healing compassion towards those of his day who were mentally ill and handicapped in other ways. Let us

pray for those similarly afflicted today—for the mentally ill, for the blind, the deaf, and the maimed; especially for anyone known personally to us:

O God, the Father of all men, give to those we now remember great courage and persistence to overcome the difficulties that can be overcome; give them grace to accept the limits that cannot be crossed. And to all of *us* give something of the active love of Our Lord—shown in His kindness and readiness to help all who needed Him.

Rupert E. Davies, *Praying Together*

*Our Homes*

506 Keep watch over our homes, O God, and make them places of goodness, security and happiness. Protect with your loving care all who are dear to us, and draw them and us closer to you; through your son who lived in an earthly home, Jesus Christ, our Lord.

Marlborough College

507 Most merciful God, protect today (tonight) our homes, our parents, our brothers and sisters and all our friends from whom we are now parted. We remember especially any who are ill, any who are in anxiety, trouble or danger. Help them to find strength and comfort. Unite us with them again, and receive our thanks for the joy of their love towards us. Through Jesus Christ our Lord.

Brentwood School

508 O Jesus Christ, our Brother, our Lord: you lived in a home at Nazareth: you obeyed your parents, worked with your father, enjoyed the company of your friends and relations. Think of our homes now, and bless them for us. Strengthen the love that we have for one another; give all that we need for our welfare and happiness. In a word, Lord, make our homes like your home; for your name's sake.

C.R.C.

*Hospitals*

509 Almighty God, whose blessed Son Jesus Christ went about doing good, and healing all manner of sickness and all manner of

disease among the people: continue, we beseech thee, this his gracious work among us in the hospitals of our land. Cheer, heal and sanctify the sick; to doctors and nurses grant skill, sympathy and patience; and send down thy blessing on all who labour to prevent suffering, and to forward thy purposes of love; through Jesus Christ our Lord.

*Prayer Book, 1928* (adapted)

*Those who Mourn*

510 Almighty God, Father of all mercies and giver of all comfort; deal graciously, we pray thee, with those who mourn, that casting every care on thee, they may know the consolation of thy love; through Jesus Christ our Lord.

*Prayer Book, 1928*

511 O God, please be very close to all those who are mourning the loss of a loved one today. May you be their comfort and their strength; through Jesus Christ our Lord.

Beryl Bye, *Prayers at Breakfast*

512 We pray, all-loving Father, that you will comfort those who mourn. We pray especially for the parents, relations and friends of. . . . Soothe them in their distress. Give them courage to face the world and go on living. In due time, heal the wounds left by this death, and give us all faith to believe that in some way physical death is part of your divine purpose and leads to a more complete life. Through your son, who died but rose again from the dead, Jesus Christ our Lord.

Marlborough College

*The Nation*

513 Almighty God who has given us this good land for our heritage, we humbly beseech you to bless us with prosperous industry, peace and safety. Save us from violence and sedition, from lying cant and vicious party politics. Defend our liberties and free speaking: preserve our unity: endue with wisdom all those to whom is entrusted the authority of government. And grant that

there may be justice at home and obedience to your laws within the nation to your honour and glory, who livest and reignest God over all.

Epsom College

514 O eternal God, through whose mighty power our fathers won their liberties of old: grant that we and all the people of this land may have grace to maintain these liberties in righteousness and peace, through Jesus Christ our Lord.

*Book of Common Prayer*, U.S. Episcopal Church

*Those in Need, Distress and Suffering*

515 Almighty and everlasting God, the comfort of the sad, the strength of them that suffer; let the prayers of all who are in distress come unto thee; and unto every person that suffers grant mercy, grant relief, grant refreshment; through Jesus Christ our Lord.

*Book of Common Prayer* (adapted)

516 O God, the strength of the weak, the friend of sinners, and the comfort of the sorrowful: grant thy mighty protection to the tempted; reveal thy grace to the fallen; maintain the faith of those who are persecuted for righteousness' sake; and give the consolation of thy presence to those who are disappointed, embittered, lonely, or in despair; for thy mercies' sake.

W. E. Orchard, in *A Book of Prayers for Schools*

517 We bring before you, O Lord, the griefs and perils of peoples and nations; the necessities of the homeless; the helplessness of the aged and weak; the sighings of prisoners; the pains of the sick and injured; the sorrow of the bereaved. Comfort and relieve them, O merciful Father, according to their needs; for the sake of thy Son our Saviour Jesus Christ our Lord.

Attributed to St. Anselm, 1033–1109

518 We commend to thy fatherly goodness all those who are in any ways afflicted or distressed in mind, body or estate, that it may please thee to comfort and relieve them according to their

several necessities, giving them patience under their sufferings and a happy issue out of all their afflictions; and this we beg for Jesus Christ his sake.

*Book of Common Prayer*

*Old People*

519 Dear God, you made the whole of life to be lived and enjoyed, so please bless all old people. Give them all that they need for friendship, comfort and occupation. Above all give them zest for life and peace in their hearts; through Jesus Christ our Lord.

C.R.C.

*Peace of the World*

520 Almighty God, from whom all thoughts of truth and peace proceed; kindle, we pray thee, in the hearts of all men the true love of peace; and guide with thy pure and peaceable wisdom those who take counsel for the nations of the earth; that in tranquillity thy Kingdom may go forward, till the earth be filled with the knowledge of thy love: through Jesus Christ our Lord.

Bishop Francis Paget, 1851–1911

521 Let us all protect one the other.
Let us all enjoy together.
Let us act valiantly together.
May spiritual knowledge ever shine before us.
Let us never hate one another.
And let Peace and Peace and Peace reign everywhere.

*The Vedas*

522 O God, who by thy son Jesus Christ hast set up on earth a kingdom of holiness; make faith to prevail over fear, and righteousness over force, and truth over the lie, and love and concord over all things; through the same Jesus Christ our Lord.

*War Prayers, 1940* (adapted)

523 We beseech thee, O Lord our God, to set the peace of Heaven within the hearts of men, that it may bind the nations also in a covenant which cannot be broken; through Jesus Christ our Lord.

*Cambridge Bede Book, 1936*

*The Police*

524 God of all wisdom and truth, bless we pray, the police men and women of this country, and guide them in carrying out their duties. Guard them in danger, and relieve their hours of monotonous waiting and walking the beat. May we serve them as they serve us. Hasten the time, Lord, when crime, dishonesty and carelessness will be abolished, and men live together in peace, love and consideration for each other. May your Kingdom come, and your will be done on earth as it is in Heaven; through Jesus Christ our Lord.

A. G. Bullivant

*The Queen and Parliaments*

525 Almighty God, the fountain of all goodness, we humbly beseech thee to bless our Sovereign Lady, Queen Elizabeth, the Parliaments in all her Dominions, and all who are set in authority under her: that they may order all things in wisdom, righteousness and peace, to the honour of thy holy name, and the good of thy Church and people; through Jesus Christ our Lord.

*Prayer Book, 1928*

*The Queen and Royal Family*

526 Almighty God, the fountain of all goodness, we humbly beseech thee to bless our most gracious Sovereign Lady Queen Elizabeth, Elizabeth the Queen Mother, Philip Duke of Edinburgh, Charles Prince of Wales, and all the Royal Family. Endue them with thy Holy Spirit; enrich them with thy heavenly grace; prosper them with all happiness; and bring them to thine everlasting kingdom; through Jesus Christ our Lord.

*Book of Common Prayer*

### *Race and Colour*

527 Hear our prayer, O God, for all who suffer because of their race or their colour. Give them strength in their suffering, and save them from fear, hatred and bitterness. Strengthen all who work to break down barriers of colour and nationality; and help us to accept all men as our brothers; through Jesus Christ our Lord.

Marlborough College

### *Scientists*

528 Direct, O Lord, with thy own loving wisdom, all men of thought and science, that they may more and more unveil the wondrous things of thy law, and draw all men to adore thee with mind and heart and soul; through Jesus Christ our Lord.

*Cuddesdon Office Book* (adapted)

### *Those at Sea*

529 O God our father, we pray for all who are at sea. In storms, give them courage; protect them from disaster; and bring them safely home. In the name of your son who stilled the tempest, Jesus Christ our Lord.

Marlborough College

530 O eternal Lord God, who alone spreadest out the heavens, and rulest the raging of the sea: be pleased to receive into thy protection all those who go down to the sea in ships, and occupy their business in great waters. Preserve them both in body and soul; prosper their labours with good success; in all time of danger be their defence, and bring them to the haven where they would be; through Jesus Christ our Lord.

*Prayer Book, 1928*

### *Sick People*

531 Almighty Father, giver of life and health: look mercifully, we beseech thee, on the sick and suffering, especially those for whom our prayers are desired, that by thy blessing upon them and upon

those who minister to them, they may be restored, if it be thy gracious will, to health of body and mind; through Jesus Christ our Lord.

*Prayer Book, 1928* (adapted)

532 Let us think of those who are sick in body, in mind or in spirit. Let us pray for them, and for all who try to help them. May God, in his mercy, give health to those who are ill; may he give skill and strength to doctors, nurses and priests; and to all who suffer with the sick may he give courage, endurance, and the knowledge of his love, in the name of the compassionate and skilful healer, our Lord, Jesus Christ.

Marlborough College

*Those who have sinned against us or we against them*

533 We offer unto Thee our prayers and intercessions, for those especially who have in any matter hurt, grieved or found fault with us or who have done us any damage or displeasure.

For all those also whom, at any time, we have vexed, troubled, burdened, and scandalized, by words or deeds, knowingly or in ignorance: that Thou wouldst grant us all equally pardon for our sins, and for our offences against each other.

Take away from our hearts, O Lord, all suspiciousness, indignation, wrath and contention, and whatsoever may hurt charity, and lessen brotherly love. Have mercy, O Lord, have mercy on those that crave thy mercy, give grace unto them that stand in need thereof, and make us such that we may be worthy to enjoy Thy grace, and go forward to life eternal.

Thomas à Kempis, 1379–1471

*Universities, Colleges and Schools*

534 Almighty God, we beseech thee with thy gracious favor to behold our universities, colleges, and schools, that knowledge may be increased among us, and all good learning flourish and abound. Bless all who teach and all who learn; and grant that in humility of heart they may ever look unto thee, who art the fountain of all wisdom; through Jesus Christ our Lord.

*Book of Common Prayer*, U.S. Episcopal Church

*Workers by Night*

535 Loving Father, we pray for those who work by night, to guard and serve us while we are sleeping: the miners, industrial workers, lighthousemen, nurses, doctors, and all the others who cannot rest at night. Watch over them, we pray, and keep them safe from danger and loneliness, for the sake of our guardian and saviour, Jesus.

A. G. Bullivant

*The World*

536 O most holy Spirit of God, from whom flows the fulness of wisdom and life: come in power and glory upon your Church and into the hearts of men; to bring to the world a new birth of holiness, new understanding of truth, and new unity in love; in the name of Jesus Christ our Lord.

National Day of Prayer, 1941 (adapted)

## THE CHURCH

537 Eternal Father, who wouldst make the Church of thy dear Son a city great and fair, the joy of the whole earth: we beseech thee, by the sending of thy Holy Spirit, direct its counsels now in all manner of wisdom, love, and might: remove perplexity, establish concord, kindle flame, and gather a people single and strong of faith: to the praise of him who with thee and the same Spirit liveth and reigneth, one God, world without end.

Lambeth Conference, 1930

538 Keep, we beseech thee, O Lord, thy Church with thy perpetual mercy; and, because the frailty of man without thee cannot but fall, keep us ever by thy help from all things hurtful, and lead us to all things profitable to our salvation; through Jesus Christ our Lord.

*Book of Common Prayer*

539 O God, our Shepherd, give to the Church a new vision and a new wisdom and fresh understanding, the revival of her bright-

ness and the renewal of her unity; that the eternal message of thy Son, undefiled by the traditions of men, may be hailed as the good news of the new age; through him who maketh all things new, Jesus Christ our Lord.

Percy Dearmer, 1867–1936, *The Sanctuary*

540 O God, who hast built thy Church upon the apostles and prophets, Jesus Christ himself being the chief corner stone, we pray today for the young national churches of Africa and the East. Prosper those who are seeking to build them up, and grant that they may bring their full enrichment to the one temple of the living God, even the Church of our Lord Jesus Christ.

Church Missionary Society, *Cycle of Prayer*

### *Clergy and People*

541 Almighty and everlasting God, who alone workest great marvels: send down upon our Bishops and clergy and all congregations committed to their charge the healthful spirit of thy grace; and that they may truly please thee, pour upon them the continual dew of thy blessing. Grant this, O Lord, for the honour of our Advocate and Mediator, Jesus Christ.

*Book of Common Prayer*

### *A Parish*

542 Almighty and everlasting God, who dost govern all things in heaven and earth; mercifully hear the prayers of us thy servants, and grant all things that are needful for the spiritual welfare of this parish. Strengthen and confirm the faithful; visit and relieve the sick and afflicted; turn and soften the wicked; rouse the careless; recover the fallen; restore the penitent; tend the children; remove all hindrances to the advancement of thy truth; and bring all to be of one heart and mind, within the fold of thy holy Church, to the honour and glory of thy blessed Son, Jesus Christ our Lord.

*Cuddesdon Office Book*

*The Spread of the Gospel*

543 O God and Father of all, whom the whole heavens adore; let the whole earth also worship thee, all kingdoms obey thee, all tongues confess and bless thee, and the sons of men love thee and serve thee in peace; through Jesus Christ our Lord.

*Memorials*

544 O God of all the nations of the earth, remember the multitudes who, though created in thine image, have not known thee nor thy Son their Saviour, Jesus Christ; and grant that by the prayers and labours of thy Church they may be delivered from all superstition and unbelief and brought to worship thee in spirit and in truth; through Jesus Christ our Lord.

St. Francis Xavier, 1506–1552 (adapted)

545 O God, who hast made of one blood all nations of men to dwell on the face of the earth, and didst send thy blessed Son, Jesus Christ, to preach peace to them that are far off, and to them that are nigh; grant that all the peoples of the world may feel after thee and find thee; and hasten, O Lord, the fulfilment of thy promise to pour out thy Spirit upon all flesh; through Jesus Christ our Lord.

Bishop Cotton, 1813–1866

*The Unity of all Christian People*

546 We beseech thee, Almighty God, to grant to the whole Christian people, unity, peace, and true concord; through Jesus Christ our Lord.

S.P.G. (adapted)

547 We know, Lord Jesus, that on the night before your death you yourself prayed to the Father for the unity of your Church. If you look at us now you will find us broken from one another by ignorance, pride and prejudice, started by our forefathers, perpetuated by us today. Please help your people to make such progress in truth, holiness and love, that we may all come closer

to you and as a result be closer to one another; so that in the end your prayer may be fulfilled and we may all be one as you and the Father are one in the unity of the Holy Spirit, world without end.

C.R.C.

## THE SCHOOL AND ITS MEMBERS PAST AND PRESENT

### *The Governors*

548 O almighty God, bless with thy wisdom and thy love the governors of this school, and grant that they may direct all according to thy will, and use all the gifts of bounty bestowed on this school to thy honour and glory and the good of thy children; through Jesus Christ our Lord.

Godolphin School

### *Those Holding Office*

549 O heavenly Father, we pray for those appointed to hold office in this school. May thy Holy Spirit direct and control them at all times in the carrying out of their duties. Fill their hearts with loyalty, courage, and patience, so that in all things they may seek thy glory and the well-being of the school; through Jesus Christ our Lord.

Source unknown

### *A House*

550 Give your grace to the members of this House, Lord, to make us honest and fair in all our dealings with others. Make us helpful to the weak, gentle with our strength, humble about our abilities, and determined to overcome our faults. May we all, together with those in other Houses, seek first your Kingdom, and obey you, our Lord Jesus Christ.

A. G. Bullivant

551 O Lord, help us to make this House a Christian place where spiritual insight, mental effort and physical vigour are all united

in your service. Give us the will to be purposeful, whole-hearted and loyal, so that our brotherly care for one another, unstained by selfishness, may shine with the light of true Christian love, worthy of your son, our master, Jesus Christ.

Marlborough College

*Those Leaving*

552 Bless, O Lord, with the gift of thy Holy Spirit those who leave this school, that they may go forth from our midst with the fire of inspiration in their lives and thy love in their hearts, to do thee true and lively service; for thine is the kingdom, the power and the glory, for ever and ever.

*An Anthology of Prayers*

553 Lord of Life, we pray for those who are leaving this school today to take a job and earn their living in the world. Guard them from the strong temptations they will surely meet, and give them wisdom in dealing with their problems. Give them a place in your world, Lord, where their abilities will be used to best advantage to their fellow-men and to the building of your Kingdom on earth.

A. G. Bullivant

*Those Leaving or who have Left*

554 O God our keeper and helper, we humbly pray thee to watch over those who are going forth (or, have gone forth) from us to enter upon their several callings in this world. May thy fatherly care shield them, the love of thy dear Son preserve them from all evil, and the guidance of thy Holy Spirit keep them in the way that leadeth to eternal life, through Jesus Christ.

C. J. N. Child

*Mutual Responsibility*

555 O almighty God, who hast gathered us together as members of one body, grant that we may realize our responsibility to one

another; may truth, honour and kindness abound amongst us; may thy blessing rest upon our work, may thy name be honoured in our midst, and thy peace guard our hearts; through Jesus Christ our Lord.

*A Book of Prayers for Schools*

### *An Old Member of the School*

556 Almighty Spirit, God of eternal wisdom, we praise your name for the life and example (and death) of . . . We see your guiding hand in his/her . . . *now name applicable qualtities such as* 'fearless championship of your cause', 'enquiring and powerful mind', 'love of mankind', 'love of all creatures', 'willingness to die for your truth', *or other qualities as applicable* . . . and his/her devotion to you in all things. Grant to us a similar devotion, and make us citizens with him/her of the Kingdom of Jesus Christ our Lord.

A. G. Bullivant

### *Old Members of the School*

557 O Lord God, bless, we pray thee, all past members of this school wherever they may be. Keep them in health and safety. Help us to build faithfully on the best traditions we have inherited from them and to hand on to those who come after us customs of right conduct and fair thought. Through Jesus Christ our Lord.

Brentwood School

### *The School*

558 Almighty God, we pray thee to give thy blessing to this school and to its members gathered here before thee. Help us to create a noble fellowship, and to build up together an honourable tradition, which shall help all who come after us in this place. Through Jesus Christ our Lord.

Brentwood School

559 We thank you, Lord, for giving us our opportunities to learn.
We thank you for our minds, our teachers and our books.
We remember that millions of children in other countries,

and many in this country, would dearly love the chances which some of us take for granted, some of us waste and some of us reject.

Help us to value our opportunities here, and to use them better; to be modest when we succeed and determined when we fail.

Show us how to contribute our best qualities generously to the enrichment of this school and its highest traditions.

Bless this school, O Lord, and all who work in it.

We ask this in the name of Jesus Christ, your son.

Marlborough College

### *A Special School Effort*

560 Lord, we ask your blessing on the . . . (school play . . . collection for . . . etc. . . . etc. . . .) and on all such enterprises. May everything be well done, and done to your glory. Bind us together in a fellowship of service, and reward us according to the worthiness of our efforts.

A. G. Bullivant

# Litanies and Acts of Worship Requiring a Spoken Response

### *A Litany of Caring*

561 READER: Let us now, in a short litany, ask God to help us to care about other people. Each section will end with the words 'We could help them if we cared'. Then please say *Teach us, O God, to care.*

Break down, O God, the wall of selfishness that makes us blind and deaf to the need of other people. We could help them if we cared:

*Teach us, O God, to care.*

The unpopular boys/girls, whom we do not want to know because we are afraid of becoming unpopular ourselves. We could help them if we cared:

*Teach us, O God, to care.*

The dull, boring people, those who are not actively disliked but simply ignored, and therefore lonely. We could help them if we cared:

*Teach us, O God, to care.*

The cleaners, servants and tradespeople whom we don't bother to treat with much courtesy, but who may be hurt by our off-handedness. We could help them if we cared:

*Teach us, O God, to care.*

The old men and women, who long for somebody young to talk to, but whom we prefer not to bother about because they are tedious. We could help them if we cared:

*Teach us, O God, to care.*

All these, and many others, we have the power and opportunity to help, O God. Your son would have used our opportunities: teach us to use them willingly, in the name of Jesus Christ our Lord.

Marlborough College

*A Litany of Dedication*

562 READER: Each section of this litany ends with the petition 'Lord, hear our prayer'. Then please say *And let our cry come unto thee.*

O God grant that we may look for the good in other people, and not for the evil, that we may listen to the voice of conscience, and not try to silence it with dishonest excuses,

Lord, hear our prayer; *And let our cry come unto thee.*

That we may remember that other people are sensitive, and not cause them pain by our thoughtlessness,

Lord, hear our prayer; *And let our cry come unto thee.*

That we may use our opportunities to learn, and not waste them through idleness,

Lord, hear our prayer; *And let our cry come unto thee.*

That we may use the wonderful gift of speech, and not abuse it with vulgarity and scandal,

Lord, hear our prayer; *And let our cry come unto thee.*

That we may heed the advice of wise people, but resist everyone who tries to lead us into evil,

Lord, hear our prayer; *And let our cry come unto thee.*

That we may be thankful for the blessing of health, and sympathetic to those who are ill or weak,
Lord, hear our prayer; *And let our cry come unto thee.*

That we may open our eyes to Creation as revealed by scientists, and rightly use the work of technicians,
Lord, hear our prayer; *And let our cry come unto thee.*

That we may appreciate the work of artists, composers and writers, who can enrich and ennoble our lives,
Lord, hear our prayer; *And let our cry come unto thee.*

That we may try to understand the Christian religion, and not lazily accept or reject ideas that need hard thought,
Lord, hear our prayer; *And let our cry come unto thee.*

Finally, that we may be modest when we succeed and courageous when we fail,
Lord, hear our prayer; *And let our cry come unto thee.*

Marlborough College

*Evening Penitence: a Litany*

563 READER: After each group of three petitions, please say *Forgive us, O God.*

O God, our Father, we have come to you tonight to say that we are sorry for all the wrong things that we have done.

For the work that we did carelessly;
For the work that we have left half-finished;
For the work that we have not even begun:
*Forgive us, O God.*

For the people we have hurt;
For the people we have disappointed;
For the people we have failed when they needed us most:
*Forgive us, O God.*

For the friends to whom we have been disloyal;
For the loved ones to whom we have been untrue;
For the promises we have broken:
*Forgive us, O God.*

For the way in which we have disobeyed you;
For the way in which we have grieved you;
For our failure to love you as you have loved us:
*Forgive us, O God.*

*Epilogues and Prayers*

*A Litany of Forgiveness and Help*

164 READER: At the end of each section, after the words 'Through your mercy', please say *Save us, O Lord.*

O Lord, open our minds to see ourselves as you see us, or even as other people see us and we see other people; and from all unwillingness to know our faults,
Through your mercy, *Save us, O Lord.*

From weakness of purpose, from want of earnest care and interest; from indolence, indifference and from all spiritual deadness of heart,
Through your mercy, *Save us, O Lord.*

From weariness in continuing struggles; from despondency in failure and disappointment; from self-conceit; from delight in supposed superiority and from all bad manners,
Through your mercy, *Save us, O Lord.*

From impatience; from retorting with irritation and taunting with sarcasm; from quickness of temper in provoking or being provoked; from love of unkind gossip and from all idle words that may do harm,
Through your mercy, *Save us, O Lord.*

When we are tempted to leave duty for amusement, or to drift into extravagance, debt or dishonesty, and in times of frailty in our flesh,
Through your mercy, *Save us, O Lord.*

When we are perplexed about what is right and best to do, O Lord, direct us with wisdom to judge rightly; but in our mistakes and misunderstandings,
Through your mercy, *Save us, O Lord.*

Chiefly, O Lord, we pray you, give us knowledge of yourself to see you in all your works, always to feel your presence, to hear and know your call; and in all our shortcomings and difficulties may we have sure faith in you, through the grace of Jesus Christ our Lord.

Bishop George Ridding, 1824–1904 (adapted)

*An Act of Intercession*

565 READER: After the words 'Lord, in thy mercy', please say *Hear our prayer.*

Let us pray for the whole Church of God in Christ Jesus, and for all men according to their needs.
Almighty God, who hast promised to hear the prayers of those who ask in faith:

(Here the reader may pray for the Church throughout the world, and especially the diocese and its bishop; for any particular need of the Church; and a short period of silence may be kept.)

Lord, in thy mercy,
*Hear our prayer.*
Grant that we who confess thy name may be united in thy truth, live together in thy love, and show forth thy glory in the world.

(Here he may pray for the nations of the world, and especially for this kingdom and Elizabeth its Queen; for all men in their various callings; and again a short period of silence may be kept.)

Lord, in thy mercy,
*Hear our prayer.*
Direct this nation and all the nations in the ways of justice and of peace, that we may honour all men, and seek the common good.

(Here he may pray for the sick, the poor, and for those in trouble; for the needs of particular persons; and again a short period of silence may be kept.)

Lord, in thy mercy,
*Hear our prayer.*
Save and comfort those who suffer, that they may hold to thee through good and ill, and trust in thy unfailing love.

(If the dead are to be commemorated, he may, at his discretion, commend the dead by name; and again a short period of silence may be kept.)

Lord, in thy mercy,
*Hear our prayer.*
Remember those who have died in faith, and grant them a share in thy eternal kingdom.

(At the end of the prayers he shall say),
Grant these our prayers, O merciful Father, for the sake of thy Son, our Saviour Jesus Christ.

*Scottish Book of Common Prayer* (adapted)

### *A Litany to Jesus*

566 READER: Jesus said 'I came that they may have life and have it more abundantly.' In this litany after each group of three invocations, please say *Hallowed be thy name* (or, if preferred, *Give us your mercy*).

Jesus, born in poverty,
Jesus, born to bring peace among men,
Jesus, workman at Nazareth,
*Hallowed be thy name* (or, *Give us your mercy*).

Jesus, friend of the poor,
Jesus, feeder of the hungry,
Jesus, healer of the sick,
*Hallowed be thy name* (or, *Give us your mercy*).

Jesus, in whom all the nations of the earth are one,
Jesus, who breaks down the barriers of colour and class,
Jesus, brother of all,
*Hallowed be thy name* (or, *Give us your mercy*).

Jesus, tempted as we are,
Jesus, constant in prayer,
Jesus, who triumphed over evil,
*Hallowed be thy name* (or, *Give us your mercy*).

Jesus, who came not to be served but to serve,
Jesus, who showed man the full extent of God's love,
Jesus, crucified for us,
*Hallowed be thy name* (or, *Give us your mercy*).

Jesus, you are alive;
Jesus, you are amongst us now;
Jesus, you are in other people when we are good to them and when we are bad;

*Hallowed be thy name* (or, *Give us your mercy*).

Giggleswick School (adapted)

### *A Litany for People who Work*

567 READER: When I say 'Thy kingdom come', please answer *Thy will be done.*

O Lord Jesus Christ, almighty and all-loving, who worked at Nazareth as a carpenter, please guide, protect and inspire all who are working at this time.

Thy kingdom come: *Thy will be done.*

Particularly we bring to you men and women who face peril and suffer pain in their work.

Thy kingdom come: *Thy will be done.*

We bring to you also those who work on land or at sea;
in offices, mines or factories;
those who buy and sell and distribute goods.

Thy kingdom come: *Thy will be done.*

Those who invent and plan and organize;
those who govern, administer, keep peace and order;
all who bear great responsibility.

Thy kingdom come: *Thy will be done.*

Journalists, writers, actors and musicians;
sportsmen and all who entertain the public;
those who are responsible for the programmes on radio and television.

Thy kingdom come: *Thy will be done.*

Those who keep house and look after children;
scholars, professors, teachers, accountants; men of law;
clergy and doctors, nurses and social workers;
all who share your work of healing and guiding and serving other people.

Thy kingdom come: *Thy will be done.*

We pray also for all who hate their work;
those whose labour is without hope, without honour, without interest;
those who are unable to work and those who cannot find employment.

Thy kingdom come: *Thy will be done.*

Giggleswick School (adapted)

*A Litany for People who Suffer*

568 READER: When I say 'For thine is the kingdom', please answer *The power and the glory.* (or, if preferred, when I say 'Help them, Lord', please answer *Have mercy upon them.*)

O Lord Jesus Christ, who loved men with the love of God and said, 'Come unto me all that travail and are heavy laden, and I will refresh you', we bring to you all who are suffering and being hurt this day. Give them courage and strength and, where you wish it, healing and an end to their suffering;

For thine is the kingdom; *The power and the glory.*

Especially we bring to you the poor, the broken and the oppressed;
all prisoners and refugees;
and those who have no homes, no friends, no shelter, no place to spend the night;

For thine is the kingdom; *The power and the glory.*

We bring you all who are ill and physically afflicted;
the deaf, the dumb, the blind, and those who cannot use their limbs;
those who are undergoing operations or who are dangerously ill;

For thine is the kingdom; *The power and the glory.*

We bring for your blessing those who are being punished, the persecuted, the unpopular;
all who are handicapped or mentally ill or distressed by fear or worry or bereavement;

For thine is the kingdom; *The power and the glory.*

We pray too for those who are hurt by their own sin; those who are soured by jealousy, weakened by lust, hardened by arrogance and pride; the lazy, the idle, the feckless; those who have been made savage by hatred; those who are the prisoners of their own selfishness and greed; the guilty, the ashamed, those in despair; all who need reassurance, forgiveness, love;

For thine is the kingdom; *The power and the glory.*

Giggleswick School (adapted)

*A Litany for Ourselves*

569 READER: When I say 'For thine is the Kingdom', please answer *The power and the glory.*

Jesus, Master, you know us by name. We bring you ourselves, our souls and bodies, our strength, our weakness, the good deeds we have done, the sins we have committed;

For thine is the Kingdom; *The power and the glory.*

We bring you the things we love and the things we hate, our hopes and fears, ambitions and temptations;

For thine is the Kingdom; *The power and the glory.*

We bring you this day with its hope, its promise, its opportunities;

For thine is the Kingdom; *The power and the glory.*

Bless all the things we do, all the people we meet, our own selves, our homes and our school;

For thine is the Kingdom; *The power and the glory.*
for ever and ever; *Amen.*

The Lord be with you;
*And with thy spirit.*
Let us bless the Lord.
*Thanks be to God.*
The grace of our Lord Jesus Christ and the love of God and the fellowship of the Holy Spirit be with us all evermore.

C.R.C.

*A Litany of Reconciliation*

570 READER: After each object of forgiveness, please answer *Father, forgive.*

The hatred which divides nation from nation, race from race, class from class,

*Father, forgive.*

The covetous desires of men and nations to possess what is not their own,

*Father, forgive.*

The greed which exploits the labours of men, and lays waste the earth,

*Father, forgive.*

Our envy of the welfare and happiness of others,

*Father, forgive.*

Our indifference to the plight of the homeless and the refugee,

*Father, forgive.*

The lust which uses for ignoble ends the bodies of men and women,

*Father, forgive.*

The pride which leads us to trust in ourselves, and not in God,

*Father, forgive.*

International Students' Festival at
Coventry Cathedral, 15th February 1964

*A Litany of Remembrance*

571 During each silent pause let us remember before God those who have been mentioned. At the end of the litany, please join in the Lord's Prayer.

Now, O God, we want to forget ourselves and to remember others;
Those who are ill and in pain;
Those who are waiting for an operation;
Those who are waiting for a doctor's diagnosis and verdict and who fear the worst:

(silence)

Those who are nervous, worried, anxious, afraid of life;
Those who are on the verge of a nervous breakdown;
Those who feel that they cannot cope with life:

(silence)

Those who are hungry and cold;
Those who are refugees with no home;
Those who are unemployed;
Those who are persecuted and those who have lost their freedom:

(silence)

Out of your great riches supply the need of those distressed in body, mind or heart.
*Our Father . . .*

*Epilogues and Prayers* (adapted)

*A Litany for Right Values*

572 READER: After each section, please join me in saying *Good Lord, deliver us.*

Give us the grace, O Lord, to value money aright;
from love of it, waste of it, and abuse of it:
*Good Lord, deliver us.*

Give us the love, O Lord, to value people aright;
from neglect of them, contempt for them, and from treating them as things:
*Good Lord, deliver us.*

Give us the honesty, O Lord, to value ourselves aright;
from pride, vain-glory, and hypocrisy:
*Good Lord, deliver us.*

Give us the faith, O Lord, to value thee aright;
from taking first place, and from forgetting thee:
*Good Lord, deliver us.*

Give us the courage, O Lord, to love our neighbour as ourselves;
from a nicely calculating heart; from the covetousness that poses as fair dealing; from casting envious eyes at our fellows' wealth:
*Good Lord, deliver us.*

Give us the will, O Lord, to serve thee as we ought;
from having other gods before thee; from the worship of graven images on cheques, on notes, and on coins:
*Good Lord, deliver us.*

Laurence Ellis

*The Way of Christ: a Litany*

573 READER: After each sentence beginning 'Jesus said', please answer *O God, incline my heart to follow in this way.* At the end of the litany please join in the Lord's Prayer.

Jesus said, Lay not up for yourselves treasures upon earth, but lay up for yourselves treasures in heaven.

*O God, incline my heart to follow in this way.*

Jesus said, Seek ye first the kingdom of God and his righteousness.

*O God, incline my heart to follow in this way.*

Jesus said, Love your enemies.

*O God, incline my heart to follow in this way.*

Jesus said, Fear not, only believe.

*O God, incline my heart to follow in this way.*

Jesus said, Except ye turn again and become as little children, ye shall not enter into the kingdom of heaven.

*O God, incline my heart to follow in this way.*

Jesus said, Ask, and it shall be given you; seek, and ye shall find; knock, and it shall be opened unto you.

*O God, incline my heart to follow in this way.*

Jesus taught, In this way you are to pray, and so, Lord, we pray: '*Our Father . . .*'

John Baillie, *A Diary of Private Prayer* (adapted)

*A Litany for Wisdom*

574 READER: Each time I say 'Give us grace, O God', please answer *that we may profit by this Word.* At the end of the litany, please join in the Lord's Prayer.

A wise man wrote,
The world is too much with us; late and soon,
Getting and spending, we lay waste our powers.
Give us grace, O God: *that we may profit by this Word.*

A wise king said,
Nothing for me is too early or too late which is in due time for thee.
Give us grace, O God: *that we may profit by this Word.*

A wise man said,
Expect great things from God, attempt great things for God.
Give us grace, O God: *that we may profit by this Word.*

A wise woman said,
He asks too much to whom God is not sufficient.
Give us grace, O God: *that we may profit by this Word.*

A wise man said,
  In His will is our peace.
    Give us grace, O God: *that we may profit by this Word.*

A wise man prayed,
  Give what thou commandest, and command what thou wilt.
    Give us grace, O God: *that we may profit by this Word.*

*Our Father . . .*

John Baillie, *A Diary of Private Prayer* (adapted)

## Extended Prayers and Meditations

*Blacks and whites make me angry, Lord*

575 Why does it make any difference to some of us? For Christ's sake, why does it, Lord? Why do people get their backs up about this colour bit?

I got very mad at a white guy today, Lord, when he came out with the old clichés during a conversation we were having. He just sat there with a damned grin on his face and started telling the old lies about Negroes. He never raised his voice. He was always a gentleman, you know, very respectable and proper, while he crucified Negroes; I felt the nails driven into me, too. I wanted to slug him, Lord, and smash his mask. I wanted to find out what was really behind it.

I don't know what to do a times like that. I'm supposed to be patient and long suffering, but I become angry, Jesus, *angry*.

And the other day I got mad at a Negro. He was so ashamed of being a Negro that he stopped being human. When I reached out to him for a human response he just burrowed further inside his brown skin and wouldn't come out.

He smiled all the time, too, Jesus, like a smiling dead man, rotting behind this mask.

I know you've done a lot to wise us up, Lord, but please keep on trying. You've even given your own self to wise us up. But, Jesus, please don't give up on us.

Please get through to the smiling white man and the smiling Negro. And get through to me, please get through to me. Who is each of us really, Jesus? Are we black and white, or are we human? They say I'm white, and sometimes black, Lord, but what do *you* say about me, and about all of us?

Malcolm Boyd, *Are you running with me, Jesus?*

### *Conformity to the life of Jesus*

576 Jesus, you were born a child of Mary in Bethlehem. Keep our hearts clean like a child's; help us to respect all women; may we never do harm in body or soul to a child.

Jesus, you lived as a boy in the Holy House of Nazareth with Joseph and Mary. Bless our homes and all whom we love.

Jesus, you spent your youth as carpenter. Help us to do our work as you would have done it.

Jesus, your whole life was spent in doing good. Help us to do no harm to anyone, in body or soul, but to be of service to other people, including any whom we do not like, or who may dislike us.

Jesus, betrayed by one of your own Apostles, Judas, deserted by the rest, and publicly denied by St. Peter, help us never to do wrong for the sake of gain, or to be cowardly because we may be laughed at or ill treated; and if we sin against you and deny our Christian faith in act or word, help us quickly to repent as St. Peter did.

Jesus, you died the terrible death of the Cross for our sake. Make us ready to sacrifice ourselves for the sake of others.

Jesus, you rose triumphantly from the dead and ascended gloriously into heaven. Help us to rise above all temptation, and live for you, and advance each day in pleasing and serving you.

*Prayer Book for Catholic Seafarers,*
*Apostleship of the Sea* (adapted)

### *A Prayer of Discipleship*

577 'Send me.'

But where, Lord? To do what?

To bring pardon where there had been injury in a life I casually brush against at my daily work? (But I had thought of mediating a teenage gang war in Chicago!)

To help turn doubt into faith in a person with whom I live

intimately in my circle of family or friends? (But I had thought of helping a tired drunk on skid row!)

To bring joy into a life, consumed by sadness, which touches the hem of my life at a drinking fountain? (But I had thought only of a far-off mission land!)

'Send me.' Send me next door, into the next room, to speak somehow to a human heart beating alongside mine. Send me to bear a note of dignity into a sub-human, hopeless situation. Send me to show forth joy in a moment and a place where there is otherwise no joy but only the will to die.

Send me to reflect your light in the darkness of futility, mere existence, and the horror of casual human cruelty. But give me your light, too, Lord, in my own darkness and need.

Malcolm Boyd, *Are you running with me, Jesus?*

*Help in Life*

578 O God, we ask you to help us never to allow the great things of life to go wrong.

Help us never to allow
Caution to become cowardice,
or courage to become recklessness.
Carefulness to become meanness,
or spending to become squandering.
Honesty to become discourtesy,
or politeness to become evasion of the truth.
Liberty to become licence,
or pleasure to become sin.

Help us never selfishly to make use of our friends, never thoughtlessly to take our loved ones for granted, never to make your love an excuse for thinking that we can do what we like. Help us always to remember how we have been loved and to try to be more worthy of it: through the love of Jesus Christ our Lord.

*Epilogues and Prayers*

*An Extended Version of the Lord's Prayer*

579 We are allowed to call you Father, O heavenly Lord God, because of your goodness to us and because your Son, Jesus Christ, has made us his brothers in the family of your Church.

May your holy name be honoured everywhere; may we learn to love you more; may more and more people come to love you—everywhere throughout the world.

May we and all other people learn to know and to do what you wish us to do.

Do not let our sins spoil your good world; but let the power of your goodness and love put all things right till all men worship you as King and God.

All things are heavenly when you are close: be close and make them heavenly amongst us on earth.

Give us day by day all that we need for our bodily welfare; food, clothing, enough money.

Forgive us our sins. We promise to try to forgive those who have sinned against us.

Please do not test us more than we are able to bear: and when we are tempted, help us to overcome the temptation.

The power of evil in the world is very strong. Give us the strength to overcome it.

You are Almighty God: you have won the victory over evil on earth. Give us the benefits of this victory and help us in all things to praise you for ever and ever.

C. R. Campling,
*The Way, The Truth and The Life* (adapted)

## MEDITATIONS BY MICHEL QUOIST

### *All*

580 I heard a priest, one who lived the Gospel, preach the Gospel.
The humble, the poor, were carried away,
The prominent, the wealthy, were shocked.
And I thought that such preaching of the Gospel would soon frighten away many of those now filling the church, and attract those now shunning it.
It occurred to me that it is a bad sign for a follower of Christ to be well thought of by conventional 'Christians'.
Rather, it would be better if we were singled out as crazy or radical.
It would be better if they pursued us, signed petitions against us, tried to get rid of us.

This evening, Lord, I am afraid.
I am afraid, for your Gospel is terrible.
It is easy to hear it preached,
It is relatively easy not to be shocked by it,
But it is very difficult to live it.

I am afraid of deluding myself, Lord.
I am afraid of being satisfied with my decent little life,
I am afraid of my good habits, for I take them for virtues;
I am afraid of my little efforts, for I take them for progress;
I am afraid of my activities; they make me think I am giving myself.
I am afraid of my clever planning; I take it for success.

I am afraid of my influence, I imagine that it will transform lives;
I am afraid of what I give; it hides what I withhold;
I am afraid, Lord; there are people who are poorer than I;
Not so well-educated,
housed,
heated,
fed,
cared for,
loved.
I am afraid, Lord, for I do not do enough for them,
I do not do everything for them.

I should give everything,
I should give everything till there is not a single pain, a single misery, a single sin in the world.
I should then give all, Lord, all the time.
I should give my life.

Lord, it is not true, is it?
It is not true for everyone,
I am exaggerating, I must be sensible!

Son, there is only *one* commandment,
For *everyone*:

You shall love with *all* your heart,
with *all* your soul,
with *all* your strength.

Michel Quoist, *Prayers of Life*

## *Lord, I Have Time*

581 All men complain that they haven't enough time. It's because they look at their lives from too human a point of view. There's always time to do what God wants us to do, but we must put ourselves completely into each moment that he offers us.

> Be most careful then how you conduct yourselves: like sensible men, not like simpletons. Use the present opportunity to the full, for these are evil days. So do not be fools, but try to understand what the will of the Lord is. (Ephesians 5.15–17)

I went out, Lord.
Men were coming out.
They were coming and going,
Walking and running.
Everything was rushing, cars, lorries, the street, the whole town.
Men were rushing not to waste time.
They were rushing after time,
To catch up with time,
To gain time.

Goodbye, sir, excuse me, I haven't time.
I'll come back, I can't wait, I haven't time.
I must end this letter—I haven't time.
I'd love to help you, but I haven't time.
I can't think, I can't read, I'm swamped, I haven't time.
I'd like to pray, but I haven't time.

You understand, Lord, they simply haven't the time.

The child is playing, he hasn't time right now on . . . Later on . . .
The schoolboy has his homework to do, he hasn't time . . . Later on . . .
The student has his courses, and so much work, he hasn't time . . . Later on . . .
The young man is at his sports, he hasn't time . . . Later on . . .
The young married man has his new house, he has to fix it up, he hasn't time . . . Later on . . .
The grandparents have their grandchildren, they haven't time . . . Later on . . .
They are ill, they have their treatments, they haven't time . . . Later on . . .

They are dying, they have no . . .
Too late! . . . They have no more time!

And so all men run after time, Lord.

You who are beyond time, Lord, you know what you are doing.
You make no mistakes in your distribution of time to men.
You give each one time to do what you want him to do.

But we must not lose time,
waste time,
kill time,
For time is a gift that you give us,
But a perishable gift,
A gift that does not keep.

Lord, I have time,
I have plenty of time,
All the time that you give me,
The years of my life,
The days of my years,
The hours of my days,
They are all mine.
Mine to fill, quietly, calmly,
But to fill completely, up to the brim,
To offer them to you, that of their insipid water
You may make a rich wine such as you made once in Cana of Galilee.

I am not asking you tonight, Lord, for time to do this and then that,
But your grace to do conscientiously, in the time that you give me, what you want me to do.

Michel Quoist, *Prayers of Life* (adapted)

*Solitude*

582 I am thinking tonight, Lord, of all the isolated ones:
Of all those who are alone, utterly alone,
Because they have never let go and been carried by anyone,
Because they have never given themselves to you, Lord;
Those who know something that others will never know;
Those who suffer from a sore that no one can ever tend;

Those who bleed from a wound that no one will ever heal;
Those who are scarred by a vicious blow that no one will ever suspect;
Those who have, locked in the terrifying silence of their hearts, a harvest of humiliations, despairs, hatreds;
Those who have hidden a mortal sin—cold sepulchres behind cheerful fronts.

The solitude of man frightens me, Lord;
Every man is alone, since he is unique;
And that solitude is sacred; he alone can break through it, confide and share confidences.
He alone can pass from solitude to communion.
And you want this communion, Lord, you want us to be united with one another,
In spite of the deep gulf that we have dug between us by sin you want us to be united as your Father and you are united.

Lord, that boy hurts me, as do all isolated ones.
Grant that I may love them enough to break through their isolation.
Grant that I may pass through the world with all doors open,
My house entirely empty, available, welcoming.

Help me to withdraw so as to embarrass no one,
That others may come in without asking,
That they may deposit their burdens without being seen.
And I'll come, silently, to get them by night,
And you, Lord, will help me to bear them.

Michel Quoist, *Prayers of Life*

*Speech*

583 Speech, Lord, is a gift, and I have no right to be quiet through pride, cowardice, negligence or apathy.
Others have a right to my words, to my soul,
For I have a message to give them from you,
And none other than I, Lord, can give it to them.
I have something to say, short perhaps, but welling up from my life, from which I cannot turn.
But my words must be true words. . . .
Forgive me, Lord, for having spoken so badly,

Forgive me for having spoken often to no purpose;
Forgive me for the days when I tarnished my lips with hollow words,
false words,
cowardly words,
words through which you could not pass.
Uphold me when I must speak in a meeting, intervene in a discussion, talk with a brother.
Grant above all, Lord, that my words may be like the sowing of seeds,
And that those who hear them may look to a fine harvest.

Michel Quoist, *Prayers of Life*

*There Are Two Loves Only*

584 There are two loves only, Lord,
Love of myself, and love of you and of others,
And each time that I love myself, it's a little less love for you and for others,
It's a loss of love,
For love is made to leave self and fly towards others,
Each time it's diverted to myself, it withers, rots and dies.
Love of self, Lord, is a poison that I absorb each day;
Love of self chooses the best part and keeps the best place;
Love of self speaks about myself and makes me deaf to the words of others;
Love of self chooses, and forces that choice on a friend;
Love of self puts on a false front, it wants me to shine, overshadowing others;
Love of self is self-pitying and overlooks the suffering of others;
Love of self advertises my ideas and despises those of others;
Love of self thinks me virtuous, it calls me a good man;
Love of self is satisfied with myself, it gently rocks me to sleep.

What is more serious, Lord, is that love of self is a stolen love.
It was destined for others, they needed it to live, to thrive, and I have diverted it.
So the love of self creates human suffering,
So the love of men for themselves creates human misery,
All the miseries of men,
All the sufferings of men:

The suffering of the boy whose mother has slapped him without cause, and that of the man whose boss has reprimanded him in front of the other workers;
The suffering of the ugly girl neglected at a dance, and that of the woman whose husband doesn't kiss her any more;
The suffering of the child left at home because he's a nuisance, and that of the grandfather made fun of because he's too old;
The suffering of the worried man who hasn't been able to confide in anyone, and that of the troubled adolescent whose worries have been ridiculed;
The suffering of the desperate man who jumps into the canal, and that of the criminal who is going to be executed;
The suffering of the unemployed man who wants to work, and that of the worker who ruins his health for a ridiculous wage;
The suffering of the father who has to pile his family into a single room next to an empty house, and that of the mother whose children are hungry while the remains of someone's party are thrown into the dustbin;
All injustices, bitternesses, humiliations, griefs, hates, despairs,
All sufferings are an unappeased hunger,
A hunger for love.
So men have built, slowly, selfishness by selfishness, a disfigured world that crushes them,
So men on earth spend their time feeding their self-love,
While around them others with outstretched arms die of hunger.
They have squandered love.
I have squandered your love, Lord.

Help me to love, Lord,
not to waste my powers of love,
to love myself less and less in order to love others more and more,
That around me, no one should suffer or die because I have stolen the love they needed to live.

Michel Quoist, *Prayers of Life* (adapted)

*The Hospital*

585 This afternoon I went to see a patient at the hospital.
From ward to ward I walked, through that city of suffering, sensing the tragedies hardly concealed by the brightly painted walls and the flower-bordered lawns.

I had to go through a ward; I walked on tiptoe, hunting for my patient.
My eyes passed quickly and discreetly over the sick, as one touches a wound delicately to avoid hurting.
I felt uncomfortable,
Like the uninitiated traveller lost in a mysterious temple,
Like a pagan in the nave of a church.
At the very end of the second ward I found my patient,
And once there, I could only stammer. I had nothing to say.

Lord, suffering disturbs me, oppresses me.
I don't understand why you allow it.
Why, Lord?
Why this innocent child who has been moaning for a week, horribly burned?
This man who has been dying for three days and three nights, calling for his mother?
This woman with cancer who in one month seems ten years older?
This worker fallen from his scaffolding, a broken puppet less than twenty years old?
This stranger, poor isolated wreck, who is one great open sore?
This woman in a cast, lying on a board for more than thirty years?
Why, Lord?
I don't understand.
Why this suffering in the World
that shocks,
isolates,
revolts,
shatters?
Why this hideous suffering that strikes blindly without seeming cause,
Falling unjustly on the good, and sparing the evil,
Which seems to withdraw, conquered by science, but comes back in another form, more powerful and more subtle?
I don't understand.
Suffering is odious and frightens me.
Why these people, Lord, and not others?
Why these, and not me?

Son, it is not I, your God, who has willed suffering, it is men.

They have brought it into the world in bringing sin,
Because sin is disorder, and disorder hurts.
There is for every sin, somewhere in the world and in time, a corresponding suffering.
And the more sins there are, the more suffering.

But I came, and I took all your sufferings upon me, as I took all your sins,
I took them and suffered them before you.
I transformed them, I made of them a treasure.
They are still an evil, but an evil with a purpose,
For through your sufferings, I accomplish redemption.

Michel Quoist, *Prayers of Life*

*The Pornographic Magazine*

586 Lord, I am ashamed of this magazine.
You must be profoundly hurt in your infinite purity.

The office workers all contributed to buy it.
The boy ran to fetch it.
And pored over it on the way back.
Here it is.
On its shining pages, naked bodies are exposed,
Going from office to office, from hand to hand;
Such foolish giggles, such lustful glances . . .
Empty bodies, soulless bodies,
Adult toys for the hardened and the soiled.

And yet, Lord, man's body *is* beautiful.
From the beginning you, the supreme Artist, held the model before you, knowing that one day you would dwell in a human body when taking on the nature of man.
Slowly you shaped it with your powerful hands; and into its inert matter you breathed a living soul.
From then on, Lord, you asked us to respect the body, for the whole body is a conveyor of the spirit,
And we need this sensitive instrument that our spirits may commune with those of our brothers.

Words, in long processions, lead us toward other souls.
A smile on our lips, the expression in our eyes, reveal the soul.

The clasp of a hand carries it to a friend,
A kiss yields it to the loved one,
The embrace of the couple unites two souls in quest of a new child of God.

But it was not enough for you, Lord, to make of our flesh the visible sign of the spirit.
Through your grace the Christian's body became sacred, and the temple of the Trinity.
A member of the Lord, and a bearer of his God,
Supreme dignity of this splendid body!

Here, Lord, before you, tonight, are the bodies of sleeping men:

The pure body of the tiny child,
The soiled body of the prostitute,
The vigorous body of the athlete,
The exhausted body of the factory worker,
The soft body of the playboy,
The surfeited body of the rich man,
The starved body of the poor man,
The neglected body of the slum child,
The feverish body of the sick man,
The painful body of the injured man,
The paralysed body of the cripple,
All bodies, Lord, of all ages.

I offer them all to you, Lord, and I ask you to bless them, while they lie in silence, wrapped in your night.
Left by their sleeping souls, they are there before your eyes, your own.
Tomorrow, shaken from their sleep, they will have to resume work.
May they be servants and not masters,
Welcoming homes and not prisons:
Not tombs, but temples of the living God.

Michel Quoist, *Prayers of Life* (adapted)

### *The Sins of Society*

587 He was in the middle of the street,
Staggering, and singing at the top of his lungs in the husky voice of a drunk.

People turned round and stopped, amused.
A policeman came silently from behind,
Grabbed him brutally by the shoulder, and took him to the police station.
He was still singing,
And people laughing.

I did not laugh, Lord.
I thought of his wife who would wait in vain for him that night.
I thought of all the other drunks of the town,
those of the pubs and the bars,
those of living-rooms and cocktail parties.
I thought of their home-coming, at night;
of the frightened youngsters,
the empty wallets,
the blows,
the cries,
the tears,
I thought of the children who would be born of drunken embraces.

Now you have spread your night over the city, Lord,
And while tragedies unfold,
The men who have

justified alcohol,
produced alcohol,
sold alcohol,

That same night sleep in peace.
I think of all those men, and I pity them;
they have produced and sold misery,
they have produced and sold sin.
I think of all the others, the crowd of others who work
to destroy and not to build,
to stupefy and not to uplift,
to debase and not to ennoble.
I think especially, Lord, of the many men who work for war,
who, to feed a family, have to work to destroy others,
who, to live, must manufacture death.
I don't ask you to keep them all from their work—that is not possible,

But, Lord,
may they question it,
may their sleep be uneasy,
may they fight in this world of disorder,
may they act as leaven,
may they be redeemers.
By all the wounded in soul and body, victims of the work of their brothers,
By all the dead for whom thousands of men have conscientiously manufactured death,
By that drunk, grotesque clown in the middle of the street,
By the humiliation and tears of his wife,
By the fear and cries of his children,
Lord, have pity on me, too often slumbering.
Lord, have pity also on the miserable men who are completely asleep and collaborate in a world where brothers kill each other to earn their bread.

Michel Quoist, *Prayers of Life*

*To Love—The Prayer of the Adolescent*

588

I want to love, Lord,
I need to love.
All my being is desire;
My heart,
My body,
yearn in the night towards an unknown one to love.
My arms thrash about and I can seize on no object for my love.
I am alone and want to be two.
I speak, and no one is there to listen.
I live, and no one is there to share my life.
Why be so rich and have no one to enrich?
Where does this love come from?
Where is it going?
I want to love, Lord,
I need to love,
Here this evening, Lord, is all my love, unused.

Listen, son,
Stop,
and silently make a long pilgrimage to the bottom of your heart.

Walk by the side of your love so new, as one follows a brook to find its source,
And at the very end, deep within you, in the infinite mystery of your troubled soul, it is I whom you will meet,
For I call myself Love, son,
And from the beginning I have been nothing but love,
And love is in you.
It is I who made you to love,
To love eternally;
And your love will pass through another self of yours,
It is she that you seek;
Set your mind at rest, she is on your way,
on the way since the beginning,
the way of my love.
You must wait for her coming,
She is approaching,
You are approaching,
You will recognize each other,
For I've made her body for you, I've made yours for her.
I've made your heart for her, I've made hers for you,
And you seek each other, in the night,
In 'my night', which will become Light, if you trust me.

Keep yourself for her, son,
As she is keeping herself for you.
I shall keep you for one another.
And, since you hunger for love, I've put on your way all your brothers to love.
Believe me, it's a long apprenticeship, learning to love,
And there are not several kinds of love:
Loving is always leaving oneself to go towards others . . .

Lord, help me to forget myself for others, my brothers,
That in giving myself I may teach myself to love.

Michel Quoist, *Prayers of Life* (adapted)

# Closing Prayers

## AFTER OTHER PRAYERS

589 Almighty God, who hast given us grace at this time with one accord to make our common supplications unto thee; and dost

promise, that when two or three are gathered together in thy name thou wilt grant their requests: fulfil now, O Lord, the desires and petitions of thy servants, as may be most expedient for them; granting us in this world knowledge of thy truth, and in the world to come life everlasting.

*Book of Common Prayer*

590 O Lord, we beseech thee mercifully to receive the prayers of thy people which call upon thee; and grant that they may both perceive and know what things they ought to do, and also may have grace and power faithfully to fulfil the same; through Jesus Christ our Lord.

*Book of Common Prayer*

591 These things, good Lord, that we pray for, give us thy grace to labour for.

Sir Thomas More, 1478–1535

## AFTER WORSHIP

592 Blessing and honour and thanksgiving and praise more than we can utter, more than we can conceive, be unto thee, O holy and glorious Trinity, Father, Son, and Holy Ghost, by all angels, all men, all creatures, for ever and ever.

Bishop Ken, 1637–1711

593 Grant, O God, that these few minutes with you may send us out again
More kind to others;
More honest with ourselves;
More loyal to you:
through Jesus Christ our Lord.

*Epilogues and Prayers*

594 Grant, O God, that what we have said and sung with our lips we may believe in our hearts; and what we believe in our hearts we may show forth in our lives; through Jesus Christ our Lord.

Source unknown

595 May God the Father bless us; may Christ take care of us; the Holy Spirit enlighten us all the days of our life.

The Lord be our Defender and Keeper of body and soul, both now and for ever to the ages of ages.

Aedelwald, a Saxon Bishop, ninth century

596 May the Lord bless you and protect you.
May the Lord smile on you and show you his favour.
May the Lord befriend you and prosper you;
now and evermore.

*Contemporary Prayers for Public Worship* (adapted)

597 Now unto the king eternal, immortal, invisible, the only wise God, be honour and glory for ever and ever.

St. Paul (1 Timothy 1.17)

598 The grace of our Lord Jesus Christ, and the love of God, and the fellowship of the Holy Spirit be with us all evermore.

St. Paul (2 Corinthians 13.14)

599 The Lord bless us and keep us, the Lord make his face to shine upon us, and be gracious unto us, the Lord lift up the light of his countenance upon us and give us peace, now and evermore.

The Jewish Blessing, *c.* seventh century B.C.

600 The Lord preserve our going out and our coming in from this time forth for ever more.

Psalm 121, verse 8

601 The peace of God, which passeth all understanding, keep our hearts and minds in the knowledge and love of God, and of his Son Jesus Christ our Lord; and the blessing of God Almighty, the Father, the Son, and the Holy Ghost, be amongst us and remain with us always.

*Book of Common Prayer* (adapted)

602 We commend ourselves unto him that is able to keep us from falling and to present us faultless before the presence of his glory with exceeding joy;

To the only wise God our Saviour, be glory and majesty, dominion and power, both now and ever.

Jude 5.25

603 READER: The Lord be with you:
RESPONSE: *And with thy spirit.*
READER: Let us bless the Lord:
RESPONSE: *Thanks be to God.*
READER: (May the souls of the faithful departed through the mercy of God rest in peace:) and may the divine assistance remain with us always.
RESPONSE: *Amen.*

604 READER: Let us depart in peace.
RESPONSE: *In the name of the Lord, Amen.*

# The Life, Death and Resurrection of Jesus Christ

605

## JESUS AND HIS MOTHER

My only son, more God's than mine,
Stay in this garden ripe with pears.
The yielding of their substance wears
A modest and contented shine:
And when they weep with age, not brine
But lazy syrup are their tears.
'I am my own and not my own.'

He seemed much like another man,
That silent foreigner who trod
Outside my door with lily rod:
How could I know what I began
Meeting the eyes more furious than
The eyes of Joseph, those of God?
I was my own and not my own.

And who are these twelve labouring men?
I do not understand your words:
I taught you speech, we named the birds,
You marked their big migrations then
Like any child. So turn again
To silence from the place of crowds.
'I am my own and not my own.'

Why are you sullen when I speak?
Here are your tools, the saw and knife
And hammer on your bench. Your life
Is measured here in week and week
Planed as the furniture you make,
And I will teach you like a wife
To be my own and all my own.

Who like an arrogant wind blown
Where he may please, needs no content?
Yet I remember how you went
To speak with scholars in furred gown.
I hear an outcry in the town;
Who carries that dark instrument?
'One all his own and not his own.'

Treading the green and nimble sward
I stare at a strange shadow thrown.
Are you the boy I bore alone
No doctor near to cut the cord?
I cannot reach to call you Lord,
Answer me as my only son.
'I am my own and not my own.'

Thom Gunn, *The Sense of Movement*

606

## THE OXEN

Christmas Eve, and twelve of the clock.
'Now they are all on their knees,'
An elder said as we sat in a flock
By the embers in hearthside ease.

We pictured the meek mild creatures where
They dwelt in their strawy pen,
Nor did it occur to one of us there
To doubt they were kneeling then.

So fair a fancy few would weave
In these years! Yet, I feel,
If someone said on Christmas Eve,
'Come; see the oxen kneel

'In the lonely barton by yonder coomb
Our childhood used to know,'
I should go with him in the gloom,
Hoping it might be so.

Thomas Hardy

## 607 HERE IS A MAN

Here is a man who was born in an obscure village, the child of a peasant woman. He worked in a carpenter's shop until he was thirty, and then for three years he was an itinerant preacher. He had no credentials but himself. While still a young man, the tide of popular opinion turned against him. His friends—the twelve men who had learned so much from him, and had promised him their enduring loyalty—ran away, and left him. He went through a mockery of a trial; he was nailed upon a cross between two thieves; when he was dead, he was taken down and laid in a borrowed grave through the pity of a friend.

Yet I am well within the mark when I say that all the armies that ever marched, and all the parliaments that ever sat, and all the kings that ever reigned, put together, have not affected the life of man upon this earth as has this one solitary life.

Anon.

## 608 THE TONGUE OF THE DUMB

TWO READINGS

*I*

You are not here, Jesus of Nazareth. So I shall just have to pretend you are.

Now I want to talk to you about my father, because the villagers say you will be passing along this road today, and they are going to bring my father to you.

There are hundreds of people here already, sitting about in groups and watching the road. All we have seen so far are three Roman soldiers and a couple of mangy camels. They have not come with father yet. He will hate all these crowds.

You see, Jesus, he is not like other men. He is big and strong and good, but he is different from all the others. He has never heard my voice. They say he has not heard his own voice since the day it was high-pitched like mother's. I suppose that is why he gets nowhere when he tries to talk. What comes out is just a sort of mumbling. I think I know what he says better than sister or mother or anyone. But it is not the words that tell me. They get lost in a babble like a foreign language.

My poor father. They push him around so when he wants to be quiet. Only my mother and I understand him. You would understand him, Jesus. He loves the Lord God, and he is clever with his hands. But he cannot join in the gossiping and grumbling of the others. He stands apart, and they despise him. Can you understand that?

This morning they wrote on a writing tablet: 'We are taking you to see the prophet.' I think he knew something of what they meant, but he looked alarmed. He cannot bear to meet strangers. You are a stranger to him, Jesus. You are a stranger to me, too, but it is good to pretend we are friends.

There is father now, surrounded by the village men. There is no place for me there. He will not see me with this crowd between us. He looks lost and sad. The crowd is thickening.

What are you going to do, Jesus of Nazareth, when you come this way? I can never be your follower again if you will not help us. I can never speak to you again.

Now the crowd in the distance is stirring. Are you really coming? Is that you with your older followers? The people are jostling and shoving, but they are making way. Our villagers are hurrying towards you, father in the middle of them. What will you do?

*2*

608 You have greeted them courteously. You seem to have told them to wait, for you are bringing father away with you, away from the crowds he hates. You are leaving the crowd and coming in this direction. How glad I am to be here. Father is too busy looking at you to notice me.

I can see everything you do. You say nothing. What use would that be? Father has been in the quiet of the grave for longer than my life.

You sigh, and look upward to heaven. Father is watching you.

You are putting your fingers into his useless ears. Father is feeling you. You are spitting on your finger, and touching his tongue. Father is tasting you.

*Be opened.* Your voice is like a trumpet sound, rousing the dead.

What has happened? Does father hear you? He stands with the strangest look on his face I have ever seen. Jesus, Jesus, can he hear you speak to him? His lips are moving. Is it the old mumbling, or does he speak to you plainly? Can he hear himself speak? Will he be able to speak to me?

The crowds are running and shouting, and here am I running faster and shouting louder than any of them. Father, my father, can you really hear me? Did you speak my name?

Father, hold me, hold me tight. I did not mean to cry.

Jesus, Master, I am your disciple. You did it. You have done all things well. You even make the deaf hear, and the dumb speak. Father and I thank you.

*Mark 7.31–37*
David Head, *Stammerer's Tongue*

609

## WHAT JESUS CONCEALED

Joy, which was the small publicity of the pagan, is the gigantic secret of the Christian. The tremendous figure which fills the Gospels towers in this respect, as in every other, above all the thinkers who ever thought themselves tall. His pathos was natural, almost casual. The Stoics, ancient and modern, were proud of concealing their tears. He never concealed His tears; He showed them plainly on His open face at any daily sight, such as the far sight of His native city. Yet He concealed something. Solemn supermen and imperial diplomatists are proud of restraining their anger. He never restrained His anger. He flung furniture down the front steps of the Temple, and asked men how they expected to escape the damnation of Hell. Yet He restrained something. I say it with reverence; there was in that shattering personality a thread that must be called shyness. There was something that He hid from all men when He went up a mountain to pray. There was something that He covered constantly by abrupt silence or impetuous isolation. There was some one thing that was too great for God to show us when He walked upon our earth; and I have sometimes fancied that it was His mirth.

G. K. Chesterton, *Orthodoxy*

610

## I AM THE MAN

1 I am the man that God has called
I am his Son and born to die

(610)

I want to live in peace for ever
Dear God, why won't you hear my cry

2 I've done your will in all you wished for
And I've been true to what you said
And now I want to be delivered
From the pain that lies ahead

3 My friends are sleeping here beside me
They don't know what lies ahead
And one has gone and sold his brother
He'll kiss and wish that he were dead

4 And then the rest will run and leave me
All alone to see it through
I only pray that you will help me
To stay and face what I must do

5 And in that hope and trust I leave it
In your hands for you are near
I know that strength and power are given
Now I know, I have no fear

Peter Allen

## 611 THE DEATH OF JESUS CHRIST

Procula. Centurion, were you at the killing of that teacher today?

Longinus. Yes, lady.

Procula. Tell me about his death.

Longinus. It is hardly fit hearing for you, my lady. . . .

Procula. Do not tell it all, then, but tell me what he said.

Longinus. The people were mocking him at first, and he prayed God to forgive them. He said: 'Father, forgive them, for they know not what they do. . . .'

Procula. Was he suffering much?

Longinus. No, lady. He wasn't a strong man. The scourging must have nearly killed him. I thought he was dead by noon, and then suddenly he began to sing in a loud voice that he was giving back his spirit to God. I looked to see God come to take him. He died singing. Truly, lady, that man was the Son of God, if one may say that. . . .

Procula. What do you think the man believed, centurion?

Longinus. He believed he was God, they say.

Procula. What do you think of that claim?

Longinus. If a man believes anything up to the point of dying on the cross for it, he will find others to believe it.

Procula. Do you believe it?

Longinus. He saw a fine young fellow, my lady; not past middle age. And he was all alone and defied all the Jews and all the Romans, and, when we had done with him, he was a poor broken-down thing, dead on the cross.

Procula. Do you think he is dead?

Longinus. No, lady, I don't.

Procula. Then where is he?

Longinus. Let loose in the world, lady, where neither Roman nor Jew can stop his truth.

John Masefield, *The Trial of Jesus*

## 612 THE KILLING

That was the day they killed the Son of God
On a squat hill-top by Jerusalem.

(612) Zion was bare, her children from their maze
Sucked by the demon curiosity
Clean through the gates. The very halt and blind
Had somehow got themselves up to the hill.

After the ceremonial preparation,
The scourging, nailing, nailing against the wood,
Erection of the main-trees with their burden,
While from the hill rose an orchestral wailing,
They were there at last, high up in the soft spring day.
We watched the writhings, heard the moanings, saw
The three heads turning on their separate axles
Like broken wheels left spinning. Round *his* head
Was loosely bound a crown of plaited thorn
That hurt at random, stinging temple and brow
As the pain swung into its envious circle.
In front the wreath was gathered in a knot
That as he gazed looked like the last stump left
Of a death-wounded deer's great antlers. Some
Who came to stare grew silent as they looked,
Indignant or sorry. But the hardened old
And the hard-hearted young, although at odds
From the first morning, cursed him with one curse,
Having prayed for a Rabbi or an armed Messiah
And found the Son of God. What use to them
Was a God or a Son of God? Of what avail
For purposes such as theirs? Beside the cross-foot,
Alone, four women stood and did not move
All day. The sun revolved, the shadow wheeled,
The evening fell. His head lay on his breast,
But in his breast they watched his heart move on
By itself alone, accomplishing its journey.
Their taunts grew louder, sharpened by the knowledge
That he was walking in the park of death,
Far from their rage. Yet all grew stale at last,
Spite, curiosity, envy, hate itself.
They waited only for death and death was slow
And came so quietly they scarce could mark it.
They were angry then with death and death's deceit.

I was a stranger, could not read these people

Or this outlandish deity. Did a God
Indeed in dying cross my life that day
By chance, he on his road and I on mine?

Edwin Muir, *Selected Poems*

613

## PIETA

Always the same hills
Crowd the horizon,
Remote witnesses
Of the still scene.

And in the foreground
The tall Cross,
Sombre, untenanted,
Aches for the Body
That is back in the cradle
Of a maid's arms.

R. S. Thomas, *Pieta*

614

## GENTLE CHRIST

1 Gentle Christ, wise and good,
We nailed him to a cross of wood,
The Son of God, he lived to save,
In borrowed stable and borrowed grave.

2 Soldiers came at Pilate's call,
Led him up into the common hall,
Took sharp thorns and made a crown.
Dressed him in a scarlet gown.

3 They spat at him and mocked him then,
Lashed his back again and again,
Laid the cross upon that back,
Forced him up the narrow track.

4 He stumbled through the city gate,
Became too weak to lift the weight,

A man who passed him, black, it's said,
Carried up his cross instead.

5 At last they came to the hanging place,
A hill we call the Eyeless Face,
They gave him drugs to kill the pain
He pushed the cup away again.

6 The soldiers hung him on the cross,
Played for his clothes at pitch and toss.
When each of them had won a share
Sitting down they watched him there.

7 The death that he died we were in it too
With the crowd or the soldiers or the High Priest's crew
We couldn't quite see where the Cross came in
With the life that would lead us away from sin.

(*Repeat verse one*)

Ewan Hooper and Ernest Marvin, *A Man Dies*

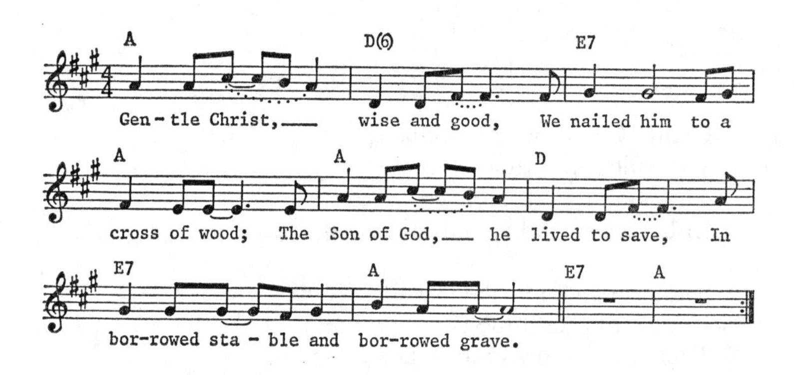


## 615 EASTER HYMN—TO ST. MARY MAGDALEN

She, Mary, who extravagantly broke
Her costly treasure, alabaster box,

She, Magdalen,
In desolation in that early dawn
Seeking in secret, seeking out the tomb,
Somehow, someway, her sorrow to assuage,
She, Magdalen, she in the garden saw,
She first, she,—ah!—the Resurrection saw,
And spoke, she first of all,
Rabboni, Lord, her heartbreak and her love.
And then,—
The April rain, the morning sun, and joy
And joy and joy and overmastering joy
Of love accepted, love returned to earth
In lilies no more Lenten, birds
All, Glory, Glory, Glory, calling, she
Alone quite speechless for her pain,
Her not-to-be-appeasèd pain, of love,
The everlasting Easter of the heart.

Katherine Watson, *The Source*

616 INTERVIEWING MARY MAGDALA

SIX READINGS

*Cass Tennel, an experienced television interviewer, tries to discover the truth about Jesus Davidson who has been executed in Jerusalem. Mary Magdala, a celebrated cabaret dancer, knew Jesus Davidson and claims that he is still alive.*

*I*

Mary Magdala sat in the chair with an easy grace, her hands folded composedly in her lap. Tall and personable, with startlingly red hair and a strongly-boned face that was handsome rather than beautiful, she was wearing a loose-fitting coat and plain shoes. The large dark eyes, the flawless complexion, the casually-dressed red hair—these things were expected. What was astonishing was her serenity; a quality of bearing that wiped away the image of the girl being stripped in the cabaret. Here was a woman of exceptional personality, who could sit still and silent in the corner of a crowded room and dominate it just by

(616 *1*) being there. I never remember seeing anyone so completely mistress of herself.

We brought her on to the screen in medium shot and dollied-in slowly, taking our time, giving the viewers an opportunity to look at her and catch the infection of her calm assurance. But what she had been like before she achieved serenity—the mental image of those long legs and that tossed red hair writhing and shaking under the staring lights of the cabaret stage—this was an electrifying thought.

'Miss Magdala,' I said then, 'thank you first of all for coming.'

She nodded. 'I'm glad to be here.'

'It's very good of you.'

This was throw-away stuff; pleasantries. But necessary pleasantries. I knew the viewers would need a moment or two to concentrate on what she was saying as well as on how she looked.

'The fact is,' I said carefully, 'we're trying to establish the truth about Jesus Davidson.'

'Yes,' she said, her voice low and clear.

There was nothing insipid about her. Whatever Davidson had done to change her he had not tamed nor diluted her spirit. Looking at her you said to yourself not: 'This is a beautiful woman,' but: 'This is a woman excitingly alive.'

'I understand you knew him well?' I said.

'Yes.'

'How well, Miss Magdala?'

'Very well.'

'Intimately?' I chose the word deliberately.

She nodded. 'Yes'.

'I see.'

She smiled at the tone of my voice, the corners of her mouth lifting, her eyebrows tilting a little. It was an amused, open smile. I could imagine the effect it must have had on the audience when she was dancing.

'Surprised, Mr. Tennel?'

'A little. You see, you are a . . .'

'I know. I'm a cabaret girl—or I was. And he is God.'

'Something like that,' I said.

She looked at me levelly. 'You don't think God concerns himself with cabaret-girls, is that it?'

But I dodged that one. It was too early in the piece to let her ask the questions, especially theological ones.

'But is he God?' I said. 'That's what we're trying to find out.'

'Oh, yes,' she said, and the confidence in her voice was a natural thing, as normal and unforced as the daylight. 'He's God. The Blessed One. The Life of the world.'

'Life?' I snatched at the word. 'But we're talking about a dead man.'

'I'm not. He was dead, certainly. But now he is alive again.'

I nodded. 'That's the rumour we've all heard, of course, but . . .'

'Not a rumour,' she said firmly. 'The truth. You said you wanted the truth about him. Well, that's it. He's alive.'

'You sound very sure of that, Miss Magdala.'

'Very sure,' she said.

'How can you be so sure?'

'Because I've seen him,' she said simply.

Looking at her like this, in close-up, I felt the conviction in her voice come through with an almost physical impact.

'Miss Magdala,' I said, 'I can see you were very attached to him.' I have had plenty of practice in this sort of thing and the implication of my words was clear enough.

But she disarmed me with one stroke.

'I love him, if that's what you mean,' she said. She was looking directly into the camera lens and her words were like the declaration of a bride at her wedding.

'Yes,' I said uncertainly. 'Yes, I see.'

I winced now, hearing my voice through the monitor speaker. I sounded as gauche as a schoolboy. I, Cass Tennel, who had reduced the most competent of actresses to embarrassed confusion in front of the camera; who had destroyed reputations for shrewdness and poise with a few carefully-chosen words. I, for whom nothing was sacred—not pain, not privacy, not grief—nothing. I sat and watched a Jewish cabaret-girl put me neatly in my place.

616

*2*

'Perhaps if you could tell us something about him,' I said. 'The kind of person he was. Would you say he was a happy man, for instance?'

'Happy?' She tasted the word doubtfully. 'No. Not really. It's not the sort of word you can use about him. It's too vulnerable, if you see what I mean?'

(616 2) 'Well, no,' I said. 'I'm not quite . . .'

'Like us,' she said. 'Trapped in a world too big for us to cope with. At the mercy of things outside our control. It wasn't like that with him. He wasn't trapped. He was free. Not a victim of circumstances but the master of them. In control—way above anything as chancy as happiness.'

'You say he was in control. You mean before he died?'

'Even before he died. You know what his name means, don't you? Jesus—Jeshua—the Conqueror. That's the only way to describe him. He was a man who had won.'

'But he didn't win. At the end, he was defeated.'

She shook her head, the bright flame of her hair swinging. 'No. That's what we thought. Last Friday afternoon that's the way it looked even to us. But now, everything's changed.'

'Since yesterday morning?'

'Yes.'

'I wonder if you could tell us what happened then, Miss Magdala? At the tomb, I mean.'

'He broke out. Nothing they could do could hold him.' She laughed, spreading her hands in a gesture of excitement. 'They sealed up the tomb, you know, and mounted a guard. It was ridiculous. Pathetic. Like tying-up a sleeping lion with cotton thread. When he wakened he just snapped the thread and strode out.'

'You say you saw him there, outside the tomb?'

'I did indeed.'

'Alive?'

'Of course.'

'Miss Magdala,' I said brutally, 'I'm sorry, but that's just not possible.'

She was quite unshaken. 'It's a miracle, Mr. Tennel. They come naturally to him, of course. I'm ashamed to think how slow we've been to recognize this.'

'It's understandable,' I said. 'I'm not much for miracles myself.'

'He performed many, Mr. Tennel. A great many.'

'So I'm told.'

'The trouble is, people misunderstood them.'

'Didn't believe in them, you mean?'

'Oh no. They believed all right. If you see a cripple get up and walk, and listen to a deaf-mute you've known all your life suddenly start singing, you haven't much option, have you? When it happens like that, in front of a crowd, you've got to believe it.' She shook her head again—that gesture of mingled frustration and excitement I was beginning to associate with people who had known Davidson. 'It was the meaning of what he did they couldn't understand. They thought he was just a man doing something extraordinary.'

'Yes,' I said.

'No. That's exactly the point. He wasn't an ordinary man. He was God. God in person, doing the things that came naturally to him. People always said, "How can this 'village nobody' work miracles?" But the real question is, "How can God walk about Israel like a man?" That's the basic miracle, Mr. Tennel, that he was here at all. Once you've seen that, the rest is perfectly logical.'

'Even a resurrection?'

'Especially that. Death can't hold God.'



## 3

I said, 'And you saw him there, in the garden outside the tomb?'

'That's right. I saw him and talked to him.' I heard the patience in her voice and smiled, watching the screen. She was right, of course. Once you had swallowed the incredible idea of God living in the world as a man, everything else was completely logical.

I said, 'How did you come to be in the garden so early in the morning? Was it pre-arranged before he died? A sort of rendezvous?'

She laughed. 'Nothing so dramatic. It was simply our first opportunity to visit his tomb. We have a strict rule about not working on the Sabbath, as I expect you know. We had to wait until first light yesterday before we could go.'

'Yes, but why did you go? Was it just a sentimental journey?'

'In a way, I suppose it was,' she said frankly. 'But practical too. We took spices and ointment and—oh, it sounds absurd now, a bunch of women in heavy mourning going to preserve a corpse. But it was all we could think of doing. We'd had to stand by and watch them take him away and kill him. And the burial on Friday was very rushed. We had to get finished before the Sabbath started at sunset. Yesterday morning we decided to do

(616 3) things properly. Give him a decent burial at least.' She smiled. 'I expect it all sounds very odd to you, Mr. Tennel. But our Jewish funeral customs are important to us.'

'I understand,' I said.

'We were terribly worried about how we were going to get into the tomb—what with that great stone slab sealing the entrance and the guard there and everything. But of course, when we got there, the guards had gone and the tomb was wide open. And when we looked inside, it was empty.'

I nodded. 'You've considered the possibility of grave-robbers?'

'It was our first thought. I remember Salome—she was one of the group—saying in that rather acid voice she puts on when she's upset, "Even when the poor soul's dead they can't leave him in peace".'

I looked at her quickly. 'They?'

'The supreme council, the Sanhedrin.'

'You thought the Sanhedrin had arranged to have the body removed?'

'Yes, of course. Who else would want to do such a thing?'

'Why the Sanhedrin?' I said.

'I don't know. Perhaps to prevent the tomb from becoming a shrine. If it hadn't been for Saul Joseph offering his own tomb they'd have buried him in quick-lime in the prison yard. That's what usually happens.'

'I wondered about that.'

She nodded. 'Mr. Joseph went personally to the Governor-General and got his permission to bury the body. The Sanhedrin were very put out about it, I believe.'

I could understand their alarm. A dead hero in a magnificent tomb was a ready-made focal point for future trouble.

'But it wasn't that at all, of course,' she said. 'We rushed back to the house and told the men. And John Zebedee and Peter Johnson went back straightaway to see for themselves. I followed behind but I hadn't a hope of catching up with them.'

I said, 'I'd like to get this quite right. It's important, I think. Are you in fact saying that the men were surprised at your news of the empty tomb?'

'And angry. Peter especially. I've never seen him so wild.'

'It would be true to say, then, that these men who were his closest friends never expected him to come back from the dead?'

'None of us did, Mr. Tennel. None of us.'

'Although he had on several occasions promised to do just that?'

'In spite of that we didn't expect to see him alive again. I'm ashamed to have to say it, but it's true.'



## *4*

'What happened when you got to the tomb the second time?'

'I saw Peter coming out. I hardly recognized him, he looked so old and beaten. John took his arm and they went off together, walking slowly. They passed right by me but I don't think either of them knew I was there. They were like men walking in their sleep.'

'And did you go after them?'

'No. I stayed on. I don't know why. I was weeping and terribly upset, and . . .'

'I quite understand, Miss Magdala. This has all been a tremendous strain on you.'

She looked at me steadily and said, 'You don't believe it, do you? You don't believe he's alive again?'

'I'm open to conviction,' I said.

She shook her head. 'You think I'm not quite myself. A little bit off-centre. You think it's all been too much of a shock for me. Well, it was a shock, finding that empty tomb. A terrible shock.'

'Yes,' I said. 'Of course.'

'The thought of them mauling him about. Dragging him out of his grave in the middle of the night and digging a hole somewhere and dropping his body in and stamping the ground down on top of him. Just for a moment or two, there by myself in the garden when the men had gone, I thought I was going out of my mind.' She smiled, a warm, sane smile. 'And then he came and spoke to me.'

'Jesus Davidson? You're sure?'

'Yes. He was suddenly there and he asked me why I was crying. He sounded so—so normal and relaxed I didn't think it was him at first. Funny isn't it, the way a familiar voice sounds strange when you don't expect to hear it? But then he spoke my name. "Mary" he said. And I knew who he was and turned round and saw him there.'

Again it was said with that devastating simplicity, as though she had wakened from a nightmare and recognized the familiar room and the figure of a parent bending over her.

'Did he say anything else?' I said.

'He gave me a message. For Peter and the men. He called them his brothers. I put my arms round him and hugged him. He was there and I was so glad to see him, and at the same time terrified in case he disappeared again. I held him tight to make sure of him. But he freed himself gently and told me to take this message back to the house.'

'What was the message? Can you tell us?'

'Oh yes. It's not a secret. We're finished with secrets now. It's all out in the open for everyone to hear. I mean, if killing him couldn't silence him, nothing can. He said "Go and tell my brothers I am ascending to my Father and yours, to my God and your God. Tell them I am going first to Galilee and they must come and meet me there." '

'And you took that message back to them?'

She nodded. 'I ran all the way. I was so excited I could hardly get the words out at first.'

'Did they understand what he meant, Miss Magdala?'

'Yes. It was exactly what he had promised. He told us all about it long before any of this happened; how he came from God and was going back to God. He told us plainly, not once but many times.'

'And yet at first, when you found the tomb empty, you didn't even consider the possibility of a resurrection.'

'I know,' she said. 'He told us exactly what would happen, and we wanted to believe him, but I don't think any of us really expected it to come true.' She shook her head. 'Looking back now over the last couple of years I think we must have broken his heart a hundred times simply by not being able to understand the truth about him and what he was trying to do for us.'



*5*

'Have the men gone north?' I said.

She nodded.

'And you? When will you go?'

'Soon. Tomorrow perhaps. Or the day after.'

I said. 'That's where it all began, isn't it? In Galilee.'

6 5) 'Yes.'

'Is that where you first met him, Miss Magdala?'

'Yes. In Tiberias. I was run-down and nervy. I'd been working too hard in the cabarets.' She looked at me calmly. 'Not the easiest kind of work, Mr. Tennel, as you can imagine. The doctor ordered a complete rest. You know the sort of thing—country air, regular meals, plenty of early nights. I went up to a little place by the lake. Right off the map and as quiet as a church.' She shrugged her shoulders and smiled. 'It sounded ideal, but after a couple of weeks of it I wasn't the slightest bit better. Worse, if anything. Depressed, no appetite, sleeping badly. I'd got to the stage where I just wasn't interested in living. The countryside was beautiful and everyone was very kind. But it was all remote somehow—out of my reach. I was there, in the middle of it, but I wasn't a part of it. I felt like a ghost.

'The doctor said it was all tied up with my life in the cabarets. Too many nights on the stage, with all those eyes watching me out of the darkness. You can't see them, you know—the spotlights take care of that. But you can feel them. It's not the pleasantest of feelings. You're on your own up there under the lights in an intense little private world. Only it isn't really private. It's like being under a microscope. After a time you begin to lose your sense of reality.

'I expect it sounds ridiculous to you, Mr. Tennel, but it had me scared. Really scared.'

I nodded. 'And then you met Davidson.'

'Yes. I didn't want to go. I didn't want to see anyone. I just wasn't interested. But they insisted. He'd got a reputation for being able to help people and they felt it was worth a try.'

'What happened,' I said, 'when you met him?'

She looked faintly surprised. 'He cured me.'

'You mean he gave you treatment? Some sort of therapy?'

She shook her head. 'It's no good, Mr. Tennel. You mustn't try to fit him into some sort of recognized category—a kind of super-psychiatrist or something. When I say he cured me, I mean just that. They brought me to him, and he set me free.'

I said cautiously, 'You mean he forgave you?'

'Of course. He forgave me, he set me free, he cured me—they all mean the same thing, Mr. Tennel. They all add up to life.'

'He accepted me as I was,' she said. 'As a person. It'd been a long time since anyone'd done that.'

(616 5) 'I find that hard to credit,' I said. 'You were famous as a dancer. Everyone in Jerusalem knew the Magdala.'

'The Magdala,' she said, the sharpness of contempt in her voice. 'A dancer. A name on a poster. A body posturing under the lights when the drums began to beat. But I'm a person, Mr. Tennel. A human being needing people, needing love. And that's how he accepted me; as a woman capable of going out of her mind.'

I said, 'But the people you were staying with in Galilee—surely they accepted you as a person too?'

She smiled. 'They were very kind to me.'

'That's something,' I said. 'To be kind to people in trouble.'

'Oh, I was grateful, Mr. Tennel. They did all they could to help me. But it wasn't enough. Nothing like enough. It never is. You know that.'

I knew that. Everyone does. Kindness can sometimes prevent a tragedy. But once the tragedy has happened, kindness—the best that is in us—is hopelessly inadequate. It can cushion but it can't cure.

'And yet,' I said, 'when this man accepted you . . .'

'That's different, isn't it?'

'How?'

'Because he's God,' she said. 'Only God is strong enough to go beyond kindness; to accept us as we are and make us whole again.'

'But what exactly did he do?' I said. 'If you could give us some idea. . . .'

'I know,' she said. 'I know what you want me to say. Shock treatment, injections, the clinical mystery of the consulting-room that makes everything credible.'

'Well,' I said uncomfortably, 'you must admit it would . . .'

She broke in crisply. 'The truth is, Mr. Tennel, he didn't do anything—not in the sense you mean. He looked at me and spoke my name. He didn't even touch me. But I felt suddenly light and empty and I thought I was going to faint. And then I was weeping, and all the strain was washing away, and I felt everything coming back into focus around me—the houses and the grass and the trees—they sort of grew up and made a place for me to stand. And the faces of my friends were clear and alive, and I heard them talking and the sounds of the town all round me. I wasn't a ghost any more. I was alive, part of the world, a person in my own right.

'It was a little resurrection,' she said. 'I understand that now. Like being born again.'

'And all this happened,' I said carefully, 'because you trusted him?'

'Yes. That's exactly right. Because I trusted him.'

'Miss Magdala,' I said, 'I'm not at all sure that I understand all of that. But this much I do understand—the sort of person you have become—your peace of mind, your happiness, indeed your basic ability to go on living—all this depends, it seems to me, on one vital fact—that Jesus Davidson was what he claimed to be.'

She nodded happily. 'Yes, Mr. Tennel. Because he is who he is, I am who I am.'

'And would it be true to say that unless he is alive now there can be no life for you?'

'For me or for any of us.'

I nodded, letting that pass. 'So it is very important to you that you saw him in the garden yesterday morning.'

'Of course.'

I said, 'Have you seen him since?'

'Not yet. But some of the others have.'

I smiled at her. 'Miss Magdala, we're most grateful to you. You've made it all vivid and . . .'

'Believable?' she said quickly, matching me smile for smile.

I hesitated. 'Worth thinking about, anyway.'

Stuart Jackman, *The Davidson Affair*

## 617 LORD OF THE DANCE

1 I danced in the morning
When the world was begun
And I danced in the moon
And the stars and the sun
And I came down from heaven
And I danced on the earth—
At Bethlehem I had my birth.

Chorus
Dance then wherever you may be,
I am the Lord of the Dance, said he,

And I'll lead you all, wherever you may be
And I'll lead you all in the dance, said he.

2 I danced for the scribe
And the pharisee
But they would not dance
And they wouldn't follow me,
I danced for the fishermen
For James and John—
They came with me
And the dance went on.

3 I danced on the Sabbath
And I cured the lame
The holy people
Said it was a shame
They whipped and they stripped
And they hung me high
And they left me there
On a Cross to die.

4 I danced on a Friday
When the sky turned black—
It's hard to dance
With the devil on your back
They buried my body
And they thought I'd gone—
But I am the dance
And I still go on.

5 They cut me down
And I leap up high—
I am the life
That'll never, never die
I'll live in you
If you'll live in me
I am the Lord
Of the Dance, said he.

Sydney Carter

Lively and rhythmic
G Em Bm Em
I danced in the morn-ing when the world was be-gun, and I
Am D
danced in the Moon and the stars_ and the sun, And I
G Em Bm Em
came down from hea-ven and I danced on the earth- At
Am D7 G G Bm
Beth-le-hem I had my birth. CHORUS: Dance then wher-
Em G Am D
-ev-er you may be, I am the Lord of the dance,said he, And I'll
G Em Bm Am D7
lead you all wher-ev-er you may be, and I'll lead you all in the
Melody of Verse 5
G Em Bm Em
Dance,said he. They cut me down and I leap up high-
Am D G Em
I am the life that'll ne-ver,ne-ver die,I'll live in you if you'll
Bm Em Am D7 G
live in me- I am the Lord of the Dance said he.
etc. Chorus

## 618 JESUS CHRIST HIS TERRIBLE DEMANDS

He was like some terrible moral huntsman digging mankind out of the snug burrows in which they had lived hitherto. In the white blaze of this kingdom of his there was to be no property, no privilege, no pride, no precedence; no motive indeed and no reward but love. Is it any wonder that men were dazzled and blinded and cried out against him? Even his disciples cried out when he would not spare them the light. Is it any wonder that the priests realized that between this man and themselves there was no choice but that he or witch-craft should perish? Is it any wonder that the Roman soldiers, confronted and amazed by something soaring over their comprehensions and threatening all their disciplines, should take refuge in wild laughter, and crown him with thorns, and robe him in purple to make a mock-Caesar of him? For to take him seriously was to enter a strange and alarming life, to abandon habits, to control instincts and impulses, to essay an incredible happiness.

H. G. Wells, *The Outline of History*

# The Christian Church and Christian Activity and Worship

## 619 CAN IT BE TRUE

1 Can It Be True!
Can it be really you?
Your words were plain
Telling us what to do
Here in this bread
And in this wine you said
Lord you are here
I should be dumb with dread!

2 There in that room,
Torture and death did loom
Dark on your heart,
Yet you withstood that gloom.
Out of your love,
From your own world above,
You left this Holy Thing,
Your endless love to prove.

3 And day by day,
You still return this way,
But we recall
There was a debt to pay.
Mine is the sin,
But I can yet begin
New life and joy
In this dear Rite to win.

4 Can It Be True?
The things they say of you:
You walked this Earth,
Sharing with friends you knew,
All that they had,
The work, the joy, the pain,
That we might find
The way to heav'n again.

5 Can It Be True?
The things they did to you:
The death, the shame,
And were your friends so few?
Yet, you returned again,
Alive and free.
Can It Be True?
My Lord, it has to be!

Brother William, S.S.F., *Songs of a Sinner*

## 620 'I SAY MY PRAYERS WHEN IT'S CALM...'

He was a very simple old sailor, the skipper of the small boat that was taking them to the Shetlands, and they were a young, lively party, actors and actresses from London on tour, going to do a night or two on the Islands. They were not above 'taking the mickey' a bit, and they thought his way of saying grace before meals very quaint and old-fashioned. However, before long a storm blew up, a really severe north-easter, and as the little ship began to pitch more and more violently, morale among the visitors got lower and lower.

A small deputation went up to ask the Captain's opinion.

'Well,' he said, 'maybe we'll get through, and maybe we won't. I never remember such a storm.' The news was greeted with dismay down below, and finally another deputation went up to the bridge to ask whether perhaps the Captain would be so good as to come and say a prayer with his terrified passengers. His reply was simple: 'I say my prayers when it's calm; and when it's rough, I attend to my ship.'

Anon.

## 621 WHEN A PRAYER MIGHT SAVE YOU

In extreme situations a need is felt to pray, as Houston prayed above House's Chimney (on K2), as Courtauld prayed when buried under the snow (on the Greenland Ice Cap Station). In a tricky position on a mountain I have felt a prayer rising in my throat and had to beat it down, because I felt that it was a request rather than a communion and that it made nonsense to ask for things in a crisis unless one's whole life was of a pattern into which such a prayer naturally fitted. But the urge was a normal and reasonable one. Those who have that type of faith believe that they are saved *because of* their prayer. I am thinking of two very fine men. One was strung upside down by the Japanese for three days during the Burma campaign; the other, when his ship was sunk by enemy action, survived thirty-six hours in the water with a broken arm. Both prayed and came through. Whether their prayer was 'answered' in the literal sense we are not discussing here. The point is that, as I believe, 'energy which but for prayer would be bound, is by prayer set free and operates in some part of the world of facts'.

Wilfrid Noyce, *They Survived*

## 622 WHITSUNDAY, 1948

*A day of splendid light and streaming wind*

These who walk seemingly indifferent
Under the glittering, exhilarating tumult
Of tall trees tossing, glancing, streaming, in the wind,
Past opulence of red, banked, pom-pom rhododendron blooms,

Fanged, piled azaleäs, hot, yellow, open in the sun,
Forget-me-nots, wild hawthorn candidissima,—
Impassive are they?—past this lavish, laughing joy,
This wealth, this colour sun-suffused, gold, green, gold, blue,
Unresting, ceaseless, quivering, sun, shadow, sun,
Light, shadow, shade again, up lifting, dipping down,
Light running, rushing, past expressing gay, hearts high,
Lord, loveliness, alive, alive—and shall these not respond?
Speak words, words wonderful, worship and praise?
Oh match they meanly this exuberance!

No, never, never, words shall be enough,
No Glory, Benedicite, be beautiful as birds,
As being thus beatified. Be, be, thy praise.
O fountain over-spilling, fall on us
Fons Vivus, Fire of Love, forever flame!
Sweep in our souls as through these leaves this light,
Sweep in our souls O wind of Pentecost!

Katherine Watson, *The Source*

623 WORSHIP

To worship is to quicken the conscience by the holiness of God, to feed the mind with the truth of God, to purge the imagination by the beauty of God, to open the heart to the love of God, to devote the will to the purpose of God. All this is gathered up in that emotion which most cleanses us from selfishness because it is the most selfless of all emotions—adoration.

William Temple, *Daily Readings*

624 DO THIS IN REMEMBRANCE OF ME

Was ever another command so obeyed? For century after century, spreading slowly to every continent and country and among every race on earth, this action has been done, in every conceivable human circumstance. Men have found no better thing than this to do for kings at their crowning and for criminals going to the scaffold; for armies in triumph or for a bride and bridegroom in a little country church; for the wisdom of the Parliament of a mighty nation or for a sick old woman afraid to die; for a school-boy sitting an examination or for Columbus setting out to discover America; in thankfulness because my father did not die of pneumonia; because the Turk was at the gates of Vienna; for the settlement of a strike; for Captain so-and-so, wounded and prisoner of war; while the lions roared in the nearby amphitheatre; on the beach at Dunkirk; tremulously, by an old monk on the fiftieth anniversary of his vows; furtively, by an exiled bishop who had hewn timber all day in a prison camp near Murmansk; gorgeously, for the canonisation of S. Joan of Arc—one could fill many pages with the reasons why men have done this, and not tell a hundredth part of them. And best of all, week by week and month by month, on a hundred thousand successive Sundays, faithfully, unfailingly, across all the parishes of christendom, the pastors have done this just to *make* the holy common people of God.

Dom Gregory Dix, *The Shape of the Liturgy*

## 625 LIGHT IN THE ASPHALT JUNGLE

SEVEN SECTIONS, SUITABLE FOR GROUPS OF READERS AND CHORAL SPEECH

*I*

I had a dream. And I saw a city,
A city that rose up out of the crust of the earth.
And its streets were paved with asphalt,
And a river of dirty water ran down along its curbs.
I saw a city. And its people knew no hope.
They were chased and herded from place to place by the churning jaws of bulldozers.
They were closed up in the anonymous cubicles of great brick prisons called housing projects.
They were forced out of work by the fearsome machines,
And by the sparseness of their learning.
They were torn in many pieces by the hostile angers of racial fears and guilt and prejudice.
Their workers were exploited. Their children had no parks to play in, no pools to swim in, no space in crowded rooms to learn in, no hopes to dream in.

And the people knew no hope.
Their bosses underpaid them. Their landlords overcharged them.
Their welfare workers despised them. Their churches deserted them.
And all of life in the city seemed dark and wild, like a jungle,
A jungle lined with asphalt. And the people sat in darkness.

625

*2*

I had a dream. And I saw a city,
A city clothed in neon-lighted darkness.
And I heard men talking. And I looked at them.
Across their chests in large golden letters—written by their own hands—
Across their chests were written the words: I am a Christian.
And the Christians looked at the city and said:
'How terrible. . . . How terrible. . . . How terrible.'
And the Christians looked at the city and said:
'That is no place to live, But some of our people have wandered there, And we must go and rescue them.
We must go and gather them, like huddled sheep into a fold;
And we will call it a City Church.'
So they built their church. And the people came,
And they walked past all the weary, broken, exploited, dying men who lined the city's streets.
Year after year they walked past,
Wearing their signs: I am a Christian.

Then one day the people in the church said:
'This neighbourhood is too bad for good Christians.
Let us go to the suburbs where God dwells and build a church there.'
And one by one they walked away, past all the weary, broken, exploited, dying men. They walked fast,
And they did not hear a Voice that said: '. . . the least of these. . . . the least of these. . . .'
And they walked by, and they went out, and they built a church.
And the church was light and lifted up, and it even had a cross.
But the church was hollow, And the people were hollow,
And their hearts (their hearts?) were as hard as the asphalt streets of the jungle.

*3*

I had a dream. And I saw a city,
A city clothed in bright and gaudy darkness.
And I saw more men with signs across their chests.
And they were Christians too. And I heard them say:
'How terrible. . . . How terrible. . . . How terrible.
The city is filled with sinners; and we are supposed to save sinners,
To save sinners. . . . To save sinners. . . . But they are so unlike us,
So bad, So dark, So poor, So strange,
But we are supposed to save them, To save them, To save them.'
And one man said
'Can't we save them without going where they are?'
And they worked to find a way to save and be safe at the same time.
Meanwhile, I saw them build a church,
And they called it a Mission, A city Mission.
And all the children came by to see what this was.
And the city missionaries who had been sent to save them gathered them in. So easy to work with children, they said,
And they are so safe, so safe.
And week after week they saved the children
(Saved them from getting in their parents' way on Sunday morning).
And in the dream the city missionaries looked like Pied Pipers,
With their long row of children stretched out behind them.
And the parents wondered if Christianity were only for children.
And when the missionaries finally came to see them,
and kept looking at the plaster falling,
and used a thousand words that had no meaning,
and talked about rescuing them from hell
while they were freezing in the apartment,
and asked them if they were saved,
and walked out, to their nice, safe neighbourhood—
When that happened, the parents knew:
This version of Christianity had no light for their jungle.
Then soon, the children saw too; it was all a children's game;
And when they became old enough they got trumpets of their own,
And blew them high and loud, And marched off
sneering, swearing, into the darkness.

625

*4*

I had a dream. And I saw Christians with guilty consciences
And I heard them say:
'What shall we do? What shall we do? What shall we do?
These people want to come to OUR church—to OUR church.'
And someone said: 'Let's build a church for THEM—for THEM,
They like to be with each other anyway.'
And they started the church, And the people walked in.
And for a while, as heads were bowed in prayer, they did not know.
But then, the prayers ended, and the people looked up, and looked around, And saw that every face was THEIR face,
THEIR face, And every colour was THEIR colour, THEIR colour.
And they stood up and shouted loudly within themselves:
'Let me out of this ghetto, this pious, guilt-built ghetto'.
And they walked out into the darkness.
And the darkness seemed darker than ever before.
And the good Christians looked and said,
'These people just don't appreciate what WE do for THEM.'

625

*5*

And just as the night seemed darkest, I had another dream.
I dreamed I saw young men walking, Walking into the heart of the city, into the depths of the darkness.
They had no signs, except their lives.
And they walked in the heart of the darkness and said:
'Let us live here and work for light.'
They said, 'Let us live here and help the rootless find a root for their lives.
Let us live here and help the anonymous find their names.'
They said, 'Let us live here and walk with the jobless until they find work.
Let us live here, and sit in the landlord's office until they give more heat and charge less rent.'
They said, 'Let us live here, and throw open the doors of this deserted church to all the people of every race and class;
Let us work with them to find the reconciliation God has brought.'

And they said, 'Let us walk the asphalt streets with the young people sharing their lives, learning their language, playing their sidewalk backyard games, knowing the agonies of their isolation.'
And they said, 'Let us live here, and minister to as many men as God gives us grace.
Let us live here, and die here, with our brothers in the jungle,
Sharing their apartments and their pain.'

And the people saw them. And someone asked who they were.
And few really knew—they had no signs—
But someone said he thought they might be Christians,
And this was hard to believe, but the people smiled;
And a little light began to shine in the heart of the asphalt jungle.

625

*6*

Then in my dream I saw the young men,
I saw the young men and women, And they were weary,
And the job was more than they could bear alone,
And I saw them turn, turn and look for help,
And I heard them call: 'Come and help us,
Come and share this joyful agony, joyful agony,
Come as brothers in the task, Come and live and work with us:
Teachers for the crowded schools, Doctors for the overflowing clinics,
Social workers for the fragmented families,
Nurses for the bulging wards, Pastors for the yearning flocks.
Workers for the fighting gangs, Christians.
Christians who will come and live here,
Here in the heart of the darkness,
Who will live here and love here, that a light may shine for all.'

'Come', I heard them call.
And I saw the good Christians across the country,
And their answers tore out my heart.
Some said, 'There isn't enough money there.'
Some said, 'It's too bad there. I couldn't raise children.'
Some said, 'I'm going into foreign missions, where things aren't quite so dark.'

Some said, 'The suburbs are so nice.'
Some said, 'But I like it here on the farm.'
Some said, Some said. . . .
And one by one they turned their backs and began to walk away.

625

## 7

At this moment my dream was shattered by the sound of a great and mighty whisper, almost a pleading sound;
And a voice said:
'Come, help me, for I am hungry in the darkness.'
And a voice said:
'Come, help me, for I am thirsty in the darkness.'
And a voice said:
'Come, help me, for I am a stranger in this asphalt jungle.'
And a voice said:
'Come, help me, for I have been stripped naked, naked of all legal rights and protection of the law, simply because I am black in the darkness.'
And a voice said:
'Come help me, for my heart is sick with hopelessness and fear in the darkness.'
And a voice said:
'Come, live with me in the prison of my segregated community, and we will break down the walls together.'
And the voices were many,
And the Voice was one.
And the Christians knew whose Voice it was.
And they turned.
And their faces were etched with the agonies of decision.
And the dream ended.

But the voice remains,
And the choice remains,
And the city still yearns for light.
And the King who lives with the least of His Brothers
in the asphalt jungle
yearns for us.

Vincent Harding

## 626 THE APATHY OF THE CHURCH

When any evil attracts public notice, or when any scheme of social progress gets less popular support than it deserves, there is sure to be talk of the 'apathy of the Church in this matter'. If every person who used the phrase would argue, 'I am a baptised Christian. Therefore I am a member of the Church. Therefore the apathy of the Church means the apathy of myself and millions like me. Therefore I must be up and doing, and trying to influence others,' all would be well.

Peter Green, *The Problem of Right Conduct*

## 627 BRINGING LIFE TO THE CHURCH

If it seems to you that the Church as organised has somehow lost sense of proportion, remember that only through the Church has the Gospel ever reached you, and that only through the Church can it reach the ages far ahead. And you will do more service to the cause of Christ by bringing in what reality you can into its life than you can ever render by staying outside and doing what seems possible to you, or you and your few friends, in isolation.

William Temple, *Daily Readings*

## 628 TALLEYRAND'S ADVICE

In the early years of the nineteenth century, the whole of France was in turmoil. The aftermath of the French revolution witnessed a flood of revolutionary ideas in the world of philosophy and religion. Talleyrand, a leading statesman and thinker, was one day approached by a friend of a philosophical turn of mind. This friend was disappointed because his attempt to establish a new religion, which he regarded as a considerable improvement on Christianity, was unsuccessful. He explained that despite all the efforts of himself and his supporters his propaganda made no headway. He asked Talleyrand's advice as to what to do.

Talleyrand replied that it was indeed difficult to found a new religion, more difficult indeed than could be imagined, so difficult that he hardly knew what to advise. 'Still', he said, after a moment's reflection, 'there is one plan which you might at least try. I should recommend you to be crucified, and to rise again on the third day.'

C. H. Robinson, *Diary of Readings* (adapted)

## 629 THE DEVIL WORE A CRUCIFIX

1 The Devil wore a Crucifix
'The Christians they are right'
The Devil said. 'So let us burn
A heretic tonight,
A heretic tonight.'

2 A lily or a swastika
A shamrock or a star
The Devil he can wear them all—
No matter what they are,
No matter what they are.

3 In red or blue or khaki
In green or black and tan
The Devil is a patriot
A proper party man,
A proper party man.

4 Whenever there's a lynching
The Devil will be there—
A witch or an apostle,
The Devil doesn't care,
The Devil doesn't care.

5 He'll beat a drum in China
He'll beat it in the west
He'll beat a drum for anyone
'A Holy war is best,
A Holy war is best.'

6 The Devil isn't down in hell
Or riding in the sky

The Devil's dead (I've heard it said)—
They're telling you a lie,
They're telling you a lie!

Sydney Carter

# God and Nature



## IN THE BEGINNING

In the beginning was the three-pointed star,
One smile of light across the empty face;
One bough of bone across the rooting air,
The substance forked that marrowed the first sun;
And, burning ciphers on the round of space,
Heaven and hell mixed as they spun.

In the beginning was the pale signature,
Three-syllabled and starry as the smile;
And after came the imprints on the water,
Stamp of the minted face upon the moon;
The blood that touched the crosstree and the grail
Touched the first cloud and left a sign.

In the beginning was the mounting fire
That set alight the weathers from a spark,
A three-eyed, red-eyed spark, blunt as a flower;

Life rose and spouted from the rolling seas,
Burst in the roots, pumped from the earth and rock
The secret oils that drive the grass.

In the beginning was the word, the word
That from the solid bases of the light
Abstracted all the letters of the void;
And from the cloudy bases of the breath
The word flowed up, translating to the heart
First characters of birth and death.

In the beginning was the secret brain.
The brain was celled and soldered in the thought
Before the pitch was forking to a sun;
Before the veins were shaking in their sieve,
Blood shot and scattered to the winds of light
The ribbed original of love.

Dylan Thomas, *Collected Poems 1934–1952*

## 631 CAROL

Garden and gardener He made
And then for seed Himself He laid
  To rectify our loss.
O red the Spring on the cruel blade
And lily-white His body splayed
  In pity on the cross.

Haunting our harvest like a thief
He hides His flesh in every sheaf,
  His blood in every fruit,
But rank the weed—Our Saviour's Grief—
We nourish into thorn and leaf
  To live by the sour root.

His is the hunger of the pyre
The seasons wither on; admire
  His great and ghostly paces
About the fume of His desire—

How many souls retreat, retire
  And turn away their faces!

Meadows whiten, stores are piled.
Again in our icy barn the Child
  Sleeps before the play.
Adore Him, now our hearts are mild,
To profit us when we have whiled
  Our innocence away.

Thomas Kinsella, *Downstream*

## 532 SPRING SOWING

About that time of the year the world opened, the sky grew higher, the sea deeper, as the summer colours, blue and green and purple, woke in it. The black fields glistened, and a row of meal-coloured sacks, bursting full like the haunches of plough-horses, ran down each one; two neat little lugs, like pricked ears, stuck up from each sack. They were opened; my father filled from the first of them a canvas tray strapped round his middle, and strode along the field casting the dusty grain on either side with regular sweeps, his hands opening and shutting. When the grain was finished he stopped at another sack and went on again. I would sit watching him, my eyes caught now and then by some ship passing so slowly against the black hills that it seemed to be stationary, though when my attention returned to it again I saw with wonder that it had moved. The sun shone, the black field glittered, my father strode on, his arms slowly swinging, the fan-shaped cast of grain gleamed as it fell and fell again; the row of meal-coloured sacks stood like squat monuments on the field. My father took a special delight in the sowing, and we all felt the first day was a special day.

Edwin Muir, *An Autobiography*

## 533 THE FORCE THAT THROUGH THE GREEN FUSE DRIVES THE FLOWER

The force that through the green fuse drives the flower
Drives my green age; that blasts the roots of trees
Is my destroyer.

And I am dumb to tell the crooked rose
My youth is bent by the same wintry fever.

The force that drives the water through the rocks
Drives my red blood; that dries the mouthing streams
Turns mine to wax.
And I am dumb to mouth unto my veins
How at the mountain spring the same mouth sucks.

The hand that whirls the water in the pool
Stirs the quicksand; that ropes the blowing wind
Hauls my shroud sail.
And I am dumb to tell the hanging man
How of my clay is made the hangman's lime.

The lips of time leech to the fountain head;
Love drips and gathers, but the fallen blood
Shall calm her sores.
And I am dumb to tell a weather's wind
How time has ticked a heaven round the stars.

And I am dumb to tell the lover's tomb
How at my sheet goes the same crooked worm.

Dylan Thomas, *Collected Poems 1934–1952*

634

## BIRTH

### TWO READINGS

*I*

On an oak chest which David had made, near to the fireplace, stood the cradle. Round the huge fire on a fireguard I hung a complete set of baby clothes to air. If I had been laying an offering on the altar of my God, I could not have felt a deeper ecstasy than in that simple act. It was humbleness, pride, joy, wonder, tenderness and seriousness, combined into an overwhelming emotion, lifting my soul nearer the truth than it had ever been before, or ever will be again. I cannot recall what I thought, but I believe in that moment I took on my motherhood.

The pain came fiercer and more often now, but I was full of restless energy. I went up and down stairs, and went down to lunch, and read aloud to John, who begged me to finish the chapter in *Treasure Island* I had begun the day before. Mrs. Townsend brought tea up to our room, and we had a sort of picnic round the fire, she and nurse talking of practical matters, but I was lost to all but my own excitement, which not even the pain could subdue. I must be doing, my soul was singing and free, my body must respond however foolishly. The fierceness of the pain stopped me in all I began; I had to hold on to anything stable, and when I looked at Mrs. Townsend's face I saw pity there. But she could not speak of her feeling to me, and I was glad she could not.

I wanted to be alone with this fierce exultation of pain. My spirit sang in triumph after each paroxysm, but my body was like a dead weight on it. I only knew that my baby and I were struggling for him to be born. He could not go back to his quiet darkness. All was changed. He had begun his perilous journey to life—I must speed him and help him; keep him with all the strength of my body and all the strength of my desire for him, pressed forwards towards the light where his soul waited for him. I did not think this, but dimly perceived it was so.

I cling on to the bed, and feel that the pain is overwhelming me. I must not let it. Nurse comes to hold me. 'No, don't touch me; go to the fire; I can smell the baby things scorching.' So by trivial ways I try to keep in touch with reality. My few garments are unbearable. I try to undress, but become confused as the waves of pain break over me, making consciousness more and more difficult to retain. But I will not let my spirit be drowned. I will not lose touch with my baby. I have a feeling that if I let go my hold on consciousness I shall be leaving him alone.

Nurse says a word of praise and encouragement, which gives me confidence in myself again. I shiver as I lie on the bed, but I use every ounce of effort and strength when the paroxysm comes, and feel again the triumphant exultation. My body labours, but my spirit is free. My baby and I are struggling to be rid of each other. That strange, secret link must be broken. He must be himself apart from me, and I must give him to mankind.

534

*2*

My body is seized by a new strangely expelling pain. I am again terribly alone—a primitive creature, without thought, without desire, without anything but this instinct to rid my womb of what encumbers it. I hear voices far away; I feel hands about me, but I am not I; I am only an elemental instinctive force bringing forth after its kind.

A pain more rending than all bears me on its crest into utter darkness. A cry, a strange unearthly cry strikes piteously at my heart, and pierces my darkness. My consciousness strives towards that cry, my soul recognizes it. It is my baby's cry, and it leads my spirit away from the dark back to the light.

Someone says 'A fine boy,' and I, wearily, 'Is he all right?' They say 'A perfect child.' Then blessed rest and content—not unconsciousness, but just a sense of fulfilment, with no remembrance of pain, nor even of the baby, who is silent.

They say 'Here is your husband,' and I hear them tell him I have been brave, and I hear his voice low and tender speaking to them or me—I do not know whom—I am too tired to listen, and when he bends over me to kiss me I cannot open my lips or my eyes for weariness. But I can smell the violets he puts on my pillow.

I don't know how long I lie like that, but after a while they give me my boy. I see he has David's fair hair and blue eyes, and I am glad; but his nose is small like mine; his ears are like his father's and covered with soft, fine down. His tiny fingers clasp my finger. His eyes are wide open: what does he see as he moves his head from side to side? The light of the winter dawn fills the room; his eyes unblinkingly seek the window, not with wonder as one coming from darkness, but as if in this strangeness the light alone is not strange.

Suddenly the realization of life and of all that may separate us comes to me, and I hold him close. I want him still to be all my own. His eyes close, and nuzzles against my breast, and with his groping mouth finds my nipple. He is soft and warm and sweet. As he draws the warm milk from me, and I feel that mysterious pleasure half spiritual, half physical, I realize that the link between us is imperishable. I am for ever his mother and he my son.

Helen Thomas, *As It Was*

## 635 i thank You God for most this amazing

i thank You God for most this amazing

day: for the leaping greenly spirits of trees
and a blue true dream of sky; and for everything
which is natural which is infinite which is yes

(i who have died am alive again today,
and this is the sun's birthday; this is the birth
day of life and of love and wings: and of the gay
great happening illimitably earth)

how should tasting touching hearing seeing
breathing any—lifted from the no
of all nothing—human merely being
doubt unimaginable You?

(now the ears of my ears awake and
now the eyes of my eyes are opened)

e. e. cummings, *Selected Poems 1923–1958*

## 636 A DOG IN THE QUARRY

The day was so bright
 that even birdcages flew open.
The breasts of lawns
 heaved with joy
and the cars on the highway
 sang the great song of asphalt.
At Lobzy a dog fell in the quarry
 and howled.
Mothers pushed their prams out of the park opposite
because babies cannot sleep
 when a dog howls,
and a fat old pensioner was cursing the Municipality:
they let the dog fall in the quarry and then leave him there,
and this, if you please, has been going on since morning.

Towards evening even the trees
 stopped blossoming
and the water at the bottom of the quarry
 grew green with death.
But still the dog howled.

(636) Then along came some boys
and made a raft out of two logs
and two planks.
And a man left on the bank
a briefcase, in which bread is planted
in the morning
so that by noon
crumbs may sprout in it
(the kind of briefcase in which documents
and deeds
would die of cramp),
he laid aside his briefcase
and sailed with them.

Their way led across a green puddle
to the island where the dog waited.
It was a voyage like
the discovery of America,
a voyage like
the quest of Theseus.
The dog fell silent,
the boys stood like statues
and one of them punted with a stick,
the waves shimmered nervously,
tadpoles swiftly
flickered out of the wake,
the heavens
stood still,
and the man stretched out his hand.

It was a hand
reaching out across the ages,
it was a hand
linking
one world with another,
life with death,
it was a hand
joining everything together,
it caught the dog by the scruff of its neck

and then they sailed back
to the music of
an immense fanfare
of the dog's yapping.

It was not a question of that one dog.

It was not a question of that park.

Somehow it was a question
of our whole childhood,
  all of whose mischiefs
  will eventually out,
of all our loves,
of all the places we loved in
  and parted never to meet again,
of every prospect
  happy as grass,
unhappy as bone,
of every path up or down,
of every raft and all the other machines
we search for at our lathes
  and drawing-boards,
of everything we are reaching out for
round the corner of the landscape.

It was not an answer.

There are days when no answer is needed.

Miroslav Holub, *Selected Poems*

## 637 STORM OVER THE ORKNEY ISLANDS: THE POWER OF WIND AND SEA

I was coming back from school when, as I passed the little pond below the house, I became aware of the intense stillness. When I went into the kitchen my mother said that she did not like the look of the weather, which surprised me, for I had loved the dull, sad stillness, the dense air which made each motionless blade of grass sweat one clear drop, the dreary immobility of the pond. A little while afterwards we heard an iron pail flying with a great clatter along the length of the house. My father and Sutherland ran out to see that all the doors and windows of the steading were fast shut. I wanted to go with them to see the storm, but my mother forbade me, saying that the wind would blow me away: I took it for a fictitious warning, for I did not know then that wind could do such things. The storm itself made very little impression on me, for I was in the house, and looking out of the windows I could not see that there was anything to see except the dull sky with its low-flying clouds, and the flattened look of everything, and the desertion of the fields. On the second day Sutherland reported that a boat anchored in the sound had dragged its anchor for several miles. This seemed to impress him and my father a good deal, and I tried to be impressed too. But what really excited me was the knowledge that this was a storm, and not merely a wind; for I thought of a storm as something different from a wind. The storm must have lasted for several days; when the wind fell news came across from Rousay that a boat returning from the mainland with two men and two women had been lost on the first day. The sea was still high, but my father and Sutherland set out in our boat, along with the other boats of Wyre and Rousay, to look for the drowned party. In the evening Sutherland talked of what the sea did to the dead, swelling their bodies and sending them to the surface on the third day. Other cases of drowning came up; at that time, when most farmers had a share in a boat and went out in the fishing season, death at sea was common in Orkney. The bodies were eventually found.

Edwin Muir, *An Autobiography*

## 638 GOD'S GRANDEUR

The world is charged with the grandeur of God.
  It will flame out, like shining from shook foil;
  It gathers to a greatness, like the ooze of oil
Crushed. Why do men then now not reck his rod?
Generations have trod, have trod, have trod;
  And all is seared with trade; bleared, smeared with toil;
  And wears man's smudge and shares man's smell: the soil
Is bare now, nor can foot feel, being shod.

And for all this, nature is never spent;
  There lives the dearest freshness deep down things;
And though the last lights off the black West went
  Oh, morning, at the brown brink eastward, springs—
Because the Holy Ghost over the bent
  World broods with warm breast and with ah! bright wings.

Gerard Manley Hopkins

## 639 DAWN CHORUS IN LIBYA

I listen with reverence to the birdsong cascading
At dawn from the oasis, for it seems to me
There is no better evidence for the existence of God
Than in the bird that sings, though it knows not why,
From a spring of untrammelled joy that wells up in its heart.
Therefore I pray that no sky-hurled hawk may come
Plummeting down,
To silence the singer, and disrupt the Song.
That rhapsodic, assured, transcending song
Which foretells and proclaims, when the Plan is worked out,
Life's destiny: the joyous, benign Intention of God.

An Arab chieftain living on the outskirts of a Libyan oasis.
Barbara Greene and Victor Gollancz,
*God of a Hundred Names*

## 640 A SHEPHERD'S LIFE

### TWO READINGS

*Leonardo is a seventeen-year-old shepherd in Sicily*

*I*

What did I do when I was little? I played leapfrog. When I was thirteen, I hired myself out as a shepherd; my father's a shepherd, and I used to help him with his sheep; when you've been tending them for a year, you know all about them.

I've tended goats as well as sheep. There are some people that goats can't abide, but they always let me handle them.

I can't count, but even when I was a long way away, I could see if one of my goats was missing. I knew every goat in my herd—it was a big herd, but I could tell every one of them apart, I could tell which kid belonged to which mother. I've tended big flocks of sheep too—flocks of a hundred or two hundred. The master used to count them to see if they were all there, but I knew they were all there without counting.

I love sheep and my sheep love me. I watch them, follow them, pet them, coax them, pick tiny beans for them to eat, and they come right up to me—they're not timid with me. When a ewe stops cropping the grass and her udders are all hard and swollen, I know she's ready to drop a lamb. She lies down, begins to bleat, and the water breaks. If everything's going well, she stops bleating, but when I see she can't manage by herself, I make the opening bigger with my hands. The lamb's feet and its tiny muzzle appear, and the moment it's born, the mother starts to lick it clean and dry it. As soon as she's finished, she gets up, and a quarter of an hour later, the lamb gets up too, and begins to suckle. I was with my father the first time I saw a lamb born, and I helped him and so I learnt what to do at lambing-time.

I love goats. I always take them where the grass is juiciest. If they can't find anything to eat, you should hear the noise they make. When the sun blazes down at midday, they all huddle together and stand in each other's shade.

If sheep nibble the berries of lords-and-ladies, they die at once. But the berries don't poison goats, so when we see lords-and-ladies growing in a field, we drive the goats ahead; as soon as they've eaten them up, we can safely graze our sheep.

To pass the time, I make a doll out of clay, and then I set it up and throw stones at it and try to knock it down. Some shepherds have reed pipes, and they play tunes on them. I haven't got a reed pipe—I don't know how to make one. I can make clay dolls, though, and knock them down, too. It's a game that all shepherds play.

640

*2*

What are stars? I've seen them often and often, but I don't know what they are. In the picture of Jesus, there are stars. The stars are some queer sort of eyes, maybe—how can I tell what they are? The moon is the Madonna. I've heard people say that the moon's the Madonna, and that's what I say, too. The sun is Our Saviour. I pray to the moon and the sun. When it's cold, I pray to the sun to come out and when the sun comes out and it's too hot, I pray to the sun to go in. 'Warm me,' I say to the sun when I'm freezing; 'give me some light,' I say to the moon when it's dark. When the sun comes out and warms me, I'm happy, and when the moon gives me light, I'm happy too. I love to watch the moon moving about in the sky. I pray to the stars as well. 'Please shine for me,' I say. I love to watch the stars.

What I like best is going back home to my village for a day, and seeing my mother and father and sisters and brothers and all my uncles. Oh, what a time I have! But I like being amongst my animals, too, I like working. I wish I were a farmer, though, so that I could sow and reap and eat as much as I liked.

Sometimes, I pray for fine weather, or I pray that it won't rain all through the winter, or that there won't be any thunderstorms. I pray to Our Father. 'Oh, dear little Father, please don't send us bad weather,' I say to him aloud.

When the wind blows, it grows cold. The wind brings the cold. What is the wind? I see the grass swaying this way and that; and that's the wind. If it's very cold, I pray to the sun. 'Please come out and warm my animals or they'll all fall sick,' I say. My mother and father taught me to pray to the sun and the moon. All us shepherds pray to them.

I've seen clouds, but I don't know what they are. The wind blows them out of the sky.

We're in the world because we have a house in it and we work in it. We eat in it too. Why do we come into the world? To work. To eat. To work. I don't know anything else. Men grow old, everything in the world grows old, the animals grow old and so do Christians. But the sun never grows old.

Danilo Dolci, *To Feed the Hungry* (adapted)

## 641 *from* BREAD AND THE STARS

How clear the stars to-night,
All the bright heaven how still!
Under dense groves of white
This glistening sheet displays
A frost of spellbound streams.

(641)

All is at rest. I gaze
Out on the paths and beams
Of night's unresting mill.

How full the clustered sky!
Beyond the uncounted crop
Of stars I still descry
Where the white millstream runs
Glittering in ghostly race
New multitudes of suns,
While here galactic space
Hangs, like a frozen drop.

Yet men to Earth are bound,
To heats from which they grew.
They sift the stars who pound
The corn with leavening yeast
Till the whole bread is made;
And plenty crowns their feast,
Wine from a cellar's shade
Preserving all that's true.

Bread of dear life, and cup
Or glass made dull by breath,
Those spinning worlds far up
Whose fiery swarms recede,
All cannot match the weight
Of your immediate need,
Brought on a man-fired plate
To break his fast to death.

Clear night, great distances,
Faith, like a pestle, drums
Your baffling silences.
Hard though the wintry crust,
What truth has man but loaves?
Bread will compel man's trust,
And not the starry groves:
Wisdom is hid in crumbs.

Vernon Watkins, *Cypress and Acacia*

# A SOLITUDE

A blind man. I can stare at him
ashamed, shameless. Or does he know it?
No, he is in a great solitude.

O, strange joy,
to gaze my fill at a stranger's face.
No, my thirst is greater than before.

In his world he is speaking
almost aloud. His lips move.
Anxiety plays about them. And now joy

of some sort trembles into a smile.
A breeze I can't feel
crosses that face as if it crossed water.

The train moves uptown, pulls in and
pulls out of the local stops. Within its loud
jarring movement a quiet,

the quiet of people not speaking,
some of them eyeing the blind man,
only a moment though, not thirsty like me,

and within that quiet his
different quiet, not quiet at all, a tumult
of images, but what are his images,

he is blind? He doesn't care
that he looks strange, showing
his thoughts on his face like designs of light

flickering on water, for he doesn't know
what look is.
I see he has never seen.

And now he rises, he stands at the door ready,
knowing his station is next. Was he counting?
No, that was not his need.

(642)

When he gets out I get out.
'Can I help you towards the exit?'
'Oh, alright.' An indifference.

But instantly, even as he speaks,
even as I hear indifference, his hand
goes out, waiting for me to take it,

and now we hold hands like children.
His hand is warm and not sweaty,
the grip firm, it feels good.

And when we have passed through the turnstile,
he going first, his hand at once
waits for mine again.

'Here are the steps. And here we turn
to the right. More stairs now.' We go
up into the sunlight. He feels that,

the soft air. 'A nice day,
isn't it?' says the blind man. Solitude
walks with me, walks

beside me, he is not with me, he continues
his thoughts alone. But his hand and mine
know one another,

it's as if my hand were gone forth
on its own journey. I see him
across the street, the blind man,

and now he says he can find his way. He knows
where he is going, it is nowhere, it is filled
with presences. He says, *I am.*

Denise Levertov

# God and Mankind

## 643 EDEN

We do not think that there ever was a beautiful garden called 'the Garden of Eden' and that two people called Adam and Eve lived in it, but we do believe that this picture gives a true idea of the place of man in the world. Man does have power over God's world, and he does change and alter it just as a gardener changes and alters a garden by digging new flowerbeds, planting new trees and so on. There is a story told of an old man who begged a farmer for the corner of a field which the plough did not reach. This bit of the field was growing wild with brambles and thistles, and the old man got to work and turned it into an allotment. He was looking after his bit of ground with his beans and his peas looking neat and tidy in their rows when the parish priest came by. The clergyman leant on the gate and exchanged a few words, and then he looked at the man's work and said, 'Well, George, you and the Almighty have made a good job of that, haven't you?' The old man looked up, spat on the ground and said, 'You should have seen it when the Almighty had it to himself'. This story brings out very well the fact that man has a part to play in God's world: God did not make the world to run itself, he made man in the world to run it.

David Cox, *What Christians Believe*

## 644 HOSPITAL FOR DEFECTIVES

By your unnumbered charities
A miracle disclose,
Lord of the Images, whose love,
The eyelid and the rose,
Takes for a language, and today
Tell to me what is said
By these men in a turnip field
And their unleavened bread.

For all things seem to figure out
The stirrings of your heart,
And two men pick the turnips up

And two men pull the cart;
And yet between the four of them
No word is ever said
Because the yeast was not put in
Which makes the human bread.
But three men stare on vacancy
And one man strokes his knees;
What is the meaning to be found
In such dark vowels as these?

Lord of the Images, whose love,
The eyelid and the rose,
Takes for a metaphor, today
Beneath the warder's blows,
The unleavened man did not cry out
Or turn his face away;
Through such men in a turnip field
What is it that you say?

Thomas Blackburn, *Living Voices*

## 645 A BUDDHIST'S FAITH

I am a religious man. I believe in God and in the Way of Buddha, and in my home I have always had a prayer-corner or prayer-room, which is the Buddhist custom. But I am not an orthodox man. I do not believe greatly in ritual, and not at all in superstition. In my life I have been on too many mountains to think that they are the home of demons. Nor do I put much stock in ghosts; and, indeed, a few years ago, I used to go out searching—unsuccessfully—for a much-talked-of lady ghost who was supposed to be haunting Toong Soong Busti. Also, and more seriously, I have known too many men of other faiths to believe that they are all wrong and Buddhists alone are all right. I am not an educated man—not a lama or scholar who can speak of matters of theology. But I feel that there is room on earth for many faiths, as for many races and nations. It is with God Himself as it is with a great mountain. The important thing is to come to Him not with fear, but with love.

*Man of Everest*, The Autobiography of Tenzing, told to James Ramsey Ullman

## 646 LOOK AT THE FACTS

When you are studying any matter or considering any philosophy, ask yourself only what are the facts and what is the truth that the facts bear out. Never let yourself be diverted either by what you would wish to believe or by what you think would have beneficial social effects if it were believed. But look only at what are the facts.

Bertrand Russell

## 647 AMEN

And God said: How do you know?
And I went out into the fields
At morning and it was true.

Nothing denied it, neither the bowed man
On his knees, nor the animals,
Nor the birds notched on the sky's

Surface. His heart was broken
Far back, and the beasts yawned
Their boredom. Under the song

Of the larks, I heard the wheels turn
Rustily. But the scene held;
The cold landscape returned my stare;

There was no answer. Accept; accept.
And under the green capitals,
The molecules and the blood's virus.

R. S. Thomas, *Pieta*

## 648 GOD AS OUR FATHER

When I find it hard to believe in a Personal God who can be called 'Father'—and who doesn't sometimes?—I always find myself pulled up short by the fact of human personality. I can't for the life of me see how personality could have been produced by a process that was merely mechanistic and impersonal. Could a being capable of love and reason and imagination somehow come from a machine which could not think or feel? Could man have emerged from the evolutionary process as the result of 'a chance accident in a backwater'?

Leslie J. Tizard, *Facing Life and Death*

649

## DON'T BE A LAZY BUM

*Advice to the Sluggard, Proverbs 6.6–19*

Take a look at the ants on the sidewalk.
Think about how they work
And you'll be with it, man.

They don't got a worker to
Check up on them—right!

They gets their own food
Then puts it away till they needs it.
Don't need no government surplus stuff.

So don't be a lazy bum
And sleep all day—
Get up and go shine shoes.

Sleep's a good thing at night,
But too much is too much—
And a lazy cat end up
on welfare—
It just sneaks up on you.

A lazy guy
Is like a hood—
You can't believe anything
He says.

He's got shifty pincers,
Always blaming someone
For his troubles,

Always trying to con a guy
And stirring up trouble.

Then before he knows what happened
Bingo—
It's too late to straighten up.

There are six things that are
No go with God:
1. Shifty pincers
2. Con artists
3. Hands that are always
Beating up on someone
4. An operator who thinks up a job
5. A stool pigeon
6. A cat who stirs up trouble.
These kind of guys are 'no go' with God.

Carl Burke, *God is for Real, Man*

650

## GODS MADE WITH HANDS

### THREE READINGS

*I*

What shape is an idol?

I worship Ganesa, brother, god of worldly wisdom, patron of shopkeepers. He is in the shape of a little fat man with an elephant's head; he is made of soapstone and has two small rubies for eyes. What shape do you worship?

I worship a Rolls-Royce sports model, brother. All my days I give it offerings of oil and polish. Hours of my time are devoted to its ritual; and it brings me luck in all my undertakings; and it establishes me among my fellows as a success in life. What model is your car, brother?

I worship my house beautiful, sister. Long and loving meditation have I spent on it; the chairs contrast with the rug, the curtains harmonize with the woodwork, all of it is perfect and holy. The ash trays are in exactly the right place, and should some blasphemer drop ashes on the floor, I nearly die of shock. I live only for the service of my house, and it rewards me with the envy of my sisters, who must rise and call me blessed. Lest my children profane the holiness of my house with dirt and noise, I drive them out of doors. What shape is your idol, sister? Is it your house, or your clothes, or perhaps even your worth-while and cultural club?

I worship the pictures I paint, brother. . . . I worship my job; I'm the best darn publicity expert this side of Hollywood. . . . I worship my golf game, my bridge game. . . . I worship my comfort; after all, isn't enjoyment the goal of life?. . . . I worship my church; I want to tell you, the work we've done in missions beats all other denominations in this city, and next year we can afford that new organ, and you won't find a better choir anywhere. . . . I worship myself. . . .

What shape is *your* idol?

650

*2*

What shape is an idol?

Need it be a man shape or a beast shape? May it not be any possible shape men can devise—anything from a dynamo to a mink coat—as long as you look to it for your salvation.

An idol is worshipped, not for its shape, but for its imagined power. The scribes and Pharisees did not succeed in stopping idolatry; they only changed its vocabulary. Instead of asking a man-shape for help, we now 'look for the salvation of society to the proper harnessing of the forces of the atom'. There are still some who kneel before images, making small offerings and promising big ones, begging for their heart's desire and watching the painted plaster face for miraculous smiles or tears. But most of us modern Christian idolaters worship gadgets instead of images. We will be happy if only we can buy the new television set or the new patent washing-machine. Lenin thought the salvation of Russia lay in electric power; Americans, having tried the dynamo in vain, now look further—to the mysterious powers of the cyclotron. The greatest idol of our time has the shape of a mushroom cloud.

*3*

650

Does it matter which of our toys we make into a god? What matters is that the thing is still a toy, an idol—a material object on which we rely to bring us happiness. Idolatry's other name is materialism. As long as we hope to be saved by the work of our own hands, we remain idolaters and the Second Commandment applies to us literally. What shape has your idol, brother? It may be quite primitive still—a rabbit's foot set in a cheap brass mounting. Or it may be subtle and civilized—a radiation perceptible only to the electron microscope. Whatever men have made, that they may worship; there are men who worship modern plumbing and hope to redeem China and India with the flush toilet.

All sins, theologians tell us, are entering wedges for the great and ultimate sin of self-worship. Why should I prefer to worship a small and limited idol, rather than a great and universal God? Perhaps because I can *own* the idol, whereas no man can own God, whose justice is incorruptible. Tom's elephant godling is supposed to answer Tom's prayers, not Dick's; and Dick's snake fetish is expected to protect Dick against Harry. The great and universal God, however, loves all men alike—how, then, dare I ask him to help me get the better of my competitors? But my Rolls-Royce sports car confers glory upon me alone, not on the lesser breeds without Rolls-Royces. Mrs. Jones's perfectly appointed house gratifies Mrs. Jones precisely because Mrs. Robinson, who lives next door, hasn't got it.

Joy Davidman, *Smoke on the Mountain*

## 651 TRUST IN GOD

If you have doubts about the existence of God or misgivings as to the kind of God He is, I do not think your need will be met by argument. It will be met only by an act of trust on your part. You must be willing to be found by the pursuing love of God which will not let you go; to face the challenge which is relentless; to move out fearlessly from your narrow self-centred life into a new, wide, spacious life with Christ at the centre—trusting not in yourself but in the all-sufficient love and power of God.

Leslie J. Tizard, *Facing Life and Death*

652

## PLAYING IT COOL

*How to Keep out of a Fight, Proverbs 15.1–7*

Playing it cool
  Will keep you out of a fight without losing face.
    But shooting your mouth off
      Will get another guy all teed up,
        And he will climb all over you.

Sometimes what a square says may be right
  And he may know something.
    It might be a good idea to listen.

A hood is always sounding off,
  Mostly about things he don't know anything about.

God is everywhere keeping watch
  And he is ready to help you.

But a fool don't pay no attention—
  He thinks
    Nobody knows anything but him.

Carl Burke, *God is for Real, Man*

# Attitudes to God, to Life and to Ourselves

653

## A CHILD'S CHARACTER

I understand more and more how true Daddy's words were when he said, 'All children must look after their own upbringing.' Parents can only give good advice or put them on the right paths, but the final forming of a person's character lies in his own hands.

*The Diary of Anne Frank*

When I was thirteen my father gave up the farm, sold off his stock and farm implements, and went to live in a small house in Kirkwall.

My year in Kirkwall was drab and sordid. I had reached the stage when boys stick together to hide the shame of their inexperience, and turn without knowing it against their parents and the laws of the house. My rough friendships were an indirect challenge to my father and mother, a hidden gesture of rebellion. I played a great deal of football; it was as if my body demanded explosive action. The place where we played was called the Craftie; it was a little field of grass, worn bare in patches, close by the slaughter-house. To us in our raw and unhappy state the slaughter-house had an abominable attraction, and the strong stench and sordid colours of blood and intestines seemed to follow us in our play. Our language and manners grew rough; even our friendship had an acrid flavour. There were savage fights in the Craftie, and the boys, crying with rage, would have killed each other if they could; yet behind their fury there was a sort of sad shame and frustration.

I do not know why boys of this age, the age of awakening puberty, should turn against everything that was pleasant in their lives before and rend it in a fit of crude cynicism. Perhaps it comes from their first distorted knowledge of the actual world, which is not the world of childhood, and a divination that all their childish games in which they played at being grown-up were of no use, something sterner being needed. Or it may be merely that I was unlucky in my friends, for I had far less worldly knowledge at the time than town boys of my age, and I was always perfectly prepared to be friendly with anyone who was friendly with me. I remember one fine summer day spent with another boy in wandering along the Wideford Burn, picking flowers and looking at birds' nests, without a single rough word. Why did I not have more days like that one in which I was perfectly happy, instead of all those days in the Craftie, when I was really miserable, though I did not know it? The Craftie seemed to hypnotize us; we kicked the football in hatred; there was a deep enmity in the bond between us.

Edwin Muir, *An Autobiography*

## 655 BUILDING A BOAT

Hughie o'Habreck, who was a skilled joiner as well as a farmer, came to build a yawl for my father. He was thickset and very strong, with a deep, rumbling voice and mutton-chop whiskers: a slow, consequential man who whenever he spoke seemed to be delivering a verdict, so that people were always asking his advice. He would stand over the growing boat and deliberate for a long time on what he should do next, at last saying in a judicial voice, as if he had just convinced himself, 'We'll do this now,' or 'We'll do that now.' He was never in a hurry; he sawed and planed and chiselled in a particular way of his own, absorbed in the thought of the boat, as if there were nothing but it and himself in the world, and his relation to it had a complete, objective intimacy. I cannot remember much about the actual building of the boat, except for the bending of the boards in steam, the slow growth of the sides as one smooth ply of wood was set on another, the sides bulging in a more swelling curve from bow to stern as the days passed in delicious slowness, the curly shavings, the scent of wood and resin, and a pot of bubbling tar into which you could thrust your hand without being burned if you dipped your hand in water first. The boat was eventually finished, and my brothers often went out in it in the evenings to fish, taking me with them.

Edwin Muir, *An Autobiography*

## 656 THE MEANING OF LIFE

What is the meaning of human life, or, for that matter, of the life of any creature? To know an answer to this question means to be religious. You ask: Does it make any sense, then, to pose this question? I answer: The man who regards his own life and that of his fellow creatures as meaningless is not merely unhappy but hardly fit for life.

Albert Einstein, *Mein Weltbild*

## 657 HEAVEN AND HELL

Heaven comes as a gift, to be accepted, not pursued;
Hell is your own choice, or, sometimes, your neighbour's.

Hell is seeing alone what you did as a mob;
Hell is the fall that comes after your pride;
Hell is letting your parents down;
Hell is envying someone else's lot;
Hell is seeing time slipping away;
Hell is the hurt look in someone's eye;
Hell is war, in its waste and futility;
Hell is seeing yourself through someone else's eyes.

> Heaven comes as a gift, to be accepted, not pursued;
> Hell is your own choice, or, sometimes, your neighbour's.

Heaven is real friendship;
Heaven is being lost in a book;
Heaven is arduous training;
Heaven is a happy marriage;
Heaven is music which says it for you;
Heaven is someone else's success;
Heaven is a letter from home;
Heaven is work well done.

> Heaven comes as a gift, to be accepted, not pursued; if you chase it, you lose it.
> Hell is your own choice, or, sometimes, your neighbour's.

Laurence Ellis

## 658 A GIRL LISTENING TO MUSIC

### TWO READINGS

*I*

The radio was on as usual. For a second she stood by the window and watched the people inside. Then she sat on the ground. This was a very fine and secret place. Close around were thick cedars so that she was completely hidden by herself. The radio was no good tonight—somebody sang popular songs that all ended in the same way. It was like she was empty. She reached in her pockets and felt around with her fingers. There were raisins and a string of beads—one cigarette with matches. She lighted the cigarette

(658 *1*) and put her arms around her knees. It was like she was so empty there wasn't even a feeling or thought in her.

One programme came on after another, and all of them were punk. She didn't especially care. She smoked and picked a little bunch of grass blades. After a while a new announcer started talking. He mentioned Beethoven. She had read in the library about that musician—his name was pronounced with an *a* and spelled with double *e*. He was a German fellow like Mozart. When he was living he spoke in a foreign language and lived in a foreign place—like she wanted to do. The announcer said they were going to play his third symphony. She only half-way listened because she wanted to walk some more and she didn't care much what they played. Then the music started. Mick raised her head and her fist went up to her throat.

How did it come? For a minute the opening balanced from one side to the other. Like a walk or march. Like God strutting in the night. The outside of her was suddenly froze and only that first part of the music was hot inside her heart. She could not even hear what sounded after, but she sat there waiting and froze, with her fists tight. After a while the music came again, harder and loud. It didn't have anything to do with God. This was her, Mick Kelly, walking in the day-time and by herself at night. In the hot sun and in the dark with all the plans and feelings. This music was her—the real plain her.

She could not listen good enough to hear it all. The music boiled inside her. Which? To hang on to certain wonderful parts and think them over so that later she would not forget—or should she let go and listen to each part that came without thinking or trying to remember? Golly! The whole world was this music and she could not listen hard enough. Then at last the opening music came again, with all the different instruments bunched together for each note like a hard, tight fist that socked at her heart. And the first part was over.

This music did not take a long time or a short time. It did not have anything to do with time going by at all. She sat with her arms held tight around her legs, biting her salty knee very hard. It might have been five minutes she listened or half the night. The second part was black-coloured—a slow march. Not sad, but like the whole world was dead and black and there was no use thinking back how it was before. One of those horn kind of instruments played a sad and silver tune. Then the music rose up angry and with excitement underneath. And finally the black march again.

But maybe the last part of the symphony was the music she loved the best—glad and like the greatest people in the world running and springing up in a hard, free way. Wonderful music like this was the worst hurt there could be. The whole world was this symphony, and there was not enough of her to listen.



*2*

It was over, and she sat very stiff with her arms around her knees. Another programme came on the radio and she put her fingers in her ears. The music left only this bad hurt in her, and a blankness. She could not remember any of the symphony, not even the last few notes. She tried to remember, but no sound at all came to her. Now that it was over there was only her heart like a rabbit and this terrible hurt.

The radio and the lights in the house were turned off. The night was very dark. Suddenly Mick began hitting her thigh with her fists. She pounded the same muscle with all her strength until the tears came down her face. But she could not feel this hard enough. The rocks under the bush were sharp. She grabbed a handful of them and began scraping them up and down on the same spot until her hand was bloody. Then she fell back to the ground and lay looking up at the night. With the fiery hurt in her leg she felt better. She was limp on the wet grass, and after a while her breath came slow and easy again.

Why hadn't the explorers known by looking at the sky that the world was round? The sky was curved, like the inside of a huge glass ball, very dark blue with the sprinkles of bright stars. The night was quiet. There was the smell of warm cedars. She was not trying to think of the music at all when it came back to her. The first part happened in her mind just as it had been played. She listened in a quiet, slow way and thought the notes out like a problem in geometry so she would remember. She could see the shape of the sounds very clear and she would not forget them.

Now she felt good. She whispered some words out loud: 'Lord forgiveth me, for I knoweth not what I do.' Why did she think of that? Everybody in the past few years knew there wasn't any real God. When she thought of what she used to imagine was God she could only see the deaf mute, Mister Singer, with a long, white sheet around him. God was silent—maybe that was why she was reminded. She said the words again, just as she would speak them to Mister Singer: 'Lord forgiveth me, for I knoweth not what I do.'

This part of the music was beautiful and clear. She could sing it now whenever she wanted to. Maybe later on, when she had just waked up some morning, more of the music would come back to her. If ever she heard the symphony again there would be other parts to add to what was already in her mind. And maybe if she could hear it four more times, just four more times, she would know it all. Maybe.

Once again she listened to this opening part of the music. Then the notes grew slower and soft and it was like she was sinking down slowly into the dark ground.

Carson McCullers, *The Heart is a Lonely Hunter* (adapted)

## 659 THE MOUNTAINS LEAD TO GOD

When I had actually started to climb, the initial time was busy with the mechanics of the new world, with the exhilarating novelty of the beauty seen from a different angle, with the new friendships, and all this compounded the attraction of the hills at that period. Later, when I came to the harder routes, I found something else, a new state of mind. This was a sudden and overwhelmingly powerful sensation of humility and gratitude, so real that I could only interpret it as being directed towards a creator. I had never been able to arrive at such a conviction through a process of reason, yet here I was forced to accept it, despite myself, through the very certainty and intensity of these emotions. I can only define such experience by using the word mystical; a manifestation of nature-mysticism: my particular relationship with the mountain, the natural order, had resulted in a profound apprehension of a transcendent order. It was the knowledge of God in his creatures. I would emphasise that the first time this experience was manifest I had made no conscious effort to achieve it; there was no act of contemplation. It just happened when I was coiling up the rope at the end of a climb; as prosaic as that.

John Emery, *The Runcible Cat*

We had with us a little store of medicines—a hundred grammes of ninety per cent alcohol, the same of pure ether, and a small bottle of iodine. I tried to swallow a little of the ether: it was like swallowing a knife. Then I tried the alcohol: it contracted my gullet. I dug a pit in the sand, lay down in it, and flung handfuls of sand over me until all but my face was buried in it.

Do not blame me if the human body cannot go three days without water. I should never have believed that man was so truly the prisoner of the springs and freshets. I had no notion that our self-sufficiency was so circumscribed. We take it for granted that a man is able to stride straight out into the world. We believe that man is free. We never see the cord that binds him to wells and fountains, that umbilical cord by which he is tied to the womb of the world. Let man take but one step too many and the cord snaps.

I have nothing to complain of. For three days I have tramped the desert, have known the pangs of thirst, have followed false scents in the sand, have pinned my faith on the dew. I have struggled to rejoin my kind, whose very existence on earth I had forgotten. These are the cares of men alive in every fibre, and I cannot help thinking them more important than the fretful choosing of a night-club in which to spend the evening. Compare the one life with the other, and all things considered this is luxury! I have no regrets. I have gambled and lost. It was all in the day's work. At least I have had the unforgettable taste of the sea on my lips.

I am not talking about living dangerously. Such words are meaningless to me. The toreador does not stir me to enthusiasm. It is not danger I love. I know what I love. It is life.

Antoine de Saint-Exupery, *Wind, Sand and Stars*

## 661 HOW TO ENJOY THE WORLD

THREE READINGS

*I*

Your Enjoyment of the World is never right, till you so Esteem it, that evry thing in it, is more your Treasure, then a Kings

Exchequer full of Gold and Silver. And that Exchequer yours also in its Place and Service. Can you take too much Joy in your fathers Works? He is Himself in evry Thing. Som Things are little on the outside, and Rough and Common: but I remember the Time, when the Dust of the Streets were as precious as Gold to my Infant Eys, and now they are more precious to the Ey of Reason.

661 *2*

You never Enjoy the World aright, till the Sea it self floweth in your Veins, till you are Clothed with the Heavens, and Crowned with the Stars: and perceiv your self to be the Sole Heir of the whole World: and more then so, becaus Men are in it who are evry one Sole Heirs, as well as you. Till you can sing and Rejoyce and Delight in GOD, as Misers do in Gold, and Kings in Scepters, you never Enjoy the World.

661 *3*

Till your Spirit filleth the whole World, and the Stars are your Jewels, till you are as Familiar with the Ways of God in all Ages as with your Walk and Table: till you are intimatly Acquainted with that Shady Nothing out of which the World was made: till you lov Men so as to Desire their Happiness, with a Thirst equal to the zeal of your own: till you Delight in GOD for being Good to all: you never Enjoy the World. Till you more feel it then your Privat Estate, and are more present in the Hemisphere, Considering the Glories and the Beauties there, then in your own Hous. Till you remember how lately you were made, and how wonderfull it was when you came into it: and more rejoyce in the Palace of your Glory, than if it had been made but to Day Morning.

Thomas Traherne, *Poems, Centuries and Three Thanksgivings*

662 REALITY

There is a reality outside the world, that is to say, outside space and time, outside man's mental universe, outside any sphere whatsoever that is accessible to human faculties.

Corresponding to this reality, at the centre of the human heart, is the longing for an absolute good, a longing which is always there and is never appeased by any object in this world.

Just as the reality of this world is the sole foundation of facts, so that other reality is the sole foundation of good.

That reality is the unique source of all the good that can exist in this world: that is to say, all beauty, all truth, all justice, all legitimacy, all order, and all human behaviour that is mindful of obligations.

Simone Weil, *Selected Essays, 1934–1943*

## 663 PLEASURE

Pleasure is a freedom-song,
But it is not freedom.
It is the blossoming of your desires,
But it is not their fruit.
It is a depth calling unto a height,
But it is not the deep nor the high.
It is the caged taking wing,
But it is not space encompassed.
Ay, in very truth, pleasure is a freedom-song.

And I fain would have you sing it with fullness of heart; yet I would not have you lose your hearts in the singing.

Some of your youth seek pleasure as if it were all, and they are judged and rebuked.

I would not judge nor rebuke them. I would have them seek.

For they shall find pleasure, but not her alone;

Seven are her sisters, and the least of them is more beautiful than pleasure.

Have you not heard of the man who was digging in the earth for roots and found a treasure?

Kahlil Gibran, *The Prophet*

## 664 HOW TO WASTE WISELY MY DAYS

To awaken each morning with a smile brightening my face; to greet the day with reverence for the opportunities it contains; to approach my work with a clean mind; to hold ever before me, even in the doing of little things, the Ultimate Purpose toward which I am working; to meet men and women with laughter on my lips and love in my heart; to be gentle, kind, and courteous through all the hours; to approach the night with weariness that ever woos sleep, and the joy that comes from work well done—this is how I desire to waste wisely my days.

Thomas Dekker

## 665 KICKING AT OUR DESTINY

Not only those who suffer cruelly, like Christ, but all of us, however soft our circumstances to an outward eye, kick at the destiny to which we are tied, and wriggle on the nails of our easy crucifixion. 'If only I were somewhere else—if I were untied from this difficult marriage—if I were released from this routine—if I could be freed from anxiety—if my health did not cramp my spirits—if only . . . then,' we say, not merely, which is obvious, 'I should be more comfortable,' but, 'then I could begin to do something, instead of merely existing; then,' we may even dare to say, 'then I could do something for God.' This is the great deception of the devil, to stop us loving, praying, working, now. It may be God's will you should fight your way out of your misfortunes; it cannot be his will that you should make them a reason to put off living as a child of God.

Austin Farrer, *Lord I Believe*

## 666 GETTING WHAT WE WANT

Life is so constituted, that many things we deeply desire we get. Our personalities and possibilities are moulded by the act of asking. 'Take what you want, and pay for it, says God'; so runs the Spanish proverb. In this we may see the inexorable judgement of God's love. Many of our most futile prayers are attempts to dodge the divinely established fact that we reap what we sow.

David Head, *He Sent Leanness*

## 667 GIVING

You give but little when you give of your possessions.

It is when you give of yourself that you truly give.

For what are your possessions but things you keep and guard for fear you may need them to-morrow?

And to-morrow, what shall to-morrow bring to the over-prudent dog burying bones in the trackless sand as he follows the pilgrims to the holy city?

And what is fear of need but need itself?

Is not dread of thirst when your well is full, the thirst that is unquenchable?

There are those who give little of the much which they have—and they give it for recognition and their hidden desire makes their gifts unwholesome.

And there are those who have little and give it all. These are the believers in life and the bounty of life, and their coffer is never empty.

There are those who give with joy, and that joy is their reward.

And there are those who give with pain, and that pain is their baptism.

And there are those who give and know not pain in giving, nor do they seek joy, nor give with mindfulness of virtue;

They give as in yonder valley the myrtle breathes its fragrance into space.

Through the hands of such as these God speaks, and from behind their eyes He smiles upon the earth.

Kahlil Gibran, *The Prophet*

## 668 THANKSGIVING FOR THE SOUL

TWO READINGS

*I*

*The Soul's Power to Comprehend Past, Present and Future*

So strangely glorious
Hast thou made my Soul:
That even Yesterday is present
To mine inward eye,

Infancy,
The days of my { Childhood,
Old Age.
We have
An endless Liberty.
Being able to see, walk, be present there,
Where neither the Eagles eye, nor the Lions thought can at all approach.
The deeds of our Progenitors,
Their Lives and Persons;
Thy ways among the Ancients,
The services of the Sun in all Generations,
The sun of Righteousness in his Rising and Eclipse;
The Creation of the World,
And the Government of Kingdoms,
Can we behold;
The day of Judgment,
The Delights of Ages,
The Sphere of time.
Nor will that contain us.
An infinite liberty we find beyond them;
Can walk in thine Eternity,
All at large;
In every moment see it wholly,
Know every where,
That from everlasting to everlasting thou art God:
Whose everlasting Glory is the Treasure of my Soul,
And thine eternal continuance a permanent
NOW;
With all its Contents
For ever enjoyed.

668 *2*

*The Soul's Power to Discern All Things and to Behold God*

A Body endless, though endued with Sense,
Can see
Only visible things,
Taste
The Qualities in Meat and Drink,

568 2) Feel
Gross or tangible Bodies,
Hear
The harshness or melody of Sounds,
Smell
The things that have Odours in them.
But those things which neither Sight, nor Smell, nor Taste, can discern, nor Feeling try, nor Ear apprehend,
The Cream and Crown and Flower of all,
Thoughts, Counsels,
Kingdoms, Ages,
Angels, Cherubims,
The Souls of Men,
Wisdom, Holiness,
Dominion, Soveraignty,
Honour, Glory,
Goodness, Blessedness,
Heroick Love,
yea
GOD HIMSELF,
Come not within the sphere of Sense:
Are all Nullities to such a Creature.
Only Souls, immortal Souls, are denied nothing.
All things are penetrable to the Soul of Man.
All things open and naked to it.
The Understanding seeth
Their { Natures,
Uses,
Extents,
Relations,
Ends,
Properties,
Services,
Even all their Excellencies.
And thee my God is she able to behold,
Who dwellest in her,
In all the Spaces of thy great Immensity;
To accompany thy Goodness, and see whatsoever thy hand is doing.

Thomas Traherne, *Poems, Centuries and Three Thanksgivings*

## 669 ENERGY

Many of the parables commend energy. The real trouble with men, Jesus seems to say, is again and again sheer slackness; they will not put their minds to the thing before them, whether it be thought or action. Thus, for instance, the parable of the talents praises energetic thinking and decisive action; and these are the things that Jesus admires—in the widow who *will* have justice—in the virgins who have thought ahead and bought extra oil—in the vigorous man who found the treasure and made sure of it—in the friend at midnight who hammered, hammered, hammered, till he got his loaves—in the 'violent' who 'take the Kingdom of Heaven by force'—in the man who will hack off his hand to enter into life. Even the bad steward he commends, because he definitely put his mind to the situation. Indecision is one of the things that in the judgement of Jesus will keep a man outside the Kingdom of God, that make him unfit for it.

T. R. Glover, *The Jesus of History* (adapted)

## 670 SELF-SATISFACTION

A man does not have to be unfaithful to his wife or dishonest in his dealings or anti-social in any other way in order to be a sinner. He has only to be satisfied with himself. It is unlikely that the Pharisee in the gospel was anything other than a thoroughly high-principled person. The basic trouble was that he had never made the effort to break through the crust of what he thought himself to be until he came upon the truth of what he really was. But there was hope for the tax-gatherer because he knew he was a sinner and was sorry.

William Purcell, *The Plain Man Looks at Himself* (adapted)

## 671 THE WHOLE TROUBLE—ORIGINAL SIN

Lucy says to Charlie Brown:

'You know what the whole trouble with you is, Charlie Brown?'

'No; and I don't want to know! Leave me alone!'

'The whole trouble with you is you won't listen to what the whole trouble with you is!'

But Lucy is not such a good listener either. On another occasion she tells Charlie Brown, 'The whole trouble with you is you don't understand the meaning of life!' 'Do *you* understand the meaning of life?' he asks her. Her reply: 'We're not talking about me, we're talking about you!'

Robert Short, *The Gospel According to Peanuts* (adapted)

672

## HAPPINESS AND VISION

*William Blake, who wrote this, was an artist, a mystic and a poet*

I feel that a man may be happy in this world and I know that this world is a world of imagination and vision. I see everything I paint in this world but everybody does not see alike. To the eye of a miser a guinea is far more beautiful than the sun and a bag worn with the use of money has more beautiful proportions than a vine filled with grapes. The tree which moves some to tears of joy is in the eyes of others only a green thing which stands in the way. As a man is, so he sees.

When the sun rises, do you not see a round disk of fire something like a gold piece? O no, no, I see an innumerable company of the Heavenly host crying 'Holy, Holy, Holy, is the Lord God Almighty.' I do not question my bodily eye any more than I would question a window concerning sight. I look through it and not with it.

William Blake

673

## LOVE, HOPE AND FAITH: MATTERS OF THE WILL

By Love, I mean respect for and goodwill to the unique value of every human being, male or female, black or white, Christian or pagan, Top person or bottom dog; and action based upon acceptance, at all times, of this equality. Love is the opposite of hate and its practise is a matter of choice—a matter of the will.

By Hope, I mean the determination to continue believing that the good wins and that therefore individual effort is worth while. Hope is the opposite of apathy and nihilism, and its practise is a matter of choice—a matter of the will.

By Faith I mean openness to the future and resolute acceptance of whatever is coming to me out of the surrounding darkness. Faith is the opposite of despair; is not to be confused with knowledge; and its practise is a matter of the will—a matter of choice.

We can really choose to be faithful, and loving and hopeful, rather than despairing and lazy and callous; it really is a matter of the will.

Mrs. Kay M. Baxter

## 674 HUMAN BEINGS WITHOUT LOVE

People think there are circumstances when one may deal with human beings without love, but no such circumstances ever exist. Inanimate objects may be dealt with without love: we may fell trees, bake bricks, hammer iron without love. But human beings cannot be handled without love, any more than bees can be handled without care. That is the nature of bees. If you handle bees carelessly you will harm the bees and yourself as well. And so it is with people. And it cannot be otherwise, because mutual love is the fundamental law of human life. It is true that a man cannot force himself to love in the way he can force himself to work, but it does not follow from this that men may be treated without love, especially if something is required from them. If you feel no love—leave people alone. Occupy yourself with things, with yourself, with anything you like, only not with men. Just as one can eat without harm and profitably only when one is hungry, so can one usefully and without injury deal with men only when one loves them. But once a man allows himself to treat men unlovingly, there are no limits to the cruelty and brutality he may inflict on others.

L. N. Tolstoy, *Resurrection*

## 675 THE IDEALISM OF YOUTH

Grown-up people reconcile themselves too willingly to a supposed duty of preparing young ones for the time when they will regard as illusion what is now an inspiration to heart and mind. It is through the idealism of youth that man catches sight of truth, and in that idealism he possesses a wealth which he must never exchange for anything else. Grow into your ideals so that life can never rob you of them.

At the present time when violence, clothed in life, dominates the world more cruelly than it ever has before, I still remain convinced that truth, love, peaceableness, meekness, and kindness are the *violence* that can master all other violence.

Albert Schweitzer, *Memoirs of Youth*

## 676 IDEALS

The old Biblical saying, 'Man does not live by bread alone', has never had a more convincing ring than it has today.

Some great thinker once said that man is an animal with a capacity for dreaming. Some people's lives only seem to prove the first part of this proposition. Yet if we look into their hearts we find that, though they have no lofty dreams, they yet dream of dreaming them.

Even a rich man is sad if he has no ideals. He may try to hide his sadness from himself and from others, but his efforts only make him sadder still.

And if even the rich are sad if they have no ideals, to those everlastingly deprived, ideals are a prime necessity. Where bread is plentiful and ideals are short, bread is not a substitute for an ideal. But where bread is short, an ideal can be bread. Simply because such is human nature—because man is a born idealist. And great ideals are born of great suffering.

Yevgeny Yevtushenko, *A Precocious Autobiography*

## 677 MAN AFIRE IN STREET IGNORED

A man whose clothes were on fire staggered from an alley shouting for help and was ignored by people in the street until a coloured man took off his jacket and smothered the flames, the Newcastle upon Tyne deputy coroner, Mr. Wilfred-Kilner, was told at an inquest yesterday.

Mr. George Charles Browning, aged 63, of West Parade, Newcastle, was set alight when he and two workmates were caught in a spray of burning oil from a switch at an electricity sub-station in Fourth Lane, Newcastle, on July 29. The jury returned a verdict of Accidental Death on Percy Redhead, aged 64, of Talbot Green, Newcastle, and Joseph Gibbons, aged 62, of Chicken Road, Wallsend, both electrical fitter's mates, who died from burns and shock.

Police-Sergeant Matthew Rowley said Mr. Browning was still in hospital. He had said that there was a big flash and a muffled explosion:

'Joe and Percy were lying there, but I couldn't do anything for them because I was myself in flames. I managed to get to Westgate Road, burning and yelling for help to a lot of people, but everybody ignored me. It was a coloured man, I think a Pakistani, who took off his jacket and put the flames out.'

*The Times*, 6th September 1968

## 678 SELF-DENIAL

Self-renunciation does not necessarily result in self-realisation. It depends on the object for which we make the sacrifice and the spirit in which it is made. Everybody who really wants something in life practises self-denial in one way or another simply because, in this life, we can't have everything. But there is nothing particularly praiseworthy in spending less on beer in order that you may put more on horses, or in denying yourself the pleasures of home life in order that you may make more money when you have enough already. And I am not sure that some people, who have given up all that life had to offer them in order to minister to the whims and selfishness of tyrannical, possessive people, had any right to make that self-martyrdom.

Nor again, does self-realization necessarily come from utter devotion to a cause. There has probably never been a better example of complete self-abandonment to a cause than that of Nazi youth, and yet the complete Nazi is a caricature of a human personality. True self-realization comes only when we give ourselves for what is supremely good.

Leslie J. Tizard, *Facing Life and Death*

## 679 GETTING AWAY FROM SIN

Within the Christian body, for which repentance of sins has from the beginning been the critical religious act, healthy-mindedness has always come forward with its milder interpretation. Repentance according to such healthy-minded Christians means getting away from the sin, not groaning and writhing over its commission.

William James, *The Varieties of Religious Experience*

## 680 CONSCIENCE

It is true that ideas of what is right and wrong vary from age to age and from place to place, but the significant thing is the abiding conviction that there *is* a distinction between right and wrong. The inner compulsion to do right and the shame we feel when we are aware of having done wrong are an experience of God.

Leslie J. Tizard, *Facing Life and Death*

# The Body

## 681 THANKSGIVING FOR THE BODY

TWO READINGS

*I*

O what Praises are due unto thee,
Who hast made me
A living Inhabitant
Of the great World.
And the Centre of it!
A sphere of Sense,
And a mine of Riches,
Which when Bodies are dissected fly away.
The spacious Room
Which thou hast hidden in mine Eye,
The Chambers for Sounds
Which thou hast prepar'd in mine Ear,

The Receptacles for Smells
Concealed in my Nose;
The feeling of my Hands,
The taste of my Tongue.
But above all, O Lord, the Glory of Speech, whereby thy Servant is enabled with Praise to celebrate thee.
For
All the Beauties in Heaven and Earth,
The melody of Sounds,
The sweet Odours
Of thy Dwelling-place.
The delectable pleasures that gratifie my Sense,
That gratify the feeling of Mankind.
The Light of History,
Admitted by the Ear.
The Light of Heaven,
Brought in by the Eye.
The Versatility and Liberty
Of my Hands and Members.
Fitted by thee for all Operations;
Which the Fancy can imagine,
Or Soul desire:
From the framing of a Needle's Eye,
To the building of a Tower:
From the squaring of Trees,
To the polishing of Kings Crowns.
For all the Mysteries, Engines, Instruments, wherewith the World is filled, which we are able to frame and use to thy Glory.

681 *2*

Every thing in thy Kingdom, O Lord,
Conspireth to mine Exaltation.
In every thing I see thy Wisdom and Goodness.
And I praise the Power by which I see it.
My body is but the Cabinet, or Case of my Soul:
What then, O Lord, shall the Jewel be!
Thou makest it the heir of all the profitable trades and occupations in the World.
And the Heavens and the Earth
More freely mine,
More profitably,

81 *2*)

More gloriously,
More comfortably
Than if no man were alive but I alone.
Yea though I am a Sinner, thou lovest me more than if thou hadst given all things to me alone.
The sons of men thou hast made my treasures,
Those Lords,
Incarnate Cherubims,
Angels of the World,
The Cream of all things,
And the sons of God,
Hast thou given to me, and made them mine,
For endless Causes ever to be enjoyed.
Were I alone,
Briars and thorns would devour me;
Wild beasts annoy me;
My Guilt terrifie me;
The World it self be a Desart to me;
The Skies a Dungeon,
But mine Ignorance more.
The Earth a Wilderness;
All things desolate:
And I in solitude,
Naked and hungry,
Blind and brutish,
Without house or harbour;
Subject unto storms;
Lying upon the ground;
Feeding upon roots;
But more upon melancholy,
Because void of thee.
Therefore thou providest for me, and for me they build, and get and provide for me
My Bread, Drink,
Clothes, Bed,
My Household stuff, { Books, Utensils, Furniture.
The use of Meats, Fire, Fuel, etc.
They teach unto me, provide for me.

Thomas Traherne, *Poems, Centuries and Three Thanksgivings*

682 **DEAFNESS**

TWO READINGS

*1*

## *Hearing and Speaking*

The ear is a very delicate piece of mechanism. First there is the drum, which waves of sound coming through the air cause to vibrate. These vibrations cause a little chain of bones to move. The bones are hinged together and so tiny that they are about the size of half a grain of barley. The third one of these bones touches a membrane stretched across a cavity which is filled with fluid, and its movement causes waves in this fluid. These waves agitate some tiny endings of nerves causing electric impulses to pass along the eighth cranial nerve to the auditory centre of the brain and the person so stimulated says, 'I hear.'

Speech and knowledge of one's native language are so common that we simply take them for granted, and forget that at one time they both had to be learned. The tiny infant has certain sounds repeated to him again and again by his mother, and though unconsciously, yet quite surely, he begins to realize that the sound 'Mummy' refers to the person who attends to his comfort and his needs, and the sound 'Daddy' refers to the other person with different characteristics such as a deeper voice. He has unconsciously made a big step forward—he has learned that persons and things have names. Soon he is learning the names of his toys, he is learning the verbal sounds of his native language. A little later on he begins to attempt to produce these sounds—he is learning to speak. And it should be noticed that two quite separate things are involved. The knowledge of meanings of words, or verbal sounds, is one thing; the ability to produce such sounds is another quite separate thing. Normally these two things are so closely linked that we do not distinguish between them, but we must do so with those born deaf.

682 *2*

## *The Deaf Child*

A totally deaf child from birth, or one who has had his hearing mechanism destroyed by disease before he has learned the meaning of words and how to pronounce them, will have two very great drawbacks. A three-year-old deaf child, who would, if he had normal hearing be prattling away, will still be unable to speak—he will be dumb and his dumbness is a direct consequence of his deafness.

It is obvious that such children cannot be educated at the ordinary school, they have to go to special schools to be taught by specially trained teachers.

On entering school the first thing the languageless, dumb child will be taught, is his own name. Written on the blackboard, the white chalk marks will be unintelligible to him as Chinese characters to us. The teacher will bend forward, draw the child's attention to her lips and pronounce his name, and point to him, himself. Then follows tedious repetition. Pointing to the written name on the blackboard, pronouncing his name with slow, clear, careful lip movements and pointing to the child himself. Again and again and again this goes on, day after day, varied with different chalk marks, different lip movements and pointing to an assortment of small toys on a desk. But the emphasis is on his own name. Then one day understanding will dawn that the silent lip movements and a certain arrangement of white chalk marks are linked together and refer to him. He has learned that he has a name. He has made a big step forward, and can now make progress in lip-reading and in the use of combinations of written letters of the alphabet. But how slow and laborious his progress will be compared with that of a hearing child!

T. H. Sutcliffe, *Soundless Worship* (adapted)

## 683 THE FIFTH SENSE

'A 65-year-old Greek Cypriot shepherd, Nicolis Loizou, was wounded by security forces early today. He was challenged twice; when he failed to answer, troops opened fire. A subsequent hospital examination showed that the man was deaf.' NEWS ITEM, 30th December 1957.

*In this poem, he speaks in hospital*

Lamps burn all the night
Here, where people must be watched and seen,
And I, a shepherd, Nicolis Loizou,
Wish for the dark, for I have been

Sure-footed in the dark, but now my sight
Stumbles among these beds, scattered white boulders,
As I lean towards my far slumbering house
With the night lying upon my shoulders.

My sight was always good,
Better than others. I could taste wine and bread
And name the field they spattered when the harvest
Broke. I could coil in the red
Scent of the fox out of a maze of wood
And grass. I could touch mist, I could touch breath.
But of my sharp senses I had only four.
The fifth one pinned me to my death.

The soldiers must have called
The word they needed: Halt. Not hearing it,
I was their failure, relaxed against the winter
Sky, the flag of their defeat.
With their five senses they could not have told
That I lacked one, and so they had to shoot.
They would fire at a rainbow if it had
A colour less than they were taught.

Christ said that when one sheep
Was lost, the rest meant nothing any more.
Here in this hospital, where others' breathing
Swings like a lantern in the polished floor
And squeezes those who cannot sleep,
I see how precious each thing is, how dear,
For I may never touch, smell, taste, or see
Again, because I could not hear.

Patricia Beer, *Loss of the Magyar*

684

## MY NEW EYES

A medical examination at school had revealed the fact that I was short-sighted. The doctor took me solemnly between his knees, looked into my face, and said, 'If you don't get some glasses, you'll be blind by the time you are fifteen, and I shall tell your parents so.'

(684) I was rather proud of this distinction. Fifteen. That was so far ahead that it meant nothing to me, except a sort of twilight at the end of my life. My parents thought otherwise, and one Saturday afternoon I was taken to a chemist's shop. Behind the shop was a room where my eyes were tested in the rough and ready way customary in those days. The chemist hung an open framework that felt like the Forth Bridge around my ears and on my nose. Lenses were slotted into this, and twisted about, while I was instructed to read the card of letters beginning with a large E.

I remember still the astonishment with which I saw the smaller letters change from a dark blur into separate items of the alphabet. I thought about it all the following week, and found that by screwing up my eyes when I was out of doors I could get to some faint approximation of that clarity, for a few seconds at a time. This made me surmise that the universe which hitherto I had seen as a vague mass of colour and blurred shapes might in actuality be much more concise and defined. I was therefore half prepared for the surprise which shook me a week later when, on the Saturday evening, we went again to the shop, and the chemist produced the pair of steel-rimmed spectacles through which I was invited to read the card. I read it, from top to bottom! I turned and looked in triumph at Mother, but what I saw was Mother intensified. I saw the pupils of her eyes, the tiny feathers in her boa necklet; I saw the hairs in Father's moustache, and on the back of his hand. Jack's cap might have been made of metal, so hard and clear did it shine on his close-cropped head, above his bony face and huge nose. I saw *his* eyes too, round, enquiring, fierce with a hunger of observation. He was studying me with a gimlet sharpness such as I had never before been able to perceive.

Then we walked out of the shop, and I stepped on to the pavement, which came up and hit me, so that I had to grasp the nearest support—Father's coat. 'Take care, now, take care!' he said indulgently (though he disapproved of all these concessions to physical weakness). 'And mind you don't break them!'

I walked still with some uncertainty, carefully placing my feet and feeling their impact on the pavement whose surface I could see sparkling like quartz in the lamplight.

The lamplight! I looked in wonder at the diminishing crystals of gasflame strung down the hill. Clapham was hung with necklaces of light, and the horses pulling the glittering omnibuses struck the granite road with hooves of iron and ebony. I could see the skeletons inside the flesh and blood of the Saturday-night shoppers. The garments they wore were made of separate threads. In this new world, sound as well as sight was changed. It took on hardness and definition, forcing itself upon my hearing, so that I was beseiged simultaneously through the eye and through the ear.

Richard Church, *Over the Bridge*

## 685 BLIND AND SEEING

*Helen Keller, who wrote this, was blind, deaf and dumb*

We differ, blind and seeing, one from another, not in our senses, but in the use we make of them, in the imagination and courage with which we seek wisdom beyond our senses.

It is more difficult to teach ignorance to think than to teach an intelligent blind man to see the grandeur of Niagara. I have walked with people whose eyes are full of light, but who see nothing in wood, sea, or sky, nothing in the city streets, nothing in books. What a witless masquerade is this seeing! It were better far to sail for ever in the night of blindness, with sense and feeling and mind, than to be thus content with the mere act of seeing. They have the sunset, the morning skies, the purple of distant hills, yet their souls voyage through this enchanted world with a barren stare.

Helen Keller, *The World we Live in*

## 686 A BLIND GIRL POT-HOLING

I laughed a great deal as my companion slithered about the place, trying not to collapse under my weight. Pot-holers are all big children. One can't be fussy underground, where everyone has to help everyone else.

'Here's a little stalactite, Colette. Feel how elegant it is.'

'It's rather rough but very pretty. And besides,' I said, 'it's my first stalactite.'

'It's calcite. One finds an enormous variety of mineral concretions in caves. These are not the most strange or the most beautiful. . . . Feel this.' Monsieur Casteret took my hand. 'It's a little cylindrical hole bored naturally in the rock. Our children used to play with it for hours when they were young, which left my wife and me free to explore the cave and make notes of what we found.'

We moved on to our right, entering a chamber with a low ceiling. Here, Monsieur Casteret told me, the prehistoric cave-dwellers had surpassed themselves. The drawings were striking in their freshness and vigour. More than twenty thousand years ago. The words ran through my mind like a refrain.

'I want you to touch the mouth of the Roaring Lion. There. . . . Follow the outline of the canine tooth with your finger. It's very well carved, very impressive—the man who carved it must certainly have seen that lion! To judge by the way he drew it he must have been horribly frightened!'

What Monsieur Casteret did not mention, in his modesty, was that he himself was the discoverer of that life-sized lion's head, in the place where it had been roaring for twenty thousand years. He had every right to be proud of it. I brushed my fingers lightly over the rock, not daring to press hard for fear of damaging a masterpiece. It was extraordinary to think that in the far, far distant past the fingers of my prehistoric brother, and his chisel of flint, had passed over that same surface. I was filled with awe.

The silence bore down on us, weighted with its age-old memories. One felt very small in the presence of so much grandeur and accumulated beauty. This was the meeting-place of God and Man and the centuries. I felt tears come into my eyes, and I imagined Monsieur Casteret's little lamp. Its soft, living light was the symbol of fire, the flame handed down to us which is also the Divine Presence in all places.

Colette Richard, *Climbing Blind*

687

## A BLIND GIRL CLIMBING

TWO READINGS

*I*

The few days that were left of my holiday were spent in initiating me into rock climbing. We went to the Rocher de l'Escalade. The sun was very hot and there were a lot of other people about, climbers and strollers.

I was roped to Raymond, who led the way to reassure me.

Piraly stood watching us at a distance and taking occasional photographs, so I had to find my holds by myself. This was something it was essential for me to learn, because I could not always have an instructor beside me.

It was not as simple as it may seem. I took care only to move one arm or leg at a time, so as not to lose my balance, and I tried to move from one hold to the next smoothly, without jerking. I can't pretend that my style was very good.

I thought of the sort of things people say about the blind—'They have such a wonderfully developed sense of touch! They're so adroit! They have a sixth sense. There's a special god for the blind.' And there were also people who would say, 'For God's sake, why do they want to go climbing rocks?'

Meanwhile there I was on the rock-face at the end of a rope, and I alone was the judge of my actions because I alone knew what it was all about.

Every climber knows that even a moment's hesitation on the part of one member can throw a rope-team out of its stride. Certainly this was different, since we were only doing a practice climb. But still, without eyes to see, one is bound at times to fumble for a few seconds before finding a protuberance which can be firmly grasped.

I had to trust to luck. My right hand seized upon a tiny hold, although there was a far better one only a few inches away from it which I could not see; my left hand sought the ideal projection but could not find it, nothing but a small bulge too near for me to be able to use it. My feet slipped, and I could not steady myself with my right hand alone. Once again I was hanging on the rope; the more I sought a foothold the more my feet slipped, while my hands fumbled blindly (the right word!) and the rope dug into my ribs.

687

*2*

If there had been an instructor beside me he would have told me what to do, but he was down below, watching and saying nothing.

His silence made me cross. I looked up and called: 'Raymond, I can't do it, I want to go down.'

Raymond knew better than anyone what the position was because he was having to sustain my full weight, but he said calmly: 'Well, come on up first, and then we'll see.'

He laughed; but my courage was failing and my muscles wouldn't obey me. I had to stop this. I was hot, scorched by the sun.

'Listen, Raymond. Piraly didn't really mean it, did he, when he said I have a natural gift for climbing? He only said it to please me.'

'Find somewhere to put your feet and rest for a moment.'

'I'm completely out of breath!'

'You're going at it too hard.'

His imperturbability restored my morale. I took his advice and rested. Then I made another effort and reached him.

'You mustn't let yourself get so upset,' he said. 'Don't fuss, you'll get the hang of it. It's bound to take a little time. You aren't doing badly. All you need is practice.'

'Are we going down now?'

'Whenever you like.'

He gave me a friendly pat on the shoulder, because I was still a little scared when it came to stepping off backwards into emptiness. I knew all about the drop below me, having just climbed up it. But having made the first step I felt wonderful.

Colette Richard, *Climbing Blind*

## Challenge and Action

688

### LOOK WELL TO THIS DAY

Look to this day!
For it is life, the very life of life.
In its busy course
Lie all the virtues and realities of your existence:
The bliss of growth,
The glory of action,
The splendour of achievement.
For yesterday is but a dream,
Tomorrow is only a vision,
But today well lived makes yesterday a dream of happiness
And every tomorrow a vision of hope.
Look well therefore to this day;
Such is the salutation to the dawn.

Third-Century Indian

I can remember many years ago my passion in life was cricket—surely the most fascinating waste of time ever conceived by a so-called civilized nation.

When one Saturday afternoon I scored a hundred in a school match, my pride knew no bounds.

On Sunday, as I strutted about, I thought that me and the Almighty in that order, were the two most important people around that day.

On Monday we had nets with the Headmaster. He was a very good player himself and he taught us with wonderful enthusiasm and patience.

In the corner of the net ground, at deep square leg stood a pink chestnut tree. It was said that no one had ever succeeded in hitting the Headmaster's accurate off breaks over it. When my turn came to bat, dreams of everlasting fame filled my already over-sized head. Having played properly for four balls, I selected the fifth, and lifting my bat as high as my young arms could manage, I swung with all my strength, half closing my eyes with exertion. Of course, I missed. I couldn't tell this story otherwise. I turned angrily to retrieve the ball. When I looked up, I found the Headmaster standing by my side.

He took me gently by the arm. 'Tommy', he said, 'you know you'll make nought far more times than you'll make a hundred. You'd better take off your pads and go back to the changing room and think about it.'

Tears filled my eyes as I fumbled with my buckles. I picked up my things and walked slowly back across the ground to the school. As I went, I became conscious that all other activity had ceased in the nets, and that twenty pairs of eyes were following my departure.

I arrived in the deserted changing room, and flinging my gear in the corner, I sat down with my head in my hands and I thought about it.

When I look back on that dismal episode, there are two things that strike me—the first I know for certain and that is, 'that I learnt more about pride and humility that day than at any other time in my life'—the other I'm not sure about to this day, and that is, 'How much the Almighty had to do with it all?'

J. R. Thompson

I realized that what mattered in the struggle for life was to overcome my fear of those who were stronger.

The ruler of our street was a boy of about sixteen who was nicknamed Red.

Red was big and broad-shouldered beyond his years.

Red walked masterfully up and down our street, legs wide and with a slightly rolling gait, like a seaman on his deck.

From under his cap, its peak always at the back of his head, his forelock tumbled down in a fiery cascade, and out of his round pock-marked face, green eyes, like a cat's, sparkled with scorn for everything and everyone. Two or three lieutenants, in peaked caps back to front like Red's, tripped at his heels.

Red could stop any boy and say impressively the one word 'money'. His lieutenants would turn out the boy's pockets, and if he resisted they beat him up hard.

Everyone was afraid of Red. So was I. I knew he carried a heavy metal knuckle-duster in his pocket.

I wanted to conquer my fear of Red.

So I wrote a poem about him.

This was my first piece of journalism in verse.

By the next day the whole street knew it by heart and exulted with triumphant hatred.

One morning on my way to school I suddenly came upon Red and his lieutenants. His eyes seemed to bore through me. 'Ah, the poet,' he drawled, smiling crookedly. 'So you write verses. Do they rhyme?'

Red's hand darted into his pocket and came out armed with its knuckle-duster; it flashed like lightning and struck my head. I fell down streaming with blood and lost consciousness.

This was my first remuneration as a poet.

I spent several days in bed.

When I went out, with my head still bandaged, I again saw Red. I struggled with myself but lost and took to my heels. At home I rolled on my bed, biting my pillow and pounding it in shame and impotent fury at my cowardice.

I made up my mind to vanquish it at whatever cost.

I went into training with parallel bars and weights. After every session I would feel my muscles; they were getting bigger, but slowly. Then I remembered something I had read in a book about a miraculous Japanese method of wrestling which gave an advantage to the weak over the strong. I exchanged a week's ration card for a textbook on ju-jitsu.

For three weeks I stayed at home, practising with two other boys. Then I went out.

Red was sitting on the lawn in our yard, playing *vingt-et-un* with his lieutenants. He was absorbed in the game.

Fear was still deep in me, urging me to go back. But I went up to the players and kicked and scattered the cards.

Red looked up, surprised at my impudence after my recent flight.

He got up slowly. 'You looking for more?' he asked menacingly.

As before, his hand dived into his pocket for the knuckle-duster. But I made a quick jabbing movement and Red, howling with pain, rolled on the ground. Bewildered he got up and came at me, swinging his head furiously from side to side like a maddened bull.

I caught his wrist and squeezed slowly, as I had read in the book, until the knuckle-duster dropped from his limp fingers. Nursing his hand, Red fell down again. He was sobbing and smearing the tears over his pock-marked face with his grubby fist.

That day Red ceased to be the monarch of our street.

And from that day on I knew for certain that one need not fear the strong. All one needs is to know the way to beat them. For every strong man there is a special ju-jitsu.

What I also learned on this occasion was that to be a poet, I had not only to write poems, but know how to stand up for them.

Yevgeny Yevtushenko, *A Precocious Autobiography*

## 691 THE BULLY AND THE PREACHER'S SON

There was a boy in school named Chuck, who was a bully. He was the first boy I heard about when we got to Pittsburgh. Before we'd unpacked our trunks I learned that Chuck always beat up the new kids, and that I had better be particularly careful because he was especially tough on preachers' kids.

Chuck had me shaking before I ever saw him. What was I going to do when we finally did meet? I asked God this question and an answer came quickly and clearly: *Not by might, nor by power, but by my Spirit.* I knew it was a Bible quotation, and I

(691) looked it up just to check on my recollection of the passage. Zechariah 4:6, it was—and then and there I took it for my motto. When the time came to face Chuck, I decided, I would simply lean on this promise; God would give me a holy boldness that would be equal to any bully.

All too soon I had a chance to test my theory. One spring afternoon I started home from school alone. I was wearing new clothes, I remember, which made it particularly important that I should not get into a fight; new clothes in our family were too carefully budgeted to be ruined in a street brawl.

Suddenly, ahead, I saw a boy walking toward me. I knew in an instant that this would be Chuck. He was strutting down the opposite side of the street. But the instant he saw me he crossed over and bore down on me like a heavy, snorting, angry bull. Chuck was an enormous boy. He must have weighed fifty pounds more than I, and he towered above me so that I had to bend my neck to look him in the eye.

Chuck stopped dead in my path, legs spread and hands on hips.

'You're the preacher's kid.'

It wasn't a question, it was a challenge, and I'll admit that in that moment all my hopes of holy boldness vanished. I was scared to the core of me.

'Not by might, nor by power, but by my Spirit. Not by might, nor by power, but by my Spirit, saith the Lord of hosts.' I kept repeating this sentence over and over to myself while Chuck commenced to give his opinion of me. First he picked on the fact that I looked stupid in my new clothes. Then he worked over the obvious truth that I was a weakling. After that he had a few words to say about preachers' kids in general.

'. . . . by my Spirit, saith the Lord.' I still had not spoken, but inside me an amazing event was taking place. I felt fear melting, and in its place came confidence and joy. I looked up at Chuck and smiled.

Chuck was getting madder and madder. His face turned red as he challenged me to fight.

Still I smiled.

Chuck started to circle me with his fist clenched, pumping his arms slowly and taking short feints toward me. In his face, though, was a hint of alarm. He could see that, for some unfathomable reason, this little shrimp was truly not afraid.

I circled, too, never taking my eye off his, and all the while I smiled.

Finally, Chuck hit me. It was a hesitant little blow that didn't hurt, and it happened to catch me on balance so I wasn't thrown. I laughed, low and secretly.

Chuck stopped his circling. He dropped his fists. He backed off and then he turned and took off down the street.

Next day at school, I began to hear how I'd beaten up the biggest bully in town. Chuck had been telling everyone. He said I was the toughest guy he ever fought. Apparently he laid it on thick, because always after that I was treated with respect by the entire school. Perhaps I should have told the kids the truth, but I never did. I had a kind of insurance policy in my reputation. And, hating to fight as I did, I wasn't about ready to turn my policy in.

David Wilkerson, *The Cross and the Switchblade*

## 692 THE CONQUEST OF EVEREST

### TWO READINGS

*I*

Time was passing and the ridge seemed never-ending. In one place, where the angle of the ridge had eased off, I tried cramponing without cutting steps, hoping this would save time, but I quickly realised that our margin of safety on these steep slopes at this altitude was too small, so I went on step-cutting. I was beginning to tire a little now. I had been cutting steps for two hours, and Tenzing, too, was moving very slowly. As I chipped steps around still another corner, I wondered just how long we could keep it up. Our original zest had now quite gone and it was turning more into a grim struggle. I then realised that the ridge ahead, instead of still monotonously rising, now dropped sharply away, and far below I could see the North Col and the Rongbuk glacier, I looked upwards to see a narrow snow ridge running up to a snowy summit. A few more whacks of the ice-axe in the firm snow and we stood on top.

My initial feelings were of relief—relief that there were no more steps to cut—no more ridges to traverse and no more humps to tantalise us with hopes of success. I looked at Tenzing and in spite of the balaclava, goggles and oxygen mask all encrusted with long icicles that concealed his face, there was no disguising his infectious grin of pure delight as he looked all around him. We shook hands and then Tenzing threw his arm around my shoulders and we thumped each other on the back until we were almost breathless. It was 11.30 a.m. The ridge had taken us two and a half hours, but it seemed like a lifetime.

692

*2*

I turned off the oxygen and removed my set. I had carried my camera, loaded with colour film, inside my shirt to keep it warm, so I now produced it and got Tenzing to pose on top for me, waving his axe on which was a string of flags—United Nations, British, Nepalese and Indian. Then I turned my attention to the great stretch of country lying below us in every direction.

To the east was our giant neighbour Makalu, unexplored and unclimbed, and even on top of Everest the mountaineering instinct was sufficiently strong to cause me to spend some moments conjecturing as to whether a route up that mountain might not exist. Far away across the clouds the great bulk of Kangchenjunga loomed on the horizon. To the west, Cho Oyu, our old adversary from 1952, dominated the scene and we could see the great unexplored ranges of Nepal stretching off into the distance. The most important photograph, I felt, was a shot down the North ridge, showing the North Col and the old route which had been made famous by the struggles of those great climbers of the 1920s and 1930s. I had little hope of the results being particularly successful, as I had a lot of difficulty in holding the camera steady in my clumsy gloves, but I felt that they would at least serve as a record. After some ten minutes of this, I realised that I was becoming rather clumsy-fingered and slow-moving, so I quickly replaced my oxygen set. Meanwhile Tenzing had made a little hole in the snow and in it he placed various small articles of food —a bar of chocolate, a packet of biscuits and a handful of lollies. Small offerings, indeed, but at least a token gift to the Gods that all devout Buddhists believe have their home on this lofty summit. While we were together on the South Col two days before, Hunt had given me a small crucifix which he had asked me to take to the top. I, too, made a hole in the snow and placed the crucifix beside Tenzing's gifts.

I checked our oxygen once again and worked out our endurance. We would have to move fast in order to reach our life-saving reserve below the South Peak. After fifteen minutes we turned to go.

Edmund Hillary, from a chapter contributed to *The Ascent of Everest*

693

## ON TOP OF EVEREST

### TWO READINGS

*I*

We stepped up. We were there. The dream had come true. . . .

What we did first was what all climbers do when they reach the top of their mountain. We shook hands. But this was not enough for Everest. I waved my arms in the air, and then threw them round Hillary, and we thumped each other on the back until, even with the oxygen, we were almost breathless. Then we looked round. It was eleven-thirty in the morning, the sun was shining, and the sky was the deepest blue I have ever seen. Only a gentle breeze was blowing, coming from the direction of Tibet, and the plume of snow that always blows from Everest's summit was very small. Looking down the far side of the mountain, I could see all the familiar landmarks from the earlier expeditions—the Rongbuk Monastery, the town of Shekar Dzong, the Kharta Valley, the Rongbuk and East Rongbuk Glaciers, the North Col, the place near the north-east ridge where we had made Camp Six in 1938. Then, turning, I looked down the long way we ourselves had come—past the south summit, the long ridge, the South Col; on to the Western Cwm, the icefall, the Khumbu Glacier; all the way down to Thyangboche, and on to the valleys and hills of my homeland.

Beyond them, and around us on every side, were the great Himalayas, stretching away through Nepal and Tibet. For the closer peaks—giants like Lhotse, Nuptse, and Makalu—you now had to look sharply downward to see their summits. And, farther away, the whole sweep of the greatest range on earth—even Kangchenjunga itself—seemed only like little bumps under the spreading sky. It was such a sight as I had never seen before and would never see again—wild, wonderful, and terrible. But terror was not what I felt. I loved the mountains too well for that. I loved Everest too well. At that great moment for which I had waited all my life my mountain did not seem to me a lifeless thing of rock and ice, but warm and friendly and living. She was a mother hen, and the other mountains were chicks under her wings. I too, I felt, had only to spread my own wings to cover and shelter the brood that I loved.

693

## 2

We turned off our oxygen. Even there on top of the world it was possible to live without it, so long as we were not exerting ourselves. We cleared away the ice that had formed on our masks, and I popped a bit of sweet into my mouth. Then we replaced the masks. But we did not turn on the oxygen again until we were ready to leave the top. Hillary took out his camera, which he had been carrying under his clothing to keep it from freezing, and I unwound the four flags from around my axe. They were tied together on a string, which was fastened to the blade of the axe, and now I held the axe up, and Hillary took my picture. Actually he took three, and I think it was lucky, in those difficult conditions, that one came out so well. The order of the flags from top to bottom was United Nations, British, Nepalese, Indian; and the same sort of people who have made trouble in other ways have tried to find political meaning in this too. All I can say is that on Everest I was not thinking about politics. If I had been I suppose I would have put the Indian or Nepalese flag highest, though that in itself would have been a bad problem for me. As it is, I am glad that the U.N. flag was on top. For I like to think that our victory was not only for ourselves—not only for our own nations—but for all men everywhere.

I motioned to Hillary that I would now take his picture. But for some reason he shook his head; he did not want it. Instead he began taking more pictures himself, around and down on all sides of the peak, and meanwhile I did another thing that had to be done on the top of our mountain. From my pocket I took the package of sweets I had been carrying. I took the little red-and-blue pencil that my daughter, Nima, had given me. And, scraping a hollow in the snow, I laid them there. Seeing what I was doing, Hillary handed me a small cloth cat, black and with white eyes, that Hunt had given him as a mascot, and I put this beside them. In his story of our climb Hillary says it was a crucifix that Hunt gave him, and that he left on top; but if this was so I did not see it. He gave me only the cloth cat. All I laid in the snow was the cat, the pencil, and the sweets. 'At home,' I thought, 'we offer sweets to those who are near and dear to us. Everest has always been dear to me, and now it is near too.' As I covered up the offerings I said a silent prayer. And I gave my thanks. Seven times I had come to the mountain of my dream, and on this, the seventh, with God's help, the dream had come true.

'Thuji chey, Chomolungma. I am grateful. . . .'

*Man of Everest*, The Autobiography of Tenzing
told to James Ramsey Ullman

## 694 MADAME CURIE PREPARES PURE RADIUM

THREE READINGS

*I*

Marie continued to treat, kilogramme by kilogramme, the tons of pitchblende residue which were sent her on several occasions from St. Joachimsthal. With her remarkable patience she was able to be, every day for four years, physicist, chemist, specialised worker, engineer and labouring man all at once. Thanks to her brain and muscle, the old tables in the shed held more and more concentrated products—products richer and richer in radium. Mme Curie was approaching the end: she no longer stood in the courtyard, enveloped in bitter smoke, to watch the heavy basins of material in fusion. She was now at the stage of purification and of the 'fractional crystallisation' of strongly radioactive solutions. But the poverty of her haphazard equipment hindered her work more than ever. It was now that she needed a spotlessly clean work-room and apparatus perfectly protected against cold, heat and dirt. In this shed, open to every wind, iron- and coal-dust was afloat which, to Marie's despair, became mixed with the products purified with so much care. Her heart sometimes constricted before these little daily accidents, which absorbed so much of her time and her strength.

Pierre was so tired of the interminable struggle that he would have been quite ready to abandon it. Of course, he did not dream of dropping the study of radium and of radioactivity. But he would willingly have renounced, for the time being, the special operation of preparing pure radium. The obstacles seemed insurmountable. Could they not resume this work later on, under better conditions? More attached to the meaning of natural phenomena than to their material reality, Pierre Curie was exasperated to see the paltry results to which Marie's exhausting effort had led. He advised an armistice.

He counted without his wife's character. Marie wanted to isolate radium and she *would* isolate it. She scorned fatigue and difficulties, and even the gaps in her own knowledge which complicated her task. After all, she was only a very young scientist: she still had not the certainty and great culture Pierre had acquired by twenty years' work, and sometimes she stumbled across phenomena or methods of calculation of which she knew very little and for which she had to make hasty studies.

So much the worse! With stubborn eyes under her great brow, she clung to her apparatus and her test-tubes.

In 1902, forty-five months after the day on which the Curies announced the probable existence of radium, Marie finally carried off the victory in this war of attrition: she succeeded in preparing a decigramme of pure radium, and made a first determination of the atomic weight of the new substance, which was 225.

The incredulous chemists—of whom there were still a few—could only bow before the facts, before the superhuman obstinacy of a woman.

Radium officially existed.

694

*2*

It was nine o'clock at night. Pierre and Marie Curie were in their little house at 108 Boulevard Kellermann, where they had been living since 1900. The house suited them well. From the boulevard, where three rows of trees half hid the fortifications, could be seen only a dull wall and a tiny door. But behind the one-storey house, hidden from all eyes, there was a narrow provincial garden, rather pretty and very quiet. And from the 'barrier' of Gentilly they could escape on their bicycles towards the suburbs and the woods.

Old Dr. Curie, who lived with the couple, had retired to his room. Marie had bathed her child and put her to bed, and had stayed for a long time beside the cot. This was a rite. When Irène did not feel her mother near her at night she would call out for her incessantly, with that 'Mé!' which was to be our substitute for 'Mamma' always. And Marie, yielding to the implacability of the four-year-old child, climbed the stairs, seated herself beside her and stayed there in the darkness until the young voice gave way to light, regular breathing. Only then would she go down again to Pierre, who was growing impatient.

The day's work had been hard, and it would have been more reasonable for the couple to rest. But Pierre and Marie were not always reasonable. As soon as they had put on their coats and told Dr. Curie of their flight, they were in the street. They went on foot, arm in arm, exchanging few words. After the crowded streets of this queer district, with its factory buildings, waste-lands and poor tenements, they arrived in the Rue Lhomond and crossed the little courtyard. Pierre put the key in the lock. The door squeaked, as it had squeaked thousands of times, and admitted them to their realm, to their dream.



*3*

'Don't light the lamps!' Marie said in the darkness. Then she added with a little laugh:

'Do you remember the day when you said to me: "I should like radium to have a beautiful colour"?'

The reality was more entrancing than the simple wish of long ago. Radium had something better than 'a beautiful colour'; it was spontaneously luminous. And in the sombre shed, where, in the absence of cupboards, the precious particles in their tiny glass receivers were placed on tables or on shelves nailed to the wall, their phosphorescent bluish outlines gleamed, suspended in the night.

'Look . . . Look!' the young woman murmured.

She went forward cautiously, looked for and found a straw-bottomed chair. She sat down in the darkness and silence. Their two faces turned toward the pale glimmering, the mysterious sources of radiation, toward radium—their radium. Her body leaning forward, her head eager, Marie took up again the attitude which had been hers an hour earlier at the bedside of her sleeping child.

Her companion's hand lightly touched her hair.

She was to remember for ever this evening of glow-worms, this magic.

Eve Curie, *Madame Curie*

## 695 THE FIRST FOUR-MINUTE MILE

The gun fired. Brasher went into the lead and I slipped in effortlessly behind him, feeling tremendously full of running. My legs seemed to meet no resistance at all, as if propelled by some unknown force.

I barely noticed the half mile, passed in 1 min. 58 sec., nor when, round the next bend, Chataway went into the lead. At three-quarters of a mile the effort was still barely perceptible: the time was 3 min. 0·7 sec., and by now the crowd were roaring. Somehow I had to run that last lap in 59 seconds. Chataway led around the next bend and then I pounced past him three hundred yards from the finish.

I had a moment of mixed joy and anguish, when my mind took over. It raced well ahead of my body and drew my body compellingly forward. I felt that the moment of a lifetime had come. There was no pain, only a great unity of movement and aim. The world seemed to stand still, or did not exist.

I felt at that moment that it was my chance to do one thing supremely well. I drove on, impelled by a combination of fear and pride.

Those last few seconds seemed never-ending. The faint line of the finishing tape stood ahead as a haven of peace, after the struggle. The arms of the world were waiting to receive me if only I reached the tape without slackening my speed. I leapt at the tape like a man taking his last spring to save himself from the chasm that threatens to engulf him.

My effort was over and I collapsed almost unconscious with an arm on either side of me. It was only then that real pain overtook me. I just went on existing in the most passive physical state without being quite unconscious. It was as if all my limbs were caught in an ever-tightening vice. I knew that I had done it before I even heard the time.

The stop-watches held the answer. The announcement came—'Result of one mile . . . time 3 minutes'—the rest lost in the roar of excitement. I grabbed Brasher and Chataway, and together we scampered round the track in a burst of spontaneous joy. We had done it—the three of us!

I felt suddenly and gloriously free of the burden of athletic ambition that I had been carrying for years. No words could be invented for such supreme happiness, eclipsing all other feelings. I thought at that moment I could never again reach such a climax of single-mindedness.

Roger Bannister, *First Four Minutes*

## 696 SAILING IN ALL WEATHERS

During the last century, transatlantic schooners operated in hundreds from the small ports of the West Country, Wales and Lancashire.

The schooners were little ships which carried fish from Newfoundland and fruit from the West Indies; their advantage over the big ships was the speed with which they could load and unload perishable cargo.

A typical schooner was well under 100 tons gross. Her crew consisted of a master, a mate and two or three seamen. On occasion, there were even fewer; there is no record of a single-handed Atlantic crossing, but it was not unknown for the crew to be as small as two. A master was paid about £6 a month, plus a share in profits, and the ordinary seamen £2 or £3. They ate well, although suffering from boils and gastric troubles because they insisted on fried food.

The schooners routinely crossed the Atlantic in all weathers, the voyage taking anything from 12 to 50 days. The Fowey schooner *Isabella* of 61 tons did six Atlantic crossings and a voyage to Spain in six months in 1899. Some schooners ranged as far as Australia and New Zealand. In heavy weather they were the wonder of big-ship sailors.

'Once', wrote the sea-captain of a clipper, 'I saw one of these ocean-going schooners showing what she could do in a howling north-Atlantic gale, with the sea running mountains high. The sailing ship I was in was under very reduced canvas. As the schooner crossed our bows less than half a mile distant we could see her leaning over until her lee gunwale was under water. Her three little scraps of sail, not much bigger than handkerchiefs, tore her along at a great pace amid a smother of foam and clouds of heavy spray and sometimes green water swept her from end to end. We could see two oilskin-clad figures at the wheel; they must have been lashed there or they would have been washed away.'

Today, as we follow the Big Jet routes over wide and apparently placid oceans we are no longer troubled by the old and justified dread of the sea that afflicted the great pioneers and sometimes drove their crews to mutiny. But by the rare glimpses we have had of Sir Francis Chichester on his solitary journey—glimpses almost exactly recapturing the sea-captain's vision of that small schooner under her three scraps of sail—it has been brought home to us that the immense wastes of the sea are still as destructive, terrifying and wonderful as they were when Columbus, Magellan and Drake first explored them.

Colin Cross, *Man against the Sea* (adapted)

# Freedom and Love

## 697 GOD MADE MAN TO BE FREE

God made man to be free,
Free within the human family.
The Commonwealth of man is still his dream.
In Charter and in Constitution,
In Petition and in Pact
He inscribes his faith
In Freedom and Equality.
Yet still the barriers rise
And prejudice is strong.
Fear and suspicion separate
And sever man from man.

Why does the dream delay?
Why is hope unfulfilled?
Man lacks the faith,
He lacks the faith of Christ,
Who lived out his belief.
Who, in a hostile world,

Revealed the potency of love.
By this one act he realized the dream
And bridged the gap that separated man from man.
The wall was down
And Jew and Gentile,
Slave and free,
Were one in Christ.

So when men dare to love
They can release a power
That heals the sad divisions of mankind.
Where men give up security and home,
To help a backward people with their skills,
There hope is born.
Where statesmen patiently negotiate,
And sacrifice advantage and prestige,
There peace can grow.
Where Negro kneels before the bullying guard,
Immune to provocation and to hate,
There love can heal.
Where men will venture on a hope
Of truth and goodness yet untried
And take Christ at his word
There God can work.

Lord, give us faith.

Jim Bates

698

## THE FREEDOM OF MAN
## HIS LORDSHIP OVER NATURE

From the first moment
When from the dark confusion
Of what was not
There flickered into being
Light,
There Freedom was.
Growing, widening
As worlds wheeled
As galaxies burst out
As life in animal and plant

Developed in complexity
So freedom grew
Until in man
It reached maturity.
Man free to conquer
Free to choose
All things beneath his feet
A master of the elements
At first a beast
Shut in by ignorance and fear,
But finding in his hand
And in his brain
A power that subdued and tamed
The wide world to his will,
Lord of the beasts
He leaves his mark
In landscape and in cultivated soil,
In conurbation and suburban sprawl,
In dam and motorway
In seared and blackened acres
And the slum
Where man makes wealth
From earth and human toil.

Physicist and Astronaut,
Industrialist and Engineer,
Artist and Architect
All praise the freedom
God has given to man.

But in his Freedom
Does man praise his God?

Jim Bates

## 699 FREEDOM AND MY NEIGHBOUR

*I*

There is a freedom that man fears
The freedom of his fellow man
In the eye of the tyrant

In the eye of the oppressed
In the eye of the neighbour
Who makes his fence too high—or low;
In the eye of the traveller in the tube
Who, like him, eyes the seat he makes for,
There is a freedom that threatens
That disturbs the freedom he has carved out for himself.
So we live
Shut in by fences, regulations, gates.
Apartheid in a thousand forms
Secures us from the freedom of the world
To invade and to destroy
Our liberty of isolation.

For freedom we build our walls,
For freedom we make our bombs,
For freedom we pass our laws,
For freedom we imprison and restrict,
For freedom we create the Ghetto.
And we shall meet no one,
And speak to no one,
And listen to no one
Who does not look as we do,
Think as we do,
Act as we do,
Except at a safe and deferential distance.

699

*2*

Christ came to make men free
Free from their isolation and their fear.
He came—
Homeless—and so at home among all;
In poverty—and so the guest of all;
In weakness—and so at the mercy of all;
Common—and so approachable by all;
A man with time for all,
A man for others.
Jesus, Son of Man.
He was in the world
And nothing came between him and the world,

So that men might be one with him,
And one with each other.

699

*3*

For in our neighbour lies
The secret of our happiness.
He alone can liberate
The generous instinct
And dispel the fear
That shuts us in.

But the man, wanting to justify himself, said:
But who is my neighbour?

I looked for my neighbour in the city,
I looked for the person who had time to be
Neighbour to me.
The churches were open, but no one was there.
The chapels were securely locked.
In the offices there was no time to talk,
In factories the din too great.
The rushing and the hazards of the street
Made conversation dangerous.
Where people lived no door stood open,
And no one stood upon the threshold
To pass the time of day.

What threshold has a flat?
How can you welcome in the passer-by
At fifteen stories up?
Where was it that men gathered and men talked,
Where they had time,
Time for each other,
And perhaps, some time for God?

Jim Bates

700

## BLACK AND WHITE MASKS

White Americans find it as difficult as white people elsewhere do to divest themselves of the notion that they are in possession of some intrinsic value that black people need, or want. And this assumption is revealed in all kinds of striking ways, from Bobby Kennedy's assurance that a Negro can become President in forty years to the unfortunate tone of warm congratulation with which so many liberals address their Negro equals. It is the Negro, of course, who is presumed to have become equal—an achievement that not only proves the comforting fact that perseverance has no colour but also overwhelmingly corroborates the white man's sense of his own value. Alas, this value can scarcely be corroborated in any other way; there is certainly little enough in the white man's public or private life that one should desire to imitate. White men, at the bottom of their hearts, know this. Therefore, a vast amount of the energy that goes into what we call the Negro problem is produced by the white man's profound desire not to be judged by those who are not white, not to be seen as he is, and at the same time a vast amount of the white anguish is rooted in the white man's equally profound need to be seen as he is, to be released from the tyranny of his mirror. All of us know, whether or not we are able to admit it, that mirrors can only lie. It is for this reason that love is so desperately sought and so cunningly avoided. Love takes off the masks that we fear we cannot live without and know we cannot live within. I use the word 'love' here not merely in the personal sense but as a state of being, or a state of grace—not in the infantile American sense of being made happy but in the tough and universal sense of quest and daring and growth. And I submit, then, that the racial tensions that menace Americans today have little to do with real antipathy and are involved only symbolically with colour. These tensions are rooted in the very same depths as those from which love springs, or murder. The white man's unadmitted private fears and longings are projected on to the Negro. The only way he can be released from the Negro's tyrannical power over him is to consent, in effect to become black himself, to become a part of that suffering and dancing country that he now watches wistfully from the heights of his lonely power.

James Baldwin, *The Fire Next Time*

701 PRAISE GOD FOR COFFEE BARS

Let us praise God for coffee bars
Praise him for

701) The dim and unreligious light of coffee bars
Praise him for the rattle of the pin table,
Praise him for the chatter and the din,
Praise him for the deep booming juke box,
Praise him for the smoke and steam.

Here the door is open
All may come
And sit and talk, or smoke in silence,
Watching, or being watched
Rub shoulders with the world,
At peace with man, . . .

There is no lock here,
There is no garden gate
That makes of hospitality
A favoured gift
Bestowed upon the few.
Here all are welcome,
Provided that they pay.
But since costs must be met,
And nothing here is perfect
Let's thank God for coffee bars
Where we can meet
And be at home among our fellow men.

Teach us, good Lord, to be more generous;
Free us from the fear, the lack of trust
That alienates us from our fellow men.
Teach us the meaning of forgiveness,
To love our enemies,
To welcome, as did Jesus
Those unlovely types
Whose pride, whose reputation, or whose smell
Makes them impossible.

And since it is our sin to shut men out
By carelessness or wilful prejudice,
Throw wide the door of our concern
To fight, to suffer and to care
With all who seek your kingdom here on earth.

Jim Bates

## FREEDOM AND FAITH

*To Colonel Alexei Leonov*

So you stepped out of your space capsule
Into nothing
Where man had never been before
You hovered in a partial vacuum
Hazarding all upon a theory.
No one had done before what you have done,
No one could be quite sure what you would meet.
Of course they made their calculations,
Caution had carefully prepared for what might be,
But no one could be sure.
Until you clambered out
Man's dream remained
A wistful longing, unfulfilled.
But you made out of it
Reality.

And so you gave man freedom to explore
A medium beyond
The envelope of atmosphere, his home.
New Worlds are his
Not only hemispheres,
Infinite of space
With only time to check his wanderings.
And all this came
From opening a door
And stepping into
The Unknown.

Lord make us men of faith
Faith to trust in what we hope for.
Faith to live by what we cannot prove
Until we risk ourselves upon it
With our lives.

Teach us by man's conquest of the world,
By those who ventured on a dream
And found new continents, new truth, new power
By faith.

Teach us to trust the hopes we have been given:
The hope of peace and welfare for mankind,
The hope that love means more than hate,
The hope that death is not the cynical denial
Of all that man has hoped for.

Teach us to take these and to live by them
And so to find that liberty from fear,
And live as free men in a world
Where man is called to live by faith
Or to withdraw,
A frightened beast, defeated by reality.

Teach us to live
As Jesus lived,
Who took the hopes of men
And made them real
By stepping out of safe convention
Into love.

And so he gave us freedom
By his faith.

Jim Bates

# Attitudes to Other People

703

## GENERATIONS' SIN

*'I thank Almighty God, son of my son,*
*that you will not meet beggars in the street*
*nor stumble in the dark on gutter-fallen drunks*
*as I did in my youth.'*

O Fathers, hear the voice of babes:
we must not hide
behind defences built around ourselves,
while men are being crucified
outside our city walls.

I do not meet one beggar in the street—
I see ten thousand on a television screen;
there are no drunkards in the gutters of my town,
and yet eyes stumble on the printed news
of drunken driving, suicides,
and starving nations sprawling
in the gutter countries of
our world.

My problem is
such people cannot touch or plead with me;
and I can switch them off,
or light the fire with them.

Chris Blackwell

704

## MY FATHER NEVER BEAT US

My father never beat us, and whether he was unlike his neighbours in that I cannot say. A distant relation of ours, Willie D., a brave and pious man, beat his family mercilessly. My father regretted his harshness, and often told of a day when he had been walking home from church with Willie and another man, talking of their children, when the other man turned to Willie and said, 'Never lift your hand to a bairn in anger. Wait, and you may change your mind.' My father admired these words, and often repeated them. Yet Willie went on thrashing his family; why I do not know; perhaps in a sort of panic, terrified what might happen to them if the evil were not driven out of them.

He came to see us once in Wyre. As I had heard so much about him I kept staring at him in guilty curiosity. He was not a big man, as I had expected, being scarcely taller than my father, but deep-chested and powerful and deliberate in his movements. He had a gentle, handsome, sad face and a grave voice, and perhaps because I knew he was so harsh to his family and yet so gentle to me I worshipped him. He must have been very attractive to women, for children are often drawn to men by the same qualities as women are. A few years later he lost his life setting out to sea in a storm which no other man would face.

The worst punishment we knew was an occasional clip across

the ears from my father's soft cap with the ear-flaps, which he always wore, outside and inside; and this never happened unless we were making an unbearable noise. Afterwards he would sit back looking ashamed. Like most gentle people he was long-suffering, but when his anger was roused it frightened us. It was roused against me only once, and that was after we left Wyre. I had been sliding on the mill-dam all one Sunday morning against his orders, and when I came back at dinner-time he threatened to thrash me with a rope-end if I did it again. I felt outraged; such a thing had never been heard of in our house before. But I knew that he was terrified that the ice might break and leave me to drown, for the mill-dam was deep. It may have been some such terrifying vision of the future that made Willie D. thrash his children, that and the common belief that evil can be beaten out of children—violently driven out with blows.

Edwin Muir, *An Autobiography*

705

## MY MOTHER

My mother had more practical sense than my father, but was just as gentle. I cannot remember ever hearing them exchanging a discourteous word or raising their voices to each other. Their form of address was 'boy' and 'lass', as it is still in Orkney among men and women, no matter of what age. My mother had a greater regard for appearances than my father, and a deeper family sense; her children were always in the right to her. She was inclined to worry, and wanted us to 'get on'. She too had passed through a religious experience as a young woman, and had a deep respect for religion, but not the spontaneous piety of my father. Yet it was she who taught me the story of Jesus out of a child's book whose name I cannot remember. It must have been written in a vein of mawkish sentiment, for it gave me the impression that Jesus was always slightly ill, a pale invalid with the special gentleness of people who cannot live as others do. My mother often lamented, as she read from this book, that she no longer had another one called *The Peep o' Day*, and for a long time I carried about an imaginary picture of it; I could see the frontispiece showing a bearded Jesus in a wide cloak, bearing a lamb in His arms. But it lay in the past, in a place I could never reach.

Edwin Muir, *An Autobiography*

## TWO READINGS

*I*

All of us when we are starting out in life have our special demons who try to kill our faith in human beings, to make us doubt the very possibility of an unselfish motive—demons with smooth, enticing hands who try to lure us for ever into the dark labyrinths of cynical distrust.

I too had such a demon.

The demon worked as an engineer in one of the mines in Kazakhstan. He was about forty-five, with a big bald head set on a squat body, and with tiny, mocking eyes.

The demon would ask me out in the evening, after work, and sit holding forth on such themes as: all men are scoundrels, or: love and friendship and all other such altruistic notions have been invented by novelists who are bastards like the rest of us in their private lives.

The demon had a woman living with him—a plain, scraggy, sad little woman with the evasive eyes of a beaten dog, who had once been a kitchen maid in the miners' canteen.

He used her as a sitting target for his contempt. Every evening when he came home she had to wash his feet, and he preferred this ritual to be performed in front of a witness. He clearly felt that it exalted him while degrading the rest of mankind in the person of this uncomplaining woman.

Thus one night when he was talking to me, he ordered her to bring a basin into which he lowered his feet, and sat wriggling his toes in the water with the utmost enjoyment.

The demon was philosophizing:

'You believe that what keeps society together is love, don't you? Well, take this woman and myself. I sleep with her though I despise her, and she hates me but sleeps with me, and, what's more, washes my feet every night. Why do we stay together? Because we need each other. I need her to sleep with and to wash my feet. And she needs me to feed and clothe her. Society is not based on love but on mutual hatred.'

I looked at the woman.

She was washing her tormentor's feet and crying, her tears falling into the dirty water, in among the playful toes.

06 *1*) The demon's arguments were abhorrent yet convincing. All the same, the more they seemed to be supported by facts, the stronger grew my resistance to them.

One day the demon took me by lorry to fetch the workmen's pay from a small town across the steppe. Our driver was a taciturn young man with a solid row of steel teeth and tattooed hands.

'Keep an eye on him, he's done time,' the demon whispered to me before we set out. 'We'll have quite a bit of money on us. I've got something here,' he patted the pocket in which he kept his revolver, 'but you'd better keep a lookout as well.'

We called at the bank. The demon carefully counted the batches of creased notes and put them away in a worn leather briefcase. Then we all three got back into the cab of the lorry—the driver, the demon with the briefcase on his knees and I.

Before us lay a journey of close on three hundred miles through nearly trackless desert.

All we could see around us was the dead glimmer of salt lakes and the desert eagles perched on telegraph poles, majestically turning their tiny heads towards us.

When we were half-way home the demon resumed his philosophizing:

'Isn't life fascinating?' he addressed the driver. 'I know that you know that there's money in my briefcase which you wouldn't mind lifting for yourself. But you also know that I've got a revolver in my pocket, and that in any case you couldn't get away even if you killed me. If it weren't for that, you'd kill me, wouldn't you, now?'

The demon giggled, pleased with himself.

The driver said nothing, though his tattooed hands tightened on the wheel.

'All men are by nature thieves and murderers,' the demon went on. 'But they're afraid of being punished. Take away punishment and everyone would steal and kill.'

Suddenly the driver jammed his foot on the brake.

I hit the windscreen with my head and when, a moment later, I recovered from the shock the revolver was in the driver's hand and pointing straight at the demon's stomach.

'Get out, you louse,' the driver said tonelessly. 'Every time you open your mouth, a lot of toads come hopping out. It stinks too much of the bog with you here. Get out and leave the money.'

He tore the briefcase from the trembling demon's hand, pushed him out and stepped on the accelerator. We drove on.

706

*2*

'You know what he's thinking about me now, don't you?' snorted the driver. 'He thinks I'm making off with the money. These crooks think everybody's like themselves. Give them half a chance and they'll foul up the whole world.'

I looked back. In the middle distance a small demon was mouthing inaudible shouts and grotesquely waving his arms as he ran after us, but he was growing smaller and smaller.

'You needn't worry about him,' the driver grunted. 'He won't get lost. That kind always fall on their feet—more's the pity.'

We travelled on.

After a while the lorry stopped.

'All the water's boiled away,' said the driver gloomily after a look at the radiator.

He glanced round him at the desert:

'There's no water here.'

He thought for a while, then came to a decision.

'I'll tell you what. You stay here and look after the lorry, while I go and get help. I'll take the money with me because you never know who might turn up. There's all sorts roaming about the steppe. You wait for me.'

He took the bundles of notes from the briefcase, stuffed them inside his shirt and walked away with long, purposeful strides.

I was alone, without food or water in the middle of the huge steppe.

Twice the sun rose and went down.

I wandered about near the lorry, chewing the harsh leaves of the desert plants for their slightly acid moisture. I became delirious. Thousands of giggling demons rose before me, with thousands of meek uncomplaining women washing their feet. And all the demons cackled in triumph:

'You see, he's left you, he won't come back. Now have you convinced yourself that all men are bastards? Now do you believe it?'

But throwing myself down in despair, I pounded the ground with my fists and shouted hysterically:

'I don't believe it! I don't believe it!'

And on the third night, when I was lying in the cab with no more strength left in me, two white, dazzling beams struck my face and small dark figures surrounded the lorry.

The door flew open, two familiar, tattooed arms were flung round me and I recognized the driver's face with its solid row of steel teeth. He was weeping with joy and shouting: 'He's alive! He's alive!'

A tattooed hand put a bottle to my lips and poured milk into my mouth.

Since then, many demons have come my way and, no doubt, many others will, but not one of them will ever shake my faith in my fellow-men.

Yevgeny Yevtushenko, *A Precocious Autobiography*

## 707 STEALING THE CHOCOLATE

The stranger did not trouble to turn his head.

'What's your name?' I asked him uncomfortably.

I was sure he was going to tell me to mind my own business; but he didn't; he rose from his seat. 'Alan Cunningham,' he said. 'We'd better go and get some lemonade. There's a place just across the street.'

I had just taken my first sip when Alan leaned forward, and pointing to a shelf directly behind Mr. Brown's head, asked, 'What are those?'

Mr. Brown turned mechanically, and at the same instant Alan lifted a large flat package of chocolate from the counter and slipped it beneath his jacket.

'Which do you mean?' asked Mr. Brown vaguely.

'Those green sweets. But it doesn't matter; I don't want any.'

There was not a glimmer of expression in his face or in his voice as he spoke. I was profoundly shocked, and what helped to trouble me was the fact that this boy had done what he had done so openly, without knowing whether I should object or not, without really knowing anything about me, and apparently without caring either.

We finished our lemonade (in my case with no great enjoyment) and came out into the sunlit street. He continued to walk beside me. Not a word about what had taken place passed between us, though the embarrassment and constraint appeared to be wholly mine.

'Shall I come round this afternoon?' he asked. 'Will you be here if I do?'

I hesitated, but he did not seem to be conscious that my reply was rather long in coming. He even put his hand on my shoulder as we walked slowly on up Mount Charles. Then I said 'Yes' but I did not look at him as I said it.

It was just before we reached the house that he took the package of chocolate from inside his jacket, and breaking it in half, handed one half to me. I shook my head and rang the bell.

'I'll chuck it away if you don't.'

'You can do as you like,' I answered. 'I don't want it.'

He stood for a moment in silence. 'Well, I'll leave it on the window sill. Somebody will see it and take it.'

Just then my eldest sister opened the door. He smiled at her and without the least hesitation, offered her the chocolate.

Forrest Reid, *Apostate*

708

## A POISON TREE

I was angry with my friend:
I told my wrath, my wrath did end.
I was angry with my foe:
I told it not, my wrath did grow.

And I water'd it in fears,
Night and morning with my tears;
And I sunned it with smiles,
And with soft deceitful wiles.

And it grew both day and night,
Till it bore an apple bright;
And my foe beheld it shine,
And he knew that it was mine,

And into my garden stole
When the night had veil'd the pole:
In the morning glad I see
My foe outstretch'd beneath the tree.

William Blake, *Songs of Experience*

## 709 STANDING IN THE RAIN

1 No use knocking on the window
There is nothing we can do, sir
All the beds are booked already—
There is nothing left for you, sir.

Chorus
Standing in the rain,
Knocking on the window,
Knocking on the window
On a Christmas day.
There he is again
Knocking on the window
Knocking on the window
In the same old way.

2 No use knocking on the window—
Some are lucky, some are not, sir.
We are Christian men and women,
But we're keeping what we've got, sir.

3 No, we haven't got a manger,
No, we haven't got a stable.
We are Christian men and women
Always willing never able.

4 Jesus Christ has gone to heaven
One day he'll be coming back, sir.
In this house he will be welcome.
But we hope he won't be black, sir.

5 Wishing you a merry Christmas
We will now go back to bed, sir!
Till you woke us with your knocking
We were sleeping like the dead, sir.

Sydney Carter

## 710 PRISONERS

In '41 Mama took me back to Moscow. There I saw our enemies for the first time. If my memory is right, nearly twenty thousand

(710) German war prisoners were to be marched in a single column through the streets of Moscow.

The pavements swarmed with onlookers, cordoned off by soldiers and police.

The crowd were mostly women—Russian women with hands roughened by hard work, lips untouched by lipstick and thin hunched shoulders which had borne half the burden of the war. Every one of them must have had a father or a husband, a brother or a son killed by the Germans.

They gazed with hatred in the direction from which the column was to appear.

At last we saw it.

The generals marched at the head, massive chins stuck out, lips folded disdainfully, their whole demeanour meant to show superiority over their plebeian victors.

'They smell of eau-de-cologne, the bastards,' someone in the crowd said with hatred.

The women were clenching their fists. The soldiers and policemen had all they could do to hold them back.

All at once something happened to them.

They saw German soldiers, thin, unshaven, wearing dirty bloodstained bandages, hobbling on crutches or leaning on the shoulders of their comrades; the soldiers walked with their heads down.

The street became dead silent—the only sound was the shuffling of boots and the thumping of crutches.

Then I saw an elderly woman in broken-down boots push herself forward and touch a policeman's shoulder, saying: 'Let me through.' There must have been something about her that made him step aside.

She went up to the column, took from inside her coat something wrapped in a coloured handkerchief and unfolded it. It was a crust of black bread. She pushed it awkwardly into the pocket of a soldier, so exhausted that he was tottering on his feet. And now suddenly from every side women were running towards the soldiers, pushing into their hands bread, cigarettes, whatever they had.

The soldiers were no longer enemies.

They were people.

Yevgeny Yevtushenko, *A Precocious Autobiography*

## 711 WHEN I NEEDED A NEIGHBOUR

When Christ came to call you, did you hear, did you hear?
When Christ came to call you, did you hear?
And the creed and the colour and the name don't matter, do you hear?

When I needed a neighbour: were you there, were you there?
When I needed a neighbour: were you there?
And the creed and the colour and the name don't matter: do you hear?

When I needed a welcome: were you there, were you there?
When I needed a welcome: were you there?
And the creed and the colour and the name don't matter: do you hear?

When I needed a listener: were you there, were you there?
etc.

When I needed a shelter: were you there, were you there?
etc.

When I needed some kindness: were you there, were you there?
etc.

When Christ asked you for service: did you hear, did you hear?
When Christ asked you for service: did you hear?
And the creed and the colour and the name don't matter: do you hear?

Sydney Carter (adapted)

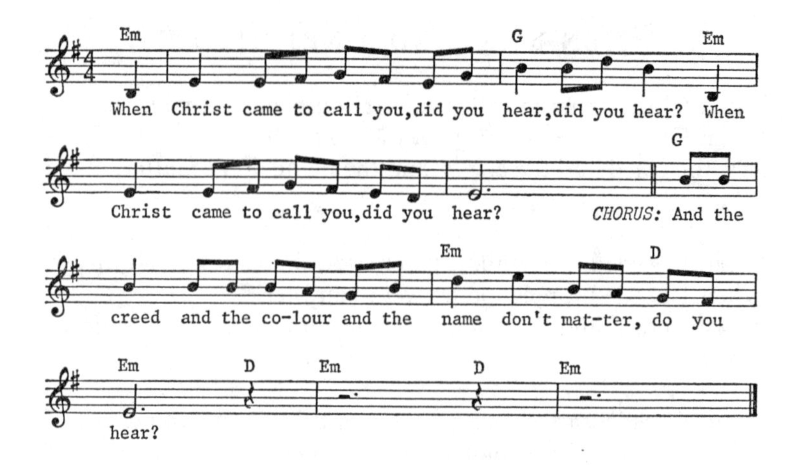


## 712 ARISTOCRACY OF THE SPIRIT

Although I came across many bad people, I grew more and more convinced that the good were in the majority, and I still believe this today. Unfortunately I also noticed that the wicked usually hang together even when they hate each other and this is their strength, whereas the good tend to be more scattered and this is their weakness.

I also arrived at a new standard by which to measure intellectuals. I realized that a man's intelligence is not the sum of what he knows but the soundness of his judgement of people and his power to understand and to help them. From this standpoint some of the most educated people I met were much less cultured than ignorant soldiers, peasants, workers, and even criminals. For me, the aristocracy of the spirit is not made up of those who can spend hours quoting everything from Plato to Kafka and Joyce, but of those whose hearts are open to others. Whilst even the most educated people, if their education only helps them to be better scoundrels, are for me the rabble.

Yevgeny Yevtushenko, *A Precocious Autobiography*

## 713 INDIFFERENCE

When Jesus came to Golgotha,
They hanged him on a tree;

713)

They drove great nails through hands and feet
And made a Calvary;
They crowned him with a crown of thorns,
Red were his wounds and deep.
For those were crude and cruel days,
And human flesh was cheap.

When Jesus came to Birmingham,
They simply passed him by;
They never hurt a hair of him,
They only let him die.
For men had grown more tender,
And they would not give him pain;
They only just passed down the street,
And left him in the rain.

Still Jesus cried, 'Forgive them,
For they know not what they do,'
And still it rained the wintry rain
That drenched him through and through.
The crowds went home and left the streets
Without a soul to see;
And Jesus crouched against a wall,
And cried for Calvary.

G. A. Studdert Kennedy, *The Unutterable Beauty*

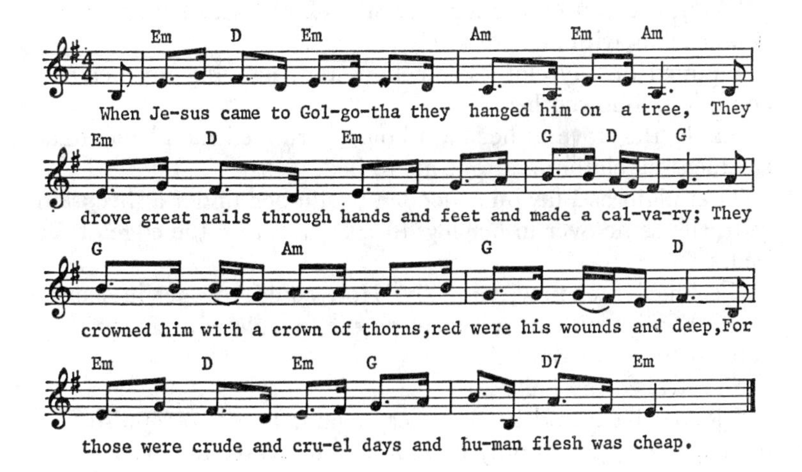

(*When he was fifteen, Yevtushenko joined a geological expedition to Siberia as a labourer*)

This cruelly harsh life was teaching me to have faith in human beings.

One day I discovered I had lice. My clothes were teeming with the filthy vermin. I was in despair, I didn't know what to do.

I ran off into the steppe and climbed down into an abandoned dig. There I took off my clothes and set about killing the lice. Somewhere high above me the grass rustled, the birds sang and the clouds billowed; while I stood hating myself, naked, alone, shivering with cold and disgust at the bottom of my pit with the frogs giving me scornful looks.

I couldn't change my clothes because I had no others.

Suddenly I started as it grew darker in the pit and, looking up through the rectangular opening, saw a young peasant woman, bare-footed and with a yoke slung over her shoulders, standing on the edge.

I leant hard against the side of the pit, wishing I could vanish into the earth, and sobbed with shame, covering my face with my hands.

There was a soft thud as the woman jumped down.

She pulled my hands away from my face. Intensely blue eyes between long black lashes looked at me with a warm kindness which is much better than pity.

'What are you crying for, you silly child?' asked the woman. 'Come along with me.'

I pulled on my clothes somehow and, hanging my head in confusion, followed her.

She lit the stove in her bath house, scrubbed me like a child, steamed my clothes and put me to bed.

That night as I lay on a wooden trestle-bed under a sheepskin coat, she came over in her nightdress and sat on the edge of the bed.

'Feeling better now, you silly? How could you get in such a state? You mustn't be afraid of people, people will always help you if you're in trouble.'

She stroked my hair.

I jerked back and began to cry again. I was so repulsive to myself, I felt I could only be repulsive to everyone else.

'What a fuss. I suppose you've got it into your head that you're disgusting. You're not in the least.'

She lay down by me under the sheepskin, her big strong body with its clean, bath-house smell of birch leaves pressed against mine.

I shall never forget her.

Ever since then I have known that if all the values in this world are more or less questionable, the most important thing in life is kindness.

I also knew another sort of human warmth, rougher and more selfconscious—the fatherly kindness of men.

The soldiers during the war, who clumsily pushed into my hand lumps of sugar stuck with shreds of tobacco; the peasants who once rescued me from an angry she-bear; the geologists who refused to let me carry my rucksack and shifted it to their own shoulders; the workmen who cured the torn blisters on my feet with herbs—all these sowed in my childhood the seeds of a deep trust in the kindness of my fellow-men.

Yevgeny Yevtushenko, *A Precocious Autobiography* (adapted)

# Helping Other People

715

## ORPHANS OF ALL AGES

### FOUR READINGS

*I*

Sister Jeanne is a big, burly, fair-skinned French peasant, with a strong face and quick blue eyes. She walks like a man and speaks her mind without fear. She has worked in Vietnam for twenty-seven years and can compare three wars in the same country. 'No one ever troubled the sisters,' she said. Sister Jeanne, and the thirty-six Catholic nuns with her, are powerless and need no protection.

Sister Jeanne's refuge is a large compound with long one-storey stucco buildings forming a square around a new, cement-covered cistern. The gravel paths are raked, the strips of grass are well tended, a few trees give shade, the place is clean and quiet.

It is also a sorrowful corner of hell, an orphanage for all ages, furnished with bare wood beds, 1,500 of them, each one a home for the homeless, the destitute, the sick, the abandoned. 'There never was such misery as now,' Sister Jeanne says. 'This last year.'

The crêche is an enormous room half-filled by cots for babies. The babies are tiny, wizened, soft skeletons, with pain already marked on their faces. They are too weak to move or cry. 'Starved,' Sister Jeanne said. 'All the little ones come to us sick from hunger. What can you expect? The people are too poor.'

In Sister Jeanne's crêche, beyond the cots of the babies, small children crawled on the floor, or sat with outstretched legs, or stood alone; all thin, all silent, all with dark, sad eyes. Sister Jeanne said: 'The misery, the misery. Everything is here. War orphans. War wounded. Tubercular. Crippled by polio. Deaf and dumb. Blind. Children of lepers. Children of refugees who cannot feed them. Men do not see the real misery of war. They do not wish to. Why don't they do something for the poor people of Saigon? It cannot go on like this.'

The Vietnamese exist as all-inclusive families, and they love children. No one could guess how many orphans are sheltered by relatives. Is it not strange that we count and proclaim only military casualties? These lonely waifs of war should be listed as wounded; and wounded for ever.

715

*2*

The school-age children were down the road at a school where the nuns teach. Older girls and women sat or lay on the hard wood beds in their building; they have nothing else to do, month after month. Most of the adults are too sick or frail or old or handicapped to work. The relatively able do maintenance jobs around the refuge and are rewarded by an extra food ration. But occupational therapy, proper medical care, any amusement are not even dreamed of: hunger rules.

Sister Jeanne talked encouragingly in Vietnamese to a girl of about sixteen, and slowly as if her back had been broken, the girl tried to raise herself to a sitting position. 'Hysterical paralysis,' Sister Jeanne said. 'Her mother was killed in their hamlet, bombs; and the girl was left alone with her father. It is curious for only two to remain in a Vietnamese family. Then one morning the girl woke and her father was dead; I don't know how. She became completely paralysed at once, but she moves a little more every day.'

Further down the long room, a middle-aged woman babbled and laughed, and a little girl of six or seven tumbled over her bed, merrily; I thought they were playing. Sister Jeanne made a quick gesture towards her head. She smiled at this cheerful pair and said, 'They have lost their reason, poor things. They are harmless and happier here; I do not want to send them to the horrible Government lunatic asylum. Many women have gone mad from their sufferings; children too.'

715 *3*

An old woman greeted Sister Jeanne as they all did, if awake, or not lying numb in sickness. Sister Jeanne patted her scrawny shoulder and pointed to the shelf under her bed. 'It is all they own in the world.' Neatly arranged, on the shelf that is part of the bed, were a cooking pot, a tin plate, a bowl, a rolled mat, folded rags of clothing, a coolie hat. By the door, the last bed belonged to a woman more emaciated than the others. She stared at the wall, unmoving. 'Yes,' Sister Jeanne said, 'Another. Lost in darkness. She has not spoken since she was brought here.'

Sister Jeanne was proud of the new cistern, her achievement. At the corners of each building a tank, the size of a telephone booth, collected rainwater, hardly sufficient for 1,500 people. 'Can you imagine how it was when the poor people wept and implored me for a drop of water and I had none?' In a test of the drinking water of all the world's capitals, according to a Vietnamese doctor, Saigon city water proved to be the most polluted. Besides it is not piped to the slum suburbs, the impure water must be brought in tins. Sister Jeanne began to build her cistern and ran out of money; anxiously, she wrote her first and only letter to US AID, which was not answered.

'Embassy ladies' rescued Sister Jeanne and finished her cistern. Though the diet of the refuge is distressingly inadequate, the people now have enough water to drink.

715 *4*

Sister Jeanne walked with me to the gate of the refuge compound. Across the unpaved road, the slum hutches spread in length and depth as far as we could see. Many of those next to the road are shops, square booths displaying cheap shabby wares, the essentials of life. At night, these shops become homes, and large families sleep somehow among the stock of cotton cloth and pots and candles and dried beans and kerosene. Sister Jeanne considered the view which faces her every day, and spoke her mind.

'Think of the heat the people have to suffer in those disgusting little houses. When there is plague or cholera among them, they hide it. How could they live if they are put in quarantine for forty days? Ports, roads, all very nice; what does it mean to those miserable people? With the bombing, there will be more and more refugees. They come to Saigon if they can because it is the safest place. And the misery grows. They will win this war only if they feed the people. They could start here in Saigon, now. Certainly there is a grenade now and then; it is also occasionally dangerous in Paris and London. The people need soup kitchens and ration cards, they must have them. And someone,' she said, speaking from her heart, 'who cares for human misery.'

Martha Gellhorn, *The Face of War*

716

## LIFE WITH THE DOSSERS

### TWO READINGS

*I*

I wasn't thrown out of school for having men in my bedroom after ten o'clock at night or anything ghastly like this. I was thrown out purely because I was wasting my own time.

I think there's always been a social conscience in me. I think it became more prominent when I got thrown out of school, because I felt rejected myself and I suddenly looked around to see how many other people were rejected. I found other young people who had similar problems to myself, family problems. Also rebels. I recognised that they were more or less in the same situation as myself, but they didn't actually worry me until I met up with the dossers. I'd been to the country for the weekend and was coming back late on Sunday night. I crossed Waterloo Station about 11.30 p.m. sort of in my togs and pearls and things, and I saw all these dirty drunk old men lying on the benches,

16 *1*) under the benches, under newspapers on the station, and I had perhaps the typical reaction of most people and thought 'how disgusting' and walked on. It suddenly occurred to me that I really was no better than them, except that I had a roof and a bed to go home to, and a hot meal in the oven for me. I was damned lucky to have this, but I felt just as rejected as they did, and I thought, how terrible, me being brought up a Roman Catholic and a Christian. How dare I walk by and say: 'God, how disgusting.' I must have been about 16 or 17, and felt very foolish because I didn't know what to say to them. I went and bought a packet of cigarettes and found two of the scruffiest men I could and sat between them, and tried to start a conversation. But they were so drunk they didn't really know what I was saying and as soon as I sat between them my Good Samaritan feelings left me.

Why?

The smell . . . it was absolutely dreadful. A smell of urine, alcohol, stale flesh, you know, and I just wanted to get up and run, but I couldn't because my two drunks on either side of me were leaning heavily on me and I knew that if I got up they'd just fall on top of each other. So I was squashed in between them and I sat there thinking: 'What do I do next?' A West Indian staggered over, he was very drunk too, a hat cocked on one side, big cheesy grin on his face, and looked me up and down and said: 'What's a nice filly like you doing here?' So I explained that I wasn't really a permanent, just temporary, and asked him what had happened to these men. And he said: 'Don't worry about us, miss. You go home, and thank the Lord you've got a home to go to.' So I said: 'Yes, but what happens to these?' And he said: 'Woman, you're trespassing on their bedroom now.' It horrified me that here were people who regarded the station as their bedroom. I just couldn't believe it. I always thought people were like me, with homes. I was so young and naïve and thought everyone had a home. I think probably for the first time in my life I got down on my knees and thanked God I had a home. I made a vow—and it was all rather dramatic because it was about three o'clock in the morning and, you know, the moon was shining—that I would do something for these people. Next morning my vow seemed rather stupid. How the devil was I going to help them? I thought: Well, I must make an effort to do something to fulfil this vow. And that was when I decided that, with the money

I was earning during the day, I would go and spend it on food, cigarettes and warm clothing and blankets and anything that I felt they would like. That was the beginning of a year of night vigils out on Waterloo Station. I had to be careful because the policeman moved them on at two, four and six. I had to be there in between the police coming and moving them on. I had quite a lot of difficulties, because it wasn't just avoiding the police, it was also avoiding my father. I knew that he wouldn't appreciate his 17-year-old daughter going and mixing with dirty drunk old men in the middle of the night. I didn't dare go down the stairs, because they creaked, so I had to climb down the drainpipe. They never knew a thing about it. I climbed down the drainpipe to a brick wall and then I used to jump from the brick wall onto the ground and get my bicycle out of the garage. There was a haversack with all these goodies and things, and I used to turn up at Waterloo Station about three-quarters of an hour later, having bicycled about six miles. It was a question of just handing out the food and going.

I did it for about a year.

716

*2*

Eventually I came to feel that by this night vigil I was never going to get to know the dossers because I was just a little charity do-gooder who turned up: it was like being a little angel from heaven. So I went looking round for something which would really take up my whole time, and I found it in the Simon Community. We started a house down in Stepney where the meths-drinkers were.

They lived on bomb-sites or in dirty filthy derelict buildings. They used to use one corner to sleep in—huddled together to keep warm—and the other corner was usually used as a lavatory. They usually brushed all rubbish aside so that they could have a little patch to sleep without having to sleep on the bottles and glass and dirty old paper.

They are regarded by everyone as a hopeless case. That's the reason why no one bothers with them. They are going to be dead in a few years. My role really was to keep them alive if they wanted to be kept alive, and a lot of them didn't. They just wanted to die off. This was going to be their only release from the hell they were living. But those that did want to stay alive I fed and kept alive that way. I used to go and con food for them at Covent Garden first thing in the morning. I was a sort of little Florence Nightingale. They were always falling in the fire. We always kept a fire going on the bomb-site to keep them warm, and one night one of my lads burnt his leg off completely. I was always taking them to hospital. When they eventually got nicked, which they inevitably did, I used to go and visit them in prison. When they were in hospital I used to visit them in hospital. And when they were dying I used to sit beside them and hold their hand.

Before a meths-drinker dies he goes blind. This is the first sign of death. He can't see and he has no possible control over his functions. I was sitting up all night beside one man, he said: 'Sal, why do you do this?' And I said: 'Well, probably I don't really know.' I muttered something about being a Christian—what one does mutter on these occasions. And he said: 'Sal, I'll be a Christian.' It was too late to say: 'Well, mate, you know, you won't be a Christian; you are going to be dead in twenty-four hours.' But the point was he was so thrilled that someone really cared. And he died peacefully.

Sally Trench, *Down among the Dead Men*, from *The Listener* (adapted)

717

## A HUMAN EXPERIMENT

TWO READINGS

*I*

This afternoon there is archery on the lawn below the terrace. The sun shines on the great house, and shaven grass bordered by rhododendrons falls meltingly away to woods, outposts of the New Forest, and to a lake with water-lilies. If you lived here all would surely be well.

All is not well, physically, with the archers. They are in their teens and twenties. Some are cruelly deformed; some are polio victims; one was paralysed at 17 in a car smash; some are severely spastic. Some of them could no more pull the string of a bow than fly—or even walk.

A Yorkshire boy with muscular dystrophy aims the arrow from a bow held for him by another Yorkshire boy who is healthy and brawny. They are both members of a party who have come down for this week from a home for the handicapped in Harrogate. Like all the others, both the healthy and the disabled, he has paid £7 to do this. There are 32 like him here, from youth clubs all over the country, spending a week with 32 young handicapped people.

It is hard work. The able-bodied rise at seven and help the disabled to wash and dress; there is no time to be either embarrassed or pitied after the first hour of the first day. Everyone here is *needed*; if *you* don't get up at seven someone else will be late for breakfast. Two girls, this afternoon, are just taking one of the spastics to give her a bath and set her hair.

After tea today there is an hour of readings. The disabled listen intently. Theresa, a spastic, lolls her head, an intermittent gagging in her throat the only other sound. But several of the healthy ones fall gently asleep; it is the only period of the day when they can be completely passive.

Photography is one of five special sessions, one of which all members attend in the mornings. The others are Gadgets and Aids, Art, Out and About, and Show Business.

Show Business is directed by a young bearded professional drama adviser. His course is built around the idea of a 'TV show', to be presented to the others on the last night. He directs able and disabled in exactly the same manner. The announcer is a congenitally deformed girl, terribly pleased at being able to walk to the microphone.

'That's good, Judy. But keep a bit of a grin going, and lift it, lift it right up out here.' It could be said to any actor. They have begun with standard limbering-up procedures. 'Shake every part of your body, as loose and relaxed as you can.' The able ones writhe in every limb; some in the chairs move their maximum three inches. But you have to remind yourself of this, already they are all just a cast.

Sometimes it's a disabled performer, sometimes not; the longer it goes on the less you notice. But there has been trouble for Theresa, who wants to sing a song by herself; and she can't.

717

*2*

Wild smiles sometimes rush across Theresa's face. On a small baby's face often the physical smile seems somehow to *precede* the actual mood of joy, almost to cause it, instead of following as it

17 2) does in a reflective adult. And this is how it is with Theresa, it moves across her face like April weather. It is the same with her tears, which are wild, as though the whole world were weeping through *her*.

At lunch a young girl Janice (who happens to be a nurse) sits feeding her with infinite patience.

Tony, from Harrogate (polio), is making a replacement for the little square board containing the letters of the alphabet, which Theresa uses to communicate. As she cannot co-ordinate her hands she often spreads her fingers over three or four letters so that no one is quite sure which one she means. So Tony is making it bigger, and he has added some words to go at the bottom, after much thought as to which would be the most useful. He has decided on THANKS, PLEASE, CAN, WILL, YOU, WHAT, HUNGRY, THIRSTY, MY, YES and NO.

At the other end of the art room Alice, who has three rudimentary and useless fingers, is painting yesterday's archery scene, with a brush held in her teeth. Her colours are mixed for her by Timmy, who is French. Perfectly healthy himself, he lives in Paris. His disabled brother and sister came last year. (There is nothing quite like this in France.) This year, on the Sunday when they were packing to come again, the disabled brother died; so Timmy has come over with the sister.

Twenty-year-old Anne is here for the day only. It is her day off from the hospital where she is training as a nurse. She embarked on this career after coming here two years ago and realising 'I must do something with my life.'

Young helpers here are not far enough outside their action to see it as any kind of a 'good deed'. They are embarrassed when asked why they do it. There's simply a unity about this life together. Ron is a spastic who can only walk with a kind of wheeled handrail to lean on, his legs jerking wildly. Out at the archery he is crawling up from one lawn to another. 'Why, Ron, mate, what you crawling down there for?' says a boy called David; there is an infinite kindness in his voice. 'Come on, let's give you a piggy-back.'

That night there is a showing of the film 'Summer Holiday' with Cliff Richard. There is a fairly unmusical joining in when the well-known pop numbers occur; and a break when someone has a seizure and is carried out.

There is a sweet-faced young girl here who once worked in a

coffee bar ('Not', she says, 'one of those rough ones. It was where ordinary people went'). One night she lifted a heavy dust-bin at home, and felt pins-and-needles in her legs. But something told her it was worse than that. She struggled upstairs—the last unaided journey she has ever made—and called her brother. She lives in a wheelchair and her legs are simply shrinking away. She says the doctors do not know what it is.

It seems irrational. Why?

And why is the blazing rhododendron so beautiful outside? Is there some love or vision that brings pain and beauty together? The participants would find this sort of speculation pompous. They don't want to know who is finding answers, who is being good and who is being done good to. They simply get on with it.

Paul Jennings, from *The Observer* (adapted)

718

## THE MAHRATTA GHATS

(*Siva, the third person of the Hindu Trinity, represents the power to destroy and to reproduce*)

The valleys crack and burn, the exhausted plains
Sink their black teeth into the horny veins
Straggling the hills' red thighs, the bleating goats
—Dry bents and bitter thistles in their throats—
Thread the loose rocks by immemorial tracks.
Dark peasants drag the sun upon their backs.

High on the ghat the new turned soil is red,
The sun has ground it to the finest red,
It lies like gold within each horny hand.
Siva has spilt his seed upon this land.

Will she who burns and withers on the plain
Leave, ere too late, her scraggy herds of pain,
The cow-dung fire and the trembling beasts,
The little wicked gods, the grinning priests,
And climb, before a thousand years have fled,
High as the eagle to her mountain bed
Whose soil is fine as flour and blood-red?

But no! She cannot move. Each arid patch
Owns the lean folk who plough and scythe and thatch
Its grudging yield and scratch its stubborn stones.
The small gods suck the marrow from their bones.
And did a thousand years go by in vain?
And does another thousand start again?

Alun Lewis, *Ha! Ha! Among The Trumpets*

## 719 FEED US NOW, O SON OF GOD

1 The people came to hear you
The poor, the lame, the blind
They asked for food to save them
And you fed them, body and mind

Chorus: Feed us now, O Son of God
As you fed them long ago

2 The ones who didn't listen
The rich, the safe, the sure
They didn't think they needed
The offering of a cure

3 And it's hard for us to listen
Things haven't changed at all
We've got the things we wanted
We don't want to hear your call

4 Yet millions still have hunger
Disease, no homes, and fear
We offer them so little
And it costs them very dear

5 So help us see the writing
Written clear upon the wall
He who doesn't feed his neighbour
Will get no food at all

Peter Allen

720

## HELP IN THE HIMALAYAS

### FIVE READINGS

*I*

*The Sherpas' Request for Help*

Shivering a little in the cold, we huddled around the smoky scrub fire. It wasn't a pleasant campsite, here on this barren windy hollow beside the Tolam Bau glacier, but we hardly noticed. For hours we had been engrossed in a discussion about the history of the Sherpa people—and their future—in a broken mixture of Nepali and English. (Sherpa is the name of the people living mostly above 7,000 feet on the south side of the Himalyan range. They originally came from Tibet, are of Mongolian origin, Mahayana Buddhist religion, and Nepalese nationality.)

In a warm flood of memory I dwelt on the many things we mountain-climbers had gained over the years from the Sherpas. Not only help in the physical sense—so many loads carried here, so many risks taken there, or so many lives (alas) lost somewhere else. But few of us had failed to learn something from the character and temperament of the men themselves—their hardiness and cheerfulness, their vigour and loyalty, and their freedom from our civilized curse of self-pity.

'Tell us, Urkien, if there were one thing we could do for your village, what should it be? I know you would like a medical clinic and believe that your farms could be improved. But if you had one choice what would it be?'

'We would like our children to go to school, sahib! Of all the things you have, learning is the one we most desire for our children. With all respect, sahib, we know you have little to teach us in strength and toughness. We do not envy you your restless spirits—perhaps we are happier and more content than you are? But knowledge for our children—that we would like to see!'

This conversation took place in October 1960. In June of the following year four of us remained behind at the conclusion of our major expedition objectives to build the first school in the village of Khumjung—at 13,000 feet on the flanks of Khumbila, the sacred mountain, only a dozen miles from the foot of Mount Everest.

720

## 2

### *People Create Goodwill*

Slowly and painfully we are seeing world-wide acceptance of the fact that the wealthier and more technologically advanced countries have a direct responsibility to help the undeveloped ones—not only through a sense of charity, but also because only in this way can we ever hope to see any permanent peace and security for ourselves.

The importance of goodwill is frequently overlooked or ignored. We should not expect people to be continuously grateful for what is being done for them—the giver-receiver relationship is always a tricky and dangerous one, and most aid is strongly flavoured with self-interest. Whereas gratitude has something of inequality about it, goodwill is an active and growing idea that a proud man need not feel ashamed to entertain. One of the most successful creators of goodwill in recent years has been the American Peace Corps. Few of the general public in an undeveloped country have any personal contact with the money or the architects of an aid project, but through organizations such as the Peace Corps they can at last obtain a direct personal relationship. With worth-while motivation, the volunteers live simply in town and village, learn the local language, work with their hands and minds alongside the local people, and at the same time build up a fund of goodwill that does much to counteract the side effects of more grandiose projects.

The basic fact is that *people* create goodwill—money cannot do it on its own. An excellent example of this is the 'Swiss' dairy in

Katmandu. This dairy treats the milk for most of Katmandu and is a worthy project indeed. The funds and equipment for the dairy were donated by the New Zealand Government under the Colombo Plan, but an enthusiastic and hard-working Swiss manages the concern, so it is called locally the 'Swiss' dairy and creates much goodwill for the Swiss as a result.

720

## 3

### *Survival in the Himalayas*

It is commonly accepted that the isolated mountain valleys of the Himalayas are Shangri-Las where there is no sickness and people live on forever. Such, alas, is not the case—or certainly not in the various Himalayan regions I have visited. Ill health and disease are just as common as in civilization, but there are no medical aids or drugs to combat them and people recover through their own natural resistance or they die. A high percentage of children never reach maturity. Most of the Sherpa mothers with two or three children have actually borne four, five or six. And the number of young mothers who don't survive childbirth is appallingly high. During the course of one of my expeditions two of my ten best Sherpas had their wives die in childbirth.

Much of this is due to dirty conditions and is aggravated by a complete lack of any sort of medical knowledge. But the rigours of the woman's life in this society must also play an important part. There's no time to rest and recuperate. Work must go on: there is food to be prepared, fields to be tilled, firewood collected and huge loads carried. A good example of this is the case of Mrs. Khunjo Chumbi, wife of one of the Khumjung headmen. Three years ago when Queen Elizabeth came on a state visit to Nepal, Mrs. Chumbi was determined to go to Katmandu despite the fact that her sixth baby was due at any moment. With a 180-mile walk in front of her she made only one concession to her condition—she reduced the work load she was carrying to a modest 30 pounds. Four days' march and sixty miles from her destination Mrs. Chumbi was forced to take shelter in a tiny tumbledown wayside cottage. She emerged an hour later holding her new son, then continued the march towards Katmandu. The journey was completed without further delay and the baby was well nourished even though his mother had been walking fourteen or fifteen miles a day.

After one night in the city it became apparent that all was not well with Mrs. Chumbi. She was having severe afterbirth pains, so we rushed her to the local mission hospital. Here an examination showed that she was still carrying the placenta. Doctors quickly acted to rectify this problem. Within twenty-four hours Mrs. Chumbi appeared smiling and happy, dressed in her best clothes, at the British Embassy garden party and achieved her desire to meet Queen Elizabeth, 'the headman of many villages'.

Mrs. Chumbi's experience ended quite happily, thanks to prompt medical treatment (and her own remarkable toughness), but in most cases there would have been only one result—the mother's death. In Sherpaland the 'weaklings' die quickly; only the tough and hardy can hope to surve.

720

## *4*

## *Doctors in the Himalayas*

Himalayan expeditions have built up a tradition of giving medical attention to all who come asking for it. We went even farther than this. With two doctors and a large supply of drugs we established a medical clinic in Khumjung for a six-month period. Our aim was not only to give immediate medical treatment to the Sherpas, but also to carry out a wider investigation with a view to establishing more long-range medical aid in the future.

From the time the walk-in started, our two doctors were kept busy. I remember particularly the evening we spent in Junbesi. One of our young Sherpas, a delightful boy, had a badly swollen leg and was in considerable pain. Phil Houghton decided he must operate. We laid the boy on a tarpaulin spread on the ground. All our porters and the entire population of the village clustered around as Phil cut the leg open and removed large quantities of fluid and blood. The poor lad was absolutely terrified and convinced he was about to die. Desmond held his hand and kept up a continual stream of encouraging comments, but we were all mighty glad when the job was finished. As the boy was showing all the signs of shock—less from the operation than from the outspoken predictions of disaster by the Junbesi villagers—I put up an extra tent, and the pale and shaking lad was slipped into a sleeping bag. Well sedated, he was left to sleep peacefully away from prying eyes. By morning he was already on the road to recovery.

Meanwhile the doctors were carrying on with a variety of patients: a boy bitten by a dog; various old ladies with pains in their tummies and chests; a singularly robust woman who said she hadn't slept for twenty-four days; and, perhaps saddest of all, a young couple with an eighteen-month-old child suffering from TB of the spine. I can still see the father's large, sad eyes filling with hopelessness as he was told that the only chance was a hospital—how could he spare the time and money for this? Being a doctor in such an area must, despite many frustrations, be a rewarding occupation. Certainly no one can bring more immediate blessing or see more spectacular results for his efforts. These people have built up no resistance to antibiotics even in their simpler forms, and the cures that can be effected at times verge on the miraculous.

720

*5*

*Practical Help*

I am firmly convinced that one of the finest ways of helping an undeveloped community is to give the opportunity for worth-while and profitable employment. Free handouts are rarely successful. Too often the money or goods go into the hands of the wealthy traders who need it least. But by creating jobs for the community, the money goes into the individual homes where it does the most good (and the traders benefit as well). Perhaps most important of all, if a man devotes his strength and skill to some worth-while task he not only feels he has earned the money honestly but he retains his pride and his independence in the process.

Edmund Hillary, *Schoolhouse in the Clouds*

# Disciples, Saints and Crusaders

721

## SCHWEITZER AND SELF-SACRIFICE

In our time there have been few men more brilliant or versatile than Schweitzer. While still in his twenties he was in the front rank of theologians and philosophers, a famous organist and a recognised authority on Bach. He could have asked so much of life. But he decided that he would devote himself to his studies and his art until he was thirty; then he would train as a doctor and go to Africa to pay what he could of the debt which he felt the white man owes to the coloured. And as he stood on the deck of the ship bringing him home for a brief furlough, he looked back to Africa and said, 'I feel myself humbled, and ask myself how I earned the privilege of carrying on such a work'. 'Whosoever will save his life shall lose it,' said Jesus, 'and whosoever will lose his life for my sake and the gospel's, the same shall find it.' These men have discovered His secret that real life is in self-giving not in bargaining.

Leslie J. Tizard, *Facing Life and Death*

722

## DANILO DOLCI
## IN THE STEPS OF ST. FRANCIS

In a society such as ours—a society of enormous numbers subordinated to an ever-expanding and almost omnipresent technology—a new Gandhi, a modern St. Francis needs to be equipped with much more than compassion and seraphic love. He needs a degree in one of the sciences and a nodding acquaintance with a dozen disciplines beyond the pale of his own special field.

Danilo Dolci is one of these modern Franciscans-with-a-degree. In his case the degree is in architecture and engineering; but surrounding this central core of specialised knowledge, there is an aura of general scientific culture. He knows what specialists in other fields are talking about, respects their methods and is willing and eager to take advice from them. But what he knows and what he can learn from other specialists is always, for him, the instrument of charity. His science is applied within a frame of reference, whose co-ordinates are an unshakable love for his fellows and a no less unshakable faith in and respect for the objects of that love. The love inspires him to use his knowledge for the benefit of the weak and unfortunate; the faith and respect keep him constantly trying to encourage the weak and the unfortunate to become self-reliant, to help them to help themselves.

When Danilo Dolci came to Sicily from the North, it was on an aesthetic and scientific pilgrimage. He was interested in ancient Greek architecture and had decided to spend a week or two at Segesta, studying the ruins. But the man with the professional interest in Doric temples was also (and primarily) the man of conscience and loving-kindness. Dolci came to Sicily for the sake of its ancient beauty; what kept him in Sicily—and Sicily is now his home—was the island's present wretchedness. What Keats called 'the giant misery of the world' is more than averagely gigantic in Sicily—particularly on the western end of the island. On Dolci's mind that first glimpse of Western Sicily's giant misery acted as a categorical imperative. Something simply had to be done about it. He settled down, some thirty miles from Palermo, in a rural slum called Trappeto, married one of his neighbours, a widow with five young children, moved into a small house with none of the usual conveniences, and from that base of operations launched his campaign against the misery that surrounded him.

Aldous Huxley, Introduction to *To Feed The Hungry*
by Danilo Dolci

## 723 A PREACHER AMONG TEENAGERS IN NEW YORK

FOUR READINGS

*I*

### *Preaching to the Gang*

I hadn't been in New York half an hour and already I was being introduced to my second street gang. Tommy gave me street directions, but I couldn't follow them. 'Boy, you *are* a rube aren't you! Nancy!' he called one of the girls standing nearby. 'Take the preacher down to the GGI's, will you?'

The GGI's met in a basement on 134th Street. To reach their 'clubroom' Nancy and I walked down a flight of cement stairs, weaving our way past garbage pails that were chained to the building, past thin cats with stiff filthy fur, past a pile of vodka bottles, until finally Nancy stopped and rapped, two-quick, four-slow, on a door.

A girl opened it. I thought at first that she was playing a joke.

She was the perfect clichéd stereotype of a tramp. She had no shoes on, she held a can of beer, a cigarette hung sideways from her lips, her hair was unkempt and the shoulder of her dress was pulled down in a deliberately revealing way. Two things kept me from laughing. This girl's face showed no signs of amusement. And she was a child, a little girl in her teens.

'Maria?' said Nancy. 'Can we come in? I want you to meet a friend.'

Maria shrugged one shoulder—the one holding her dress up—and opened the door wider. The room inside was dark and it took me a while to realize that it was filled with couples. Boys and girls of high-school age sat together in this cold and ill-smelling room and I realized with a jolt—Tommy was right: I was a rube—that Maria had probably not taken off her own shoes, nor pulled down her own dress. Someone switched on a wan overhead light bulb. The kids slowly untangled themselves and looked up with the same bored eyes I'd seen in the faces of the first gang I'd met, the Rebels.

'This is that preacher that was kicked out of the Farmer trial,' said Nancy.

Immediately, I had their attention. More important, I had their sympathy. That afternoon I had a chance to preach my first sermon to a New York gang. I didn't try to get a complicated message over to them, just that they were loved. They were loved as they were, there, amid the vodka bottles and the weary searching sex. God understood what they were looking for when they drank and played with sex, and He yearned for them to have what they were looking for: stimulation and exhilaration and a sense of being sought after. But not out of a cheap bottle in a cold tenement basement. God had so much higher hopes for them.

Once, when I paused, a boy said, 'Keep it up, Preach. You're coming through.'

It was the first time I heard the expression. It meant that I was reaching their hearts, and it was the highest compliment they could have paid my preaching.

723

## 2

### *The Drug Addict*

I would have left that basement hideout, half an hour later, with a feeling of great encouragement, except for one thing. There, among the GGI's, I had my first encounter with narcotics. Maria—she turned out to be President of the GGI Debs, the girl-gang attached to the GGI's—interrupted me when I said God could help them toward a new life.

'Not me, Davie. Not me.'

Maria had put down her glass, and she had pulled her dress back up over her shoulder.

'Why not you, Maria?'

In answer, she simply pulled up her sleeve and showed me her inner arm at the elbow.

I didn't understand. 'I don't follow you, Maria.'

'Come here.' Maria walked over beneath the light bulb and held out her arm. I could see little wounds on it like festered mosquito bites. Some were old and blue. Some were fresh and livid. I suddenly knew what this teen-age girl was trying to say to me. She was a dope addict.

'I'm a mainliner, Davie. There's no hope for me, not even from God.'

I looked around the room to see if I could catch in the other youngsters' eyes a sense that Maria was being melodramatic. No one was smiling. In that one fleeting glance into the faces of a circle of kids, I *knew* what I was later to find out in police statistics and hospital reports: medicine does not have an answer to drug addiction. Maria had expressed the opinion of the experts: there was virtually no hope for the 'mainline' addict, the one who injects heroin directly into the bloodstream.

Maria was a mainliner.

723

## *3*

### *The Tough Gang Leaders and the Skinny Preacher*

'I am a country preacher,' I told them, 'three hundred miles from home, and I have a message for you.'

Nobody was listening. Directly in front of me a boy and girl were doing the Fish, the grinding hips that brought whistles and clapping from onlookers. Others picked it up, cigarettes hanging sideways from their mouths, bodies quivering with excitement. It was hardly the setting for a sermon.

In despair, I bowed my head.

'Lord,' I said, 'I can't even get their attention. If You are doing a work here, I will have to ask You even for this.'

33) While I was still praying, the change began.

It was the smallest children who settled down first. But when I opened my eyes I noticed that a lot of the older boys who had been leaning up against the school fence, smoking, had straightened up, taken their hats off and were now standing with heads slightly bowed.

I was so startled by the sudden silence that I was at a loss for words.

When finally I did begin to speak, I chose John 3.16 as my text: 'For God so loved the world that He gave His only begotten Son that whosoever believeth in Him should not perish, but have everlasting life.' I told them that God loved them as they were, right then. He knew what they were. He knew their hatred and their anger. He knew that some of them had committed murder. But God also saw what they were going to be in the future, not only what they had been in the past.

That was all. I had said what I had to say, and I stopped.

A heavy, eloquent silence hung over the street. I could hear the flag flapping in a light breeze. I told the boys and girls then that I was going to ask for something special to happen to them. I was going to ask for a miracle, that in the next moment their lives be completely changed.

I bowed my head again and prayed that the Holy Spirit do His work. I raised my head. Nobody moved. I asked if there was anyone who wanted to come up front where we could talk. No response.

It was an awkward situation. I had made an experiment in letting the Spirit lead, and He didn't seem to be leading anywhere.

And then suddenly I heard myself saying, without any intention on my part:

'All right, now. They tell me that you've got a couple of pretty tough gangs here in Fort Greene. I want to talk to your Presidents and your Vice-Presidents. If you are so big and tough, you won't mind coming up and shaking hands with a skinny preacher.'

I still don't know why I said it, but as I look back on it now, it was perhaps the best thing I could possibly have said. For a minute, nobody stirred. Then from the rear someone called,

'What's the matter, Buckboard? You scared?'

Slowly a big coloured boy left his station at the rear of the crowd and started to work forward. A second boy followed. This one was carrying a cane, and both were wearing sunglasses. On their way through the crowd they picked up two more boys and all four grouped themselves in front of the piano stool.

The big one stepped forward another few inches.

'Slip me some skin, Preacher,' he said. 'I'm Buckboard, President of the Chaplains.'

I was still innocent of the slang of New York, and when he held out his hand I tried to grasp it. 'Just slip it, Preach,' said Buckboard, and he slid his open palm along mine. He stood for a minute, examining me curiously. 'You're all right, Preacher,' he said.

Buckboard then introduced me to his Vice-President, Stagecoach, and to his two War Lords.

723

## *4*

### *The Gang Leaders Kneel*

I told the four boys it wasn't I who was coming through but the Holy Spirit. I told them He was trying to reach inside their pride . . . 'and your arrogance, too,' I said, looking directly in their eyes, 'and your complacency. That's all just a shell to hide the real, scared, lonely you. The Holy Spirit wants to get inside that shell and help you start all over again.'

'What we supposed to do, man?'

I looked at Jimmy, but his expression didn't help me. In a church I might have asked these boys to come forward and kneel at the altar. But how could you ask anyone to do that on a public street, in front of friends?

Still, maybe it was just such a bold step that was needed. The chance in their lives that we were asking was drastic, so maybe the symbol had to be drastic too.

'What are you supposed to do?' I said. 'Why, I want you to kneel down right here on the street and ask the Holy Spirit to come into your lives so that you will become new men. "New creatures in Christ" is what the Bible says: this can happen to you too.'

There was a long pause. For the first time I was vaguely aware of the crowd that was waiting, very quietly, to see what was going to happen. Finally Stagecoach said, in a voice that was strangely hoarse:

'Buckboard? You want to? I will if you will.'

And before my astonished eyes, these two leaders of one of the most feared fighting gangs in all of New York slowly dropped to their knees. Their War Lords followed their lead. They took their hats off and held them respectfully in front of them. Two of the boys had been smoking. Each took his cigarette out of his mouth and flipped it away, where it lay smouldering in the gutter while I said a very short prayer.

'Lord Jesus,' I said, 'here are four of your own children, doing something that is very, very hard. They are kneeling here before everyone and asking You to come into their hearts and make them new. They want You to take away the hate, and the fighting, and the loneliness. They want to *know* for the first time in their lives that they are really loved. They are asking this of You, Lord, and You will not disappoint them. Amen.'

Buckboard and Stagecoach got up. The two War Lords followed. They did not lift their heads. I suggested they might want to get off by themselves for a while, maybe find a church somewhere.

Still without speaking, the boys turned and started to make their way through the crowd. Someone called out,

'Hey, Buckboard! What's it like when you got religion?'

Buckboard told them to lay off and he was taunted no more. I suppose if someone had really rubbed him the wrong way, he wouldn't have been saved enough to take it non-violently.

David Wilkerson, *The Cross and the Switchblade*

## 724 A CHRISTIAN MISSIONARY IN CHINA

SIX READINGS

*I*

*Gladys Aylward is Appointed*

(*In accordance with ancient custom, the feet of Chinese children were bound very tight in bandages and could not grow properly*)

With a contemptuous flick of his fan the Mandarin said: 'It must be *you* who become foot inspector.'

'Me!' repeated Gladys in a strangulated voice. At moments like these her conversation seemed to fail her.

'You are the only woman in the province with big feet. You must take the job! It is very simple. You will travel from village to village and tell the people of the Government's decree. You will assemble the women in the centre of the village or in their houses and inspect their feet. If the feet of the infants are bound, you will unbind them. You will be armed with my authority and report to me personally. Do you agree?'

As he talked, Gladys's thoughts fell into place. She wondered why she hadn't thought of it before. A mule out to the most distant villages? A guard to protect her? It was an opportunity without parallel for her to visit every part of the province, preaching wherever she went. But would he accept this?

'You must realize, Excellency,' she said, 'that if I accept this position I shall try and convert the people of this province to Christianity wherever I go!'

There was a short silence. The retainers in the background appeared frozen in horror. She wondered if she had committed an unpardonable error. Then he said quietly: 'I care nothing for your religion or to whom you preach. This is a matter for the conscience of each individual. But it is important that you should do this work. The Central Government is impatient.'

Gladys was knowledgeable enough about local conditions by that time to realize that the Central Government was probably demanding facts and figures about the incidence of foot-binding from this mountain province. She smiled inwardly. This was certainly something to write home about; a foot inspector on the payroll of the Mandarin.

She bowed low. 'I am anxious to be of assistance,' she said. 'I will gladly accept the position.'



## 2

### *The Children's Feet*

Gladys Aylward never forgot the first village at which she arrived as official foot inspector.

A small dark-eyed girl, aged about three, clung to her mother's trousers and looked nervously up at Gladys. A single glance was sufficient to tell that her feet were bound.

'That one,' said Gladys, trying to insert a note of authority into her voice. 'Unbind her feet!'

Two women neighbours and a grandmother had now appeared in the room. The mother took the child on her lap and all four women began to undo the bandages.

To cover her own nervousness, Gladys maintained a running commentary, which she improvised as each fold of cloth fell away.

'That's it. Come on now. Hurry up! If God intended little girls to have horrible stubby little feet, He'd have made them like that in the first place, wouldn't He? Feet are to walk with, not to shuffle up and down with, aren't they? I don't care if the husbands say you should do it or not. They should try it sometime, and see if they like hobbling about on little club feet. Any other man who tells you to do it goes to prison at once; that's the law now.'

The last bandage dropped, revealing tiny white feet with toes bent downwards and up into the soles.

'Look at those feet!' exclaimed Gladys. 'Disgraceful, absolutely disgraceful! How d'you expect the poor child to walk properly with those feet?'

She almost pushed the women away, and, kneeling down, gently prised the toes up and away from the sole. The child regarded her with wide, timid eyes.

'There,' said Gladys softly.

She massaged the foot tenderly. Suddenly there was a quick liquid giggle of sound from the child, who wriggled with delight.

The spell was broken.

724

## 3

### *Riot in the Prison*

The Governor of the prison, small, pale-faced, his mouth set into a worried line, met her at the entrance. Behind were grouped half a dozen of his staff.

'We are glad you have come,' he said quickly. 'There is a riot in the prison; the convicts are killing each other.'

'So I can hear,' she said. 'Why don't you send the soldiers in to stop it?'

'The convicts are murderers, bandits, thieves,' said the Governor, his voice trembling. 'The soldiers are frightened. There are not enough of them. You must go in and stop the fighting!'

(724 3) Gladys's mouth dropped open. 'Are you mad! If I went in they'd kill me!'

'But how can they kill you? If you preach the truth, if your God protects you from harm, then you can stop this riot.'

Gladys stared at him. Oh, these stupidly simple people! How could she go into the prison? By the sounds, louder now, a small human hell had broken loose. How could she? 'I must try,' she said to herself. 'I must try. O God, give me strength.'

'The key!' snapped the Governor. 'The key, quickly.'

One of his orderlies came forward with a huge iron key. Literally she was pushed inside. The door closed behind her. She heard the great key turn. She was locked in the prison with a horde of raving criminals who by their din sounded as if they had all gone completely insane. A dark tunnel, twenty yards long, stretched before her. At the far end it appeared to open out into a courtyard. She could see figures racing across the entrance. With faltering footsteps, she walked through it and came to an abrupt standstill.

The courtyard was about sixty feet square, with queer cage-like structures round all four sides. Within its confines a writhing, fiendish battle was going on. Several bodies were stretched out on the flagstones. One man, obviously dead, lay only a few feet away from her, blood still pouring from a great wound in his scalp. There was blood everywhere. Inside the cage-like structures small private battles were being fought. The main group of men, however, were watching one convict who brandished a large, bloodstained chopper. As she stared, he suddenly rushed at them and they scattered wildly to every part of the square. No one took any notice whatsoever of Gladys. The man rushed again; the group parted; he singled one man out and chased him. The man ran towards Gladys, then ducked away. The madman with the axe halted only a few feet from her. Hardly realizing what she was doing, she took two angry steps towards him.

'Give me that chopper,' she said furiously. 'Give it to me at once!'

The man turned to look at her. For three long seconds the wild dark pupils staring from bloodshot eyes glared at her. He took two paces forward. Suddenly, meekly, he held out the axe. Gladys snatched the weapon from his hand and held it rigidly down by her side. The other convicts—there must have been fifty or sixty men cowering there—stared from every corner of the courtyard. All action was frozen. Gladys knew that she must clinch her psychological advantage.

'All of you!' she shouted. 'Come over here.' She screamed at them, gabbled at them like an undersized infuriated sergeant-major, like a schoolmarm with a class of naughty children. 'Get into line at once. Come on, form up in front of me!'

Obediently the convicts shambled across, forming into a ragged group before her. There was silence. Then suddenly her fear had gone. In its place was an immense, soul-searing pity that pricked the tears into her eyes. They were so wretched.

724

## *4*

### *God and War*
### (*In 1937 the Japanese invaded Northern China*)

With her Bible, Gladys moved through villages sometimes occupied by the Japanese, and sometimes by the Nationalists. They were unaware that she took careful notice of their dispositions, that she passed this information back to the Nationalist troops, and even led them to where she knew the enemy would be. She knew exactly what she was doing, and was not ashamed of her actions. She was Chinese by adoption. Had she been in London, and England in danger, she would have acted in the same way. Her heart had reached the fighting stage, even though she could not entirely quieten her conscience.

It was almost dark when she returned to the village where she had first met the Nationalist troops. The village elder met her outside his house; 'General Ley is here,' he whispered. 'He is anxious to meet you.'

She had heard much of General Ley, but had never met him. He was a legendary figure in the province; a Roman Catholic priest, a European, though from what country he came she did not know.

When the Japanese invaded Shansi he was not content to sit back and rely upon God's mercy. With militant Christian fury he had found weapons for his parishioners and struck back; now he was the leader of a large guerilla force. They lived in the mountains, and fought the Japanese whenever and wherever they could.

Listening to the weariness in his voice, it was not difficult for

(724 4)

Gladys to divine his inner despair because the same conflict existed in her own heart. 'We shall kill many Japanese,' he said unemotionally. He had gone straight to the heart of the matter.

'We shall kill many Japanese,' he repeated.

Their eyes met across the lamp. She understood this agonizing dilemma of his Christian conscience. She, too, in the quietness of her prayers had tried to find some clear path to follow.

Should he—should they—stand aside and let the forces of evil reach with black fingers into every corner of the province, or should he—should they—take up the sword, and in the name of God strike at the evil?

'I have heard much about you, Ai-weh-deh,' he said quietly.

'What have you heard?'

'At times you make journeys behind the Japanese lines to gather information for the Chinese armies. That is true, is it not?'

'Yes,' she said.

'Do you not feel that you are betraying the position that God has given you?' he demanded coldly.

'I don't understand.' She looked at him in bewilderment, the anger slowly rising inside her. Then the words cascaded out.

'God recognizes the difference between right and wrong,' she said stormily. 'We can recognize the difference, can't we? The Japanese are wicked. Our Lord drove the moneylenders out from the temple with whips. The Japanese sweep through our countryside looting, burning and killing. We must drive them out, too, with every means in our power. They are my people they kill; my people legally, morally, spiritually, and I shall go on doing what I can to protect and help them—'

She stopped suddenly in the middle of her tirade, conscious that he was smiling.

'We ask ourselves these questions, Ai-weh-deh, do we not? And even though we answer them to our own satisfaction, even though we can clear our consciences at any man-made inquisition, we are still not quite certain how we would answer at the Courts of God. Are we, Ai-weh-deh?'

She did not answer. She knew he did not need an answer. He was examining his own conscience aloud.

'I am a Christian priest,' he said slowly. 'I am in this country to teach the ignorant and aid the sick, and bring the word of God to those who have never heard it. And yet on the battlefield I see the corpses of the men I have helped to kill—yes, killed myself with these own two hands. Yet what is the use of neutrality? There is fighting in every part of the world, Ai-weh-deh, against a common enemy of evil, and unless every man takes up arms—spiritual, moral and physical arms—and fights in the best way he is equipped to fight, how can we ever defeat it? How can a Christian man stand by while it continues? I cannot, and I shall not!'

724

## *5*

### *A Christian who would not Break*

*(Before the Japanese invasion, another missionary, called David Davis, had lived two days' journey away from the town where Gladys Aylward had been working)*

It was to be many long years before she heard the full story of David Davis.

Two weeks after the Japanese occupied Tsehchow they arrested him. For some Oriental reason known only to themselves, they were determined to make him admit he was a spy. Their methods were quite simple. They starved him, kept him without sleep, and beat him viciously at regular intervals.

Two of his Christian converts they tied to beams and tortured in an effort to induce them to declare that David Davis had conspired against the Japanese. Both refused to condemn him. Both they killed. They were simple men; they could not understand why they were being tortured into confessing an untruth, which they knew, and the Japanese knew, was an untruth. They died keeping faith. The Japanese had no grounds for suspicion regarding David, but he was a European and a Christian, and they distrusted both. Why had he spied for the Nationalists? Why? Why? Why? Day and night he was made to kneel facing a plain wall, and if he fell asleep he was woken every hour by blows.

For three months this treatment continued; they did not even dent his spirit or his determination,

Then he was placed in a steel cage with a concrete floor and concrete back wall with twenty other prisoners. It was a few feet square. They were jammed together in a hot, stinking mass. Day and night an electric bulb glared down upon them. At dawn—they knew it was dawn because the warden would give a single order, 'Kneel'—they would kneel, facing the wall. They would stay in that position for hours; if they moved or spoke they were savagely beaten. Then they would get an order, 'Stand!' With heads bent, because the cell was too low for anyone to stand upright, they would crouch immobile. At night came the last order, 'Lie down!' and they would lie on the concrete floor in a packed, contorted row. Once every two or three days bowls of maize would be passed in, and a little water. Every few days David Davis was taken out for questioning. He was told that if he admitted to being a spy he would at once be given better quarters and better treatment. He refused. He knew that they were trying to drive him mad; he also knew that while he was sane they could never defeat him. Even in the depths of his deepest physical misery there was a kind of exaltation in his suffering. If the Japanese had understood even vaguely the mystique of Christianity, which had produced an unending succession of martyrs since that Good Friday when Jesus Christ was nailed to a Cross, they might have known that they were wasting their efforts. There was a core in the spirit of this man from the mountains of Wales which no physical degradation could destroy. For six months, filthy, lice-ridden, they kept him in this cell, heaped together with those other pitiful fragments of humanity. He saw neither sun nor moon, nor knew the passing of night into day.

At length it was the Japanese who admitted defeat. He was transferred into another cell which held only three prisoners; he was accorded slightly better treatment. He spent that time converting one of his fellow-prisoners to Christianity. Two years after he had been arrested he was sent to the coast to be repatriated as a civilian.

Today he lives at Ely, a suburb of Cardiff, in a small house, running his own church and community. He carries scars on his face from his encounters with the Japanese. But no scars internally.

There is no malice or vengefulness in the soul of David Davis.

724

## 6

### *Interviewing Gladys Aylward*

(*Alan Burgess, the author of* 'The Small Woman', *concludes his book by telling how he came to hear of Gladys Aylward*)

When I first read of Gladys Aylward's arrival, I was writing and producing a dramatized series of true stories for a BBC feature entitled 'The Undefeated'. In the hope that she might have a

24 6) story which would fit into this pattern, I went to see her at her home in Edmonton. I explained my purpose, and Gladys shook her head very seriously, and said that she was quite certain that nothing had happened to her which could possibly make a radio play.

'But, surely,' I said, 'in twenty years in China you must have had many strange experiences?'

'Oh yes,' said Gladys, 'but I'm sure people wouldn't be interested in them. Nothing very exciting happened.'

It was at least fifteen minutes more before she confessed that she had 'once taken some children across the mountains'.

The rest of the conversation went in this manner, a verbatim memory which I have never forgotten:

'Across the mountains? Where was this?'

'In Shansi in north China; we travelled from Yangcheng across the mountains to Sian.'

'I see. How long did it take you?'

'Oh, about a month.'

'Did you have any money?'

'Oh no, we didn't have any money.'

'I see. What about food? How did you get that?'

'The Mandarin gave us two basketfuls of grain, but we soon ate that up.'

'I see. How many children did you say there were?'

'Nearly a hundred.'

I became conscious that I was saying, 'I see,' rather often, and actually I was not 'seeing' anything at all, except that I was on the brink of a most tremendous story.

It was not mock modesty on the part of Gladys Aylward; the stories she had been telling in China were, to her, the greatest in the world, taken straight from the pages of the New Testament; that her own adventures might be worth setting down, she had simply not considered.

Since then, during the years she has been in England, she has been travelling around the country, lecturing and preaching at churches and schools and mission halls. She has been a second mother to scores of Chinese students from Singapore and Hong Kong arriving in England to study; and she has played a large part in helping to set up a hostel in Liverpool for Chinese nationals and Chinese seamen. As always, she has lived frugally, and simply, and from day to day.

She is one of the most remarkable women of our generation, and although one can never enter completely into the heart and mind of a fellow human being, it is clear that she possesses that inner exaltation, that determination to go on, unto death, which adversity, torture, brainwashing and hardship cannot eradicate from the human soul, and which is the natural corollary of faith.

I thank Miss Gladys Aylward for telling me her story, and for allowing me to set it down. I can only hope that I have done this small woman justice.

Alan Burgess, *The Small Woman* (adapted)

## 725 HELPING THE HOMELESS CHILDREN OF NAPLES

SEVEN READINGS

*I*

### *A Young Priest Plans to Live in the Gutter*

One day, towards the beginning of 1950, Mario Borrelli presented himself for an interview with his ecclesiastical superior, Cardinal Ascalesi, Archbishop of Naples.

Borrelli was twenty-eight, then, remember, a youngster from the *bassi* with the oil of his anointing hardly dry on his nervous fingers, Ascalesi was an old man, wise in the world and in the Church, burdened with the manifold distresses of his people. . . .

He listened, patiently, while Borrelli made his request.

It was an odd one in any language. He wanted to take off his *soutane*. He wanted to go out and live in the streets with the *scugnizzi*. He wanted to understand their lives, their psychology, to make himself their friend, one day, perhaps, to bring them to live with him and teach them to live decently.

The old Cardinal pursed his thin lips and frowned. . . .

'No, my son. No! Before we can begin new works like this one, we must set in order what we have already—the parishes, the schools, the orphanages. There is work under your hand. Do that and rest content that you are serving God as he wishes to be served.'

Borrelli was angry. Because he was a Neapolitan, the anger was swift and incontinent.

25 *1*) 'Your excellency does not understand. How can he, when he does not see? These are children, the little ones of Christ! They sleep on the gratings and in the beds of prostitutes. They pimp and steal and lend themselves to murder and violence. They live like animals in the forest, friendless and alone. And Your Excellency tells me to forget them. . . . No! If the Church refuses this work, it is not the Church of God!'

Old and grey and terrible, the Cardinal sat in his high-backed chair and looked down at the small, boyish fellow who challenged him; challenged, too, the ancient power of the Church which he represented. . . .

White-faced and trembling, Borrelli waited. . . . It seemed an age before the old man spoke again. His voice was strangely gentle.

'To redeem the children is one thing. To take them off the streets and give them a home—this I can approve. But the other—to live with them on the streets, to become in a sense a partner in their misdeeds—this I cannot understand. Why do you want to do it?'

Borrelli relaxed a little. There was still hope. . . .

'Your Excellency, you must understand something of what the life of the streets does to these children. You must know that to be a *scugnizzo* is to have a man's soul in the body of a child. It is to have suffered in that body the rape of innocence, the pain of hunger, the bleak, desert cold of the city. To be a *scugnizzo* is to live without love, to trust no one, because the one you trust will snatch the bread from your mouth or the cigarettes from your pocket. To be a *scugnizzo* is to know that every woman is a whore, and every man a thief, that every policeman is a sadist and every priest a liar. If I went among them as I am now, they would laugh at me or spit in my face. If I offered them a home they would tell me that the *carabinieri* offer them a home, too—in a house of correction. I should never come within a hand's reach of them. Believe me, Your Excellency. . . .' His voice trembled and he threw out his arms in a passionate gesture of appeal. 'Believe me! I was born in the *bassi*. I know!'

Cardinal Ascalesi sat in his high-backed chair and pondered. . . . Then, softly and deliberately, he gave his verdict.

'I need time to consider this matter. Come back to see me in ten days. Meantime—' His voice faltered a little and his tired eyes softened. 'Meantime, pray for me, my son. Pray for both of us. You may go.' . . .

2

## *Evidence for the Cardinal*

Mario Borrelli went home and prayed. That night, as he lay wakeful in his narrow bed, the idea came to him. He looked at his watch. It was still an hour to midnight. Time enough yet to make contact with the man he needed. In a flurry of excitement, he slipped out of bed, dressed himself, left the house and hurried to the nearest bar to make a telephone call.

An hour later, he was drinking coffee and talking excitedly with a photographer from a Neapolitan daily. The project they framed was shatteringly simple.

In the ten days and nights that were left, Borrelli and the photographer would walk the city together. They would photograph what they saw—the homeless waifs sleeping in the streets, the urchin packs cooking the food over fires in the alleys, the nightly interrogations in the *questura*. Then they would show the photographs to Cardinal Ascalesi.

Ten days later, Mario Borrelli stood before the old man and watched him poring over the glossy prints spread out on the desk. The Cardinal's face was haggard as he scanned the devastating evidence before him. Then he straightened up and spread his hands over the photographs, as if to shut them out of his sight. His grey mouth was tight with anger. When he spoke his voice was strong with conviction.

'Even had you not shown me these, I should have given you permission for your work. Now that I have seen them, I am doubly sure that it is a good work.' . . .

Borrelli's tight face broke into an urchin grin. He felt free and happy, and, like all his people, he wanted to shout and sing and tell the whole wide world. But the Cardinal was a great man and demanded a great respect. So Borrelli mastered his joy and began to tell the Cardinal of his friend, Spada, young like himself, a priest of the diocese of Naples. He was not, like Borrelli, a thrusting, combative man, but his heart was full of love for children, and when the urchins came one day to the house they hoped to have, they would have much need of love and fatherly care.

The Cardinal nodded his approval. . . .

One hour and a half later, Mario Borrelli stood in the streets of the city and looked about him. It was his city now and the children of the city were his children. If he failed them, there was no one else to whom they could turn. He shivered though the sun was warm. He felt suddenly lonely and afraid.

He turned into an old grey church and knelt a long time in prayer.

725

## 3

### *Borrelli Joins the Scugnizzi, the Urchins*

A few days later the *scugnizzi* of the Piazza Mercato turned a speculative eye on a new arrival.

He was working his way up from the direction of the waterfront, picking up cigarette butts as he came. He wore a filthy shirt, patched in many places. . . . His face was grimy and unshaven and he wore a greasy peaked cap on the back of his head.

At the corner of the Piazza he stopped, leaned against the wall, took out a half smoked cigarette and lit it with a wax match that he scraped against the stone. He smoked slowly, shoulder against the angle, legs crossed, bright eyes darting this way and that appraising the trade in the Piazza.

The boys studied him carefully, noting the broken nose and the tight mouth and the insolent tilt of the head. A *guappo* this one—cocky, tough, dangerous possibly. They hadn't seen him before. . . .

They let him smoke for a few moments and they studied every gesture he made. They saw how he held his cigarette between the thumb and the forefinger. They saw how he blew the smoke out of the corner of his mouth. How he spat into the puddle, how he cleaned his nose by pinching it between two fingers and then wiping it on his sleeve. They saw how he scratched his thighs and his armpits like a man accustomed to lice in his clothes.

No doubt about it, he was one of the boys. Now it was time to make contact.

A weedy youth with a dark, Arab face detached himself from one of the groups of loungers and sauntered across the Piazza. Out of the corner of his eye, Borrelli watched him come. His stomach knotted a little, but no flicker of fear showed itself in his bright eyes. The youth came abreast, opened a packet of American cigarettes, stuck one in his mouth, shoved the packet into his pocket and then asked for a match. Borrelli took the glowing butt

(725 3) from his mouth and held it against the tip of the other's cigarette. Then he put it back in his own mouth. He did not move from his lounging posture.

The youth grunted his thanks and leaned on the wall beside Borrelli. He spoke out of the corner of his mouth in the slurred and sing-song dialect of Naples.

'I haven't seen you before.'

Borrelli shrugged expressively.

'Naples is a big town. I haven't seen you either.'

The dark youth blew out a cloud of smoke and considered the matter. The accent was right, the words were right. You can't fake the dialect of the streets. The attitude was right, too. The fellow was a *guappo* all right. You couldn't rattle him. Best to take him easy.

'You in business?'

'Sort of.'

'Got any contacts?'

Borrelli cocked his head on one side and gestured vaguely.

'Enough for me.'

'What sort of contacts?'

Without haste, Borrelli fished in his pockets and brought out, in succession, a packet of American cigarettes, a cheap ring with a synthetic stone, a dollar bill and a grimy address book with a few scrawled names and telephone numbers. The sallow youth studied them a moment, then nodded approvingly. Contraband, theft or receiving, a few girls. It was enough for one man. This one obviously knew how to look after himself. But there was something else he had to know.

'Ever been in gaol?'

Borrelli grinned, crookedly, and spat on the ground.

'Not yet. But I need a change of air.'

Ah! Now we were come to the nub of it. The police had been on the tracks of this fellow, so he was moving his camp. That made him more co-operative, more susceptible to a proposition. The youth fished in his pocket and brought out his own cigarettes.

'Here, have one of these.'

'Thanks.'

'What's your name?'

'Mario.'

'Mine's Carlucciello. I run things round here.' He waved an

expansive hand at the seedy bustle of the Piazza Mercato. 'Like to meet some of the boys?'

'Sure.'

Mario Borrelli heaved himself off the wall, hitched up his belt and sauntered across the crowded square with Carlucciello. His face was still the cocky indifferent mask which the *guappo* presents to his fellows. But inside he was grinning like a schoolboy. He had passed the first test. He was in.

Mario Borrelli had become a *scugnizzo*.

725

## *4*

### *Living with the Scugnizzi*

The longer Borrelli lived with the *scugnizzi*, the more he understood that the house he hoped to build for them would have to be of a very special kind.

These were a special kind of children—half men, half boys. To pen them in an institution would be an intolerable cruelty. They would stifle with fear or burst into a frenzy of revolt. . . .

He must make a place to which they would return willingly, because it was better than anything they could find in the streets. He must give them security with freedom and food without a price ticket. On the street they had found friendship and a small store of love. This he must not destroy but preserve, adding to it his own love and the abundant gentleness of his friend Spada, who was tramping the streets every day looking for a vacant place to house them. . . .

He looked at them again squatting over the dying warmth. . . .

As he watched them, one of the little ones began to tremble violently. His teeth chattered and he tried to draw closer to the tin dish full of coals. Borrelli moved forward and bent over him.

'*Cos' è Nino?* What's the matter?'

The tiny simian face looked up at him. The dark eyes were full of tears, but Nino was too much of a man to cry.

'I'm cold, Mario. I'm cold.'

Borrelli lifted him in his arms and sat back in the angle of the wall, cradling the wasted body in his arms. Suddenly the child was wrenched with a spasm of coughing. His tiny chest caved in, his belly muscles knotted, then he vomited on the pavement. The priest wiped the boy's mouth with his hand—a handkerchief is an unbelievable luxury among the urchins—then he looked down at the vomit. It was mucus, dark and clotted and stained with little gouts of blood. Nino was in an advanced stage of tuberculosis.

Blind rage took hold of the priest and he cursed this dark city that crucified its children or shouldered them off its sidewalks to cough their hearts out in a gutter. Then the rage left him and he prayed—prayed for the courage and the strength and the wisdom to lead these lost ones out of the desert into a place of rest and refreshment. And, as he prayed, he held the sick child against his breast, trying to warm him with his own body, while all the time the bleak wind stirred along the alleys and the thin brown cats prowled among the rubbish heaps.

All the time the others watched him, their wary eyes full of dumb admiration. They were glad to have this Mario in their band. He gave them courage and a sense of security. He was different from the others, though they had no words to describe the difference.

How could they? Mario Borrelli had brought love to the children of the streets, but the word itself was still a strangeness and a mockery.

725

## *5*

### *The Scugnizzi see Borrelli as a Priest*

It was late at night when Mario Borrelli went back to the *scugnizzi*. . . .

He had stripped off his urchin's rags and dressed himself in his priestly black. In his breast pocket was the small sheaf of photographs, the proof of his good faith. He walked slowly through the dark lanes of the *bassi*, praying a little, fearing much. A life's work depended on the outcome of the next ten minutes. . . .

He turned into a narrow lane. It was a cul-de-sac. At the end of it, just settling themselves for sleep, were the boys of his band.

They looked up when they heard his footfall, and when they saw that he was a priest, they cowered back, blank-faced and staring like small frightened animals. He took off his hat and stood looking down at them.

He grinned, cheerfully, and asked them in dialect:

'Don't you remember me? Mario?'

They stared at him with dumb hostility. He took a torch out of his pocket and shone it on his stubbly face.

'Look! It's really me. You know me, don't you? You, Carlucciello? You, Tonino? You, Mozzo?'

At the sound of their names they started and stared at one another in disbelief. Carlucciello heaved himself to his feet, lounged over to him and stared insolently into his eyes. Nino, the sick one, coughed and spat and groaned unhappily. Then Carlucciello spoke:

'You look like Mario, sure. But you're not. What do you want here? Why don't you get back to your convent?'

The boys tittered uneasily. Carlucciello was a real *guappo*. He knew how to handle the priests. Borrelli grinned and fished in his pockets for the bunch of photographs. He fanned them out and handed them to Carlucciello.

'First I want to show you that I really am Mario. Go on! Take a look at those. Use the torch if you want to.'

Carlucciello took the torch and then, squatting, shone it on the photographs while the others crowded round, chattering uneasily and looking from the glossy prints to the white face of the priest standing above them. Borrelli talked, too.

'You remember now, don't you? That's the one that was taken the night after we met the sailors outside Filomena's place. That's the one where we were eating chocolate that Mozzo pinched from the American car. That's the one where Nino was sick and he was sleeping in my arms all night. You know me, don't you, Nino? I got the medicines for you, didn't I, and the big pills that made you feel better?'

The small wasted child looked up at him.

'It's Mario all right. How would he know all these things, if he was someone else?'

Carlucciello stood up again. His eyes were hostile. He handed back the prints and the torch without a word. Then, after a long minute, he spoke. His voice was quiet and angry and the little group shifted uneasily.

'All right, Mario, what's the game? Yesterday you were one of us, today you're a black crow. What's the story?'

'The story comes later, Carlucciello. I'm a priest, sure. Why and how I'll tell you later. Right now I've come to tell you that I found a place for us—it's not much, but there are beds and blankets and a fire and food. It was the best I could do. Nino's sick. If he stays on the streets, he'll die. I'd like you to come and have a look. If it doesn't please you, you can leave. It's your place, not mine.'

Carlucciello's dark face was twisted with anger and contempt. He had trusted this fellow like a brother and now he turned out to be a dirty priest. Carefully, he filled his mouth with spittle then voided it full in the face of Mario Borrelli. Then he threw back his head and laughed. The sound echoed horribly along the empty lane.

The other boys watched in tense amazement. These were the leaders. Of the two, Mario was closer to them, but not this way, not in this hated garb of authority. They watched to see what he would do.

725

## 6

### *The Scugnizzi Decide*

Carefully Borrelli wiped the spittle from his face. He shoved the torch into his pocket and, still holding the prints in his hand, squatted down against the wall, heedless of the mud and filth that soiled his black cassock.

When he spoke, his voice was quiet and controlled.

'If you'd done that to me yesterday, Carlucciello, I'd have broken your nose and you know it. I could still do it. You know that, too. But I've let you have your fun. Now sit down here and listen. Is that fair or isn't it?' . . .

They hesitated a moment then squatted beside him. Borrelli took Nino in his arms and cradled him against his breast in the old way. After a moment Carlucciello squatted again, but a little apart. He would listen, sure. But he was too wise to be taken in by shabby tricks like this one.

Borrelli sat a moment in silence, considering his words. They had to be the right words, or the boys would race away from him and he would never come near them again. He said, simply:

. . . 'This place I've got isn't much, but it keeps the rain out. There's straw for you to sleep on and a blanket apiece. There's wood for a fire and enough food to give you a good meal. You can stay there the night and leave in the morning. If you like it, you can come back again, any time, for a feed and a bed. It's better than the street, isn't it?'

The boys nodded, silently. They looked at Carlucciello, but

he was staring at the ground drawing a dirty picture in the mud with his finger.

Borrelli went on:

'I'm going there now. I don't want to force you to come. You can follow me or stay here, just as you want. The only thing is, I'm carrying Nino. It's a long way and he's sick. I'm going to try to get a doctor and medicine for him. That's all. From here on, it's up to you.'

Abruptly he stood up, hoisted Nino onto his shoulders and carried him pick-a-back down the dark alley. He heard the whispers and the scuffling but he did not look back. He plodded onwards, head down, arms behind his back supporting the puny child who clung to his shoulders like a monkey.

It was not until he reached the Via San Gennaro that he dared to look behind.

The boys were a dozen yards away, padding along his tracks. A long, long way behind, but still following, was the skinny stooping figure of Carlucciello.

His heart leapt. His mouth split into a grin as wide as a water melon and he started to whistle the jaunty little tune of the 'Duckling and the Poppy-flower'.

The Pied Piper of Naples was bringing his children home.

725

## 7

### *The House of the Urchins*

The first thing that strikes the visitor to the House of the Urchins is its poverty. This poverty is a daily indictment of the selfishness and social indifference of wealthy Italians. Here are two young men keeping a hundred and ten homeless boys and ten paid helpers for less than a dollar a day each. . . .

The place looks poor. It is an old grey building in a back street and it looks out on rows of tenements with washing strung from the balconies and chickens pecking among the dust heaps. There are bedrooms with rows of chipped iron cots, each with two blankets and a pair of unbleached sheets and a tiny towel.

There is a small dispensary where the senior boys administer first aid. There are a couple of classrooms and a dining room and a small kitchen with a cooking range but no refrigerator. There is a bathroom with a cold shower and a row of hand-and-foot basins but no hot water. . . .

There is a long narrow room with a television set where the youngsters sit entranced every evening at five-thirty. There is a pocket-handkerchief yard at the back of the Church. . . .

The boys' food is rough but plentiful—*pasta* with the inevitable tomato sauce, meat once a week, soup, bread and jam, occasional fruit. . . . The boys' clothes are poor and patched, but warm and serviceable. They don't wear uniforms, they can't afford them. . . . But when the young ones go to school each has a clean smock so that he is indistinguishable from all the others of his class.

When Padre Spada takes you round on a tour of inspection, you sense the diffidence and the pathetic pride as he tells you how much has been done and with how little. . . . Most of it has been paid for by the sale of scrap iron and old clothes and by a trickle of private charity, sporadic and uncertain like all good works in Naples.

The place is clean and the boys are clean, in a rough and ready sort of way. The building is centuries old. The plaster cracks off and the tufa walls shed a fine grey dust that settles on everything. The boys play in an unpaved courtyard between the high walls of crumbling tenements.

Yet they are happy. They are free to walk out at any time. They stay because they want to stay, because they have found a warmth and a love stronger even than the call of the streets. They are proud of themselves and of their house, and this pride is the more striking for the poverty in which it flourishes.

It is little, you say, pitifully little after five years' heart-break and sacrifice. True. But when you think of the ruinous beginning and the rank indifference of the gentry of Naples, it is a very great thing indeed.

Morris West, *Children of the Sun* (adapted)

# People and Society



## I DREAM A WORLD

I dream a world where man
No other will scorn,

Where love will bless the earth
And peace its paths adorn.
I dream a world where all
Will know sweet freedom's way,
Where greed no longer saps the soul
Nor avarice blights our day.
A world I dream where black or white,
Whatever race you be,
Will share the bounties of the earth
And every man is free,
Where wretchedness will hang its head,
And joy, like a pearl,
Attend the needs of all mankind.
Of such I dream—
Our world!

Langston Hughes

727

## THE SERENE PEOPLE

Perhaps the most remarkable and the least known of earthly paradises is the small kingdom of Hunza in the Himalayas.

A fair-skinned population of 18,000 live there in a fertile and almost inaccessible valley not far from the Sinkiang border, 8,000 feet up. A legend tells that they are the descendants of three deserters from the army of Alexander the Great, who settled here with Persian wives: this may incline us to believe that pacifism is hereditary, because these people have had no war in 2,000 years. They have no money, no crime, and no diseases. They rarely die before ninety. Their mental control over their bodies is almost unbelievable: childbirth is painless; and toothache, a joke; they keep their numbers stationary without contraceptives, and without abortion, by sheer abstinence, though a recent visitor there saw a new-born son of a chuckling father aged eighty-nine. Their diet, which consists mostly of apricots and raw vegetables, may have something to do with their unshakeable serenity. It is almost unbelievable that human nature *can* be like this. Hunza sounds like Aldous Huxley's imaginary island, but unlike the fictitious characters there, the Hunza people have no art—only serenity!

Dennis Gabor, *Inventing the Future*

# A GIRL IN HIDING

## FOURTEEN READINGS

## FROM *The Diary of Anne Frank*

### *Introduction*

*Anne Frank was Jewish. When the Nazis invaded Holland in 1940, the Frank family went into hiding in order to escape from the Nazi persecution of the Jews. Anne, the youngest, began her diary on her thirteenth birthday and continued it until a few days before the family was betrayed to the police in August 1944. Except for her father, the whole family died in German concentration camps not long before the end of the war. But the diary, though it expresses a recurrent sense of danger, is illuminated by the longing for freedom and the hope of deliverance. It is perhaps the most moving book ever written by so young an author.*

### *I*

### *Into Hiding*

Wednesday, 8th July, 1942

Into hiding—where would we go, in a town or the country, in a house or a cottage, when, how, where?

These were questions I was not allowed to ask, but I couldn't get them out of my mind. Margot and I began to pack some of our most vital belongings into a school satchel. The first thing I put in was this diary, then hair-curlers, handkerchiefs, school books, a comb, old letters; I put in the craziest things with the idea that we were going into hiding. But I'm not sorry, memories mean more to me than dresses.

Mummy called me at 5.30 the next morning. Luckily it was not so hot as Sunday; warm rain fell steadily all day. We put on heaps of clothes as if we were going to the North Pole, the sole reason being to take clothes with us. No Jew in our situation would have dreamt of going out with a suitcase full of clothing. I had on two vests, three pairs of knickers, a dress, on top of that a skirt, jacket, summer coat, two pairs of stockings, lace-up shoes, woolly cap, scarf and still more; I was nearly stifled before we started, but no one inquired about that.

Margot filled her satchel with school books, fetched her bicycle and rode off into the unknown, as far as I was concerned. You see I still didn't know where our secret hiding-place was to be. At seven-thirty the door closed behind us. Moortie, my little cat, was the only creature to whom I'd said farewell. She would have a good home with the neighbours.

There was one pound of meat in the kitchen for the cat, breakfast things lying on the table, stripped beds, all giving the impression that we had left helter-skelter. But we didn't care about impressions, we only wanted to get away, only escape and arrive safely, nothing else.

728

## 2

### *The Hiding Place*

Friday, 21st August, 1942

The entrance to our hiding-place has now been properly concealed. Mr. Kraler thought it would be better to put a bookcase in front of our door (because a lot of houses are being searched for hidden bicycles), but of course it had to be a movable bookcase that can open like a door. Mr. Vossen made the whole thing. We had already let him into the secret and he can't do enough to help. If we want to go downstairs, we first have to bend down and then jump, because the step has gone. The first three days we were all going about with masses of lumps on our foreheads, because we all knocked ourselves against the low doorway. Now we have nailed a cloth filled with sawdust against the top of the door. Let's see if that helps!

I'm not working much at present; I'm giving myself holidays until September. Then Daddy is going to give me lessons; it's shocking how much I've forgotten already. There is little change in our life here. Mr. Van Daan and I usually manage to upset each other, it's just the opposite with Margot whom he likes very much. Mummy sometimes treats me just like a baby, which I can't bear. Otherwise things are going better. I still don't like Peter Van Daan any better, he is so boring; he flops lazily on his bed half the time, does a bit of carpentry and then goes back for another snooze. What a fool!

It is lovely weather and in spite of everything we make the most we can of it by lying on a camp-bed in the attic, where the sun shines through an open window.

# 3

## *Persecution*

19th–28th November, 1942

Countless friends and acquaintances have gone to a terrible fate. Evening after evening the green and grey army lorries trundle past. The Germans ring at every front door to inquire if there are any Jews living in the house. If there are, then the whole family has to go at once. If they don't find any, they go on to the next house. No one has a chance of evading them unless one goes into hiding. Often they go round with lists, and only ring when they know they can get a good haul. Sometimes they let them off for cash—so much per head. It seems like the slave hunts of olden times. But it's certainly no joke; it's much too tragic for that. In the evenings when it's dark, I often see rows of good, innocent people accompanied by crying children, walking on and on, in charge of a couple of these chaps, bullied and knocked about until they almost drop. No one is spared—old people, babies, expectant mothers, the sick—each and all join in the march of death.

How fortunate we are here, so well cared for and undisturbed. We wouldn't have to worry about all this misery were it not that we are so anxious about all those dear to us whom we can no longer help.

I feel wicked sleeping in a warm bed, while my dearest friends have been knocked down or have fallen into a gutter somewhere out in the cold night. I get frightened when I think of close friends who have now been delivered into the hands of the cruellest brutes that walk the earth. And all because they are Jews!

Yet we shall still have our jokes and tease each other, when these horrors have faded a bit in our minds. It won't do us any good, or help those outside, to go on being as gloomy as we are at the moment. And what would be the object of making our 'Secret Annexe' into a 'Secret Annexe of Gloom'? Must I keep thinking about those other people, whatever I am doing? And if I want to laugh about something, should I stop myself quickly and feel ashamed that I am cheerful? Ought I then to cry the whole day long? No, that I can't do. Besides, in time this gloom will wear off.

Added to this misery there is another, but of a purely personal kind; and it pales into insignificance beside all the wretchedness I've just told you about. Still, I can't refrain from telling you that lately I have begun to feel deserted. I am surrounded by too great a void. I never used to feel like this, my fun and amusements, and my girl friends completely filled my thoughts. Now I either think about unhappy things, or about myself. And at long last I have made the discovery that Daddy, although he's such a darling, still cannot take the place of my entire little world of bygone days.

728

## 4

### *Mother and Daughter: Estrangement*

Friday, 2nd April, 1943

Oh, dear, I've got another terrible black mark against my name. I was lying in bed yesterday evening waiting for Daddy to come and say my prayers with me, and wish me good-night, when Mummy came into my room, sat on my bed and asked very nicely, 'Anne, Daddy can't come yet, shall I say your prayers with you tonight?' 'No, Mummy,' I answered.

Mummy got up, paused by my bed for a moment and walked slowly towards the door. Suddenly she turned round, and with a distorted look on her face said, 'I don't want to be cross, love cannot be forced.' There were tears in her eyes as she left the room.

I lay still in bed, feeling at once that I had been horrible to push her away so rudely. But I knew too that I couldn't have answered differently. It simply wouldn't work. I felt sorry for Mummy; very, very sorry, because I had seen for the first time in my life that she minds my coldness. I saw the look of sorrow on her face when she spoke of love not being forced. It is hard to speak the truth, and yet it is the truth; she herself has pushed me away, her tactless remarks and her crude jokes which I don't find at all funny, have now made me insensitive to any love from her side. Just as I shrink at her hard words, so did her heart when she realized that the love between us was gone. She cried half the night and hardly slept at all. Daddy doesn't look at me and if he does for a second, then I can read in his eyes the words, 'How can you be so unkind, how can you bring yourself to cause your Mother such sorrow?'

They expect me to apologize: but this is something I can't apologize for because I spoke the truth and Mummy will have to know it sooner or later anyway. I seem, and indeed am, indifferent both to Mummy's tears and Daddy's looks, because for the first time they are both aware of something which I have always felt. I can only feel sorry for Mummy, who has now had to discover that I have adopted her own attitude. For myself, I remain silent and aloof; and I shall not shrink from the truth any longer, because the longer it is put off, the more difficult it will be for them when they do hear it.

728

## 5

### *Mother and Daughter: Looking Back*

Sunday, 2nd January, 1944

This morning when I had nothing to do I turned over some of the pages of my diary and several times I came across passages dealing with the subject 'Mummy' in such a hot-headed way that I was quite shocked, and asked myself:

'Anne, is it really you who mentioned hate? Oh, Anne, how could you!' I remained sitting with the open page in my hand, and thought about it and how it came about that I should have been so brimful of rage and hate that I had to confide it all in you. I have been trying to understand the Anne of a year ago and to excuse her, because my conscience isn't clear as long as I leave you with these accusations, without being able to explain, on looking back, how it happened.

I suffer now—and suffered then—from moods which kept my head under water (so to speak) and only allowed me to see the things subjectively without enabling me to consider quietly the words of the other side, and to answer them as the words of one whom I, with my hot-headed temperament, had offended or made unhappy.

I hid myself within myself, I only considered myself and quietly wrote down all my joys, sorrows, and contempt in my diary. This diary is of great value to me, because it has become a book of memoirs in many places, but on a good many pages I could certainly put 'past and done with'.

I used to be furious with Mummy, and still am sometimes. It's true that she doesn't understand me, but I don't understand her either. She did love me very much and she was tender, but as she landed in so many unpleasant situations through me, and was nervy and irritable because of other worries and difficulties, it is certainly understandable that she snapped at me.

I took it much too seriously, was offended, and was rude and aggravating to Mummy, which, in turn, made her unhappy. So it was really a matter of unpleasantness and misery rebounding all the time. It wasn't nice for either of us, but it is passing.

I just didn't want to see all this, and pitied myself very much; but that, too, is understandable. Those violent outbursts on paper were only giving vent to anger which in a normal life could have been worked off by stamping my feet a couple of times in a locked room, or calling Mummy names behind her back.

The period when I caused Mummy to shed tears is over. I have grown wiser and Mummy's nerves are not so much on edge. I usually keep my mouth shut if I get annoyed, and so does she, so we appear to get on much better together.

I can't really love Mummy in a dependent child-like way—I just don't have that feeling.

I soothe my conscience now with the thought that it is better for hard words to be on paper than that Mummy should carry them in her heart.

728

## *6*

### *After a Year and a Half in Hiding*

Friday, 24th December, 1943

When someone comes in from outside, with the wind in their clothes and the cold on their faces, then I could bury my head in the blankets to stop myself thinking, 'When will we be granted the privilege of smelling fresh air?' And because I must not bury my head in the blankets, but the reverse—I must keep my head high and be brave—the thoughts will come, not once, but oh, countless times. Believe me, if you have been shut up for a year and a half, it can get too much for you some days. In spite of all justice and thankfulness, you can't crush your feelings. Cycling, dancing, whistling, looking out into the world, feeling young, to know that I'm free—that's what I long for; still, I must show it, because I sometimes think if all eight of us began to pity ourselves, or went about with discontented faces, where would it lead us? I sometimes ask myself, 'Would anyone, either Jew or non-Jew, understand this about me, that I am simply a young girl badly in need of some rollicking fun?' I don't know, and I couldn't talk about it to anyone.

728

## 7

### *Anne and Peter: Making Friends*

Thursday, 6th January, 1944

My longing to talk to someone became so intense that somehow or other I took it into my head to choose Peter.

Sometimes if I've been upstairs into Peter's room during the day, it always struck me as very snug, but because Peter is so retiring and would never turn anyone out who became a nuisance, I never dared stay long, because I was afraid he might think me a bore. I tried to think of an excuse to stay in his room and get him talking, without it being too noticeable, and my chance came yesterday. Peter has a mania for cross-word puzzles at the moment and hardly does anything else. I helped him with them and we soon sat opposite each other at his little table, he on the chair and me on the divan.

It gave me a queer feeling each time I looked into his deep blue eyes, and he sat there with that mysterious laugh playing round his lips. I was able to read his inward thoughts. I could see on his face that look of helplessness and uncertainty as to how to behave, and, at the same time, a trace of his sense of manhood. I noticed his shy manner and it made me feel very gentle; I couldn't refrain from meeting those dark eyes again and again, and with my whole heart I almost beseeched him: oh, tell me, what is going on inside you, oh, can't you look beyond this ridiculous chatter?

When I lay in bed and thought over the whole situation, I found it far from encouraging, and the idea that I should beg for Peter's patronage was simply repellent. One can do a lot to satisfy one's longings, which certainly sticks out in my case, for I have made up my mind to go and sit with Peter more often and to get him talking somehow or other.

Whatever you do, don't think I'm in love with Peter—not a bit of it! If the Van Daans had had a daughter instead of a son, I should have tried to make friends with her too.

## *8*

728

### *Anne and Peter: Looking*

Sunday, 13th February, 1944

Since Saturday a lot has changed for me. It came about like this. I longed—and am still longing—but now something has happened, which has made it a little, just a little, less.

To my great joy—I will be quite honest about it—already on Sunday morning I noticed that Peter kept looking at me all the time. Not in the ordinary way, I don't know how, I just can't explain.

I used to think that Peter was in love with Margot, but yesterday I suddenly had the feeling that it is not so. I made a special effort not to look at him too much, because whenever I did, he kept on looking too and then—yes, then—it gave me a lovely feeling inside, but which I mustn't feel too often.

I desperately want to be alone. Daddy has noticed that I'm not quite my usual self, but I really can't tell him everything. 'Leave me in peace, leave me alone,' that's what I'd like to keep crying out all the time. Who knows, the day may come when I'm left alone more than I would wish!

728

## *9*

### *Anne and Peter: Help*

Sunday, 19th March, 1944

We talked about how we neither of us confide in our parents, and how his parents would have loved to have his confidence, but that he didn't wish it. How I cry my heart out in bed, and he goes up into the loft and swears. How Margot and I have only really just begun to know each other well, but that, even so, we don't tell each other everything, because we are always together. Over every imaginable thing—oh, he was just as I thought!

Then we talked about 1942, how different we were then. We just don't recognize ourselves as the same people any more. How we simply couldn't bear each other in the beginning. He thought I was much too talkative and unruly, and I soon came to the conclusion that I'd no time for him. I couldn't understand why he didn't flirt with me, but now I'm glad. He also mentioned how much he isolated himself from us all. I said that there was not much difference between my noise and his silence. That I love peace and quiet too, and have nothing for myself alone, except my diary. How glad he is that my parents have children here, and that I'm glad he is here. That I understand his reserve now and his relationship with his parents, and how I would love to be able to help him.

'You always do help me,' he said. 'How?' I asked very surprised. 'By your cheerfulness.' That was certainly the loveliest thing he said. It was wonderful, he must have grown to love me as a friend, and that is enough for the time being.

728

*10*

*Anne and Peter: Love*

Friday, 28th April, 1944

We were, as usual, sitting on the divan, our arms around each other's waists. Then suddenly the ordinary Anne slipped away and a second Anne took her place, a second Anne who is not reckless and jocular, but one who just wants to love and be gentle.

I sat pressed closely against him and felt a wave of emotion come over me, tears sprang into my eyes, the left one trickled on to his dungarees, the right one ran down my nose and also fell on to his dungarees. Did he notice? He made no move or sign to show that he did. I wonder if he feels the same as I do? He hardly said a word. Does he know that he has two Annes before him? These questions must remain unanswered.

At half-past eight I stood up and went to the window, where we always say good-bye. I was still trembling, I was still Anne number two. He came towards me, I flung my arms round his neck and gave him a kiss on his left cheek, and was about to kiss the other cheek, when my lips met his and we pressed them together. In a while we were clasped in each other's arms, again and again, never to leave off. Oh, Peter does so need tenderness. For the first time in his life he has discovered a girl, has seen for the first time that even the most irritating girls have another side to them, that they have hearts and can be different when you are alone with them. For the first time in his life he has given of himself and, having never had a boy or girl friend in his life before, shown his real self. Now we have found each other.

For that matter, I didn't know him either, like him having never had a trusted friend, and this is what it has come to.

Am I only 14? Am I really still a silly little schoolgirl? Am I really so inexperienced about everything? I have more experience than most; I have been through things that hardly anyone of my age has undergone. I am afraid of myself, I am afraid that in my longing I am giving myself too quickly. How, later on, can it ever go right with other boys? Oh, it is so difficult always battling with one's heart and reason; in its own time, each will speak, but do I know for certain that I have chosen the right time?

728

*II*

*Growing Up: Popularity*

Tuesday, 7th March, 1944

If I think now of my life in 1942, it all seems so unreal. It was quite a different Anne who enjoyed that heavenly existence to the Anne who has grown wise within these walls. Yes, it was a heavenly life. Boy friends at every turn, about twenty friends and acquaintances of my own age, the darling of nearly all the teachers, spoilt from top to toe by Mummy and Daddy, lots of sweets, enough pocket money, what more could one want?

You will certainly wonder by what means I got round all these people. Peter's word 'attractiveness' is not altogether true. All the teachers were entertained by my cute answers, my amusing remarks, my smiling face, and my questioning looks. That is all I was—a terrible flirt, coquettish and amusing. I had one or two advantages, which kept me rather in favour. I was industrious, honest and frank. I would never have dreamt of cribbing from anyone else. I shared my sweets generously, and I wasn't conceited.

Wouldn't I have become rather forward with so much admiration? It was a good thing that in the midst of, at the height of, all this gaiety, I suddenly had to face reality, and it took me at least a year to get used to the fact that there was no more admiration forthcoming.

How did I appear at school? As one who thought of new jokes and pranks, always 'king of the castle', never in a bad mood, never a cry-baby. No wonder everyone cycled with me, and was nice.

Now I look back at that Anne as an amusing, but very superficial girl, who has nothing to do with the Anne of today. Peter said quite rightly about me: 'If ever I saw you, you were always surrounded by two or more boys and a whole troupe of girls. You were always laughing and always the centre of everything!'

What is left of this girl? Oh, don't worry, I haven't forgotten how to laugh or to answer back readily. I'm just as good, if not better, at criticizing people, and I can still flirt if . . . I wish. That's not it though. I'd like that sort of life again for an evening, a few days, or even a week; the life which seems so carefree and gay. But at the end of that week, I should be dead-beat and would be only too thankful to listen to anyone who began to talk about something sensible. I don't want followers, but friends, admirers who fall not for a flattering smile but for what one does and for one's character.

I know quite well that the circle around me would be much smaller. But what does that matter, as long as one still keeps a few sincere friends?

Yet I wasn't entirely happy in 1942 in spite of everything; I often felt deserted, but because I was on the go the whole day long, I didn't think about it and enjoyed myself as much as I could. Consciously or unconsciously, I tried to drive away the emptiness I felt with jokes and pranks. Now I think seriously about life and what I have to do. One period of my life is over for ever. The carefree schooldays are gone, never to return.

I don't even long for them any more; I have outgrown them, I can't just only enjoy myself as my serious side is always there.

728

*12*

*Growing Up: Changing Myself*

Tuesday, 7th March, 1944

The first half of 1943: my fits of crying, the loneliness, how I slowly began to see all my faults and shortcomings, which are so great and which seemed much greater then. During the day I deliberately talked about anything and everything that was farthest from my thoughts, tried to draw Daddy to me; but could not. Alone I had to face the difficult task of changing myself, to stop the everlasting reproaches, which were so oppressive and which reduced me to such terrible despondency.

Things improved slightly in the second half of the year, I became a young woman and was treated more like a grown-up.

I started to think and write stories, and came to the conclusion that the others no longer had the right to throw me about like an india-rubber ball. I wanted to change in accordance with my own desires. But *one* thing that struck me even more was when I realized that even Daddy would never become my confidant over everything. I didn't want to trust anyone but myself any more.

728

## *13*

### *Growing Up: Happiness*

Tuesday, 7th March, 1944

At the beginning of the New Year: the second great change, my dream. And with it I discovered my longing, not for a girl friend, but for a boy friend. I also discovered my inward happiness and my defensive armour of superficiality and gaiety. In due time I quietened down and discovered my boundless desire for all that is beautiful and good.

And in the evening, when I lie in bed and end my prayers with the words, 'I thank you, God, for all that is good and dear and beautiful,' I am filled with joy. Then I think about 'the good' of going into hiding, of my health and with my whole being of the 'dearness' of Peter, of that which is still embryonic and impressionable and which we neither of us dare to name or touch, of that which will come some time; love, the future, happiness and of 'the beauty' which exists in the world; the world, nature, beauty and all, all that is exquisite and fine.

I don't think then of all the misery, but of the beauty that still remains. This is one of the things that Mummy and I are so entirely different about. Her counsel when one feels melancholy is, 'Think of all the misery in the world and be thankful that you are not sharing in it!' My advice is: 'Go outside, to the fields, enjoy nature and the sunshine, go out and try to recapture happiness in yourself and in God. Think of all the beauty that's still left in and around you and be happy!'

I don't see how Mummy's idea can be right, because then how are you supposed to behave if you are going through the misery yourself? Then you are lost. On the contrary, I've found that there is always some beauty left—in nature, sunshine, freedom, in yourself; these can all help you. Look at these things, then you find yourself again, and God, and then you regain your balance.

And whoever is happy, will make others happy too. He who has courage and faith will never perish in misery!

728

## *14*

### *Ideals*

Saturday, 15th July, 1944

It's really a wonder that I haven't dropped all my ideals because they seem so absurd and impossible to carry out. Yet, I keep them, because in spite of everything I still believe that people are really good at heart. I simply can't build up my hopes on a foundation consisting of confusion, misery, and death. I see the world gradually being turned into a wilderness, I hear the ever-approaching thunder, which will destroy us too, I can feel the sufferings of millions and yet, if I look up into the heavens, I think that it will all come right, that this cruelty too will end, and that peace and tranquillity will return again.

In the meantime, I must uphold my ideals, for perhaps the time will come when I shall be able to carry them out.

*The Diary of Anne Frank* (adapted)

729

## INCIDENT

Once riding in old Baltimore,
  Heart-filled, head-filled with glee,
I saw a Baltimorean
  Keep looking straight at me.

Now I was eight and very small,
  And he was no whit bigger,
And so I smiled, but he poked out
  His tongue and called me, 'Nigger'.

I saw the whole of Baltimore
  From May until December:
Of all the things that happened there
  That's all that I remember.

Countee Cullen, *On These I Stand*

# SAY THIS CITY HAS TEN MILLION SOULS

Say this city has ten million souls,
Some are living in mansions, some are living in holes:
Yet there's no place for us, my dear, yet there's no place for us.

Once we had a country and we thought it fair,
Look in the atlas and you'll find it there:
We cannot go there now, my dear, we cannot go there now.

In the village churchyard there grows an old yew,
Every spring it blossoms anew:
Old passports can't do that, my dear, old passports can't do that.

The consul banged the table and said;
'If you've got no passport you're officially dead':
But we are still alive, my dear, but we are still alive.

Went to a committee; they offered me a chair;
Asked me politely to return next year:
But where shall we go to-day, my dear, but where shall we go
to-day?

Came to a public meeting; the speaker got up and said:
'If we let them in, they will steal our daily bread';
He was talking of you and me, my dear, he was talking of you
and me.

Dreamed I saw a building with a thousand floors,
A thousand windows and a thousand doors;
Not one of them was ours, my dear, not one of them was ours.

Stood on a great plain in the falling snow;
Ten thousand soldiers marched to and fro:
Looking for you and me, my dear, looking for you and me.

W. H. Auden, *Collected Shorter Poems 1927–1957*

# TELEPHONE CONVERSATION

The price seemed reasonable, location
Indifferent. The landlady swore she lived
Off premises. Nothing remained
But self-confession. 'Madam,' I warned,
'I hate a wasted journey—I am African.'
Silence. Silenced transmission of
Pressurized good-breeding. Voice, when it came,
Lipstick coated, long gold-rolled
Cigarette-holder pipped. Caught I was, foully.
'HOW DARK?' . . . I had not misheard. . . . 'ARE YOU
  LIGHT
OR VERY DARK?' Button B. Button A. Stench
Of rancid breath of public hide-and-speak.
Red booth. Red pillar-box. Red double-tiered
Omnibus squelching tar. It *was* real! Shamed
By ill-mannered silence, surrender
Pushed dumbfoundment to beg simplification.
Considerate she was, varying the emphasis—
'ARE YOU DARK? OR VERY LIGHT?' Revelation came.
'You mean—like plain or milk chocolate?'
Her assent was clinical, crushing in its light
Impersonality. Rapidly, wave-length adjusted,
I chose. 'West African sepia'—and as afterthought,
'Down in my passport.' Silence for spectroscopic
Flight of fancy, till truthfulness clanged her accent
Hard on the mouthpiece. 'WHAT'S THAT?' conceding
'DON'T KNOW WHAT THAT IS.' 'Like brunette.'
'THAT'S DARK, ISN'T IT?' 'Not altogether.
Facially, I am brunette, but madam, you should see
The rest of me. Palm of my hand, soles of my feet
Are a peroxide blonde. Friction, caused—
Foolishly madam—by sitting down, has turned
My bottom raven black—One moment madam!'—sensing
Her receiver rearing on the thunderclap
About my ears—'Madam,' I pleaded, 'wouldn't you rather
See for yourself?'

Wole Soyinka

732

Christians, above all others, should be concerned with social problems and social injustices. Down through the centuries the church has contributed more than any other single agency in lifting social standards to new heights. Child labour has been outlawed. Slavery has been abolished. The status of woman has been lifted to heights unparalleled in history, and many other reforms have taken place as a result of the influence of the teachings of Jesus Christ. The Christian is to take his place in society with moral courage to stand up for that which is right, just and honourable.

Billy Graham, *Peace with God*

733

## A NEGRO TEACHER IN THE EAST END OF LONDON

### TWO READINGS

*I*

There was the sound of tittering from the back row, and glancing towards it I noticed that Denham and Sapiano, one of his cronies, were amusing themselves with something which Denham had in his half-open desk. I walked over and pulled the lid of the desk fully open; inside was a copy of *Weekend Mail* which featured an enlarged picture of a well-favoured young woman in the briefest of bikinis; Denham was busy with his pencil in a way which defeated the already limited purpose of the scanty costume.

I picked up the paper and closed the desk. Denham leaned back in his chair and smiled at me insolently—he had wanted me to find it. Without a word I tore the disgusting thing to shreds, walked back to my desk and dumped them into the waste-basket. As I turned away from him I distinctly heard the muttered 'F—ing black bastard'. I continued with the lesson as if nothing had happened.

Denham's face was now a picture of vicious anger. He had wanted a row, that he might in some way upset the class, and he felt checked. The others looked at me in alarm when I tore up the paper—they were familiar with Denham's reputation, and

(733 *1*) their surprised, anxious faces warned me that something unpleasant was in store.

I was soon to find out what it was.

On Thursday morning the class seemed to be in the grip of some excitement and expectancy. During recess they stood about the classroom in little whispering groups which fell silent as I approached, but I could read no special significance into this. The lessons proceeded more or less normally, but heavily.

In the afternoon, we went down to the gym for the usual P.T. period. The equipment was neatly arranged around the cleared dining hall; vaulting horse, buck, jumping standards, medicine balls, boards, several pairs of boxing gloves slung by their laces across the vaulting horse. The boys were, with one exception, barefoot and wearing only blue shorts. Sapiano sat on a low form, his right arm bandaged from elbow to wrist.

'Line up in the centre, will you,' I began.

They eagerly obeyed, forming two neatly graded lines. But then Denham stepped forward.

'Please, Sir.'

'Yes, Denham?'

'Can't we have boxing first to-day, please, Sir?'

'Why, Denham?'

'Oh, nothing, Sir, just feel we'd like to have a bit of a change, Sir.'

'Oh, very well,' I replied. 'Get yourselves into pairs according to size.'

The pairing was completed in a moment as if by prearrangement; only Denham remained unpaired.

'My partner's crippled, Sir.' He indicated the bandaged Sapiano. 'Will you have a go with me?'

At this the others, as if on cue, moved quietly towards us, watchful, listening.

'You can wait and have a bout with Potter or one of the others.'

The pieces were falling into place, the penny had finally and fatefully dropped.

'They'll be done in, Sir, I don't mind having a knock with you.'

'Go on, Sir, take him on.'

This chorus of encouragement was definitely not in my best interest.

'No, Denham, I think you'll have to skip it for today.'

Denham looked at me pityingly, slipped the gloves off his large hands and casually dropped them at my feet. He had made his point. Looking quickly at the others I could read the disappointment and disgust in their faces. They thought I was afraid, scared of the hulking, loutish fellow.

733

*2*

'Okay, let's go.'

I took a pair of gloves from the horse. Potter stepped over and expertly secured the laces for me while Sapiano, strangely unhampered by his mysterious injury, did the same for Denham. The others meanwhile ranged themselves along the wall, silent and expectant.

As we began to box it became clear that Denham's reputation as a boxer was thoroughly justified; he was fast and scored easily, though his blows were not delivered with his full weight. I tried to dodge and parry as best I could, being only concerned with riding this out for a while until I could reasonably stop it. I had stupidly allowed myself to be lured into this one, and it was up to me to extricate myself with as little damage to either dignity or person as I could.

'Come on, Sir, go after him.' I recognised Patrick Fernman's voice. Disappointment was poignant in it; they must all be somewhat surprised at my lame efforts.

Suddenly Denham moved in and hit me in the face; the blow stung me and I could feel my eyes filling up with tears; the salt blood in my mouth signalled other damage. I was angry now, this was no longer a pleasant little affair—the fellow meant business. It may have been the sight of the blood on my face, or the insistent urging of his cronies to 'Go arter 'im'; whatever it was, it spelled Denham's undoing. Guard open, he rushed in and I hit him; my gloved fist sank deep into his solar-plexus, and the air sighed out of him as he doubled up and collapsed on the floor.

There was a moment of stunned silence, then Potter and some others rushed to help him.

'Hold it. Leave him where he is and line up quickly for vaulting. Clarke, collect the gloves and stack them by the door.'

To my amazement they obeyed without demur, while I hurried

to Denham and helped him over to a low form against the wall; he was only winded and would soon be right as rain. When he was comfortable I continued with the P.T. lesson, which went without a hitch; the boys were eager to do their best, and went through the various movements without recourse to my prompting or direction; they now looked at me as if I had suddenly and satisfactorily grown up before their very eyes.

At the end of the lesson I dismissed class and went over to Denham; he still looked a bit green.

'That was just a lucky punch, old man; no harm meant. Why don't you pop up to the washroom and soak your head in some cold water? You'll feel a lot better.'

'Yes, Sir.' His voice was shaky, but there was no hesitation or mimicry about the 'Sir'. I helped him to his feet and he signalled to Potter, who went off with him towards the washroom.

That incident marked a turning point in my relationship with the class. Gradually Denham's attitude changed, and like it that of his cronies. He could still be depended on to make a wise-crack or comment whenever the opening presented itself, but now these were more acceptable to all of us, for they were no longer made in a spirit of rebellion and viciousness. He appeared clean and more and more helpful and courteous, and with this important area of resistance dispelled the class began to move into high gear. Moreover, I suddenly became aware of an important change in my own relationship to them. I was experiencing more than a mere satisfaction in receiving their attention, obedience and respect with their acceptance of my position as their teacher. I found myself liking them, really liking them, collectively and singly. It was a delight to be with them, and more and more I had occasion to wonder at their generally adult view-point.

E. R. Braithwaite, *To Sir, With Love*

## 734 A NEGRO TEACHER AND HIS WHITE PUPILS

(*He is taking them to see an exhibition of costume in the Victoria and Albert Museum*)

At Whitechapel we changed to a District Line for South Kensington. At that time of morning there were not many seats available, and the children were strung out among two carriages in groups of three or four. I was sandwiched near a door with Moira Joseph, Barbara Pegg and Pamela Dare, who were chattering excitedly to me about the things we were likely to see. They were especially anxious to look at some very fine complicated hand-stitching about which Gillian had told them, and it pleased me to be so closely identified with their lively enthusiasm. At Cannon Street two elderly, well-dressed women joined the train, and stood in the crowd close to us. The stare of disapproval they cast in our direction was made very obvious; and soon they were muttering darkly something about 'shameless young girls and these black men'.

I felt annoyed and embarrassed, and hoped the girls were too absorbed in discussion to notice the remarks, which were meant to be overheard.

Barbara Pegg who was closer to them than the others, was the first to hear them. She bent forward and whispered to Pamela, who moved around until she had changed places with Barbara and was next to the women. Suddenly she turned to face them, her eyes blazing with anger.

'He is our teacher. Do you mind?'

She had intended her voice to carry, and it did. The women looked away, shocked and utterly discomfited, as other people on the train turned to stare at the defiantly regal girl and the blushing busybodies who probably wished that they could sink through the floor.

E. R. Braithwaite, *To Sir, With Love*

## 735 A NEGRO TEACHER ASKS FOR A ROOM

TWO READINGS

*I*

The address was one of a terrace in a rather dingy street, but the pavement outside the front door was, like its neighbours, scrubbed white, and the brass door knocker and lace window curtains bore testimony to the occupant's attention to cleanliness. Some of these local folk were as houseproud as duchesses. I knocked and presently the door was opened by a large, red-faced smiling woman.

'Good evening. I'm here to enquire about the room.'

Immediately the smile was replaced by the expression of cold withdrawal I had come to know so well.

'Sorry, I'm not letting.'

'Mr. Pinkus told me about it just a few moments ago,' I persisted.

'Sorry, I've changed me mind.' Her arms were folded across her stomach, and the set face and bulk of her added to the finality of her words.

'Who's it, Mum?' a girlish voice enquired from somewhere behind her.

'Some darky here asking about the room.' Her mouth spat out the words as if each one was intended to revile.

Embarrassed to the point of anger, I was turning away when there was a sudden movement behind her and a voice cried in consternation:

'Oh Gawd, Mum, it's Sir, it's me teacher.' Beside the woman's surprised face I caught a glimpse of the startled, freckled countenance of Barbara Pegg. 'Oh me Gawd. . . .'

735

*2*

One afternoon, after the class was ended for the day, I was alone in my classroom correcting papers, when there was a knock and Mrs. Pegg entered. I stood up and invited her to come in.

'Good afternoon, Mrs. Pegg.'

'Good afternoon, Sir. I see you've remembered me.'

I did not reply to this, but waited for her to continue.

'I want to talk to you about the room, Sir. You see I didn't know that you was Babs' teacher, you know what I mean.'

I knew what she meant then, and I knew what she meant now.

'I think we'll just forget about the whole thing, Mrs. Pegg.'

'But I can't forget about it, Sir. Babs has been after me day and night to come and talk to you about it. You can have the room if you like, Sir.'

'That's all right, Mrs. Pegg. I've changed my mind about the room.'

'Have you got another one somewhere else locally, Sir?'

'No, Mrs. Pegg, I've decided to remain where I am, at least for the present.'

'What shall I tell Babs, Sir? She'll think you're still mad at me, that's why you won't have the room.'

35 2) There was very real concern in her voice. Barbara must be quite a girl, I thought, to be able to put the fear of God into someone as massive and tough-looking as her mother.

'Leave it to me, Mrs. Pegg. I will have a word with Barbara and explain the situation to her.'

'Oh Sir, I'd be glad if you would; I didn't mean no harm that day, and she won't let me forget it.'

I was finally able to get rid of her. I did not believe for one moment that she cared whether I found a room or not, but, as was characteristic of so many of these women, she would have willingly submerged her own opinions and prejudices to please her daughter. I was not, on reflection, bitter about Mrs. Pegg's refusal.

It was understandable that in the present state of things a mother might be disinclined to have a male lodger sharing the same small house with her teen-age daughter; my being a negro might even strengthen that disinclination, though it could not excuse her crudely discourteous behaviour. What really mattered was that Barbara did not share her mother's snap prejudices; if the young ones were learning to think for themselves in such things, then even that painful incident had been worth something.

Later that day I found an opportunity to talk with Barbara. I mentioned that her mother had wanted me to take the room but that I had decided to stay where I was.

'But you would have had it at first, Sir, if me Mum had let you?'

'That's true, Miss Pegg, but you know we all change our minds about things.'

'Are you still mad at Mum, Sir?' She wanted so desperately to be reassured.

'No, I was a bit annoyed at first, but not now. I think it is very generous of both of you to make the offer and I am grateful. Tell you what, if I need to move at any time, I'll let you know and if the room is available I'll have it. How's that?'

'That's okay, Sir.'

'Good, now we'll forget the whole thing until then, shall we?'

'Yes, Sir.'

She smiled, completely relieved. She was a good kid, and perhaps would, in due course, be able to teach her mother a few more lessons in the essential humanities.

E. R. Braithwaite, *To Sir, With Love*

# A NEGRO TEACHER AND HIS COLOURED PUPIL

## THREE READINGS

### *I*

(*Seales is the son of a white mother and a coloured father*)

On December 6th, Seales was not in his place and I marked him absent. Just before recess he came in and walked briskly to my table.

'Sorry I can't stay, Sir, but my mother died early this morning and I'm helping my Dad with things.'

As if those words finally broke all his efforts to be strong and grown-up, his face crumpled and he wept like the small boy he really felt. I got up quickly and led him unresisting to my chair, where he sat, his head in his hands, sobbing bitterly.

I gave the news to the class; they received it in shocked silence, in that immediate sympathy and compassion which only the young seem to know and experience, and then many of them were weeping too.

I spoke comfortingly to Seales and sent him home; then I went to see Mr. Florian to acquaint him with the circumstances.

After recess, as I was about to begin our History lesson, Barbara Pegg stood up; she had been asked by the class to say that they had agreed to make a collection among themselves to purchase a wreath or other floral token of sympathy, to be sent to Seales' home. I said I was agreeable, providing I was allowed to contribute also. We learned that the funeral was fixed for the Saturday. Barbara collected contributions throughout the week, and by Friday morning had nearly two pounds. I was delighted at this news, and after assembly we discussed together the type of floral token they wished to purchase and the nearest florist from whom it could be obtained. Then I remarked:

'Which of you will take it over to his home?'

Their reaction was like a cold douche. The pleasantly united cameraderie disappeared completely from the room, and in its place was the watchful antagonism I had encountered on my first day. It was as if I had pulled a thick transparent screen between them and myself, effectively shutting us away from each other.

It was ugly to see; I felt excluded, even hated, but all so horribly quickly.

'What's the matter with you?' My voice was loud in my ears. 'What's suddenly so awful about the flowers?'

Moira stood up. 'We can't take them, Sir.'

'What do you mean, Miss Joseph? Why can't you take them?'

She looked quickly around the room as if pleading with the others to help her explain.

'It's what people would say if they saw us going to a coloured person's home.' She sat down.

There it was. I felt weak and useless, an alien among them. All the weeks and months of delightful association were washed out by those few words.

Nothing had really mattered, the teaching, the talking, the example, the patience, the worry. It was all as nothing. They, like the strangers on buses and trains, saw only the skins, never the people in those skins. Seales was born among them, grew up among them, played with them; his mother was white, British, of their stock and background and beginnings.

All the hackneyed clichés hammered in my head. A coloured boy with a white mother, a West Indian boy with an English mother. Always the same. Never an English boy with a Negro or West Indian father. No, that would be placing the emphasis on his Englishness, his identification with them.

It was like a disease, and these children whom I loved without caring about *their* skins or *their* backgrounds, they were tainted with the hateful virus which attacked their vision, distorting everything that was not white or English.



*2*

They were quiet in the classroom. I wanted to say something, but no words came. Jacqueline Bender rose.

'Sir, I don't think you understood just now. We have nothing against Seales. We like him, honest we do, but if one of us girls was seen going to his home, you can't imagine the things people would say. We'd be accused of all sorts of things.' She sat, evidently overcome by this long speech.

'Thank you for making that so clear, Miss Bender. Does the same thing apply to the boys as well?'

They were not defiant now, but their eyes were averted.

'I'll take them.' Pamela stood up, tall and proudly regal.

'Why should you, Miss Dare? Aren't you afraid of what might be said of you?'

'No, Sir, gossips don't worry me. After all, I've known Larry, I mean Seales, since in the Infants.'

'Thank you, Miss Dare. The funeral is at ten o'clock. I'll take my usual train and perhaps I'll see you there. Thank you.'

On Saturday morning I caught an early bus from Brentwood. I sat on the top deck in the rearmost seat, disinclined to see or be seen, to speak or be spoken to; withdrawn and wishing only to be as far removed from white people as I possibly could be. I had given all I could to those children, even part of myself, but it had been of no use. In the final analysis they had trotted out the same hoary excuse so familiar to their fathers and grandfathers: 'We have nothing against him personally, but . . .' How well I knew it now! If he'd been pimp or pansy, moron or murderer, it would not have mattered, providing he was white; his outstanding gentleness, courtesy and intelligence could not offset the greatest sin of all, the sin of being black.



## *3*

They had been glib at the Students' Council, and bright and persuasive. It had sounded great coming from them, that talk of common heritage and inalienable rights; glib and easy, until they were required to do something to back up all the talk, and then the façade had cracked and crumbled because it was as phoney as themselves. Crucify him because he's black; lynch him because he's black; ostracise him because he's black; a little change, a little shift in geographical position and they'd be using the very words they'd now so vociferously condemned.

The whirr and rattle of the bus was a rhythmic percussion syncopating the anger in my heart into a steady, throbbing hate, until I felt rather light-headed. I disembarked outside the London Hospital and walked towards Commercial Road and Priddle Street where the Seales lived. As I turned into the narrow roadway I could see the drearily ornate hearse parked there, and the small group of curiosity-seekers who somehow always materialize to gape open-mouthed on the misery of others. And then I stopped, feeling suddenly washed clean, whole and alive again. Tears were in my eyes, unashamedly, for there, standing in a close, separate group on the pavement outside Seales' door was my class, my children, all or nearly all of them, smart and self-conscious in their best clothes. Oh God, forgive me for the hateful thoughts, because I love them, these brutal, disarming bastards, I love them.

I hurried over to join them to be again with them, a part of them. They welcomed me silently, pride and something else shining in their eyes as they gathered close around me. I felt something soft pressed into my hand, and as I looked round into the clear, shining eyes of Pamela Dare, I dried my own eyes with the tiny handkerchief.

E. R. Braithwaite, *To Sir, With Love*

## 737 WHAT WE WANT

Modern man seems, if anything, to have too many wishes and his only problem seems to be that, although he knows what he wants, he cannot have it. All our energy is spent for the purpose of getting what we want, and most people never question the premise of this activity: that they know their true wants. They do not stop to think whether the aims they are pursuing *are* something they themselves want. In school they want to have good marks, as adults they want to be more and more successful, to buy a better car, to go places, and so on. Yet when they do stop to think in the midst of all this frantic activity, this question may come to their minds: 'If I do get this new job, if I get this better car, if I can take this trip—what then? What is the use of it all? Is it really I who want all this? Am I not running after some goal which is supposed to make me happy and which eludes me as soon as I have reached it?'

People tend to get rid as soon as possible of these disturbing thoughts. They feel that they have been bothered by these questions because they were tired or depressed—and they go on in the pursuit of the aims which they believe are their own.

But 'know thyself' is one of the fundamental commands that aim at human strength and happiness.

Erich Fromm (adapted)

When we survey our lives and endeavours, we soon observe that almost the whole of our actions and desires is bound up with the existence of other human beings. The individual, if left alone from birth, would remain primitive and beastlike in his thoughts and feelings to a degree that we can hardly conceive. The individual is what he is and has the significance that he has not so much in virtue of his individuality, but rather as a member of a great human community, which directs his material and spiritual existence from the cradle to the grave.

A man's value to the community depends primarily on how far his feelings, thoughts, and actions are directed towards promoting the good of his fellows. We call him good or bad according to his attitude in this respect. It looks at first sight as if our estimate of a man depended entirely on his social qualities.

And yet such an attitude would be wrong. It can easily be seen that all the valuable achievements, material, spiritual, and moral, which we receive from society have been brought about in the course of countless generations by creative individuals. Someone once discovered the use of fire, someone the cultivation of edible plants, and someone the steam engine.

Only the individual can think, and thereby create new values for society, nay, even set up new moral standards to which the life of the community conforms. Without creative personalities able to think and judge independently, the upward development of society is as unthinkable as the development of the individual personality without the nourishing soil of the community.

The health of society thus depends quite as much on the independence of the individuals composing it as on their close social cohesion.

Albert Einstein, *Mein Weltbild*

## 739 ALCOHOL

If alcohol, instead of being a beneficent gift from the gods in the remote past, were invented today by a research chemist, there is little doubt it would immediately be stringently controlled by law. But because our society has lived with it so long, we can control it, and tolerate those effects we can't control. For example, it is estimated that there are about 100,000 acute alcoholics in England and Wales, and the upkeep of those that are in prison or who cannot work, with their families, costs the nation about £6 million a year. Less acute alcoholics are probably three times as numerous, and their absenteeism and poor work costs, at a moderate estimate, another £35 million a year. Alcohol probably causes some 1,200 deaths on the roads and 50,000 injuries a year. In Scotland alcoholism is the cause of admission to mental hospital of one patient in five. In Glasgow 15,000 crimes a year are committed under the influence of this drug, and in the three worst wards of the city six per cent of all males are arrested every year for being drunk and incapable. These things happen around us and we are not worried. Our society spends £20 million a year advertising alcohol on TV and in the press, and 340,000 people work at the manufacture and distribution of alcohol—half as many again as work in all gas, electricity and water supply industries.

Peter Laurie, *Drugs*

# Wealth

## 740 WEALTH AND HUMANITY

I am absolutely convinced that no wealth in the world can help humanity forward, even in the hands of the most devoted worker in this cause. The example of great and pure individuals is the only thing that can lead us to noble thoughts and deeds. Money only appeals to selfishness and irresistibly invites abuse.

Can anyone imagine Moses, Jesus, or Gandhi armed with the money-bags of Carnegie?

Albert Einstein, *Mein Weltbild*

## 741 MONEY

Some eminent person once said that money is the means to freedom. But it seems to me that money always was and is the means of making people slaves. Those who have none are slaves because they need it in order to live. And those who have it and spend their nerves and energy on getting more or at least keeping what they have are slaves just as much.

I witnessed the currency reform of 1947. When the rumour spread that it was imminent, people mobbed the shops and bought up everything. I saw a man loading four lavatory seats on a car because the hardware shop had nothing else left. I saw a woman staggering, puffing and sweating under the weight of a plaster Venus. The day the reform was officially announced, I saw an old man running down the street, screaming in hysterics as he scattered bank notes on the pavement and trampled on them.

Yevgeny Yevtushenko, *A Precocious Autobiography*

# Suffering

## 742 JOY AND SUFFERING

Joy and suffering are two equally precious gifts which must both of them be savoured to the full, each one in its purity without trying to mix them. Through joy, the beauty of the world penetrates our soul. Through suffering it penetrates our body. We could no more become friends of God through joy alone than one becomes a ship's captain by studying books on navigation. The body plays a part in all apprenticeships. On the plane of physical sensibility, suffering alone gives us contact with that necessity which constitutes the order of the world, for pleasure does not involve an impression of necessity. It is a higher kind of sensibility which is capable of recognising a necessity in joy, and that only indirectly through a sense of beauty. In order that our being should one day become wholly sensitive in every part to this obedience which is the substance of matter, in order that a new sense should be formed in us which enables us to hear the universe as the vibration of the word of God, the transforming power of suffering and of joy are equally indispensable. When either of them comes to us we have to open the very centre of our soul to it.

Simone Weil, *Waiting on God*

## 743 SUFFERING AND SYMPATHY

Many works of art have their origin in an experience of suffering—often in a kind of inward frustration and despair. Artists, as a matter of fact, are not usually very articulate about this, but Van Gogh the painter spoke of attending 'the free lectures of the College of Misery'. He likened himself to a bird in a cage in springtime. Whilst other birds in the open are building their nests and feeding their young, 'The children who clean out his cage think that he has everything he needs, but the bird looks at the storm-laden sky and revolts against his fate. I am cooped up in a cage and lack nothing, you idiots.' Van Gogh felt trapped. But he knew how he could be released from his inward frustration.

'Do you know what takes away the cage? Every profound relationship, brotherhood, friendship, love. They open the cage like a magic key. He who creates sympathy, creates life!'

Robert C. Walton, from *The Problem of Suffering*

744

## FOUR WALLS

Four great walls have hemmed me in.
Four strong, high walls:
Right and wrong,
Shall and shan't.

The mighty pillars tremble when
My conscience palls
And sings its song—
I can, I can't.

If for a moment Samson's strength
Were given me I'd shove
Them away from where I stand;
Free, I know I'd love
To ramble soul and all,
And never dread to strike a wall.

Again, I wonder would that be
Such a happy state for me . . .
The going, being, doing, sham—
And never knowing where I am.
I might not love freedom at all;
My tired wings might crave a wall—

Four walls to rise and pen me in
This conscious world with guarded men.

Blanche Taylor Dickinson

745

## THE DAILY GRIND

If Nature says to you,
'I intend you for something fine,
For something to sing the song
That only my whirling stars can sing,
For something to burn in the firmament
With all the fervour of my golden sun,
For something to moisten the parched souls
As only my rivulets can moisten the parched,'

What can you do?

If the System says to you,
'I intend you to grind and grind
Grains of corn beneath millstones;
I intend you to shovel and sweat
Before a furnace of Babylon;
I intend you for grist and meat
To fatten my pompous gods
As they wallow in an alcoholic nectar,'

What can you do?

Naught can you do
But watch that eternal battle
Between Nature and the System.
You cannot blame God,
You cannot blame man;
For God did not make the System,
Neither did man fashion Nature.
You can only die each morning,
And live again in the dreams of the night.
If Nature forgets you,
If the System forgets you,
God has blest you.

Fenton Johnson

There is a young man,
who lives in the world of progress.
He used to worship a God,
Who was kind to him.
The God had a long white beard,
He lived in the clouds,
but all the same,
He was close to the solemn child,
who had secretly
shut Him up, in a picture book.

But now,
the man is enlightened.
Now he has been at school,
and has learnt to kick a ball,
and to be abject
in the face of public opinion.
He knows too,
that men are hardly removed from monkeys.
You see, he lives in the light
of the twentieth century.

He works twelve hours a day
and is able to rent a room,
in a lodging house that is not a home.
At night he hangs a wretched coat
up on a peg on a door,
and stares at the awful jug and basin
and goes to bed.
And the poor coat,
worn to the man's shape,
round-shouldered and abject,
watches him asleep,
dreaming of all the essential, holy things,
that he can hope to obtain
for two pound ten a week.

Very soon, he will put off his body,
like the poor dejected coat

that he hates.
And his body will be
worn to the shape
of twelve hours' work a day,
for two pounds ten a week.

If he had only known,
that the God in the picture book,
is not an old man in the clouds,
but the seed of life in his soul,
the man would have lived.
And his life would have flowered,
with the flower of limitless joy.

But he does not know,
and in him
the Holy Ghost,
is a poor little bird in a cage,
who never sings,
and never opens his wings,
yet never, never
desires to be gone away.

Caryll Houselander, *The Flowering Tree*

## 747 THE GIFT OF COURAGE

On the whole it is true to say that suffering, courageously borne, lifts morale not only for the person himself but also for everybody else. I have seen patients in a ward who were undoubtedly among the most severely afflicted by disease or injury, but whose courage was not only an example but a tremendous source of comfort to everybody else. And I have seen people go down to an operating theatre the braver because they had seen somebody else go down the week before who set a good example. Courage, like fear, like cowardice, can be infectious. So showing courage in suffering can be a gift to the world. It is a gift which doctors are always glad to receive from their patients.

David Stafford-Clark, from *The Problem of Suffering*

(*After two years of imprisonment in Buchenwald Concentration Camp*)

This for me is the first lesson of the camp—that it made beasts of some men and saints of others. And the second lesson of the camp is that it is hard to predict who will be the saint and who the beast when the time of trial comes.

Men famous and honoured in pre-war France, regarded as natural leaders, showed neither spirit nor authority in the camp. Other men, of seemingly mediocre brains and character, who would never have been noticed in ordinary times, shone out like beacons as the true leaders. Under the stresses and strains imposed by life in the camp, only one thing prevailed—strength of character. Cleverness, creativeness, learning, all went down; only real goodness survived.

Sooner or later weakness of fibre was revealed in a man, and sooner or later it destroyed him. Self-discipline was essential, and this is the basis of character. For instance—the question of the open fire. It had been very tempting, especially in the cold winter nights, to go and lie by the open braziers in our blockhouse. But it was fatal. A man began by lying some distance from the fire, on the outer ring. But the fire drew like a magnet. He would go closer to the flames, until finally he would get as near as he possibly could. The contrast between the heat of the fire at night and the cold of the roll call in the morning was too much for these poor human frames. It was only a matter of time before it killed them.

The fact that every prisoner knew this did not prevent a great many from succumbing. If a prisoner began habitually to leave his bunk in the night and lie down to sleep on the floor around the fire, you knew that he had decided, even if he had not faced his own decision, that death was preferable to discomfort.

As I write about the temptation of the fire, which symbolises all the temptations of the camp, I think of P., a famous scientist who was among us. P. had begun the downhill path by selling his margarine ration to obtain cigarettes. He could not afford this deficiency in fat, as he well knew, and it became necessary for him to obtain heat from the fire. Gradually P. moved from the outside circle of the sleepers to the centre. Every night he got a little nearer. For a week or so he slept as close to it as he could get. And then, because he had failed to discipline his craving for cigarettes, he died.

It seemed to me that those men displayed most character who had the capacity for living on their own and that these men possessed something which is easiest described as religion, faith, or devotion. I saw that leadership exercised by Christians. I saw it in communists, too. It was displayed by people who had no religious faith or political creed in any formal sense, but who still had some inner core which gave them a belief in life, when the rest of us were lost.

The camp showed me that a man's real enemies are not ranged against him along the borders of a hostile country; they are often among his own people—indeed, within his own mind. The worst enemies are hate and greed, and cruelty. The real enemy is within.

Pierre d'Harcourt, *The Real Enemy*

## 749 THE FELLOWSHIP OF PAIN

Suffering is an initiation into human experience which we can never know at second-hand. No matter how much we see of suffering, no matter how much we read or hear of what others have to say about it, there is something that cannot be imparted. Perhaps that was one reason why Plato said that a physician should not be a man who has always enjoyed robust health. It is only by your own suffering that you are admitted to the fellowship of pain.

Leslie J. Tizard, *Facing Life and Death*

## 750 BABIY YAR

(*The stresses fall as follows: Bábiy Yar; Belostók*)

*Introduction*

*Babiy Yar is the name of a ravine near Kiev where many thousands of Jews were massacred and buried during the Second World War. The*

(750) *'Society of the Russian People' was a notorious organization in pre-Revolutionary Russia, responsible for pogroms directed against the Jews. Belostok was formerly part of the Russian Empire, and is nowadays included within the frontiers of Poland.*

Over Babiy Yar
there are no memorials.
The steep hillside like a rough inscription.
I am frightened.
Today I am as old as the Jewish race.
I seem to myself a Jew at this moment.
I, wandering in Egypt.
I, crucified. I perishing.
Even today the mark of the nails.
I think also of Dreyfus. I am he.
The Philistine my judge and my accuser.
Cut off by bars and cornered,
ringed round, spat at, lied about;
the screaming ladies with the Brussels lace
poke me in the face with parasols.
I am also a boy in Belostok,
the dropping blood spreads across the floor,
the public-bar heroes are rioting
in an equal stench of garlic and of drink.
I have no strength, go spinning from a boot,
shriek useless prayers that they don't listen to;
with a cackle of 'Thrash the kikes and save Russia!'
the corn-chandler is beating up my mother.
I seem to myself like Anna Frank
to be transparent as an April twig,
and am in love, I have no need for words,
I need for us to look at one another.
How little we have to see or to smell
separated from foliage and the sky,
how much, how much in the dark room
gently embracing each other.
They're coming. Don't be afraid.
The booming and banging of the spring.
It's coming this way. Come to me.
Quickly, give me your lips.
They're battering in the door. Roar of the ice.

Over Babiy Yar
rustle of the wild grass.
The trees look threatening, look like judges.
And everything is one silent cry.
Taking my hat off
I feel myself slowly going grey.
And I am one silent cry
over the many thousands of the buried;
am every old man killed here,
every child killed here.
O my Russian people, I know you.
Your nature is international.
Foul hands rattle your clean name.
I know the goodness of my country.
How horrible it is that pompous title
the anti-semites calmly call themselves,
Society of the Russian People.
No part of me can ever forget it.
When the last anti-semite on the earth
is buried for ever
let the International ring out.
No Jewish blood runs among my blood,
but I am as bitterly and hardly hated
by every anti-semite
as if I were a Jew. By this
I am a Russian.

Yevgeny Yevtushenko, *Selected Poems*

751 PRISONERS OF THE JAPANESE

(*The experiences of Captain Ernest Gordon, based on his book* 'The Miracle on the River Kwai')

FIVE READINGS

*I*

*The Degraded Prisoners*

During a large part of the Second World War, I was a prisoner of war on the banks of a jungle river in Thailand. We were working on the infamous 'Death Railway', the 250 mile track which the Japanese were forcing prisoners to build. Of 62,000 Allied prisoners engaged on the job, some 12,400 died from starvation and brutality. Many thousands more will suffer from the experience for the rest of their lives.

The Japanese had promised that their British captives would be reduced to a lower level than any coolie in Asia, and they kept their word. Failure to salute the Japanese sentries, or bow as required, brought severe beatings. 'Looking Arrogant' was cause enough for a clubbing. Under such treatment, plus mounting exhaustion and illness, our morale weakened. In a matter of weeks, tough men were reduced to skeletons. Almost all developed jungle ulcers, the sort that eat the flesh away to the bone. Yet illness excused no prisoner from back-breaking work.

As men will under such circumstances, many of us 'tried religion'. We read our Bibles, flocked to religious services. We prayed for our deliverance. When nothing happened, the little faith we had summoned up glimmered and died, and bitterness took its place. Not even God—if there was God—cared about us. Some men took to stealing one another's food, a few resorted to treachery. The Japanese found it amusing to watch the once proud white soldiers destroying one another. Then something happened.

751

## 2

### *Death and Life*

It all started with a small group of other ranks. Among the leaders were two corporals. One, a lad named Miller, was from my own unit: the other, Denis Moore, from the Royal Corps of Signals. Neither lived to see the end of the war; Miller died of dysentery on a ship taking him and other prisoners to Japan. It was said that Moore was crucified, literally, by a Japanese officer who hated him for his radiant spirit that refused to break under torture.

To these two men largely belongs the credit for effecting one of the most wondrous changes I ever witnessed. Not in me alone, but in that entire camp of some 3,000 men.

I owe them more: my life. One day in 1944 after more than two years on the Death Railway, I collapsed. I was desperately ill, paralysed from the waist down. Only half conscious, I was aware of the two medical orderlies in charge of the hospital bending over me and overheard one say, 'He's not long for the road, all we can do is make his end as easy as possible.' Corporals Miller and Moore also overheard this sentence of death. They took me from the hospital, built me a little bamboo shack, shared their food with me, took turns in nursing me. In two and a half months they had given me back my life. But, more important, they gave me another life.

Under their care I became aware that these lads had something that the rest of us had missed, something that could not be beaten out of them, or starved, or kicked. That something was the greatest force on earth—LOVE. Love that quite literally 'casts out fear', Love that loses life in order to gain it.

751

## 3

### *The Way to God*

Suddenly, I knew that I and all the others in Chungkai must have Christian love, must carry it as well as receive it or we would perish.

Corporal Miller showed me, one night during the last stages of my convalescence, the way to that love and that meaning. We were talking about man's age-old quest for meaning in life. Impatiently I cried, 'But how can any man find meaning in this hell?'

Quietly he replied, 'Sir, an unknown poet once wrote a little poem that explains it all. He said,

> "I sought my soul, but my soul I could not see,
> I sought my God, but my God eluded me,
> I sought my brother—and found all three."

On my feet again I found myself involved in that search. I was asked to lead a discussion group on Christianity. My own faith had been a weak, inadequate thing based on casual church attendance at home and soon I found that I was not so much teacher as the one being taught. The meetings, held at night, started with about a dozen men, grew to scores, then to hundreds.

Those classes determined the need for action, not mere talk. Spontaneously there spread the most thrilling examples of redemptive service I've ever known. We formed teams of masseurs, who went about among the sick whose muscles had atrophied from long disuse, and massaged them back to life. Other teams went about merely spreading cheer, performing what little services seemed necessary.

The focal point of this activity was the church. Out of bamboo we erected a house of worship. Services were held by the flickering light of a lamp made from an old tin. The lamp stood in front of a rough wooden cross—its very shape drawing men's gaze upwards towards God, and outwards towards mankind.

751

## *4*

### *Prayer*

Christmas 1944 at Chungkai in sharp contrast to the lonely bitterness of the two previous Nativities was a happy occasion. We had spent many evenings arranging get-togethers and exchanging gifts. The cooks, by heroic efforts, had contrived a delicious Christmas pudding—made from fermented rice, lime skins and palm sugar.

The special service for Christmas was the most movingly reverent of my life.

Nowhere was the change in attitude more manifest than in our prayers. We learned to pray for others more than ourselves. When we did pray for ourselves it was not to *get* something, but to release some power within us. When we prayed, 'Yea, though I walk through the valley of the shadow of death', we were not pitying ourselves; we were affirming something, 'I will fear no evil.'

Gradually we learned to pray that hardest of all prayers: for our enemies. I shall never forget the time when a young N.C.O., leading us in the Lord's Prayer, arrived at the line, 'Forgive us . . . as we forgive them that trespass against us', only to hear himself voicing it alone. Pausing a moment, he repeated the phrase—and this time a hundred voices spoke it with him, firmly, resolutely.

751

## *5*

### *Compassion*

Our hatred of the Japanese ebbed away. We began to see them in better perspective, to understand what forces had operated to make them what they were. And with understanding came compassion.

An incident that happened during the final months of imprisonment revealed to me how far we had come from hatred. I had been placed in charge of a company being transferred to a working site. On the way we were shunted on to a siding near a small village, when a trainload of Japanese soldiers pulled in. They were casualties from the fighting in Burma and in a pitiful plight: indescribably filthy, ragged, starving, their wounds full of maggots.

My men's action was as instinctive as it was compassionate. With no order from me and in defiance of our Japanese guards, they moved over to clean the soldiers' wounds, give them their own rations of rice, share with them what money they had. To our men these were no longer enemies, only fellow sufferers.

Ernest Gordon, *Miracle on the River Kwai* (adapted)

# Death and Eternity

752

## IN TIME OF DEATH

'We have this treasure in earthen vessels', writes St. Paul, and we all know how easily earthen vessels can be broken: we cannot escape the sickening, heart-rending and often shocking 'breakability' of life. Each of you may recall some time when as a child you were enjoying yourself tremendously—a real game, a pretend game—but then the plans of adults, time for tea or time for bed, broke the joy of the moment. Treasure, yes; but in earthen vessels: at any moment it could be broken.

Particularly do we see in the death of a young person that we have our treasure in *earthen vessels* . . . (words may be said now about the person himself). . . . Here indeed is human treasure broken with terrible suddenness.

'But it is not destroyed': this is the message of the Christian Gospel. The Christian faith says clearly that God is *with us* in all this. He is not remote and apart. He is part of this breakable life, and he suffers this aspect of life with us. Indeed at one time in the history of man the whole treasure of God's love was contained for a while in one earthen vessel, the person and life of Jesus Christ. And this treasure was not lost, nor changed nor destroyed by death. The body was broken, but the resurrection showed for all time that the treasure is unbreakable, imperishable and eternal.

Let us give thanks to God for the fulness of (. . . .'s) life and the love which we have had for him. Jesus said, 'I am come that they might have life, and that they might have it more abundantly.' Let us rejoice in the knowledge that with him the *treasure of . . . .'s life* is not destroyed but fulfilled.

R. S. Ingamells, at the funeral of Peter Beattie

## 753 THE FIRST EXPLOSION OF THE ATOMIC BOMB 16TH JULY, 1945

By two o'clock in the morning all those taking part in the experiment were in their places. They were assembled in the Base Camp, some ten miles from Point Zero where there stood the high scaffolding on which the new, still untested weapon had been placed—the bomb on which they had been working for the last two years and had now finally brought to completion. They tried on the dark glasses with which they had been provided and smeared their faces, by artificial light, with anti-sunburn cream. They could hear dance music from the loudspeakers distributed throughout the area. From time to time the music was interrupted by news of the progress of the preparations.

During the ensuing period of waiting, which seemed an eternity, hardly a word was spoken. Everyone was giving free play to his thoughts. But so far as those who have been asked can remember, these thoughts were not apocalyptic. Most of the people concerned, it appears, were trying to work out how long it would be before they could shift their uncomfortable position and obtain some kind of view of the spectacle awaited. Fermi, experimental-minded as ever, was holding scraps of paper, with which he meant to gauge the air pressure and thereby estimate the strength of the explosion the moment it occurred. Frisch was intent on memorizing the phenomenon as precisely as possible, without allowing either excitement or preconceived notions to interfere with his faculties of perception. Groves was wondering for the hundredth time whether he had taken every possible step

(753) to ensure rapid evacuation in the case of a disaster. Oppenheimer oscillated between fears that the experiment would fail and fears that it would succeed.

Then everything happened faster than it could be understood. No one saw the first flash of the atomic fire itself. It was only possible to see its dazzling white reflection in the sky and on the hills. Those who then ventured to turn their heads perceived a bright ball of flame, growing steadily larger and larger. 'Good God, I believe that the long-haired boys have lost control!' a senior officer shouted. Carson Mark, one of the most brilliant members of the Theoretical Division, actually thought—though his intelligence told him the thing was impossible—that the ball of fire would never stop growing till it had enveloped all heaven and earth. At that moment everyone forgot what he had intended to do.

Groves writes: 'Some of the men in their excitement, having had three years to get ready for it, at the last minute forgot those welders' helmets and stumbled out of the cars where they were sitting. They were distinctly blinded for two to three seconds. In that time they lost the view of what they had been waiting for over three years to see.'

People were transfixed with fright at the power of the explosion. Oppenheimer was clinging to one of the uprights in the control room. A passage from the *Bhagavad Gītā*, the sacred epic of the Hindus, flashed into his mind.

> If the radiance of a thousand suns
> were to burst into the sky,
> that would be like
> the splendour of the Mighty One—

Yet, when the sinister and gigantic cloud rose up in the far distance over Point Zero, he was reminded of another line from the same source:

> I am become Death, the shatterer of worlds.

Sri Krishna, the Exalted One, lord of the fate of mortals, had uttered the phrase. But Robert Oppenheimer was only a man, into whose hands a mighty, a far too mighty, instrument of power had been given.

It is a striking fact that none of those present reacted to the phenomenon as professionally as he had supposed he would. They all, even those—who constituted the majority—ordinarily without religious faith or even any inclination thereto, recounted their experiences in words derived from the linguistic fields of myth and theology. General Farrell, for example states:

The whole country was lighted by a searing light with an intensity many times that of the midday sun. Thirty seconds after the explosion came, first, the air blast pressing hard against the people and things, to be followed almost immediately by the strong, sustained, awesome roar which warned of doomsday and made us feel that we puny things were blasphemous to dare tamper with the forces heretofore reserved to the Almighty.

Robert Jungk, *Brighter Than a Thousand Suns*

## 754 CREATION IN REVERSE

In the end, man destroyed the heaven that had been called earth. For the earth had been beautiful and happy until the destructive spirit of men moved upon it. This was the seventh day before the end.

For man said, 'Let me have power in the earth,' and he saw that power seemed good, and he called those who sought power 'great leaders', and those who sought only to serve others and bring reconciliation 'weaklings', 'compromisers', 'appeasers'. And this was the sixth day before the end.

And man said, 'Let there be a division among all people, and divide the nations which are for me from the nations which are against me.' And this was the fifth day before the end.

And man said, 'Let us gather our resources in one place and create more instruments of power to defend ourselves; the radio to control men's minds, conscription to control men's bodies; uniforms and symbols of power to win men's souls.' And this was the fourth day before the end.

And man said, 'Let there be censorship to divide the propaganda from the truth.' And he made two great censorship bureaux to control the thoughts of men; one to tell only the truth he wishes known at home, and the other to tell only the truth that he wishes known abroad. And this was the third day before the end.

And man said, 'Let us create weapons which can kill vast numbers, even millions and hundreds of millions, at a distance.' And so he perfected germ warfare and deadly underwater arsenals, guided missiles, great fleets of war planes and destructive power to the extent of tens of thousands of millions of tons of T.N.T. And it was the second day before the end.

And man said, 'Let us make God in our own image. Let us say God does as we do, thinks as we think, wills as we will, and kills as we kill.' So man found ways to kill with atomic power and dust, even those as yet unborn. And he said 'This is necessary. There is no alternative. This is God's will.'

And on the last day, there was a great noise upon the face of the earth, and man and all his doings were no more, and the ravished earth rested on the seventh day. . . .

Anon.

## 755 AN ATOMIC EXPERIMENT

Slotin had been busy testing the interior mechanism of the experimental bomb. It consisted of two hemispheres which would come together at the moment of release, thereby enabling the uranium they contained to unite in a 'critical mass'.

Such experiments were assigned to the group in the charge of Frisch, the discoverer of fission, who had been brought to Los Alamos from England. Slotin was one of the members of this group. He was in the habit of experimenting without taking any special protective measures. His only instruments were two screwdrivers, by means of which he allowed the two hemispheres to slide towards each other on a rod, while he watched them with incessant concentration. His object was to do no more than just reach the critical point, the very first step in the chain reaction, which would immediately stop the moment he parted the spheres again. If he passed the point or was not quite quick enough in breaking contact, the mass might become supercritical and produce a nuclear explosion.

But the daring young scientist thoroughly enjoyed risking his life in this way. He called it 'twisting the dragon's tail'. Ever since his earliest youth he had gone in search of fighting, excitement, and adventure.

On 21 May 1946, Slotin was carrying out an experiment, similar to those he had so often successfully performed in the past. It was connected with the preparation of the second atom-bomb test, to be performed in the waters of the South Sea atoll of Bikini. Suddenly his screwdriver slipped. The hemispheres came too close together and the material became critical. The whole room was instantly filled with a dazzling, bluish glare. Slotin, instead of ducking and thereby possibly saving himself, tore the two hemispheres apart with his hands and thus interrupted the chain reaction. By this action he saved the lives of the seven other persons in the room. He had realized at once that he himself would be bound to succumb to the effects of the excessive radiation dose which he had absorbed. But he did not lose his self-control for a moment. He told his colleagues to go and stand exactly where they had been at the instant of the disaster. He then drew on the backboard, with his own hand, an accurate sketch of their relative positions, so that the doctors could ascertain the degree of radiation to which each of those present had been exposed.

As he was sitting with Al Graves, the scientist who, except himself, had been most severely infected by the radiation, waiting at the roadside for the car which had been ordered to take them to the hospital, he said quietly to his companion: 'You'll come through all right. But I haven't the faintest chance myself.' It was only too true. Nine days later the man who had experimentally determined the critical mass for the first atom bomb died in terrible agony.

The recording card of the neutron counter had been left behind in Slotin's laboratory. It showed a thin red line which rose steadily till it stopped abruptly at the instant of the catastrophe. The radiation had become so strong at that moment that the delicate instrument could no longer register it.

Robert Jungk, *Brighter Than a Thousand Suns*

756

## NO MAN IS AN ISLAND

(*A man who has been very ill hears a bell tolling*)

Perchance he for whom this bell tolls may be so ill, as that he knows not it tolls for him; and perchance I may think myself so much better than I am, as that they who are about me, and see my state, may have caused it to toll for me, and I know not that. The Church is Catholic, universal, so are all her actions; all that she does belongs to all. When she baptizes a child, that action concerns me; for that child is thereby connected to that Head which is my Head too, and engraffed into that body, whereof I am a member. And when she buries a man, that action concerns me. As therefore the bell that rings to a sermon, calls not upon the preacher only, but upon the congregation to come; so this bell calls us all; but how much more me, who am brought so near the door by this sickness. The bell doth toll for him that thinks it doth; and though it intermit again, yet from that minute, that that occasion wrought upon him, he is united to God. Who casts not up his eye to the sun when it rises? but who takes off his eye from a comet when that breaks out? Who bends not his ear to any bell, which upon any occasion rings? but who can remove it from that bell, which is passing a piece of himself out of this world? No man is an island, entire of itself; every man is a piece of the continent, a part of the main; if a clod be washed away by the sea, Europe is the less, as well as if a promontory were, as well as if a manor of thy friends or of thine own were. Any man's death diminishes me, because I am involved in mankind. And therefore never send to know for whom the bell tolls; it tolls for thee.

John Donne, *Sermons*

## 757 THOUGHTS ON REMEMBRANCE SUNDAY

(*Introduction to the Two Minutes' Silence*)

We want to live. We did not ask to be born into a world of guns and bombs. We do not want to fight. Leave us alone, you statesmen and rulers, let us live our lives in peace. We want to live.

So did they, the boys, girls, men and women who lived, suffered and died in the wars. Of course they wanted to go on living; and yet, for some strange, inscrutable reason that God alone knows, they were destined for wounds and slaughter. God let them be killed. Before they died, many of them had to endure hell on earth. Somehow they struggled on. Where did they find the strength? Some, in the people they loved, or the country they loved, or the sheer animal will to survive; some, in their faith in God.

There were those who believed that they were giving themselves to build a world for us. They died for the future, for an ideal world that we could live in, an earth at peace. Now it is our turn to strive for peace on earth. War is not only made by statesmen. It is made by us, ordinary people who strive to achieve our own selfish ends, quarrelling and hating as we pursue our petty, sordid, self-seeking quest. We *can* make peace, with God's help, if we have faith, and hope, and love for one another. *We* are responsible for peace. Let us begin here, to build what the dead of the wars left unfinished. Perhaps we were not worth dying for: but without their sacrifice we would not be alive today.

Let us thank God for them, and let us honour them, in silence.

Michael Davis

## 758 AND DEATH SHALL HAVE NO DOMINION

And death shall have no dominion.
Dead men naked they shall be one
With the man in the wind and the west moon;
When their bones are picked clean and the clean bones gone,
They shall have stars at elbow and foot;
Though they go mad they shall be sane,
Though they sink through the sea they shall rise again;
Though lovers be lost love shall not;
And death shall have no dominion.

And death shall have no dominion.
Under the windings of the sea
They lying long shall not die windily;
Twisting on racks when sinews give way,
Strapped to a wheel, yet they shall not break;
Faith in their hands shall snap in two,
And the unicorn evils run them through;
Split all ends up they shan't crack;
And death shall have no dominion.

And death shall have no dominion.
No more may gulls cry at their ears
Or waves break loud on the seashores;
Where blew a flower may a flower no more
Lift its head to the blows of the rain;
Though they be mad and dead as nails,

Heads of the characters hammer through the daisies;
Break in the sun till the sun breaks down,
And death shall have no dominion.

Dylan Thomas, *Collected Poems 1934–1952*

759

## THE YOUNG AND THE DEAD

What the dying old man sought, probably, was the comfort of human communication. And it is here that believers, unbelievers, and the 'don't knows' may find common ground. Here, too, there is hopeful evidence that at least some of the young are ready to challenge the taboo with which the present generation of elders may be trying to shroud death. A woman who lost her undergraduate son in an accident comments that 'in moments of crisis one realises how near the surface are primitive superstitions. I felt people were embarrassed when I talked about Richard; some, I felt, almost shunned me with fear, as if some of my bad luck might brush off on to them.' But, she says:

'Richard's young friends talked and laughed about the things he had said and done. It was a humbling experience to be comforted by the young. Though I knew newspaper reports to be distorted, some of it sticks, like the insistence that the young of today are promiscuous, when the vast majority are, in fact, very faithful to each other. I leaned on his friends shamelessly and they never let me down. Thinking back to when I was their age during the war, I realised that I'd never gone to see the parents of my contemporaries who had been killed. I had been too afraid.'

Undergraduates, it may be suggested, are a sophisticated minority. But then there is the charwoman who lost two boys in a road accident and found their secondary modern school friends kept calling and talking to her about them. Though she was shocked at first by this 'openness', she now thinks it helped.

And a visitor from the United States, where avoidance is sometimes carried to extremes of fantasy by the pretence that death is pleasant, recounts a similar experience. Her husband died suddenly while they were on holiday in a remote area. A youth who drove her to a railway station some distance away asked her how it had happened. 'Instead of sitting there silent, he kept me talking about it practically the whole way. It was only after he'd gone that I realised what he'd done and how I would never have dreamed of doing that in his place.'

Perhaps the young are rejecting the fantasy, are finding out for themselves anew that life cannot have meaning if the reality of death is not included, and that only by sharing some of the experiences of the dying can we ourselves learn how to die—and come to accept that death is something that will happen to us.

Laurence Dobie, from *The Observer Review*

760

### LIFE AFTER DEATH

The problem of a future after death can have no effect upon the data of any real problem in life. The problem is to raise oneself in this life to the level of eternal things, by struggling free from bondage to what is perpetually renewed and destroyed. And if everything disappears when we die, it is all the more important not to bungle this life which is given us, but to manage to have saved one's soul before it disappears. I am convinced that this is the real thought of Socrates and Plato (as also of the Gospel) and that all the rest is only symbols and metaphors.

Simone Weil, *Seventy Letters*

## Fables and Legends

761

### DOIN' THE RIGHT THING—NOT JUST PROMISIN'

*The Parable of the Two Sons, Matthew 21. 28–30*

There was a guy who had two sons. He told his oldest son to go clean up the back yard.

The son was a wise guy and said, 'I ain't gonna to do it.' But he didn't mean it that way. So when no one was lookin', he went and put the rubbish in the garbage cans, and made the back yard shine.

But the old man didn't know this, so he told the young son to go clean up the back yard. So he said, 'Sure, dad.' But he didn't do it. He just went up to the corner and hung around.

So which guy obeyed his father?
The first son, of course.

Jesus told this story because he wanted people to know that doin' the right thing is more important than promisin' to do it and not doin' it.

Of course, the kid was wrong to talk back to his father like that. But at least it will be easy for his father to forgive him 'cause he did what he was told in the end. But the most important part is that he was sorry for what he said to his father. At least he wasn't two-faced about it. Maybe that's what Jesus means when he says that sinners will get into the kingdom of God, before someone like the younger son.

Carl Burke, *God is for Real, Man*

762

## LEGEND

The blacksmith's boy went out with a rifle
and a black dog running behind.
Cobwebs snatched at his feet,
rivers hindered him,
thorn branches caught at his eyes to make him blind
and the sky turned into an unlucky opal,
but he didn't mind,
I can break branches, I can swim rivers, I can stare out any
  spider I meet,
Said he to his dog and his rifle.

The blacksmith's boy went over the paddocks
with his old black hat on his head.
Mountains jumped in his way,
rocks rolled down on him,
and the old crow cried, 'You'll soon be dead.'
And the rain came down like mattocks.
But he only said
I can climb mountains, I can dodge rocks, I can shoot an old
  crow any day,
and he went on over the paddocks.

When he came to the end of the day the sun began falling.
Up came the night ready to swallow him,

like the barrel of a gun,
like an old black hat,
like a black dog hungry to follow him.
Then the pigeon, the magpie and the dove began wailing
and the grass lay down to pillow him.
His rifle broke, his hat blew away and his dog was gone
and the sun was falling.
But in front of the night the rainbow stood on the mountain,
just as his heart foretold.
He ran like a hare,
he climbed like a fox;
he caught it in his hands, the colours and the cold—
like a bar of ice, like the column of a fountain,
like a ring of gold.
The pigeon, the magpie and the dove flew up to stare,
and the grass stood up again on the mountain.

The blacksmith's boy hung the rainbow on his shoulder
instead of his broken gun.
Lizards ran out to see,
snakes made way for him,
and the rainbow shone as brightly as the sun.
All the world said, Nobody is braver, nobody is bolder,
nobody else has done
anything to equal it. He went home as bold as he could be
with the swinging rainbow on his shoulder.

Judith Wright

## 763 DAEDALUS AND ICARUS

*The First Men to Fly*

The inventor Daedalus, tired of Crete and of his long absence from home, was filled with longing for his own country, but he was shut in by the sea. Then he said: 'The king may block my way by land or across the ocean, but the sky, surely, is open, and that is how we shall go. King Minos may possess all the rest, but he does not possess the air.' With these words, he set his mind to sciences never explored before, and altered the laws of nature. He laid down a row of feathers, beginning with tiny ones, and gradually increasing their length, so that the edge seemed to

(763) slope upwards. In the same way, the pipe which shepherds used to play is built up from reeds, each slightly longer than the last. Then he fastened the feathers together in the middle with thread, and at the bottom with wax; when he had arranged them in this way, he bent them round into a gentle curve, to look like real birds' wings. His son Icarus stood beside him and, not knowing that the materials he was handling were to endanger his life, laughingly captured the feathers which blew away in the wind, or softened the yellow wax with his thumb, and by his pranks hindered the marvellous work on which his father was engaged.

When Daedalus had put the finishing touches to his invention, he raised himself into the air, balancing his body on his two wings, and there he hovered, moving his feathers up and down. Then he prepared his son to fly too. 'I warn you, Icarus,' he said, 'you must follow a course midway between earth and heaven, in case the sun should scorch your feathers, if you go too high, or the water make them heavy if you are too low. Fly halfway between the two. And pay no attention to the stars: take me as your guide, and follow me!'

While he was giving Icarus these instructions on how to fly, Daedalus was at the same time fastening the novel wings on his son's shoulders. As he worked and talked the old man's cheeks were wet with tears, and his fatherly affection made his hands tremble. He kissed his son, whom he was never to kiss again: then, raising himself on his wings, flew in front, showing anxious concern for his companion, just like a bird who has brought her tender fledgelings out of their nest in the treetops, and launched them into the air. He urged Icarus to follow close, and instructed him in the art that was to be his ruin, moving his own wings and keeping a watchful eye on those of his son behind him. Some fisher, perhaps, wielding his quivering rod, some shepherd leaning on his staff, or a peasant bent over his plough handle caught sight of them as they flew past and stood fixed in astonishment, believing that these creatures who could fly through the air must be gods.

The boy Icarus began to enjoy the thrill of swooping boldly through the air. Drawn on by his eagerness for the open sky, he left his guide and soared upwards, till he came too close to the blazing sun, and it softened the sweet-smelling wax that bound his wings together. The wax melted. Icarus moved his bare arms up and down, but without their feathers they had no purchase on the air. Even as his lips were crying his father's name, they were swallowed up in the deep blue waters. The unhappy father, a father no longer, cried out: 'Icarus!' 'Icarus,' he called. 'Where are you? Where am I to look for you?' As he was still calling 'Icarus' he saw the feathers on the water, and cursed his inventive skill.

Ovid, *Metamorphoses*

## 764 A COOL SQUARE COMES TO THE RESCUE

*The Story of the Good Samaritan, Luke 10. 33–37*

A man was going from his apartment in the project to his friend's house. While he was walking, a couple of muggers jumped him in a dark place. He didn't have very much, so they took his wallet and clothes and beat on him and stomped on him—they almost killed him.

Before long a hood came by, but he didn't give a care. Besides, the cops might ask him questions, so he beat it out of there. Next came a squeak—never gave the poor guy a second look. After a while a real cool square comes along. He sees the character, feels sorry for him. So he puts a couple of Band-aids on, gives him a drink and a lift in his car. The square even put him up in a room some place. Cost him two bucks, too!

So who do you think the best guy was? Well, you got the message, bud. But you don't have to be a square to show love, and to be sorry for someone and to help a guy. But get with it, man—this is what God wants you to do.

Carl Burke, *God is for Real, Man*

## 765 COPING WITH GRANDPA

Once upon a time there was a little old man. His eyes blinked and his hands trembled; when he ate he clattered the silverware distressingly, missed his mouth with the spoon as often as not, and dribbled a bit of his food on the tablecloth. Now he lived with his married son, having nowhere else to live, and his son's wife was a modern young woman who knew that in-laws should not be tolerated in a woman's home.

'I can't have this,' she said. 'It interferes with a woman's right to happiness.'

So she and her husband took the little old man gently but firmly by the arm and led him to the corner of the kitchen. There they set him on a stool and gave him his food, what there was of it, in an earthenware bowl. From then on he always ate in the corner, blinking at the table with wistful eyes.

One day his hands trembled rather more than usual, and the earthenware bowl fell and broke.

'If you are a pig,' said the daughter-in-law, 'you must eat out of a trough.' So they made him a little wooden trough, and he got his meals in that.

These people had a four-year-old son of whom they were very fond. One suppertime the young man noticed his boy playing intently with some bits of wood and asked what he was doing.

'I'm making a trough,' he said, smiling up for approval, 'to feed you and Mamma out of when I get big.'

The man and his wife looked at each other for a while and didn't say anything. Then they cried a little. Then they went to the corner and took the little old man by the arm and led him back to the table. They sat him in a comfortable chair and gave him his food on a plate, and from then on nobody ever scolded when he clattered or spilled or broke things.

One of Grimm's fairy tales, this anecdote has the crudity of the old simple days: the modern serpent's tooth method would be to lead Grandpa gently but firmly to the local asylum, there to tuck him out of sight as a case of senile dementia. But perhaps crudity is what we need to illustrate the naked and crude point of the Fifth Commandment: honour your parents lest your children dishonour you. Or, in other words, a society that destroys the family destroys itself.

Joy Davidman, *Smoke on the Mountain*

## 766 THE EMPEROR'S NEW CLOTHES

### THREE READINGS

*I*

Many years ago there was an Emperor who was so excessively fond of new clothes that he spent all his money on them.

(766 *1*) Life was very gay in the great town where he lived; hosts of strangers came to visit it every day, and among them one day two swindlers. They gave themselves out as weavers, and said that they knew how to weave the most beautiful stuffs imaginable. Not only were the colours and patterns unusually fine, but the clothes that were made of the stuffs had the peculiar quality of becoming invisible to every person who was not fit for the office he held, or if he was impossibly dull.

'Those must be splendid clothes,' thought the Emperor. 'By wearing them I should be able to discover which men in my kingdom are unfitted for their posts. I shall distinguish the wise men from the fools. Yes, I certainly must order some of that stuff to be woven for me.'

He paid the two swindlers a lot of money in advance so that they might begin their work at once.

They did put up two looms and pretended to weave, but they had nothing whatever upon their shuttles. At the outset they asked for a quantity of the finest silk and the purest gold thread, all of which they put into their own bags while they worked away at the empty looms far into the night.

'I should like to know how those weavers are getting on with the stuff,' thought the Emperor; but he felt a little queer when he reflected that anyone who was stupid or unfit for his post would not be able to see how it was getting on. Everybody in the town knew what wonderful power the stuff possessed, and everyone was anxious to see how stupid his neighbour was.

'I will send my faithful old minister to the weavers,' thought the Emperor. 'He will be best able to see how the stuff looks, for he is a clever old man and no one fulfils his duties better than he does!'

So the good old minister went into the room where the two swindlers sat working at the empty loom.

'Heaven preserve us!' thought the old minister, opening his eyes very wide. 'Why I can't see a thing!' But he took care not to say so. The swindlers pointed to the empty loom, and the poor old minister stared as hard as he could but he could not see anything, for of course there was nothing to see.

'Good heavens!' thought he, 'is it possible that I am a fool? I have never thought so and nobody must know it. Am I not fit for my post? It will never do to say that I cannot see the stuff.'

'Well, sir, you don't say anything about the stuff,' said the one who was pretending to weave.

'Oh, it is beautiful! quite charming!' said the old minister looking through his spectacles; 'this pattern and these colours! I will certainly tell the Emperor that the stuff pleases me very much.'

'We are delighted to hear you say so,' said the swindlers, and then they named all the colours and described the peculiar pattern. The old minister paid great attention to what they said, so as to be able to repeat it when he got home to the Emperor.

Then the swindlers went on to demand more money, more silk, and more gold, to be able to proceed with the weaving; but they put it all into their own pockets—not a single strand was ever put into the loom, but they went on as before weaving at the empty loom.

766

*2*

The Emperor soon sent another faithful official to see how the stuff was getting on, and if it would soon be ready. The same thing happened to him as to the Minister; he looked and looked but as there was only the empty loom, he could see nothing at all.

'Is not this a beautiful piece of stuff?' said both the swindlers, showing and explaining the beautiful pattern and colours which were not there to be seen.

'I know I am not a fool!' thought the man, 'so it must be that I am unfit for my good post! It is very strange though! However one must not let it appear!' So he praised the stuff he did not see, and assured them of his delight in the beautiful colours and the originality of the design. 'It is absolutely charming!' he said to the Emperor. Everyone in the town was talking about this splendid stuff.

Now the Emperor thought he would like to see it while it was still on the loom. So, accompanied by a number of selected courtiers, among whom were the two faithful officials who had already seen the imaginary stuff, he went to visit the crafty impostors, who were working away as hard as ever they could at the empty loom.

'It is magnificent!' said both the honest officials. 'Only see, your Majesty, what a design! What colours!' And they pointed to the empty loom, for they thought no doubt the others could see the stuff.

'What!' thought the Emperor; 'I see nothing at all! This is

terrible! Am I a fool? Am I not fit to be Emperor? Why, nothing worse could happen to me!'

'Oh, it is beautiful!' said the Emperor. 'It has my highest approval!' and he nodded his satisfaction as he gazed at the empty loom. Nothing would induce him to say that he could not see anything.

The whole suite gazed and gazed, but saw nothing more than all the others. However they all exclaimed with his Majesty, 'It is very beautiful!' and they advised him to wear a suit made of this wonderful cloth on the occasion of a great procession which was just about to take place. 'It is magnificent! gorgeous! excellent!' went from mouth to mouth; they were all equally delighted with it. The Emperor gave each of the rogues an order of knighthood to be worn in their buttonholes and the title of 'Gentlemen Weavers'.

766

### *3*

The swindlers sat up the whole night, before the day on which the procession was to take place, burning sixteen candles; so that people might see how anxious they were to get the Emperor's new clothes ready. They pretended to take the stuff off the loom. They cut it out in the air with a huge pair of scissors, and they stitched away with needles without any thread on them. At last they said: 'Now the Emperor's new clothes are ready!'

The Emperor, with his grandest courtiers, went to them himself, and both the swindlers raised one arm in the air, as if they were holding something, and said: 'See, these are the trousers, this is the coat, here is the mantle!' and so on. 'It is as light as a spider's web. One might think one had nothing on, but that is the very beauty of it!'

'Yes!' said all the courtiers, but they could not see anything, for there was nothing to see.

'Will your imperial majesty be graciously pleased to take off your clothes,' said the impostors, 'so that we may put on the new ones along here before the great mirror.'

The Emperor took off all his clothes, and the impostors pretended to give him one article of dress after the other, of the new ones which they had pretended to make. They pretended to fasten something round his waist and to tie on something; this was the train, and the Emperor turned round and round in front of the mirror.

'How well his majesty looks in the new clothes! How becoming they are!' cried all the people round. 'What a design, and what colours! They are most gorgeous robes!'

'The canopy is waiting outside which is to be carried over your majesty in the procession,' said the master of the ceremonies.

'Well, I am quite ready,' said the Emperor. 'Don't the clothes fit well?' and then he turned round again in front of the mirror, so that he should seem to be looking at his grand things.

The chamberlains who were to carry the train stooped and pretended to lift it from the ground with both hands, and they walked along with their hands in the air. They dared not let it appear that they could not see anything.

Then the Emperor walked along in the procession under the gorgeous canopy, and everybody in the streets and at the windows exclaimed, 'How beautiful the Emperor's new clothes are! What a splendid train! And they fit to perfection!' Nobody would let it appear that he could see nothing, for then he would not be fit for his post, or else he was a fool.

None of the Emperor's clothes had been so successful before.

'But he has got nothing on,' said a little child.

'Oh, listen to the innocent,' said its father; and one person whispered to the other what the child had said. 'He has nothing on; the child says he has nothing on!'

'But he has nothing on!' at last cried all the people.

The Emperor writhed, for he knew it was true, but he thought 'the procession must go on now', so he held himself stiffer than ever, and the chamberlains held up the invisible train.

Hans Andersen

767

## KING MIDAS

*The King with the Golden Touch*

The god Bacchus granted King Midas the right to choose himself a gift—a privilege which Midas welcomed, but one which did him little good, for he was fated to make poor use of the opportunity he was given. He said to the god: 'Grant that whatever my person touches be turned to yellow gold.' Bacchus, though sorry that Midas had not asked for something better,

767) granted his request, and presented him with this life-destroying gift.

The king went off cheerfully, delighted with the misfortune which had befallen him. He tested the good faith of Bacchus' promise by touching this and that, and could scarcely believe his own senses when he broke a green twig from a low-growing branch of oak, and the twig turned to gold. He lifted a stone from the ground and the stone, likewise, gleamed pale gold. He touched a sod of earth and the earth, by the power of his touch, became a lump of ore. The dry ears of corn which he gathered were a harvest of golden metal, and when he plucked an apple from a tree and held it in his hand, you would have thought that it was an apple of gold. If he laid his finger on the pillars of his lofty doorways, they were seen to shine and glitter, and even when he washed his hands in clear water, the trickles that flowed over his palms became a golden shower. He dreamed of everything turned to gold, and his hopes soared beyond the limits of his imagination.

So he exulted in his good fortune, while servants set before him tables piled high with meats, and with bread in abundance. But then, when he touched a piece of bread, it grew stiff and hard: if he hungrily tried to bite into the meat, a sheet of gold encased the food, as soon as his teeth came in contact with it. He took some wine, itself the discovery of the god who had endowed him with his power, and adding clear water, mixed himself a drink: the liquid could be seen turning to molten gold as it passed his lips.

Wretched in spite of his riches, dismayed by the strange disaster which had befallen him, Midas prayed for a way of escape from his wealth, loathing what he had lately desired. No amount of food could relieve his hunger, parching thirst burned his throat, and he was tortured, as he deserved, by the gold he now hated. Raising his shining arms, he stretched his hands to heaven and cried: 'Forgive me, father Bacchus! I have sinned, yet pity me, I pray, and save me speedily from this disaster that promised so fair!'

The gods are kind: when Midas confessed his fault, Bacchus restored him to his former state, cancelling the gift which, in fulfilment of his promise, he had given the king. 'And now,' he said, 'to rid yourself of the remaining traces of that gold which you so foolishly desired, go to the river close by the great city of Sardis.

Then travel upstream till you come to the water's source. There, where the foaming spring bubbles up in great abundance, plunge your head and body in the water and, at the same time, wash away your crime.' The king went to the spring as he was bidden: his power to change things into gold passed from his person into the stream, and coloured its waters.

Ovid, *Metamorphoses*

## 768 THE SADHU AND THE SNAKE

### THREE READINGS

*I*

(*A sadhu is a man who has given up all worldly possessions and devotes his life to meditation*)

I was at one time ambitious of becoming a musician. I came near being one. It was years and years ago. I was living at the time in Kumbum, a small village eighty miles from Malgudi. A master musician lived there. When he played on the flute, it was said, the cattle of the village followed him about. He was perhaps the greatest artist of the century, but quite content to live in obscurity, hardly known to anyone outside the village, giving concerts only in the village temple, and absolutely satisfied with the small income he derived from his ancestral lands. I washed his clothes, swept his house, ran errands for him, wrote his accounts, and when he felt like it he taught me music. His personality and presence had a value all their own, so that even if he taught only for an hour it was worth a year's tuition under anyone else. The very atmosphere around him educated one.

After three years of chipping and planing my master felt that my music was taking shape. He said, 'In another year, perhaps, you may go to the town and play before a public, that is, if you care for such things.' You may be sure I cared. Not for me the greatness of obscurity. I wanted wealth and renown. I dreamt of going to Madras and attending the music festival next year, and then all the districts round would ring with my name. I looked on my bamboo flute as a sort of magic wand which was going to open out a new world to me.

I lived in a cottage at the end of the street. It was my habit to sit up and practise far into the night. One night, as I was just losing myself in *bhairavi raga*, there came a knock at the door. I felt irritated at the interruption.

'Who is there?' I asked.

'*A sadhu*: he wants a mouthful of food.'

'At this hour! Go, go. Don't come and pester people at all hours.'

'But hunger knows no time.'

'Go away. I have nothing here. I myself live on my master's charity.'

'But can't you give a small coin or at least a kind word to a *sadhu*?'

'Shut up,' I cried, glared at the door, and resumed my *bhairavi*.

Fifteen minutes later the knocks were repeated. I lost my temper. 'Have you no sense? Why do you disturb me?'

'You play divinely. Won't you let me in? You may not give me food for my stomach but don't deny me your music.'

I didn't like anyone to be present when I practised, and this constant interruption was exasperating. 'Don't stand there and argue. If you don't go at once, I will open the door and push you out.'

'Ah, bad words. You needn't push me out. I am going. But remember, it is your last day of music. Tomorrow you may exchange your flute for a handful of dried dates.'

768

*2*

I heard his wooden clogs going down the house steps. I felt relieved and played for about ten minutes. But my mind was troubled. His parting words . . . what did he mean by them? I got up, took the lantern from its nail on the wall, and went out. I stood on the last step of my cottage and looked up and down the dark street, holding the lantern. I turned in. Vaguely hoping that he might call again, I left the door half open. I hung up the lantern and sat down. I looked at the pictures of gods on the wall and prayed to be protected from the threat of the unseen mendicant. And then I was lost in music once again.

Song after song flowed from that tiny bamboo and transformed my lonely cottage. I was no longer a petty mortal blowing through a piece of bamboo. I was among the gods. The lantern on the wall became a brilliant star illuminating a celestial hall, and I came to the snake-song in *punnaga varali*. I saw the serpent in all its majesty: the very venom in its pouch had a touch of glory: now I saw its divinity as it crowned Shiva's head: Parvathi wore it as a wristlet: Subramanya played with it: and it was Vishnu's couch. The whole composition imparted to the serpent a quality which inspired awe and reverence.

And now what should I see between the door and me but a black cobra! It had opened its immense hood and was swaying ecstatically. I stopped my song and rubbed my eyes to see if I was fully awake. But the moment the song ceased, the cobra turned and threw a glance at me, and moved forward. I have never seen such a black cobra and such a long one in my life. Some saving instinct told me: 'Play on! Don't stop.' I hurriedly took the flute to my lips and continued the song. The snake, which was no less than three yards from me, lifted a quarter of its body, with a gentle flourish reared its head, fixed its round eyes on me, and listened to the music without making the slightest movement. It might have been a carven snake in black stone.

768

## *3*

And as I played with my eyes fixed on the snake I was so much impressed with its dignity and authority that I said to myself, 'Which god would forgo the privilege of wearing this in His hair? . . .' After playing the song thrice over, I commenced a new song. The cobra sharply turned its head and looked at me as if to say, 'Now what is all this?' and let out a terrible hiss, and made a slight movement. I quickly resumed the snake-song and it assumed once again its carven posture.

I attempted to change the song once or twice, but I saw the snake stir menacingly. I vainly tried to get up and dash out, but the snake nearly stood up on its tail and promised to finish me. And so I played the same song all night. By and by I felt exhausted. My head swam, my cheeks ached through continuous blowing, and my chest seemed to be emptied of the last wisp of breath. I knew I was going to drop dead in a few seconds. It didn't seem to matter very much if the snake was going to crush me in its coils and fill me with all the venom in its sac. I flung down the flute, got up, and prostrated before it crying, 'Oh, *Naga Raja*, you are a god; you can kill me if you like, but I can play no more.'

When I opened my eyes again the snake was gone. The lantern on the wall had turned pale in the morning light. My flute lay near the doorway.

Next day I narrated my experiences to my master. He said, 'Don't you know you ought not to play *punnaga varali* at night? Now you can never be sure you will not get the snake in again if you play. And when he comes he won't spare you unless you sing his song over again. Are you prepared to do it?'

'No, no, a thousand times no,' I cried. The memory of that song was galling. I had repeated it enough to last me a lifetime. 'If it is so, throw away your flute and forget your music. You can't play with a serpent. It is a plaything of Gods. Throw away your bamboo. It is of no use to you any more.' I wept at the thought of this renunciation. My master pitied me and said, 'Perhaps all will be well again if you seek your visitor of that night and beg his forgiveness. Can you find him?'

I put away my flute. I have ever since been searching for an unknown, unseen mendicant, in this world. Even today if, by God's grace, I meet him, I will fall at his feet, beg his forgiveness, and take up my flute again.

R. K. Narayan, *An Astrologer's Day*

## 769 CHOPSTICKS

In Korea there is a legend about a native warrior who died and went to heaven. 'Before I enter,' he said to the gatekeeper, 'I would like you to take me on a tour of hell.' The gatekeeper found a guide to take the warrior to hell. When he got there he was astonished to see a great table piled high with the choicest foods. But the people in hell were starving. The warrior turned to his guide and raised his eyebrows.

'It's this way,' the guide explained. 'Everybody who comes here is given a pair of chopsticks five feet long, and is required to hold them at the end to eat. But you just can't eat with chopsticks five feet long if you hold them at the end. Look at them. They miss their mouths every time, see?'

The visitor agreed that this was hell indeed and asked to be taken back to heaven post-haste. In heaven, to his surprise, he saw a similar room, with a similar table laden with very choice foods. But the people were happy: they looked radiantly happy.

The visitor turned to the guide. 'No chopsticks, I suppose?' he said.

'Oh yes,' said the guide, 'they have the same chopsticks, the same length, and they must be held at the end just as in hell. But you see, these people have learned that if a man feeds his neighbour, his neighbour will feed him also.'

John P. Hogan, *Here and There*

770

## CIRCE

*The Enchantress who Turns Men to Beasts*

I was one of the twenty-two sailors sent by Ulysses to the house of which we knew nothing. We had no sooner arrived, and were standing at the entrance to this house of Circe the enchantress, when we were frightened by a horde of wild animals, a thousand strong, wolves and bears and lionesses, rushing to meet us. But there was no need to be afraid of them, for none wanted to injure us in any way. On the contrary, they even wagged their tails affectionately and fawned upon us, as they escorted us along, until we were received by servant girls, who led us through marble-roofed halls to their mistress.

Circe was sitting in a handsome private apartment, raised on a majestic throne, with a gold-embroidered cloak wrapped round her, over her gleaming robes. Handmaids were with her, arranging their mistress' herbs, separating into baskets the flowers and variegated grasses, that lay scattered about in no proper order. Circe, the goddess, herself directed them as they worked, for she knew the virtues of each leaf, and what kinds mixed well together. Carefully she watched and weighed the herbs she measured out.

When she saw us, and received our greetings, she bade us welcome, and her smiling face seemed to augur well. Immediately she gave orders for a concoction of toasted barley, honey, strong wine, and cheese to be prepared, and to these ingredients she added juices whose taste would be concealed by the sweetness of the rest. We took from the goddess' hand the cups she gave us, and drained them greedily, for we were parched. As soon as we had done so, the dread goddess touched our hair lightly with her wand and at that—ashamed though I am, I shall tell you—my body began to bristle with stiff hairs, and I was no longer able to speak, but uttered harsh grunts instead of words. My body bent forward and down, until my face looked straight at the ground, and I felt my mouth hardening into a turned-up snout, my neck swelling with muscles. My hands, which had lately held the goblet, now left prints, like feet, upon the ground.

With the others, who had suffered the same fate (such is the power of magic drugs!) I was shut up in a sty, and then we saw that our fellow-sailor Eurylochus was the only one who had not been turned into a pig. He alone had avoided the cup that was offered him. Had he not done so, I should still, to this day, be one of that bristling herd, for Ulysses would never have learned from him of the disaster that had overtaken us, and come to Circe for revenge.

Mercury, bringer of peace, had given Ulysses a white flower, that grows from a black root. With this and heaven's warnings to defend him, he entered Circe's home, and was invited to drink the treacherous cup. But when she tried to stroke his hair with her wand, he thrust her back, and frightened off the terrified goddess with drawn sword. Then Ulysses insisted that we, his companions, be restored to our true shape. We were sprinkled with the juices of some mysterious herb, possessing more wholesome properties than the last: then Circe tapped our heads with wand reversed, and chanted spells to counteract her previous charms. The more she recited, the more we raised ourselves erect, lifting ourselves up from the ground. Our bristles fell out; the split disappeared from our cloven hooves; shoulders, upper arms, and forearms, were restored to their proper shape. With tears of joy we embraced Ulysses, who was himself in tears, and the first words we uttered were expressions of gratitude.

Ovid, *Metamorphoses*

## 771 THROWIN' A PARTY FOR JUNIOR

*The Prodigal Son's Return, Luke 15. 11–32*

There was a rich guy who had two sons. Junior says, 'Hey, Dad, how's about giving me my share of your dough now, why wait until you kick off?'

(771) His father says, 'OK, man,' and gave him half his money. So Junior starts off to have a good time. At first, he's got lots of friends, a white Cadillac, two suits, and what he eats is real class, and beer at every meal. But, pretty soon the money is all gone and he's dead broke.

So he's got no friends, no money, no nothin'; and, man, oh man, is he hungry, and no pad to sleep in. He goes over to the stockyards to look for a job, and gets one feeding the pigs. The boss don't pay very much, and the pigs get more food than he does.

So Junior thinks this over and says, 'I must be some kind of a nut. I was better off at home. It wasn't so bad at that. I guess I'll go home and tell 'em I'm sorry I made a real goof of this one.'

All the time this is goin' on, Dad's thinkin' about it, too. He's plenty worried about Junior getting mixed up with queers and winos and he wishes that Junior would come home. So he watches out the window every night.

Then one day he sees Junior way down the end of the long block. Dad runs like crazy to meet him. Junior starts to tell his dad how sorry he is and that he made a goof to do what he did. But his dad tells him to knock it off and come home and get some clean rags on and we'll have a big supper. Dad's pretty happy to see the little cat 'cause he thought Junior was dead, and that he would never see him again.

While this was happenin', the other son had stayed home and worked. He was out workin' his paper route when Junior came home. When he gets home from his papers he sees a wild party. So he says, 'What gives?' Some guy says, 'Your brother came home, and your dad's throwing a party.' This makes him mad, and he says, 'To hell with that jazz,' and won't even go into the house.

Dad comes out and tries to talk him into it. He says, 'I stay home and sell papers and keep this place clean, and you don't buy me a damn thing. Junior here chickens out on his big plans and you throw a party and say "Glad to see you home." Well, I say to hell with him.'

The old man's not so dumb and gets on to what happens here and knows that he's just jealous. So he says, 'My boy, you just settle down a minute. I always loved you, and I love your brother too. I thought he was a gone cat and was dead, but he ain't and I'm happy. I could always see you but him I couldn't. This party is for me, I'm so happy.' That's how God feels when people come back to him.

Carl Burke, *God is fo: Real, Man*

772

## A FABLE FOR TOMORROW

There was once a town in the heart of America where all life seemed to live in harmony with its surroundings. The town lay in the midst of a chequerboard of prosperous farms, with fields of grain and hillsides of orchards. In autumn, oak and maple and birch set up a blaze of colour. Then foxes barked in the hills and deer silently crossed the fields.

Along the roads, laurel, viburnum and alder, great ferns and wild flowers delighted the traveller's eye through much of the year. Even in winter the roadsides were places of beauty, where countless birds came to feed on the berries. The countryside was, in fact, famous for the abundance and variety of its bird life; people travelled from great distances to observe them. Others came to fish the streams which flowed clear and cold out of the hills and contained shady pools where trout lay. So it had been from the days many years ago when the first settlers raised their houses, sank their wells and built their barns.

Then a strange blight crept over the area and everything began to change. Some evil spell had settled on the community: mysterious maladies swept the flocks of chickens; the cattle and sheep sickened and died. Everywhere was a shadow of death. The farmers spoke of much illness among their families. In the town the doctors had become more and more puzzled by new kinds of sickness appearing among their patients. There had been several sudden and unexplained deaths, not only among adults but even among children, who would be stricken suddenly while at play and die within a few hours.

There was a strange stillness. The birds, for example—where had they gone? Many people spoke of them, puzzled and disturbed. The feeding stations in the backyards were deserted. The few birds seen anywhere were moribund; they trembled violently and could not fly. It was a spring without voices. On the mornings that had once throbbed with the dawn chorus of scores of bird voices there was now no sound; only silence lay over the fields and woods and marsh.

On the farms the hens brooded, but no chicks hatched. The farmers complained that they were unable to raise any pigs—the litters were small and the young survived only a few days. The apple trees were coming into bloom but no bees droned among the blossoms, so there was no pollination and there would be no fruit.

The roadsides, once so attractive, were now lined with browned and withered vegetation as though swept by fire. These, too, were silent, deserted by all living things. Even the streams were now lifeless. Anglers no longer visited them, for all the fish had died.

In the gutters under the eaves and between the shingles of the roofs, a white granular powder still showed a few patches; some weeks before it had fallen like snow upon the roofs and the lawns, the fields and streams.

No witchcraft, no enemy action had silenced the rebirth of new life in this stricken world. The people had done it themselves.

This town does not actually exist. Yet every one of these disasters has actually happened somewhere, and many real communities have already suffered a substantial number of them. A grim spectre has crept upon us almost unnoticed, and this imagined tragedy may easily become a stark reality we all shall know.

Rachel Carson, *Silent Spring*

# Short Readings

## 773 LOVE AND HATE

Love makes everything lovely; hate concentrates itself on the one thing hated.

George Macdonald

## 774 GOD AND OUR NEIGHBOUR

We cannot know whether we love God, although there may be strong reasons for thinking so, but there can be no doubt about whether we love our neighbour or no.

Saint Theresa

## 775 ATTITUDES TO CHILDREN: A CONTRAST

Self-contained flat available. No dogs. No children.
Furnished flats to let. Couples with children need not apply.

Advertisement

Let the children come to me and do not try to stop them; for the kingdom of God belongs to such as these. Whoever does not accept the kingdom of God like a child, will never enter it.

Jesus Christ

## 776 HOW TO BE FIRST: A CONTRAST

'How can you create the big impression without seeming to show off? Drive a grandmobile. The big impression is built in.'

Advertisement

'If anyone wants to be first, he must make himself last of all and servant of all.'

Jesus Christ

## 777 UNHAPPINESS

We have no right to make unhappy those whom we cannot make good.

The Marquis de Vauvenargues

778 TRUSTING GOD

Trusting God is the first step in getting wised up
And only some kind of a nut
Don't want to learn new things.

Carl Burke, *God is for Real, Man*
(based on Proverbs 1.7)

779 YOUR FATHER

You better listen to what your old man is saying; maybe he's right, you may learn something.

Carl Burke, *God is for Real, Man*
(based on Proverbs 4.1)

780 RULES

It's good to know how far you can go and where
the lines are, and to have somebody tell you what
the score is if they don't get mad about it. And
you're a retard if you don't listen.

Carl Burke, *God is for Real, Man*
(based on Proverbs 12.1)

781 EXCUSES

Ya can always find an excuse if you get caught, only ya get in deeper.

Carl Burke, *God is for Real, Man*
(based on Proverbs 18.1)

782 SUPERIORITY

A show-off always gets slapped down
and Mr. High and Mighty with him.

Carl Burke, *God is for Real, Man*
(based on Proverbs 16.18)

783 PRAISE

It is a sure sign of mediocrity to be niggardly with praise.

The Marquis de Vauvenargues

784 WHAT ARTISTS BELIEVE

Artists, in a way, are religious anyhow. They have to be: if by religion one means believing that life has some significance, and some meaning, which is what I think it has. An artist couldn't work without believing that.

Henry Moore

785 ART AND RELIGION

In a way, a painter's, a sculptor's art is an expression of his religion.

Henry Moore

786 FRAGRANT GARDENS FOR THE BLIND

Some blind people may boycott a scented garden to be planted in Regent's Park, London, because they feel it 'smacks of segregation'. Mr. George Miller, a blind journalist, said yesterday: 'If the public sees blind people feeling and smelling plants and flowers they will think, "Oh, the poor things, they are blind." This is just the sort of sympathy we do not want.'

*The Times* (adapted)

787 A BLIND GARDENER

A totally blind man has just won for the second year running the best kept garden competition run by the Nottingham Corporation.

*The Times* (adapted)

788 HUMILITY

The only wisdom we can hope to acquire
Is the wisdom of humility: humility is endless.

T. S. Eliot, *Four Quartets*

## 789 LEARN TO KNOW YOURSELF

A man has many skins in himself, covering the depths of his heart. Man knows so many things; he does not know himself. Why, thirty or forty skins or hides, just like an ox's or a bear's, so thick and hard, cover the soul. Go into your own ground and learn to know yourself there.

Meister Eckhart

## 790 IGNORANCE OF SELF

In other living creatures ignorance of self is nature; in man it is vice.

Boethius

## 791 SELF-KNOWLEDGE

As the light grows, we see ourselves to be worse than we thought. We are amazed at our former blindness as we see issuing from our heart a whole swarm of shameful feelings, like filthy reptiles crawling from a hidden cave. But we must be neither amazed nor disturbed. We are not worse than we were; on the contrary, we are better.

François Fénelon

## 792 PEACE

The peace of the world is always uncertain unless men keep the peace of God.

T. S. Eliot

## 793 GOD'S SERVICE

God forces no one, for love cannot compel, and God's service, therefore, is a thing of perfect freedom.

Hans Denk

794 GOD IN HIS CREATION

I believe that God is in me as the sun is in the colour and fragrance of a flower—the light in my darkness, the voice in my silence.

Helen Keller, who became blind and deaf in infancy, and did not know there was such a thing as human speech.

795 DETACHMENT

Those who speak ill of me are really my good friends.
When, being slandered, I cherish neither enmity nor preference,
There grows within me the power of love and humility.

Kung-chia Ta-shih

796 CHARITY AND SELF-SEEKING

When a man practises charity in order to be reborn into heaven, or for fame, or reward, or from fear, such charity can obtain no pure effect.

Sutra

797 GOD AND PROFIT

Some people want to see God with their eyes as they see a cow, and to love Him as they love their cow—for the milk and cheese and profit it brings them. This is how it is with people who love God for the sake of outward wealth or inward comfort. They do not rightly love God, when they love Him for their own advantage.

Meister Eckhart

798 JACOB

Isn't it the greatest possible disaster, when you are wrestling with God, not to be beaten?

Simone Weil

799 ART

It is not difficult to understand the beauty of certain Negro sculptures when one knows that a Negro sorcerer spends seven days in prayer before making a fetish.

Simone Weil

800 RELIGIONS

To die for God is not a proof of faith in God. To die for an unknown and repulsive convict who is a victim of injustice, that is a proof of faith in God.

Simone Weil

801 HOW WE KNOW GOD

The heart has its reasons, which reason knows not, as we feel in a thousand instances.

It is the heart which is conscious of God, not the reason. This then is faith: God sensible to the heart, not to the reason.

Blaise Pascal

802 THE INSTINCT FOR WORSHIP

It cannot be that the instinct which has led to the erection of cathedrals, and of churches in every village, is wholly mistaken and misleading. There must be some great truth underlying the instinct for worship.

Sir Oliver Lodge

803 WISDOM

The first step of wisdom is to know what is false.

Latin Proverb

804 WAR

Weapons of war are tools of evil; those who truly admire them are murderers at heart.

Taoist saying

805 SLANDER

The slanderous tongue kills three: the slandered, the slanderer, and him who listens to the slander.

The Talmud

806 WRONG-DOING

There is not a single offence which does not, directly or indirectly, affect many others besides the actual offender. Hence, whether an individual is good or bad is not merely his own concern but really the concern of the whole community, nay, of the whole world.

Mahatma Gandhi

807 POLITICS AND RELIGION

For me, politics bereft of religion are absolute dirt, ever to be shunned. Politics concern nations and that which concerns the welfare of others must be one of the concerns of a man who is religiously inclined, in other words, a seeker after God and Truth. God and Truth are convertible terms and if anyone told me that God was a God of untruth or a God of torture I would decline to worship Him. Therefore in politics also we have to establish the Kingdom of Heaven.

Mahatma Gandhi

808 MAN'S GREATNESS

Man becomes great exactly in the degree in which he works for the welfare of his fellow-men.

Mahatma Gandhi

809 HUMAN NATURE

Human nature will find itself only when it fully realizes that to be human it has to cease to be beastly or brutal.

Mahatma Gandhi

## 810 THE WORD

His was the Word that spake it,
He took the bread and brake it,
And what that Word doth make it,
I do believe and take it.

Queen Elizabeth I

## 811 GRUMBLING

I had no shoes to my feet and I grumbled, until I met a man along the road with no feet.

Indian proverb

## 812 SELF

The true value of a human being is determined primarily by the measure and the sense in which he has attained liberation from the self.

Albert Einstein

## 813 LOVE: THE SUBTLEST FORCE

The more efficient a force is, the more silent and the more subtle it is. Love is the subtlest force in the world.

Mahatma Gandhi

## 814 SELF-RESTRAINT AND SACRIFICE

Man is superior to the brute inasmuch as he is capable of self-restraint and sacrifice, of which the brute is incapable.

Mahatma Gandhi

## 815 SACRIFICE AND JOY

No sacrifice is worth the name unless it is a joy. Sacrifice and a long face go ill together.

Mahatma Gandhi

## 816 TROUBLE

Do you think anything on earth can be done without trouble?

Mahatma Gandhi

## 817 A VALIANT SPIRIT

Strength of numbers is the delight of the timid. The valiant of spirit glory in fighting alone.

Mahatma Gandhi

## 818 LOVE: THE HUMBLEST FORCE

Love is the strongest force the world possesses and yet it is the humblest imaginable.

Mahatma Gandhi

## 819 MAN AND RELIGION

No doubt religion has to answer for some of the most terrible crimes in history. But that is the fault not of religion but of the ungovernable brute in man.

Mahatma Gandhi

## 820 A DEFINITION OF GOD

That which gives one the greatest solace in the midst of the severest fire is God.

Mahatma Gandhi

## 821 RELIGION AND MORALITY

There is no such thing as religion overriding morality. Man, for instance, cannot be untruthful, cruel and incontinent and claim to have God on his side.

Mahatma Gandhi

822 JUSTICE AND SYMPATHY

No one can be just who is without sympathy.

The Marquis de Vauvenargues

## 823 SORRY NO COLOURED: AND A COMMENT

Attractive bed-sitter, electric fire, Belling cooker, own meter. Business person. Sorry no coloured. Near Brent station, buses.

Advertisement

Always treat others as you would like them to treat you.

Jesus Christ

## 824 NO COLOURED: AND A COMMENT

Bed-sitting room, two divans, furnished, kitchen, fridge, Ascot etc; business couple or two business ladies. No coloured. 5½ guineas.

Advertisement

Compassion is the chief law of human existence.

Fyodor Dostoevsky

## 825 ENGLISH ONLY: AND A COMMENT

Divan room, near buses, Tube; every convenience; English only. £2 5*s*. 0*d*.

Advertisement

And all must love the human form,<br>
In heathen, turk, or jew;<br>
Where Mercy, Love and Pity dwell<br>
There God is dwelling too.

William Blake

# INDEXES

# NOTE

Detailed notes on the use of the three indexes are given on page xi of the Introduction.

For ease of reference the following type conventions are used throughout:

Bible themes are in bold type . . . . . . **Numerals 1 to 106**
Prayers are in italic type . . . . . . *Numerals 107 to 604*
Readings are in roman type . . . . . Numerals 605 to 825

The diagram below shows a typical entry in the Readings index. The other two indexes follow the same principle but in a different order.

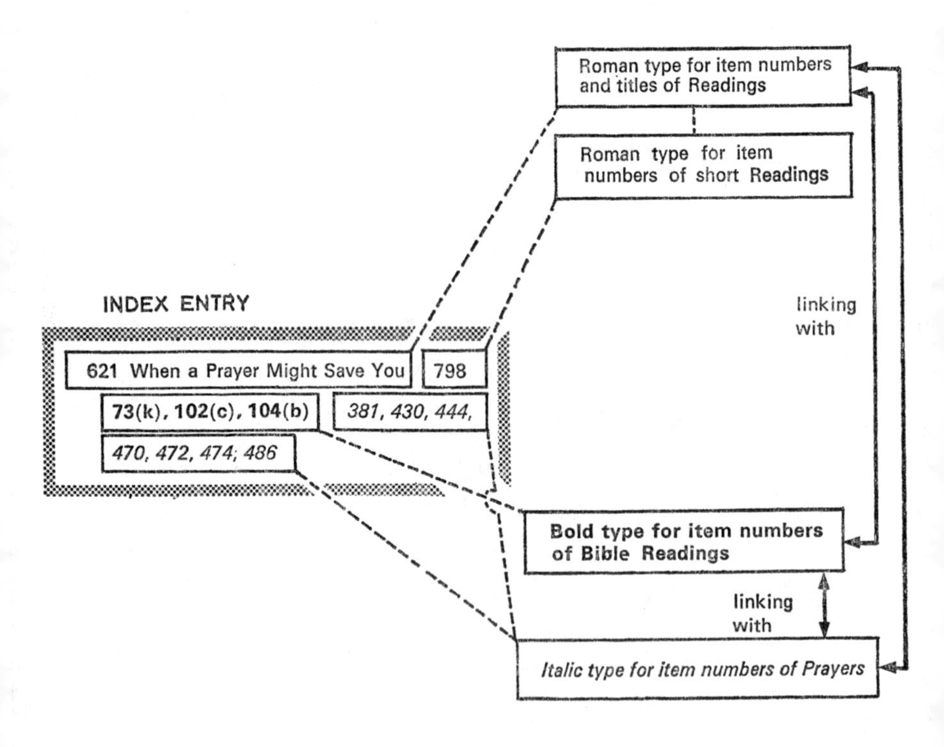

# Bible Index


**1 The Beatitudes 1**
(a) *134, 289, 400, 566* 606, 607, 730, 735
(b) *170, 211, 386, 420, 441, 572* 625, 737
(c) *203, 263, 328* 718, 737, 767, 768
(d) *382–3, 388–90, 412* 676, 718, 767, 768
(e) *201, 334, 386, 406, 411* 707, 739, 748, 767

**2 The Beatitudes 2** *510–2, 515–8, 568*
(a) *340, 498* 743, 749, 759
(b) *169, 181, 368, 397, 522* 743, 749, 759
(c) *236, 369* 743, 749, 759
(d) *175, 366* 736, 749
(e) *232, 479* 644, 742, 749, 759

**3 The Beatitudes 3** *398–401*
(a) *170, 439, 441* 763
(b) *170, 252–3, 266–7* 729, 735
(c) *324, 379, 416, 456* 690, 691
(d) *114, 179, 256, 424* 644, 689, 768
(e) *210, 281, 433, 459* 689, 720, 768
(f) *289, 400, 479, 566, 576* 607, 689
(g) *111, 181* 679, 691

**4 The Beatitudes 4**
(a) *168, 417, 443* 646, 678, 750
(b) *166, 255, 417, 516, 568* 680, 806
(c) *240, 418, 483–4* 738, 814, 822
(d) *383, 427, 482* 675, 737
(e) *395, 428, 485* 680, 738
(f) *171, 240, 265, 385, 433, 561* 678, 797
(g) *193, 198, 245, 328, 375, 433, 580* 677, 720, 735, 750

**5 The Beatitudes 5**(i)
(a) *179, 182, 184, 186, 209, 264, 469* 710, 715
(b) *175, 188, 256, 270, 571* 611, 612, 617, 713
(c) *165, 188, 272, 533* 773
(d) *184, 255, 270–1, 561* 618, 706
(e) *192, 258, 274* 713, 751

**6 The Beatitudes 5**(ii) *488–9, 492–6, 499, 505, 509–12, 515–9, 527, 531–3, 542, 568, 571, 582, 585*
(a) *198, 252* 730, 731, 735
(b) *272* 636, 644
(c) *170, 175, 188, 253, 273. 281, 561* 625, 715, 769
(d) *171, 265, 269* 644, 719, 720, 738, 751
(e) *172, 193, 244, 462* 677, 719, 720, 730, 732, 738, 769

**7 The Beatitudes 6** *240, 245–7, 417, 443*
(a) *395, 486, 573* 706, 737
(b) *201–2, 275, 427* 675, 702
(c) *427–8, 485* 676, 796
(d) *109, 401, 403* 678, 724(6), 815
(e) *168, 377, 563* 712, 789, 791
(f) *107, 109, 111, 374* 706, 728 (14), 729

**8 The Beatitudes 7**
(a) *192, 265–8, 500, 520–3, 601* 728 (11–14), 757
(b) *144, 145, 163, 230, 415, 529, 530* 637, 757
(c) *110, 176, 206, 229, 601* 638
(d) *140, 206, 192* 735, 773, 813, 822
(e) *177, 277, 570* 706
(f) *147–8, 259–62, 277* 704, 728 (4–5)

**9 The Beatitudes 8**
(a) *175, 298, 301, 384, 480* 706, 724 (5), 728 (1–3), 745
(b) *368, 382, 479* 721, 724 (3), 816, 820
(c) *122, 381, 385* 815, 822
(d) *122, 200, 368, 375, 414* 706, 745, 751
(e) *145, 368, 375–7, 448* 702, 745
(f) *134, 479* 654, 679, 728 (6), 736, 745

**10 The Bible** *325, 357*
(a) *152, 445, 449, 486* 617, 619, 793, 797
(b) *168, 291, 450, 580* 606, 607, 801, 803
(c) *134, 210, 479* 606, 607, 610, 619
(d) *134, 156, 466* 616, 617

**11 A Christian Community** *157–8, 277, 358–60, 363, 550–1, 558–9*
(a) *189–201, 238, 283, 521, 569* 679, 739, 813
(b) *146, 255, 262, 555* 703, 712, 808
(c) *280, 431–2, 533, 548–9, 555, 562* 680, 807
(d) *192, 255, 269* 676, 746, 808

**12 Christian Living**
- (a) *110, 112, 427–8, 439* 664, 736, 789, 821
- (b) *202, 386, 465, 468* 645, 661, 662
- (c) *192 444, 448, 473, 479, 482* 661, 664, 679, 742, 751, 765
- (d) *240, 483, 539, 542* 661, 742
- (e) *142, 198, 244, 388, 396, 573, 578* 661, 704, 746

**13 Compassion** *488–9, 492–6, 499, 505, 509–12, 515–19, 527, 531–3, 542, 568, 571, 582, 585*
- (a) *256, 257, 268, 281, 383* 703, 715, 768, 823
- (b) *252, 258, 269* 703, 715, 768, 824
- (c) *253, 273, 281, 385, 436, 575* 703, 711, 712, 715, 768, 774
- (d) *208, 212, 255, 272, 279* 625, 699, 711, 712, 736, 768, 774
- (e) *254, 270, 301* 658, 715, 742, 743, 768, 825

**14 Detachment** *200–4, 263, 386, 411–412, 572–4, 580*
- (a) *116, 118–9, 122, 199* 664, 728 (11–14), 740, 796
- (b) *122, 289, 410* 728 (11–14), 823, 825
- (c) *328, 333–4, 383* 625, 667, 740, 741, 767
- (d) *202, 465, 468* 647, 665, 667, 672, 740
- (e) *185, 334, 404* 667, 740, 741, 767
- (f) *170–1, 419* 680, 741, 767

**15 Eternal Life** *123*
- (a) *184* 642, 794, 810
- (b) *110, 120, 124, 132, 153–5* 647, 668, 746
- (c) *150–1, 304, 326* 642, 748
- (d) *282. 302, 476, 486* 685, 715, 728 (11–14)
- (e) *175, 479* 648, 681
- (f) *166–174, 182 followed by 162 and 164* 727, 739

**16 The Eucharist 1** *107 (349–353), 444*
- (a) *189, 303* 619, 642
- (b) *134, 152* 619, 624
- (c) *184, 304* 619, 641, 644
- (d) *464, 479, 483* 619, 624, 626, 644
- (e) *482, 486–7* 624, 627, 647

**17 The Eucharist 2** *107 (349–353), 444*
- (a) *286, 306, 357* 619, 641, 810
- (b) *136, 146, 208, 479* 619, 624, 810
- (c) *110, 146* 619, 624, 641, 810
- (d) *111, 165–183, 184, 190, 533* 619, 624, 641, 644
- (e) *111, 165–183, 184, 190, 533* 619, 641, 647, 810

**18 The House of God**
- (a) *162, 544–5* 639, 728
- (b) *111, 116* 625, 626, 627, 647, 648
- (c) *133, 168, 190, 403* 615, 625, 647
- (d) *190, 198, 311–2, 337, 447*

**19 Faith** *210, 474, 484–7*
- (a) *144, 215, 247* 656, 724, 736
- (b) *145, 281* 682, 724
- (c) *185, 211, 408, 413, 424–5, 459, 471* 732, 801
- (d) *149, 155, 269, 274* 615, 616, 818
- (e) *115, 194, 319, 455* 620, 651, 691, 728 (14), 801
- (f) *239, 240, 313, 449–60* 651, 751

**20 Laws and Commandments: Old Testament** *449–460*
- (a) *239, 240* 649, 660, 665, 669
- (b) *171, 292, 433* 649, 673, 707, 780
- (c) *248, 419, 473* 636, 639
- (d) *410, 489, 491* 636, 639
- (e) *242, 248, 282* 673, 698, 731, 744
- (f) *284, 446, 479* 728 (11–14), 744

**21 Laws and Commandments: New Testament**
- (a) *122, 123, 126, 143, 391, 442, 445, 452, 467–8* 618, 700, 730
- (b) *258, 270–1, 406, 413, 449, 466* 744, 748
- (c) *255–6, 265, 270–1, 561* 744, 751
- (d) *264, 396–7, 433–5, 583* 676, 781
- (e) *402–3, 416, 450, 454, 459* 744, 780
- (f) *279, 281, 451–5, 515–8* 724, 774
- (g) *401, 403, 519* 765, 821
- (h) *265, 309, 401, 406, 459* 645, 733
- (i) *294, 452, 459, 468, 479* 618, 643, 700, 769
- (j) *198, 257, 269, 272–4, 280–1, 289, 294, 584, 588* 645, 813
- (k) *198, 257, 269, 272–4, 280–1, 289, 294, 584, 588* 642, 713, 751, 769

**22 Martyrdom**
- (a) *175, 298, 301, 375–6, 479, 576* 711, 747, 750, 800
- (b) *175, 189, 298, 301, 341–2, 381–5* 700, 814, 815
- (c) *122, 189, 298, 301, 341–2, 381–5* 730, 747
- (d) *156, 189, 298, 301, 341–2, 381–5* 728, 747, 800

**23 Membership: Baptism and Confirmation** *347–8, 463*
- (a) *447, 544, 573* 635, 736
- (b) *445, 472, 543* 635, 751
- (c) *446, 452, 545* 625, 751
- (d) *177, 180, 189, 311, 382, 448, 576* 627, 751

**24 Men for God**
- (a) *189–202* 723, 725
- (b) *189–202* 751, 762
- (c) *197–8* 725, 751, 762
- (d) *238–41* 751, 762

(e) *577* 724, 736
(f) *381–5* 748, 751

**25 Missionaries** *328, 341, 346, 316, 317, 543–5, 577*
(a) 723, 774
(b) 626, 722
(c) 626, 776
(d) *189–202, 320* 722, 723
(e) *189–202, 320, 542* 702, 752

**26 The Ten Commandments 1 and 2: Worship**
(a) *109, 116, 120, 132–3, 197–202, 244, 441* 650, 802
(b) *115, 170, 174, 240, 404, 474* 650, 753
(c) *111, 404, 434–5, 439, 457* 650, 781
(d) *163, 166, 168, 177, 417, 457, 482* 650, 767
(e) *110, 395, 404, 409, 438–9, 459, 481* 650, 767
(f) *124, 197, 201, 395, 427–8* 626, 650

**27 The Ten Commandments 3: God's Name** *121, 130, 473*
(a) *119, 129, 409, 471* 630, 638, 648
(b) *140, 184, 479, 566* 605, 613
(c) *113, 117, 314–5, 592, 595* 628, 751
(d) *113, 126, 315, 566* 622, 668
(e) *107, 403, 423* 618, 624, 625, 629
(f) *108, 128, 576, 579* 607, 615

**28 The Ten Commandments 4: The Sabbath (i)** *581*
(a) *132, 372, 425, 453*
(b) *142, 426, 438, 449, 450, 481*
(c) *142, 426, 438, 449, 450, 481*
(d) *417, 452, 596, 599, 601*

**29 The Ten Commandments 4: The Sabbath (ii)**
(a) *170, 398, 403, 431*
(b) *145, 171, 217, 396, 399, 403, 407, 572*
(c) *187, 256, 263, 403, 480*
(d) *182, 269, 402–3, 405*

**30 The Ten Commandments 4: The Sabbath (iii)**
(a) *286, 455, 473, 536*
(b) *302–4*
(c) *208, 351, 445, 472, 537, 593*
(d) *203–4, 385–7, 392–4, 468*

**31 The Ten Commandments 5: Honouring Parents** *147–8, 259–61, 506–8*
(a) 653, 704, 705, 728 (4–5)
(b) *254, 392–4, 438–9* 765, 821
(c) *162–3, 167, 394, 448* 704, 822
(d) *438* 634, 704, 705, 728 (4–5), 761, 765

**32 The Ten Commandments 6: Murder**
(a) *258, 274, 406–7, 570* 697, 748
(b) *171, 270, 274* 652, 699, 708
(c) *263, 271–2, 298* 652, 708, 821
(d) *168, 175, 403* 708, 821
(e) *164, 175, 192, 236, 294, 476* 708, 710
(f) *123, 162, 175, 192, 265, 498* 708, 710

**33 The Ten Commandments 7: Adultery** *107, 190, 417, 588*
(a) *168, 187, 427* 806
(b) *182, 423, 432* 806
(c) *168, 464* 791, 806
(d) *171, 184, 464* 792, 798, 809
(e) *194, 202, 234, 427* 789, 809

**34 The Ten Commandments 8: Stealing**
(a) *114, 163, 203, 397, 411* 707, 774, 806
(b) *143, 204, 243, 263* 707, 808, 812, 814
(c) *142, 198, 264, 273, 494, 571* 707, 781, 806

**35 The Ten Commandments 9: Truth** *583*
(a) *324, 374, 377, 395–6* 766, 781
(b) *170, 385, 397, 522* 766, 803, 806
(c) *168, 182, 217, 226, 403, 486, 578* 646, 766, 821
(d) *171, 374, 383–4, 433* 766, 791, 806, 821
(e) *175, 182, 432, 435–6, 522, 578* 766, 789
(f) *177, 275, 383, 396, 522* 766, 798
(g) *311, 313, 324–5, 331, 466* 733, 766, 812, 814

**36 The Ten Commandments 10: Covetousness** *203–4, 386*
(a) *275, 406, 408* 776, 808
(b) *227, 383, 411* 796, 806, 809, 812
(c) *407, 570* 806, 814
(d) *412, 441, 572* 797, 812

**37 Vocation: God Calls People to His Service 1** *189–202, 577*
(a) *210–2, 248, 467* 711, 762
(b) *240, 248, 382, 452, 459* 723, 750
(c) *219, 452, 454* 712, 801
(d) *115, 218, 357* 702, 778
(e) *215, 248, 382, 465* 713, 793
(f) *249, 384, 446, 449* 700, 723

**38 Vocation: God Calls People to His Service 2** *189–202, 577*
(a) *244, 316–7, 385* 651, 778
(b) *334, 382, 466* 651, 801
(c) *203–4, 383, 387, 411–2, 572* 709, 812, 814
(d) *320, 448, 466* 762, 793, 821
(e) *218, 244, 320, 382, 384, 398–400* 733, 788

**39 Advent: The Coming of Christ (i)** *282–6*

**Kingdom of God:** *252–3, 265–8, 500–504, 513, 520–3*
- (a) *448, 455, 505, 513–9, 531–2* 639, 701, 726
- (b) *111, 171, 466* 776, 791
- (c) *181, 444–5, 489* 656, 668
- (d) *197, 452, 485* 727, 825

**40 Advent: The Coming of Christ (ii)** *282–6*
- (a) *166–174, 176–183, 329, 457, 483* 618, 709
- (b) *128, 323, 484* 605, 631, 634
- (c) *107, 134, 289* 606, 631
- (d) *479, 482–7* 607, 713, 793

**41 An Advent Carol Service** *282–6*

**42 A Christmas Carol Service** *287*

**43 Christmas** *134, 287–9, 400*
- (a) *286* 631
- (b) *236* 613
- (c) *468, 484* 606, 631
- (d) *357, 471, 487* 701, 751
- (e) *226, 315, 445, 466* 605
- (f) *198* 734

**44 Epiphany: The Shining Light** *290–291*
- (a) *482, 483* 662
- (b) *409, 484* 824
- (c) *459, 485* 825
- (d) *320, 543–5* 701
- (e) *445, 482* 728 (11–14)
- (f) *447, 466*

**45 Septuagesima: Creation** *117, 118, 120, 124, 410*
- (a) *132, 141* 631, 643, 648, 681, 753
- (b) *149, 155, 489* 632, 681
- (c) *125, 127, 489* 630, 633, 754
- (d) *131, 150, 153* 630, 639, 754
- (e) *130, 149, 151, 154* 630, 698, 754

**46 Sexagesima: The Fall** *166–174, 176–183, 293, 563, 564*
- (a) *374, 396–7, 401, 416, 435* 671, 753
- (b) *374, 396–7, 401, 416, 435* 753, 773
- (c) *187, 252–3, 258* 770, 791
- (d) *232, 419, 422, 430, 470* 638, 770
- (e) *175, 268, 297, 430, 470*

**47 Quinquagesima: Christian Love** *252–81, 294, 468, 561, 570–1, 584, 586*
- (a) *107, 206, 215, 272, 301, 482* 714, 728 (7–10), 755
- (b) *123, 142, 208, 273, 338, 446, 478* 636, 714, 728 (7–10)
- (c) *111, 165, 186–8, 398–9* 714
- (d) *128, 140, 145, 157–8, 339, 546–7, 593* 627, 681
- (e) *122, 218, 274, 310, 461, 546–7* 627, 705, 714

**48 Lent 1** *295, 296, 464, 573, 576*
- (a) *134, 289, 400, 566* 676, 709
- (b) *111, 200, 243, 328, 331, 382, 573* 675, 676, 678, 696
- (c) *386–7, 448, 480* 812
- (d) *188, 256–7, 265, 368, 399, 415, 479* 629
- (e) *175, 188, 298, 300, 372, 459, 475* 734

**49 Lent 2** *295, 296, 464, 573, 576*
- (a) *141, 194, 386, 392–4* 632
- (b) *151, 206, 372, 456* 632, 810
- (c) *148, 154, 372, 409* 754, 770
- (d) *155, 451, 459* 638, 678
- (e) *210, 349–353, 468* 633

**50 Lent 3** *115, 295, 296, 319, 580*
- (a) *445, 456* 607
- (b) *170, 303, 318* 615
- (c) *226, 461, 466* 685
- (d) *134, 482, 487* 609
- (e) *303, 318* 619
- (f) *297, 298, 466, 475–6* 614

**51 Lent 4** *109, 581*
- (a) *182, 412, 417, 427, 438* 650
- (b) *166, 439, 441, 470* 625, 650
- (c) *170, 396–7, 433* 625, 650, 781
- (d) *379, 427, 452, 472* 650
- (e) *181, 382, 472*

**52 Lent 5** *295, 296, 398–401, 576, 579*
- (a) *131, 428, 481, 537, 572* 629, 692, 754
- (b) *274, 483, 539, 567* 607, 610
- (c) *416, 458, 473, 520* 629
- (d) *270, 298, 436, 542* 609, 618
- (e) *175, 271, 300, 500, 522* 617
- (f) *175, 300, 501, 503–4* 611, 614

**53 Palm Sunday and Holy Week** *297–298, 536, 588*
- (a) *399–400, 415, 483* 691
- (b) *422, 479* 710, 728 (1–3, 6)
- (c) *205, 207, 473* 641
- (d) *198, 420* 636
- (e) *189, 474, 479* 605, 607

**54 Palm Sunday** *130, 297–8, 430*
- (a) 755
- (b) 635

**55 The Events of Holy Week** *297–8, 479, 584*
- (a) *459, 527, 543–5* 650, 676
- (b) *403, 409, 413, 433, 487* 671, 676
- (c) *398, 403, 407, 433* 673, 675
- (d) *184, 188, 381–5, 388–90* 615, 616
- (e) *300, 411* 650, 678

**56 Maundy Thursday** *479, 584*
- (a) *107, 111, 349–53, 547* 619, 641
- (b) *166–74, 182, 366, 468* 607, 731, 774
- (c) *181, 381–5, 396–7, 464, 480* 610

**57 Good Friday and Holy Saturday** *479, 533, 568, 585*
(a) *175, 299–301, 366, 475–6* 614
(b) *175, 299–301, 366, 475–6* 611, 612, 614, 747, 759
(c) *369, 222–37* 788, 800

**58 Easter 1** *302–4*
(a) *121, 433, 448 486* 613, 758
(b) *125, 444, 468* 619, 758
(c) *128, 357, 471, 482, 487* 628, 758
(d) *129, 226, 318–9, 461, 484, 487* 619, 673, 758
(e) *144, 286, 445* 793, 797
(f) *134, 142, 189–202, 330–1* 756
(g) *133, 315, 472, 478, 543–5* 775, 776

**59 Easter 2** *302–4*
(a) *447, 459, 473, 543–5* 628
(b) *433 505, 509, 515–8, 531–2* 801, 803
(c) *398, 450, 452, 455* 801, 803
(d) *319, 453, 459* 628, 758
(e) *450, 468, 486* 631, 673, 752, 758, 759
(f) *110, 121, 306, 472* 668, 752

**60 The Ascension** *305–8*
(a) *110 452, 459* 759, 801
(b) *126, 189, 444* 759, 801
(c) *123 190, 467* 810
(d) *133, 202, 468* 728 (6)
(e) *194, 208, 466* 813, 825

**61 Whitsun 1** *309–313, 463*
(a) *107, 536, 537* 622, 760
(b) *112, 184, 452, 536* 697
(c) *130, 195, 251, 459* 686, 734, 760
(d) *196, 198, 257, 270–4, 294, 468, 547* 673, 674, 756, 764
(e) *197, 215, 443, 536* 695, 699, 760

**62 Whitsun 2** *309–13*
(a) *107, 168, 450, 537* 728 (11–14), 760
(b) *443, 447, 452, 539* 622, 760
(c) *190, 239, 249, 401, 482, 574* 685, 694
(d) *110. 240, 401* 694 755
(e) *448, 451, 536, 543* 686, 693, 760

**63 Trinity** *314, 315, 592, 598, 601*
(a) *113, 118, 121, 125–30, 133, 189–202, 409, 577* 623, 672, 797
(b) *113, 118, 121 125–30, 132, 133, 543* 635, 672, 694
(c) *197, 325, 329, 468, 471, 484* 686
(d) *144, 162–3, 270–4, 410, 468* 636, 674, 714, 729

**64 St. Andrew (November 30th)** *316, 317, 540, 543–5*
(a) *189–202, 541* 655, 793
(b) *262, 346, 478* 775, 793
(c) *217, 218, 269, 372, 542* 756, 797
(d) *192, 252, 265 436, 568* 701, 797

**65 St. Thomas (December 21st)** *318, 319*
(a) *110, 123, 456, 465, 479* 797, 801
(b) *181, 229, 232, 485* 797, 801
(c) *111, 120, 460, 483* 635, 637, 659, 693
(d) *111, 113, 116, 122, 155* 788, 801
(e) *115, 200, 239, 240, 381–5* 692, 793, 801
(f) *144, 149–54, 184, 468* 692, 793, 801
(g) *145, 192, 298, 602* 727

**66 The Conversion of St. Paul (January 25th)** 2 *320*
(a) *115, 145, 170, 175* 750, 792, 793
(b) *168, 182, 185, 577* 657, 723
(c) *170, 163, 182, 189, 197* 723, 793, 813, 818
(d) *171, 188, 268, 279, 488* 697, 723
(e) *145, 181, 192, 200, 229, 583* 723, 813, 818

**67 The Conversion of St. Paul 2** *320*
(a) *123, 181, 444–8, 449–60* 657
(b) *184, 366, 445, 461, 468* 654, 687, 723
(c) *144, 272–4, 410, 468, 584* 697, 723, 728 (7–10)
(d) *157–8, 255, 277, 280, 358–60, 363, 521, 550–1* 627, 792, 813
(e) *142, 155, 190, 200, 382* 723, 793
(f) *122, 134, 289, 398–401, 566* 731, 788, 818
(g) *202, 206, 222, 237, 380, 469, 576 592* 687, 813, 818

**68 The Presentation of Christ in the Temple, or, the Purification of St. Mary the Virgin (February 2nd)** *189–202, 218, 321, 481, 562*
(a) *445, 476, 482* 771
(b) *427, 436, 485* 705
(c) *123, 207, 481, 483–4* 657, 793
(d) *438, 444, 487* 751, 793

**69 St. Matthias (February 24th)** *189–202, 322, 341, 580*
(a) *111, 168, 172, 479*
(b) *129, 130, 131, 401, 577*
(c) *376–8, 401, 433*
(d) *427, 541, 543–5*

**70 The Annunciation of the Blessed Virgin Mary (March 25th)** *218, 323*
(a) *125–9, 143, 346, 417, 543–5* 635, 770
(b) *444–8* 605
(c) *119, 121–4, 467* 634, 771
(d) *184, 189, 190, 192,* 607
(e) *116, 118, 197* 605, 634

**71 St. George (April 23rd)**
(a) *198, 200, 324, 521, 522* 723, 724

**72 St. Mark (April 25th)** *249, 325, 357*
(a) *205–6, 236, 238* 625, 626, 627

(b) *189, 208, 543–5* 625, 626, 627
(c) *192, 200, 215, 543–5* 625, 626, 627
(d) *152, 197, 230, 232* 625, 626, 627

**73 St. Philip and St. James (May 1st)** *326, 337*
(a) *134, 200 262, 317* 626, 627
(b) *141, 372, 392–4, 579* 638, 641, 719
(c) *107, 115, 239–40, 461* 724, 801
(d) *112, 193, 200, 202, 207, 217, 241–244. 250–1, 462, 561, 571* 715, 776, 821
(e) *170, 248, 252–5, 257, 269, 280–1, 289, 416, 566, 580* 701, 716, 717, 719, 740, 741
(f) *112, 193, 200, 202, 207, 217, 241–244, 250–1, 462, 561, 571* 715, 716, 717, 724
(g) *108, 170, 374–8, 583* 706, 731, 795
(h) *166, 175, 182–3, 441, 451, 586, 587* 715, 716, 717, 776
(i) *201, 334, 386, 406, 411–2* 716, 725, 740, 741, 776
(j) *115, 145, 368, 380–5, 414, 415, 569* 687, 692
(k) *111, 163, 172, 180. 415, 563–4, 565, 589–91* 621, 791

**74 St. Barnabas (June 11th)** *200–4, 327, 328, 333–4, 386, 411, 412*
(a) *383, 503*
(b) *384, 572*
(c) *427, 537, 541*
(d) *382, 543–5*
(e) *111, 300, 543–5*
(f) *175, 298, 343*
(g) *341, 504, 543–5, 596*

**75 The Nativity of St. John the Baptist (June 24th)** *323*
(a) *181, 182, 282, 284*
(b) *484, 487*
(c) *459, 482*
(d) *472, 483*
(e) *452, 462, 485, 486*
(f) *319, 509, 515–8, 585* 716, 751
(g) *309–13, 347–8, 447–8* 723, 724

**76 St. Peter (June 29th)** *330–331*
(a) *142, 189–202, 207, 221, 543–5* 716, 725
(b) *238–240, 472, 474* 687, 696
(c) *409, 445, 450. 539, 540* 722, 725
(d) *116, 373, 449, 466*
(e) *119, 123, 125–30, 468, 479* 607, 727
(f) *145, 168, 180, 182*
(g) *175, 181, 205, 208, 262, 275–6, 374, 381, 396–7, 433, 563–4*
(h) *175, 181, 205, 208, 262, 275–6, 374, 381, 396–7, 433, 563–4*
(i) *128, 302–4*
(j) *128, 302–4*
(k) *189–302, 519, 537–45*
(l) *166, 190, 197, 309–13*
(m) *269, 270, 379, 410, 436, 488, 505* 724
(n) *223, 226, 236, 387, 396, 535* 724
(o) *278, 309, 428*
(p) *281, 431, 509* 724
(q) *274, 279, 432* 724
(r) *342, 387, 395, 419* 724

**77 St. Mary Magdalen (July 22nd)** *332*
(a) *415, 417, 426, 430, 436, 586* 616
(b) *210, 302–4, 391* 615, 616
(c) *184* 616
(d) *118, 123, 128, 444, 479* 616

**78 St. James the Apostle (July 25th)**
(a) *185, 197, 204, 212, 221, 581* 725, 746
(b) *192, 246, 382, 443* 747, 748
(c) *175, 214, 235* 610, 747, 748
(d) *145, 206, 342* 749, 751

**79 St. Matthew (September 21st)**
(a) *334, 386, 397, 411–2, 452*
(b) *189, 192, 542–5*

**80 St. Michael and All Angels (September 29th)**
(a) *192, 199, 200, 324, 335, 347*
(b) *122, 145, 184, 335*

**81 St. Luke (October 18th) 1**
(a) *336, 499, 505, 509, 531–2, 567, 585* 682, 683, 684, 715. 720
(b) *336, 427, 537, 561, 571*
(c) *336, 432, 443*
(d) *336, 382, 426, 442, 529–30*

**82 St. Luke 2**
(a) *193, 269, 329, 462, 473* 731, 778
(b) *401, 428, 441, 451, 457* 666, 716, 720
(c) *184, 459, 461, 468, 479, 564* 777, 810
(d) *252, 265, 543–5* 716, 825
(e) *145, 165, 217, 252–5, 272–4, 279, 527, 561, 575* 715, 716, 717, 732, 756
(f) *111, 122, 163, 172, 202, 443–4, 566* 705, 717, 720
(g) *114, 182, 128, 184, 474, 563* 773, 777

**83 St. Simon and St. Jude (October 28th)** *337*
(a) *189–204, 478–81, 577*
(b) *189–204, 478–81, 577* 724, 756
(c) *189–204, 478–81, 577* 724
(d) *310–3, 458–9*
(e) *537–9, 546–7*

**84 All Saints' Day (November 1st)** *156, 338–41*
(a) *122, 126, 133, 483, 537*

(b) *144, 303, 446*
(c) *130, 145, 363, 503–4, 513–4* 717
(d) *118, 121–2, 125–30, 483, 537* 726
(e) *111, 149, 194, 201, 227, 240, 273, 427* 724
(f) *302–6, 369, 395, 410, 468, 497–8* 758
(g) *302–6, 369, 395, 410, 468, 497–8* 758
(h) *302–6, 369, 395, 410, 468, 497–8*
(i) *302–6, 369, 395, 410, 468, 497–8*

**85 Harvest Thanksgiving** *117, 120, 124, 131–2, 135–9, 141, 150–3, 567*
(a) *185–202, 219, 241–4, 270–3* 633, 663, 693
(b) *185–202, 219, 241–4, 270–3*
(c) *185–202, 219, 241–4, 270–3* 638
(d) *205, 428, 443, 452, 572* 632, 751
(e) *203–4, 254–5, 263, 411–2, 568*

**86 The Beginning of Term** *110, 115, 118, 142, 148, 151, 157–8, 205–7, 240, 250, 358–60, 364, 409, 446, 506–8, 548–51, 558–9, 600*
(a) *189–202, 215–6, 456* 688
(b) *140, 262, 275–7, 280, 432, 555*
(c) *140, 262, 275–7, 280, 432, 555*

**87 An Important School Occasion** *113, 143, 156–7, 194, 363, 367, 488, 548, 554, 556–9, 592*
(a) *149, 195, 249, 482–3*
(b) *313, 445–8, 452, 459* 646, 693, 694, 803
(c) *313, 445–8, 452, 459* 646, 803
(d) *313, 445–8, 452, 459* 790, 791
(e) *145, 503–4* 693, 694, 695, 783
(f) *151, 197, 313, 444, 472, 536* 647
(g) *192, 382* 687, 691

**88 The End of Term** *156–7, 169, 176–180, 185, 361–2, 506–8, 552–4, 599, 601*
(a) *155* 691, 727
(b) *272* 724

**89 The Journey to the Promised Land; Many Difficulties are Overcome** *569*
(a) *115, 122, 134, 181, 239, 430* 696, 725
(b) *114, 190, 372, 448* 725
(c) *117, 183, 207, 448* 725
(d) *118, 145, 197, 205, 427* 725
(e) *116, 123, 154, 192, 215–6* 725

**90 The People's Reluctance to Enter the Promised Land** *572–3*
(a) *240, 374–8, 427–8, 443*
(b) *245–8, 278, 374–8, 398*
(c) *185, 245–8, 382*
(d) *185, 206, 384, 430*
(e) *185, 199, 385*
(f) *191, 195, 239, 347, 444* 726

**91 Lessons from the Book of Daniel 1: Discipline**
(a) *181, 190–1, 200, 238, 248–9, 276, 372, 381, 386, 480, 580, 587* 772
(b) *181, 190–1, 200, 238, 248–9, 276, 372, 381, 386, 480, 580, 587* 772

**92 Lessons from the Book of Daniel 2: Loyalty to God**
(a) *300, 379, 381–5, 428, 438, 470, 479, 483, 594* 772
(b) *300, 379, 381–5, 428, 438, 470, 479, 483, 594* 772, 820
(c) *300, 379, 381–5, 428, 438, 470, 479, 483, 594* 772, 820

**93 Lessons from the Book of Daniel 3: Reverence**
(a) *111, 118, 401, 404, 452, 490* 719
(b) *111, 118, 401, 404, 452, 490* 719
(c) *111, 118, 401, 404, 452, 490* 719

**94 Lessons from the Book of Daniel 4: Faith**
(a) *300, 381–5. 427, 463, 480–2* 728 (1–3, 6)
(b) *300, 381–5, 427, 463, 480–2* 675, 728 (1–3, 6)

**95 Lessons from the Book of Daniel 5: Penitence and Hope** *166–83*
(a) *181, 533*
(b) *454, 472*
(c) *462, 536*

**96 The Book of Jonah (The Reluctant Missionary)** *543–5*
(a) *436, 443, 465, 487, 529–30* 625, 720, 723, 724
(b) *181, 397, 455, 465, 529–30* 625, 720, 723, 724
(c) *398, 445, 469* 625, 720, 723, 724
(d) *265, 274, 410, 489, 491, 527* 625, 699, 720, 723, 724

**97 The Good Shepherd** *539*
(a) *192, 248, 273, 284, 330, 403, 524, 534, 549* 640, 720
(b) *235, 240, 444, 469, 478, 483* 640, 681, 684, 728 (7–10), 762
(c) *235, 240, 444, 469, 478, 483* 720
(d) *229, 473, 479* 617, 640, 721
(e) *274–6, 330, 541*

**98 Some Stories which Illustrate what Jesus does for Men (From Mark)** *144*
(a) *134, 236, 264, 366, 431–2, 505, 515–8, 568, 585* 609, 682, 683, 684, 717
(b) *155, 166, 182, 176–80, 515–8, 587* 658, 683, 684, 725, 771
(c) *181, 206, 229, 415, 424, 426, 430, 463, 529–30* 620, 771
(d) *265, 366, 370–1, 377, 413, 429, 436, 487, 493, 499* 682, 683, 725

(e) *155, 215, 226, 373, 409, 448* 656, 662, 725

**99 Some Stories which Illustrate what Jesus Does for Men 2 (From John)** *164*

(a) *111, 184, 194, 287, 352, 442, 484* 718, 728 (7–10), 771

(b) *109, 168, 190, 352, 433, 478* 772, 791

(c) *391, 402, 443, 448* 660, 813

(d) *351, 372, 455–6, 473* 641, 818

(e) *123, 239, 453, 465, 472, 474, 486, 573* 684, 717

**100 Opposition to Jesus 1** *145, 165, 374, 376–7, 403, 479, 566*

(a) *182, 258, 269* 609

(b) *175, 188, 257, 263, 273* 732

(c) *169, 186, 296–7* 682

(d) *168, 187, 259–61, 425, 581*

**101 Opposition to Jesus 2** *145, 165, 479, 576*

(a) *168, 264, 273, 570*

(b) *173, 182, 296–7* 609

(c) *168, 175, 255, 406–8* 772

(d) *175, 256, 270–1, 279, 298, 300, 433, 475–6* 617

(e) *175, 256, 270–1, 279, 298, 300, 433, 475–6*

**102 The Sermon on the Mount**

(a) *196, 198, 215, 226 459, 466–7, 482* 703

(b) *107, 115, 217, 254, 257, 269, 485* 761

(c) *108, 112, 118, 123, 129, 400, 444, 451, 461, 474, 579* 620, 621

(d) *377, 406–8, 432, 436, 461, 547, 587* 671, 725

(e) *468, 565, 579* 659, 725

(f) *451, 454–5, 462, 481* 653, 677, 721, 725, 732

(g) *470, 473, 482, 486, 572* 658, 688, 725

**103 Parables of Jesus 1 : The Kingdom**

(a) *117, 201, 427, 443, 487* 632, 726

(b) *119, 125, 137, 243, 473* 653, 659, 718

(c) *121, 126, 447, 459, 461* 725

(d) *118, 197, 328, 386, 580* 721, 812

**104 Parables of Jesus 2: Prayer and Forgiveness**

(a) *242, 245–6, 427, 461, 485, 573* 751

(b) *114–5, 165, 174, 416* 670

(c) *187, 255–6, 258, 264, 279, 533, 571*

(d) *163, 180, 184, 448, 469, 570*

**105 Parables of Jesus 3: How to Treat Other People**

(a) *135, 145, 197, 217, 269, 369, 568, 582* 677, 699, 764

(b) *186–7, 203–4, 252–5, 386, 561* 764

(c) *134, 186–7, 202, 265, 280–1, 570–1* 688, 726

**106 Parables of Jesus 4: Response to God and Use of His Gifts**

(a) *114, 206, 349, 451, 584* 665

(b) *142, 150, 152, 155, 158, 185, 207, 238, 242–4, 250–1, 562, 581* 643, 649, 669, 761

(c) *154, 185, 239–40, 567* 649, 669

(d) *154, 243, 245–7, 462* 649, 698

(e) *115, 199, 200, 251, 367, 468*

# Prayer Index

*107–115* *OPENING PRAYERS*

*116–33* *PRAYERS OF PRAISE* **27**(a) (d), **45**, **62**(a) (b), **70** (a) (c), **77**(d), **85**(a) (b) (c), **89** 617, 630, 635, 638–41, 661–2

*125–9* *From the Psalms* **21**(a), **45**, **60**(d) 617, 635–6

*130* *Man the Viceroy of God* **45** (b) (e), **62**(a) (c), **84**(c) 638, 643, 655–6, 667, 692, 698, 785, 793

*131* *Harvest Song* **45**(d), **85**, **103** (a) (b) (c) 632, 638, 640, 785

*132* *God's Boundless Care for His Creation* **15** (b) (c), **26**(f), **28**(a), **45**(a) 630–1, 635

*133* *Summons to Praise* **60**(d), **63** (a) (b) 617, 635, 805

*134–58* *PRAYERS OF THANKSGIVING*

*134* *For the Life and Teaching of Jesus Christ* **10**(a), **43**, **98–9** 607, 609, 619

*135–9* *For Food: Graces* **12**(b), **17** (b) (c), **85**, **89**(b) (c), **91**(a) (b) 641, 719

*140* *Friendship* **12**, **47**, **86**(c), **105** 609, 673, 674

*141–4* *General Thanksgiving* **12**(d), **70**(a), **85**(a) (b) (e) 635, 640, 661, 684, 805

*145* *For the Goodness of Other People* **4**(e), **9**(d), **61**(c), **87** (b) (e) 694, 714, 721–5, 755

*147–8* *For Homes* **8**(f), **31** 704, 705, 728, 771

*149–54* *For Life and the Gifts of Life* **15**(c), **19**(d), **49**(b) (c) (e), **85**(c), **106**(b) 609, 640, 655–656, 660–1, 686–7, 693, 701

*155* *Personal Thanksgiving and Penitence* **19**(d), **65**(a) (b) (d), **88**(a), **104**(b) 664, 753, 770

*156* *For the Saints* **22**(d), **84** 721–5

*157–8* *Thanksgiving for the School* **11**, **47**(d), **86–8**, **106**(b)

*159–88* *PRAYERS OF CONFESSION AND FORGIVENESS*

*159–61* *Absolution* **5**, **8**(c), **15**(f), **18**(a), **19**(d), **31**(c), **32**(f), **56**(b), **63**(d)

*162–4* *Assurance of Forgiveness* **5**, **8**(c), **15**(f), **18**(a), **19**(d), **31**(c), **32**(f), **56**(b), **63**(d), **73**(k), **82**(g), **95**(a) (b), **99**(c) (d) 658, 761, 771, 811

*165* *As We Forgive Them* **5**, **47**(c) 697, 708, 735, 751 (5), 779

*166–74* *Prayers of Confession* **4**(a) (b), **5**, **15**(f), **39**(b), **40**(a), **41**(d), **46**, **51**(b) (c), **61**(b), **73**(g) (h) (k), **97**(c), **104**(b) 658, 670–1, 679–80, 748

*175* *By the Cross* **46**, **55**(c) (d) (e), **56**(c), **57**(a) (b), **67**(f) 611–4

*176–80* *For Forgiveness, See Absolution and Assurance of Forgiveness*

*181* *Prayer of Repentance and Trust* **3**(g), **65**(b), **67**(a), **89**(a), **98**(c), **102**(e) 697

*182* *Sins* **15**(f), **32–6**, **51**(a–c), **73**(h), **82**(g) 670–1

*183* *Besetting Sins* **15**(f), **32–6**, **51**(a–c), **73**(h), **82**(g) 670–1

*184* *Thanksgiving for Forgiveness* **15**(a), **19**(f), **65**(d) (g), **77**(c), **82**(g), **97**(b) 679. 771

*185* *Time Wasted* **14**(e), **19**(c), **76**(a), **106**(b–d) 643, 669, 688, 739

*186–8* *Unkindness* **46**(c), **48**(d) (e), **55**(d), **100**(b), **105** 654, 690, 729

*189–204* *PRAYERS OF SELF-DEDICATION* **9**, **14**(d), **22**, **23**(a), **24–5**, **37–8**, **44**(f), **64**, **66**, **68** (c), **69**(d), **71**, **76**, **92–5**, **96** 610, 623, 618, 688, 694, 715, 721–5, 751, 761, 764

*202* 661

*203–4* *Possessions* **1**, **14**, **30**(d), **34**,

| | |
|---|---|
| | **36**(b) (d), **38**(c), **74**(a) 650, 737, 741, 766, 767 |
| *205–21* | *MORNING PRAYERS* 664, 688 |
| *206* | *Collect for Peace* **8**, **47**(a), **67**(g), **89**(d) 699, 786 |
| *207* | *God's Gift* **68**(c), **76**(a), **106**(b) 664 |
| *208–16* | *God's Presence and Guidance throughout the Day* **11**(a), **89**, **97**, **98**(c), **99**(e), **106**(b) (c) 620, 688 |
| *217* | *A Good Deed* **29**(b), **35**(c), **82**(e) 643, 723–4, 764 |
| *218–9* | *Thanksgiving and Dedication* **37**(d), **38**(e), **70**, **85**(a) (b) 668, 693 |
| *220* | *On Waking* 688 |
| *221* | *Blessing on Work* 688 |
| *222–37* | *EVENING PRAYERS* |
| *238–51* | *IN ACTIVITIES AND WORK* **34**(b), **38**(a), **61**(c), **68**(c), **73**(f), **81**(a), **82**(f), **86**(b), **87**(e), **97**(a), **102**(a), **106** 649, 655, 664, 669, 676, 681–2, 684, 687–9, 692–3, 695–6, 698, 776, 786, 801 |
| *238* | *Daily Life* |
| *239–40* | *For God's Grace and Help* **38**(a) |
| *241–3* | *Work* **106** 643 |
| *244* | *Work as Prayer* 655 |
| *245–7* | *Perseverance* 687, 695 |
| *248* | *Sense of Responsibility* 106 |
| *249* | *In Studies and Enquiries* **87**(a–f) |
| *282–315* | *THE CHURCH'S YEAR* |
| *250–1* | *The Use of Talents* 106 |
| *252–81* | *ATTITUDE TO AND RELATIONSHIP WITH OTHER PEOPLE* **13**, **47**, **82**(a) (e), **105** **121**(e), 674, 699, 703–14, 715–30, 721–5, 769 |
| *252–3* | *Against Barriers of Class, Race and Colour* **64**(d), **73** (e), **105**(b) 700, 711, 726, 729, 731, 733–6, 780, 802, 814 |
| *254* | *Caring for Old People* **31**(b) 703, 709 716, 719, 765 |
| *255* | *Caring about People* **13**(c), **73**(e) 677, 703, 709, 712, 715, 717, 719, 730, 764, 769, 775, 782, 801 |
| *256* | *Against Condemning Others* **21**(c), **82**(c) 701, 706, 751 (5), 790 |
| *257* | *For Courtesy* **12**(e), **21**(j) (k), **61**(e) 675, 712, 714, 769 |
| *258* | *Against Envy and Hatred* **32**(a), **100**(a) 701, 708, 710, 726, 751 (5) |
| *259–61* | *In Family Life* **8**(f), **31** 605, 704–5, 728(4–5), 825 |
| *262* | *Friendship* **11**(b), **73**(g), **86**(b) (c) 712, 720, 728(7–10) |
| 263 | *For Generosity* **1**(c), **32**(c), **34**(b), **55**(d), **85**(e) |
| *264* | *Human Understanding* **5**(a), **34**(c), **102**(d), **104**(c) 677, 690–1, 701, 712, 716–7, 782, 795 |
| *265–8* | *A Sense of International Brotherhood* **3**(b), **8**, **13**(a), **32**(f), **46**(c), **96**(d), **64**(d) 711, 726, 730, 750, 780 |
| *269* | *Kindness* **13**, **21**(j) (k), **29**(d), **76**(m), **102**(a), **105**(a) 706, 714, 717, 719 |
| *270–1* | *Love of Enemies* **5**(b–e), **102**(d) 706, 710, 751 |
| *272–4* | *Love of People* **56**(b), **63**(d) 701, 703, 709, 714, 716, 733, 769, 783, 797–9 |
| *275–6* | *Loyalty* **7**(c), **9**(c), **35**(f), **92** 720 |
| *277* | *Peace in Community* **11** 726, 733–6, 751 |
| *278* | *Responsibility* **97a**, **106** 707, 760 |
| *279* | *Sensitivity to Other People* **82**(e), **100**(d), **105**(c) 709, 711–2, 764 |
| *280–1* | *Towards Those Who Serve Us* **3**(d–g) 711, 769 |
| *282–6* | *Advent* **39**, **40**, **41** 605, 607, 631, 717 |
| *287–9* | *Christmas* **42–3** 606–7, 627, 631 |
| *290–1* | *Epiphany* **44** 609 |
| *292* | *Septuagesima* **45** 630, 631–632, 634–5, 637 |
| *293* | *Sexagesima* **46** 638, 671, 753–4, 777, 824 |
| *294* | *Quinquagesima* **47** 636, 705, 710, 711, 714, 728(7–10), 751, 784 |
| *295–6* | *Ash Wednesday and Lent* **48–55** 629, 675, 676, 678, 709 |
| *297–8* | *Palm Sunday and Holy Week* **50**(f), **53–6** 613–4 |
| *299–301* | *Good Friday* **57** 611–2, 614, 628 |

*302–4* *Easter* **58–9** 615–6, 628, 758–9
*305–8* *Ascension Day* **60** 609, 616–617
*309–13* *Whitsunday* **61–2** 618, 622, 746
*314–5* *Trinity* **63** 623, 648, 668
*316–46* *SAINT'S DAYS*
*316–7* *St. Andrew* **64** 618, 721–2, 724
*318–9* *St. Thomas* **65** 619, 646–7, 746
*320* *The Conversion of St. Paul* **66–7** 629, 665, 723
*321* *The Presentation of Christ in the Temple (The Purification of the Blessed Virgin Mary)* **68** 697, 721
*322* *St. Matthias* **69**
*323* *The Annunciation of the Blessed Virgin Mary* **70** 605, 634–5
*324* *St. George* **71** 723
*325* *St. Mark* **72**
*326* *St. Philip and St. James* **73** 626–7 719
*327–8* *St. Barnabus* **74** 667, 721–2, 725, 733–6
*329* *St. John Baptist* **75** 618, 716
*330–1* *St. Peter* **76** 618–20, 711
*332* *St. Mary Magdalen* **77** 615–616
*333* *St. James the Apostle* **78** 725, 749
*334* *St. Matthew* **79** 628
*335* *St. Michael and All Angels* **80** 672
*336* *St. Luke* **82** 711, 716–7, 720–1, 723 (2), 724
*337* *St. Simon and St. Jude* **83** 627
*338–9* *All Saint's Day* **84** 672, 706, 712
*340* *All Soul's Day* **84**(f) (g) (i) 758–60
*341* *Saints, Martyrs and Missionaries of the Church of England* **84** 625
*342* *A Martyr* **22** 612, 742, 747, 750
*343* *A Bishop* **97**(e)
*344–5* *A Christian Teacher* **67** 654, 656, 723(3)
*346* *A Missionary* **25** 721–5
*347–357* *CHURCH AND STATE OCCASIONS*
*347–8* *Before a Confirmation* **23–4, 61–2** 618–9, 722, 784
*349–53* *Approach to the Eucharist* **16–17** 619, 621, 623–4, 823
*354* *Before a General Election* **4**(a), (b) (c) (g), **8**(a) (e), **39** 727, 737–8, 740–1
*355* *Remembrance Day* **2**(a) (c), **15**(a) 752–3, 757–60, 810
*356* *At the Laying of a Wreath on Remembrance Sunday* 757
*357* *Before the Study of Scripture*
*358–65* *SCHOOL TERM*
*358–60* *At the Beginning of Term* **11, 47**(d) (e), **86** 649, 651–3, 657
*361* *At the End of Term* **88** 675–676, 756
*362* *At the End of Term (or Week)* **88** 675–676, 756
*363* *On Founder's Day* **87**
*364* *After a Short Holiday* **14**(d), **18**(d), **21**(j) 620, 635, 640
*365* *For the Remainder of the Term* **14**(d), **18**(d), **21**(j) 620, 635, 640
*366–78* *FEELINGS, SENSES, FACULTIES*
*366* *Sorrow* **2**(d) (e), **67**(b), **95**(c), **98**(a) 614, 742, 747, 749
*367* *Success* **87, 106**(e) 629, 788
*368* *Suffering* **9**(a) (d) (e) (f), **95**(c) 614, 742, 747 ,749
*369* *Tragedy and Bereavement* **2**(a) (c), **84**(f–i) 752
*370–1* *Hearing* **98**(d) 608, 681–3
*372* *Hunger and Food* **14**(d), **28**(a), **49**(b) (c), **99**(c), **103**(a) 641, 715, 718–9
*373* *Sight* **76**(d), **98**(e), **102**(a) (d) 640(2), 642, 672, 684, 685–7
*374–5* *Speech* **7**(f), **9**(d), **35**(a), (d), **69**(c), **73**(g), **98**(d), **100**(c) 608, 682, 731
*376–8* *Words* **7**(f), **9**(d), **35**(a) (d), **69**(c), **73**(g), **98**(d), **100**(c) 608, 682, 731
*379–443* *CONCERNING VIRTUES, VICES AND VALUES*
*379* *Boldness* **3**(c), **76**(l) (m)(n), **92, 94** 686–7, 690–1, 723 (3), 819
*380* *Cheer* **9**(c), **67**(g), **70**(e) 640, 664, 727, 787

*381–5* *Courage* **9**(c) (d) (e), **22, 24, 71, 81**(d), **91–2, 94** 607, 620 677, 690–3, 695–6, 720, 723–724, 747–8, 751

*386* *Detachment* **1, 14, 36** 625, 650, 666, 676, 740–1, 810

*387* *Freedom* **12**(d), **38**(c), **76**(r) 640, 657, 663, 697–9, 744, 786, 808, 812

*388–90* *Generosity* **1**(d) (e), **12**(e), **19**(d), **30**(d), **55**(d) 667, 711, 768, 805

*391* *Gladness* **21**(a), **77**(b) (c) (d) 639–40, 727–8, 809

*392–4* *Gratitude* **27**(f), **70**(a) (c), **85** 615–6, 642, 787

*395* *High Purpose and Lofty Aspiration* **4, 7, 12**(e), **26, 99**(e) 646, 669 676, 722, 800

*396–7* *Honesty* **2**(b), **21**(d), **34, 100** (c) 646, 651, 707, 766, 781, 792, 796

*398–401* *Humility* **3, 38**(e), **47**(c), **56** (b), **67**(f) 652, 670–1, 689, 788, 791

*402* *Sense of Humour* **21**(d) (e), **29**(d), **102**(b) (d) 609

*403* *Hypocrisy* **6**(e), **18**(c), **21**(f), **32**(d), **35**(c), **97**(a) 670–1, 766, 807

*404* *Idle Pleasures* **14**(e), **26, 93** 625, 661, 663, 666, 812, 822

*405* *Independence* **13**(a) (b), **29** (d), **91–3** 675, 677, 819

*406–8* *Jealousy* **1**(e), **19**(c), **21**(c), **32**(a), **36, 55**(c) 763, 767, 824

*409* *Knowledge* **87** 646, 656

*410* *Love of Life* **14**(b), **45, 63**(d) 623, 633, 635, 640, 658, 660, 673–4, 693

*411–2* *Attitude to Money* **1**(e), **14, 34, 36**(b) (c) (d), **74, 85**(e), **106**(b) 650, 737, 740, 741 767

*413* *Open-mindedness* **29, 55**(b), **98**(d) (e) 645–6, 817

*414* *For Patience* **9, 73**(j) 616, 779, 716

*415* *For Peace* **8, 53**(a), **73**(j) (k), **77, 98**(c) 651–2, 726–7

*416* *Against Pride* **1**(d), **3, 104**(b) 682, 689, 815

*417* *For Purity* **4, 7, 33** 615–6, 678–80

*418* *Faith in the Right* **3**(c), **4**(c), **91–4** 691, 706, 723–4, 824

*419–20* *Against Selfishness* **1**(b), **14** (f), **20**(e) 625, 667, 703, 713, 717, 784

*421* *Mastery of Self* **6**(a), **46**(d), **91–4, 106**(b) (c) 653, 692, 812

*422–3* *For True Self-esteem* **6**(a), **46**(d), **91–4** 653, 692–6

*424* *A Sense of Proportion* **21**(e), (f) (g) (h) (i), **102** (g) 629, 656, 661–3

*425* *For Sensitivity to Goodness* **3**(d), **19, 28**(a), **99**(c) (d), **100**(d) 683–5, 701, 714

*426* *For Serenity* **77, 81**(b) (d), **82**(f) 647, 651, 727, 742, 779, 803

*427–8* *Single-mindedness* **4, 7, 24, 51**(d), **71, 76**(e), **82**(a) (b), **103**(d) 675–6, 724–5, 728, 737

*429* *That We May Help the Deaf* **13, 98**(d) 608, 681–3, 717

*430* *Strength in Weakness* **46**(d) (e), **54, 56**(b), **89, 98, 102**(g) 607, 620–1, 687, 690–1, 742

*431* *Tact* **3**(d), **11, 12**(e) 642

*432* *Trust* **11**(b) (c), **35**(e), **76**(g), **81**(c), **86**(b) (c) 706, 712, 714

*433–5* *Truth* **35, 55**(b), **69**(c), **73**(g) **76**(g) (h) 646, 662, 707, 796

*436–7* *Unselfishness* **8**(d) (f), **12**(a), (e), **13, 31**(b), **61**(e) **73** 607, 667, 702, 703, 728

*438–9* *A sense of values* **3**(a), **26, 31**(d), **51, 92, 102**(g) 739, 740, 741, 766, 767

*440* *Technology* **26**(e), **45**(e) 630, 635, 643

*441* *The World* **1**(b), **14, 26**(a) (e) (f), **36**(b), (c) (d), **73**(h), **85**(c) 632, 659, 660, 661, 718, 720

*442* *Worry* **14**(d), **21**(a), **81**(d), **102**(e) 621, 640

*443* *Zeal* **7, 62**(b), **74, 85**(d), **90, 96**(a) (b), **106** 626, 669, 693

*444–8* *COME CLOSE, O GOD* **12**(c), **17, 20**(f), **39**(c), **58**(e), **60**(b), **67**(a), **70**(b), **90**(f), **97**(b)(c) 620, 621, 647, 651, 687

*444* **47**(b) 691

*445* **66**(b) 659

*446* **37**(a), **87**(a) (f) 642

*447* **62**(b), **75**(g) 622

*448* **9**(f), **38**(d), **89**(c) 751

*449–460* *GRACE TO KNOW AND DO THE WILL OF GOD* **19, 20, 21, 37, 38, 44**(f), **61**(e), **62**(c) (d), **67**(a), **71, 76, 89** 618, 642, 645, 646, 647, 665, 680, 683

*461–74* *SPIRITUAL GIFTS*

*461* *Increase of Faith* **19, 47**(e), **50**(c), **82**(c), **102**(c), **103**(c), **104** 607, 612, 648, 789

*462* *Good Works* **6**(e), **82**(a), **102** (f), **106**(d) 618, 629, 769

*463–5* *Grace* **67**(a), **71, 80**(a), **99**(c) (d) 656, 657, 662

*466–7* *The Light of Christ* **38**(d), **43** (e), **44, 39, 102**(a) 642, 683, 684, 685, 686–7, 694, 785

*467* 653, 654

*468* *The Love of God* **9**(f), **12**(b), **13**(e), **15**(c) (d) (e) (f), **47, 56**(b), **67**(b), **77**(c) (d), **97** 615, 673, 784, 786

*469* *Mercy* **5, 6, 96**(c), **104**(d) 651, 662, 673

*470* *Protection* **3**(c), **89, 92, 94, 97**(d), **99**(e) 621, 691

*471* *Revelation* **10, 19**(c), **27**(a), **37**(a), **40**(d), **58**(c) 645, 646, 647, 648, 658, 659, 672, 685, 778

*472* *Strength* **24**(a) (b), **91, 92**(i), **94, 99**(d) (e) 620, 648, 687, 690, 691, 778

*473* *True Religion* **12**(c), **20**(c), **27, 30**(a), **52**(c), **97**(d), **103** (b) 657, 777

*474* *Trust* **19, 53**(e), **76**(b), **99**(e), **102**(c) 620, 621, 651, 673

*475–81* *JESUS CHRIST*

*475* *Why is reality about you so shocking to us, Lord?* **48**(e), **50**(f), **57** 611. 612

*476* *You're hanging on a cross again, Jesus* **15**(c) (d) (e) 611

*477–80* *Friendship and Discipleship* **3**(e) (f), **4**(g), **5**(d) (e), **8**(c), **9**(f), **12**(c), **18**(d), **24, 25, 37, 38, 67**(a) (e), **74, 96** 607, 613, 724

*481* *The Service of Christ* **3**(e) (f), **4**(g), **5**(d) (e), **8**(c), **9**(f), **12**(c), **18**(d), **24, 25, 37, 38, 67**(a) (e), **74, 96** 607, 613, 724

*482–7* *TRUE RESPONSE TO GOD* **4, 12**(c) (d), **16**(e), **19, 40**(d) 627, 643, 657, 658, 663, 668, 688, 697, 709, 719, 720, 793–4

*483* **37**(d), **65**(c)

*484* **44**(e)

*485* **65**(b)

*486* **15**(d), **99**(e) 646

*487* **16**(e), **68**(c), **96**(a)

*488–536* *ALL SORTS AND CONDITIONS OF MEN AND CREATURES*

*488* **66**(d), **76**(m), **104**(a) (b)

*489* *Animals and Pets* **20**(d), **45** (b), **96**(d) 636, 639

*490* *Atomic Power* **45**(b), **93, 95** 643, 698, 753, 754, 755, 763

*491* *Birds* **20**(d) 639

*492* *Children* **3**(d), **6**(b), **24**(b) (c) (d), **31**(a), **37**(a) (e) 715, 725, 728, 729, 734–6, 775

*493* *Children who are Deaf* **3**(d), **6**(e), **19**(e), **81**(a), **98**(d) 608, 682, 725

*494* *Children who are Destitute* **3** (d), **6**(b), **97** 713, 715, 723, 724 (2) and (6), 725, 728

*495* *Children in Other Countries* 723, 724, 725

*496* *Christian Aid* **4**(g), **13**(d), **38** (c) (e) 713, 716, 718, 719, 720, 724, 725, 769

*497–8* *For the Dead* **15**(c) (f), **84** (a–e) (f–i), **97**(b) 615, 752

*499* *Schools for the Deaf* **81**(a), **98**(a) 608, 682, 725

*500* *For Disarmament* **8**(a), **39, 41**(a–d) 753, 754, 755, 803, 810

*501* *Government* **3**(b), **4, 8**(a), **20, 39, 97**(a) 803

*502* *Local Government* **3**(b), **4, 8**(a), **20, 39, 97**(a) 803

*503* *Great Men and Women* **4, 7** (e), **8**(a), **11**(c), **24**(a) (e), **41**(c), **97**(a) 694

*505* *For the Handicapped* **6, 13, 19**(b) (e), **76**(m), **81**(a), **98** (a) (d) (e) 608, 642, 644, 681, 687, 715–7, 776

506–8 *Our Homes* **8**(f), **12**(e), **31** 605, 634, 653–4, 671, 704, 705
509 *Hospitals* **13**, **39**(a), **59**(a) (b), **81**(a), **98**(a) (b) (d) (e) 644, 683, 684, 715, 717
510–2 *Those who Mourn* **2**, **84** 752, 759
513–4 *The Nation* **39**, **84**(c), **90**(f), **92**, **93**, **95** 804
515–8 *Those in Need, Distress and Suffering* **2**, **5**, **6**, **13**, **47**, **73** (d) (f), **77**, **81**(a), **97**, **98**, **99**, **105** 713, 715, 716, 717, 725, 730, 749, 758, 759, 765
519 *Old People* **21**(g), **76**(k) (p) 713, 715, 765
520–3 *Peace of the World* **3**(b), **8**(a), **39**, **40**(a) 753, 757, 772
524 *The Police* **11**(c), **20**(b) (c), **21**
525 *The Queen and Parliaments* **11** (c), **21**, **97**
526 *The Queen and Royal Family* **11**(c), **21**, **97**
527 *Race and Colour* **3**(b), **8**(d), **82**(e), **96**, **102**(d) 729, 730, 731, 733–6
528 *Scientists* **87** 643, 650, 694
529–30 *Those at Sea* **8**(b), **81**(d) 696
531–2 *Sick People* **6**, **13**, **19**(a) (b) (c) (e), **39**(a), **59**(a) (b), **81** (a), **98**(a) (d) (e) 644, 683, 715–7, 749
533 *For those who have sinned against us or we against them* **2**(c), **5**, **77**(a) (c) (d) **95**(a), **104**(c) (d), 610, 614, 657, 736, 751
534 *Universities, Colleges and Schools* **62**(c) (d), **87**, **97**(a), **102**(g) 675
535 *Workers by Night* **76**(m) 763
536 *The World* **39**, **53**(a) (b), **87** (f), **95**(c) 658, 772
537–47 *PRAYERS FOR THE CHURCH* **12**(d), **18**, **27**(c), **30**(a) (c), **52**(a), **62**, **69**(a), **74**, **76**(a) (c) (e) (q) (v), **81**(b) (c), **84** (a), **89**, **90**, **97** 626, 627
541 *Clergy and People* **12**(d), **18**, **27**(c), **30**(a) (c), **52**(a), **62**, **69**(a), **74**, **76**(a) (c) (e) (q) (v), **81**(b) (c), **84**(a), **89**, **90**, **97** 626, 627
542 *A Parish* **12**(d), **18**, **27**(c), **30** (a) (c), **52**(a), **62**, **69**(a), **74**, **76**(a) (c) (e) (q) (v), **81**(b) (c), **84**(a), **89**, **90**, **97** 626, 627
543–5 *The Spread of the Gospel* **18** (c), **23**, **25**, **27**(c), **44**(d), **59** (a), **82**(d), **102**(a), **103**(a) (b) (c) 626, 627, 724
546–7 *The Unity of all Christian People* **8**(c) (d) (e) (f), **47**(d) (e), **61** (c) (d)
548–60 *PRAYERS FOR THE SCHOOL AND ITS MEMBERS PAST AND PRESENT* **11**, **12**, **86**, **87**, **88**, **97**, **102**(b) (d) (f) (g), **103**, **104**, **105**, **106**
548 *The Governors*
549 *Those Holding Office*
550–1 *A House*
552–3 *Those Leaving*
554 *Those Leaving or who have Left*
555 *Mutual Responsibility* **11**(c), **86**(c)
556 *An old Member of the School*
557 *Old Members of the School*
558–9 *The School*
560 *A Special School Effort*
561 *A Litany of Caring* **6**, **13**, **21** (c), **47**, **73**(d) (e) (f), **105** 677, 712, 714, 720
562 *A Litany of Dedication* **106**(b) 665, 666, 679, 694
563 *Evening Penitence* **5**(d), **73** (k), **76**(g) (h), **82**(c) (g) 610, 614
564 *A Litany of Forgiveness and Help* **5**(a) (d) (e), **46**(d) (e) 629, 663
565 *An Act of Intercession* **73**(j), (k), **102**(e), **104**(a) (b) 621
566 *A Litany to Jesus Part 1* **3**(f), **55**(d) (e), **56**(b) (c), **57**(a) 613, 614, 617, 619
567 *A Litany for People Who Work* **28**(d), **34**(b) (c), **38**(a), **106** (e) 643, 655, 694–6, 773–4
568 *For People who Suffer* **2**, **6**, **13**, **64**(d), **105**(a) 642, 676, 716, 723–4, 728, 730, 749
569 *Litany For Ourselves* **11**(a), **73**(j), **89**
570 *A Litany of Reconciliation* **5**, **47**, **104**(c) (d) 629, 740, 750, 757

*571* *A Litany of Remembrance* **5** (**b**), **6, 13, 47** 715, 724

*572* *A Litany for Right Values* **1** (**b**), **14, 26, 36, 90–4, 102** 719, 741, 767–8

*573* *The Way of Christ: A Litany* **12**(e), **48, 49, 99**(e) 645

*574* *A Litany for Wisdom* **62**

*575* *Blacks and Whites make me angry, Lord* **13**(**c**) 700, 731, 814

*576* *Conformity to the Life of Jesus* **3**(**f**), **22**(a), **23**(**d**) 611, 612

*577* *A Prayer of Discipleship* **24–5, 37–8, 63**(a), **83**(a)

*578* *Help in Life* **12**(**e**), **35**(c)

*579* *An Extended Version of the Lord's Prayer* **7, 52, 102**(e)

*580* *All* **10**(**b**), **69**. **73**(e), **91, 103** (**d**) 721, 722

*581* *Lord, I have Time* **26**(**e**), **28, 51, 78**(**a**), **106**(b) 688

*582* *Solitude* **6, 13, 105**(a) 642

*583* *Speech* **21**(**d**), **35, 73**(g) 731, 813

*584* *There are Two Loves Only* **21** (**j**), **47, 55, 56, 66**(e), **67**(a) 674, 703, 720, 743

*585* *The Hospital* **57, 81** (a), **75**(**f**), **98**(a) 715

*586* *The Pornographic Magazine* **7**(**b**) (**f**), **33, 47, 73**(**h**), **77**(a) (**c**) 681

*587* *The Sins of Society* **92, 93, 98**(**b**), **102**(a) 643, 739

*588* *To Love—The Prayer Of The Adolescent* **7**(**f**), **33**(e), **21** (j) (**k**) 728 (7–10)

*589–91* *After Other Prayers*

*592–604* *After Worship*

# Reading Index


605 Jesus and his Mother **42**(e), **43**(e), **70**(e) *149, 259, 260, 283, 285*

606 The Oxen **42**(g) *287, 288, 289*

607 Here is a Man **40**(d), **56**(b), **76**(e) *282, 315, 382, 430, 436, 461, 479*

608 The Tongue of the Dumb (1–2) **98**(d) *370, 371, 374, 376, 429, 493, 499, 505, 583*

609 What Jesus Concealed **98**(a), **100**(a), **101**(b) *140, 149, 198, 264, 306, 402*

610 I am the Man **56**(c), **78**(c) *142, 189, 192, 193, 212*

611 The Death of Jesus Christ **5**(b), **57**(b) *299, 300, 301, 475, 576*

612 The Killing 819 **5**(b), **57**(b) *299, 300, 301, 461, 476, 479*

613 Pieta **43**(b), **58**(a) *175, 297, 477, 479, 480*

614 Gentle Christ **57**(a) (b) *297, 299, 300, 301, 366, 368*

615 Easter Hymn—to St. Mary Magdalen 818 **19**(d), **55**(d), **77**(b) *302, 303, 304, 392, 417, 419, 420, 468.*

616 Interviewing Mary Magdala (1–6) 818, 820 **19**(d), **55**(d), **77**(a) (b) (c) (d) *392, 417, 419, 420, 421, 423, 468, 485, 487*

617 Lord of the Dance 815 **5**(b), **97**(d), **101**(d) *125, 133, 208, 286, 289, 306, 311*

618 Jesus Christ his Terrible Demands 816 **5**(d), **21**(a) (i) *210, 263, 286, 379, 459, 474, 566, 577*

619 Can it be True **56**(a), **58**(b) (d) *119, 134, 315, 350, 351*

620 'I say my prayers when it's calm . . .' **19**(e), **98**(c), **102**(c) *381, 430, 444, 472, 474, 486*

621 When a Prayer Might Save You 798 **73**(k), **102**(c), **104**(b) *381, 430, 444, 470, 472, 474, 486*

622 Whitsunday 783, 799 **61**(a), **62**(b) (e) *309, 310, 311, 312, 313*

623 Worship 797 **63**(a) *312, 313, 315, 410*

624 Do This in Remembrance of Me **16**(e), **17**(b) (e) *349, 350, 351, 352, 353*

625 Light in the Asphalt Jungle (*1–7*) **6**(c) (e), **13**(d), **14**(c) *294, 382, 383, 384, 385, 386, 419, 421, 436, 437*

626 The Apathy of the Church **25**(b) (c), **26**(f) *248, 250, 379, 443, 481, 539*

627 Bringing Life to the Church **47**(d) (e), **67**(d) *481, 482, 539, 545*

628 Talleyrand's Advice 800 **58**(c), **59**(a) (d) *301, 302, 303 304*

629 The Devil Wore a Crucifix **48**(d), **52**(a) (c) *461, 462, 463, 464, 564, 570*

630 In the Beginning **45**(c) (d) (e) *116, 117, 118, 120, 122, 124, 132*

631 Carol 783 **43**(a), **45**(a), **59**(e) *116, 117, 121, 286, 289*

632 Spring Sowing **45**(b), **49**(a) (b), **85**(c) *120, 123, 124, 128, 441, 471*

633 The Force that Through the Green Fuse Drives the Flower 784, 794 **45**(c), **49**(e), **85**(a) *116, 117, 121, 124, 130, 132*

634 Birth (1–2) **31**(d), **41**(e), **70**(c) (e) *116, 117, 120, 121, 125, 127, 132, 142*

635 I thank You God for most this amazing **63**(b), **65**(c), **70**(a) *116, 118 120, 121, 125, 126, 127, 133*

636 A Dog in the Quarry **47**(b), **53**(d), **63**(d) *116, 117, 118, 119, 125, 126, 127, 489*

637 Storm over the Orkney Islands **8**(b), **65**(c) *117, 121, 124, 130, 131, 529, 530*

638 God's Grandeur **8**(c), **46**(d), **49**(d), **85**(c) *117, 118, 120, 123, 129, 132*

639 For Birds **18**(a), **20**(c), **39**(a), **45**(d) *116, 118, 120, 124, 491*

640 A Shepherd's Life (1–2) **97**(a) (b) (d) *117, 119, 120, 123 124, 131, 149, 193, 195*

641 *from* Bread and the Stars 783, 810 **16**(c), **17**(a) (e), **99**(d) *117, 120, 127, 135, 136, 210. 286, 351, 353, 372.*

642 A Solitude **15**(a) (c), **21**(k) *373, 375, 394, 431, 446, 453, 466, 505. 568, 582*

643 Eden **21**(i), **45**(a), **106**(b) *145, 185, 196, 198, 200, 217, 243, 567, 587*

644 Hospital for Defectives **2**(e), **3**(d), **6**(d) *255, 269, 281, 505, 509, 518, 531*

645 A Buddhist's Faith **12**(b), **21**(h) (j) *192, 202, 244, 413, 452, 456, 573*

646 Look at the Facts 803 **35**(c), **87**(b) (c) *395, 409, 450, 451, 456*

647 Amen **14**(d), **15**(b), **87**(f) *426, 445, 448, 454, 459, 471, 566*

648 God as Our Father **15**(e), **27**(a), **45**(a) *210, 461, 465, 466, 467, 471, 472*

649 Don't be a Lazy Bum **106**(b) (c) (d) *238, 241, 242, 243, 245, 246, 250*

650 Gods Made with Hands (1–3), 802 **26**(a) (b) (c) (d) (e) (f) *165, 166, 172, 173, 174, 176, 190, 195, 201, 202, 203, 386, 411, 412*

651 Trust in God 778, 801 **19**(e) (f), **38**(a) (b) *444, 447, 448, 465, 466, 467, 469, 474*

652 Playing it Cool **31**(c), **32**(b) (c) *277, 399, 400, 415, 416, 421, 426*

653 A Child's Character **31**(a), **102**(f), **103**(b) *219. 240, 248, 250, 278*

654 The Pain of Growing Up **5**(c), **9**(f), **67**(b) *186, 187, 188, 189, 190, 193, 197, 198*

655 Building a Boat **64**(a) *154, 193, 195, 198, 567*

656 The Meaning of Life **39**(c), **98**(e) *112, 194, 202, 215, 409, 445*

657 Heaven and Hell 773 **66**(b), **67**(a), **68**(c) *255, 258, 259, 262, 266, 277, 281, 456, 533*

658 A Girl Listening to Music (1–2) **13**(e), **98**(b), **102**(g) *145, 176, 410, 452, 471, 479, 482, 483, 536*

659 The Mountains Lead to God **65**(c), **102**(e), **103**(b) *410, 441, 446, 448, 449, 471*

660 Dying of Thirst in the Desert **20**(a), **65**(e) (f), **99**(c) *120, 149, 207, 387, 410, 441*

661 How to Enjoy the World (1–3) **12**(b) (c) (d) (e) *117, 120, 128, 149, 197, 266, 273, 441*

662 Reality 784 **12**(b), **42**(i), **44**(a) *432, 445, 461, 463, 466, 469*

663 Pleasure 793 **41**(a) (c), **85**(a) *129, 194, 387, 484, 486, 487*

664 How to Waste Wisely my Days **12**(a) (c), **14**(a) *122, 128, 142, 155, 207, 212, 380*

665 Kicking at Our Destiny **14**(d), **106**(a) *457, 461, 465, 472, 484, 562*

666 Getting what We Want **82**(b) *169, 458, 465, 479, 483, 562*

667 Giving 796 **14**(c) (d) (e) *263, 388, 389, 390, 419, 420, 421, 436, 437*

668 Thanksgiving for the Soul (1–2) 794 **15**(b), **39**(b), **59**(f) *189, 218, 309, 311, 315, 386*

669 Energy **106**(b) (c) *185, 241, 247, 250, 311, 395, 428, 443*

670 Self-Satisfaction **104**(b) *165, 398, 400, 401, 403*

671 The Whole Trouble—Original Sin **46**(a), **102**(d) *160, 165, 170, 173, 183, 398, 399, 403*

672 Happiness and Vision 785 **14**(d), **63**(a) (b), **98**(e) *120, 130, 373, 466, 467, 471*

673 Love, Hope and Faith 814 **58**(d), **59**(e), **61**(d) *192, 194, 410, 461, 468, 469, 474, 480, 522*

674 Human Beings without Love 813 **61**(d), **63**(d) *192, 194, 198, 410, 584*

675 The Idealism of Youth 821 **4**(d), **7**(b), **94**(b) *381, 387, 395, 427. 428, 466, 484, 522*

676 Ideals **1**(d), **7**(c), **11**(d) *201, 382, 386, 395, 427, 472, 568*

677 Man Afire in Street Ignored **4**(g), **6**(e), **102**(f), **105**(a) *193, 200, 253, 255, 269, 273, 561*

678 Self-Denial 815 **4**(a) (f), **7**(d) *189, 190, 194, 195, 197. 199, 201*

679 Getting away from Sin **3**(g), **9**(f), **11**(a), **12**(c) *168, 169, 183, 184, 189, 192, 562, 577*

680 Conscience 821 **4**(b) (e), **11**(c), **14**(f) *449, 450, 454, 456, 457, 459*

681 Thanksgiving for the Body (1–2) **15**(e), **45**(a) (b), **47**(d), **97**(b) *137, 371, 373, 376, 429, 505, 586*

682 Deafness (1–2) **81**(a), **98**(a) (d), **100**(c) *370, 371, 374, 376, 377, 378, 429, 493, 499, 505*

683 The Fifth Sense **81**(a), **98**(a) (b) (d) *370, 371, 429, 505, 509, 531, 532*

684 My New Eyes **81**(a), **97**(b), **98**(a) (b), **99**(e) *373, 466, 467, 505, 509, 532*

685 Blind and Seeing 786 **15**(d), **50**(c), **62**(c) *124, 128, 373, 466, 471*

686 A Blind Girl Pot-Holing 787 **61**(c), **62**(e), **63**(c) *117, 120, 129, 373, 386, 471*

687 A Blind Girl Climbing (1–2) 786 **67** (b) (g), **73**(j), **76**(b), **87**(g) *246, 373, 379, 430, 444, 472, 474, 505*

688 Look Well to this Day **86**(a), **102** (g), **105**(c) *185, 189, 221, 238, 561, 581*

689 A Cricketer's Pride 782 **3**(d) (e) (f) *165, 183, 398, 399, 400, 401, 416*

690 The Bully 782 **3**(a) (b) (c) *151, 238, 240, 243, 246, 247, 430*

691 The Bully and the Preacher's Son **3** (g), **53**(a), **87**(g), **88**(a) *192, 238, 240, 243, 430, 444, 456, 470*

692 The Conquest of Everest (1–2) **52** (a), **65**(e) (f), **73**(j) *130, 205, 240, 246, 251, 384, 393, 428.*

693 On Top of Everest (1–2) **62**(e), **65** (c), **85**(a), **87**(b) (e) *132, 218, 238, 247, 394, 410, 430, 443, 470*

694 Madame Curie Prepares Pure Radium (1–3) **62**(c) (d), **63**(b), **87**(b) (e) *116, 118, 124, 145, 149, 150, 503, 528, 562, 567*

695 The First Four-Minute Mile **61**(e), **87**(e) *189, 196, 240, 246. 247, 428, 443, 567*

696 Sailing in all Weathers 788 **48**(b), **76**(b), **89**(a) *240, 246, 421, 529, 530, 567*

697 God Made Man to be Free 792 **61** (b), **66**(d), **67**(c) *168, 170, 175, 192, 194, 197, 252, 253, 265*

698 The Freedom of Man, His Lordship Over Nature **45**(e), **20**(e), **106**(d) *122, 132, 142, 149, 268, 387, 490*

699 Freedom and my Neighbour **13**(d), **61**(e), **96**(d), **105**(a) *252, 253, 254, 255, 261, 263, 387*

700 Black and White Masks **21**(a) (i), **22**(b), **37**(f) *252, 253, 255, 265, 266, 267, 274, 281, 575*

701 Praise God for Coffee Bars **39**(a), **43**(d), **44**(d), **64**(d) *270, 271, 273, 274, 279, 281*

702 Freedom and Faith **7**(b), **9**(e), **25** (e), **37**(d) *192, 197, 198, 311, 436, 443*

703 Generations' Sin 774 **11**(b), **13**(a) (b) (c), **102**(a) *294, 388, 419, 421, 436, 568, 584*

704 My Father Never Beat Us 779 **8**(f), **12**(e), **31**(a) (c) (d) *147, 148, 259, 260, 261, 277, 399, 425*

705 My Mother **31**(a) (d), **47**(e), **68** (b), **82**(f) *147, 148, 259, 260, 261, 277, 399, 425*

706 Faith in People (1–2) 795 **7**(a) (f), **8**(e) (f), **9**(a), **12**(a), **13**(d), **73**(g) *279, 281, 418, 427, 432, 464, 472*

707 Stealing the Chocolate 781 **1**(e), **20**(b), **34**(a) (b) (c) *396, 397, 432, 433, 435, 472*

708 A Poison Tree **32**(b) (c) (d) (e) (f) *168, 170, 172, 180, 192, 198, 266*

709 Standing in the Rain **13**(d), **38**(c), **40**(a), **41**(d), **48**(a) *253, 255, 263, 265, 272, 273, 274*

710 Prisoners 804 **5**(a), **32**(e) (f), **53**(b) *252, 253, 255, 263, 264, 265, 266, 269, 279*

711 When I Needed a Neighbour **13**(c) (d), **22**(a), **37**(a) *253, 255, 263, 269, 281, 388, 389, 390*

712 Aristocracy of the Spirit **7**(e), **11**(b) **13**(c) (d), **37**(c) *256, 258, 272, 273, 274, 279, 561*

713 Indifference 822 **5**(b) (e), **21**(k), **37**(e), **40**(d) *193, 196, 200. 419, 494, 496, 517, 519, 521*

714 Kindness 775 **47**(b) (c) (e), **63** (d) *149, 193, 197, 380, 389, 419, 421, 521*

715 Orphans of All Ages (1–4) **5**(a), **6**(c), **13**(a) (b) (c) (e), **15**(d), **73**(d), **81**(a), **82**(e) *193, 254, 281, 372, 421, 487, 492, 494, 505, 509, 517, 519, 531, 532, 571, 585*

716 Life with the Dossers 811 **75**(f), **76**(a), **82**(b) (d) (e) *193, 419, 496, 505, 515, 517, 521, 532, 568*

717 A Human Experiment (1–2) 776, 811 **82**(e) (f), **84**(c), **98**(a), **99**(e) *193, 198, 281, 419, 421, 429, 505, 509, 515, 531, 532*

718 The Mahratta Ghats **1**(c) (d), **99** (a), **103**(b) *197, 263, 266, 273, 281, 372, 441, 496*

719 Feed Us Now, O Son of God **6**(d) (e), **93**(a) (b) (c) *200, 273, 281, 372, 388, 421, 487, 496, 572*

720 Help in the Himalayas (1–5) **3**(e), **4**(g), **6**(d) (e), **81**(a), **82**(b) (f), **96**(a) (b) (c) (d), **97**(a) (c) *194, 197, 200, 255, 263, 266, 268, 273, 281, 421, 441, 487, 496, 561, 584*

721 Schweitzer and Self-Sacrifice 812 **9**(b), **97**(d), **102**(f), **103**(d) *189, 198, 253, 263, 268, 281, 386, 580*

722 Danilo Dolci in the Steps of St. Francis **19**(b), **25**(b) (d) (f) *238, 242, 250, 294, 372, 383, 395, 421, 580*

723 A Preacher among Teenagers in New York (1–4) 777 **25**(a) (d), **37**(b) (f), **66**(b) (c) (d) (e), **67**(b) (c) (e), **71** (a) *192, 196, 208, 215, 217, 240, 245, 248, 294, 382, 383, 384, 385, 401, 447, 494, 568*

724 A Christian Missionary in China (1–6) **71**(a), **73**(c) (f), **76**(m) (n) (p) (q) (r), **83**(b) (c), **84**(e), **88**(b) *192, 197, 198, 208, 215, 217, 240, 245, 248, 379, 421, 430, 455, 494, 496, 566, 568, 571*

725 Helping the Homeless Children of Naples (1–7) 817 **89**(a) (b) (c) (d) (e), **98**(a) (b) (d) (e), **102**(d) (e) (f) (g), **103**(c) *192, 197, 198, 215, 217, 240, 246, 248, 421, 465, 492, 493, 494, 495, 496, 499, 515, 517*

726 I Dream a World 822 **39**(a), **84**(d), **90**(f), **103**(a), **105**(c) *253, 255, 256, 264, 265, 266, 267, 268, 387*

727 The Serene People **15**(f), **39**(d), **65**(g), **76**(e), **88**(a) *253, 254, 255, 264, 266, 269, 380, 391, 426*

728 A Girl in Hiding (1–3, 6) **9**(a) (f), **18**(a), **22**(d), **53**(b), **60**(d), **94**(a) (b) *387, 415, 492, 494, 496, 517, 518, 522, 568*

A Girl in Hiding (cont.) (4–5) **8**(f), **31** (a) (d) *148, 259, 260, 261, 277, 388*

A Girl in Hiding (cont.) (7–10) **47**(a) (b), **67**(c), **97**(b) *380, 388, 391, 392, 398, 401, 419, 420, 426, 427, 436, 589*

A Girl in Hiding (cont.) (11–14) 790, 791 **8**(a), **14**(a) (b), **15**(d), **20**(f), **44**(e), **62**(a) *119, 129, 192, 197, 207, 215, 250, 262, 264, 268, 277, 582*

729 Incident 823 **3**(b), **7**(f), **63**(d) *187, 252, 253, 255, 269, 270, 273, 492, 527*

730 Say this City has Ten Million Souls **1**(d), **6**(a) (e), **21** (a), **22**(c) *252, 253, 265, 269, 516, 517, 518, 527, 568*

731 Telephone Conversation **20**(e), **56** (b), **67**(f), **73**(g), **82**(a) *192, 252, 253, 269, 273, 527*

732 Christians and Society **6**(e), **82**(e), **100**(b), **102**(f) *170, 189, 193, 197, 200, 441, 564*

733 A Negro Teacher in the East End of London (1–2) **21**(h), **35**(g), **38**(e) *252, 253, 381, 382, 383, 384, 527*

734 A Negro Teacher and his White Pupils 805 **43**(f), **48**(e), **61**(c) *252, 253, 374, 376, 377, 414, 419, 466, 527*

735 A Negro Teacher Asks for a Room (1–2) 824 **1**(a), **3**(b), **4**(g), **8**(d) *171, 192, 198, 252, 253, 273, 461, 479, 527*

736 A Negro Teacher and his Coloured Pupil (1–3) 825 **2**(d), **9**(f), **12**(a), **13**(d), **19**(a), **23**(a) *252, 253, 255, 265, 269, 274, 279, 281, 527*

737 What We Want 789 **1**(b) (c), **4**(d), **7**(a) *201, 203, 204, 386, 411, 412, 427, 428*

738 Society and Personality **4**(c) (e), **6**(d) (e) *189, 190, 191, 192, 193, 194, 195, 196*

739 Alcohol **1**(e), **11**(a), **15**(f) *164, 168, 175, 184, 185, 192, 587*

740 Wealth and Humanity **14**(a) (c) (d) (e) *203, 204, 411, 412, 439, 441, 570*

741 Money **14**(c) (d) (e) (f) *203, 204, 411, 412, 439, 441, 572*

742 Joy and Suffering **2**(e), **12**(c) (d), **13**(e) *125, 274, 368, 392, 420, 426, 430, 436*

743 Suffering and Sympathy **2**(a) (b) (c), **13**(e) *270, 273, 279, 281, 447, 584*

744 Four Walls 780 **20**(e) (f), **21**(b) (c) (e) *171, 187, 191, 198, 240, 242, 248, 387*

745 The Daily Grind **9**(a) (d) (e) (f) *247, 250, 301, 368, 414, 426*

746 The Young Man **11**(d), **12**(e), **15** (b), **25**(f) *201, 219, 311, 312, 315, 427, 428, 436*

747 The Gift of Courage **22**(a) (c) (d), **57**(b) *200, 215, 240, 379, 382, 383, 384, 385*

748 The Real Enemy is Within 778 **1**(e), **5**(e), **15**(c), **21**(b) *258, 270, 271, 281, 382, 386*

749 The Fellowship of Pain **2**(a) (b) (c) (d) (e) *368, 515, 516, 517, 518, 532, 568*

750 Babiy Yar 728 (14) **4**(a) (g), **22**(a), **24**(f), **37**(b) *272, 273, 274, 279, 281, 570*

751 Prisoner of the Japanese (1–5) **5** (d) (e), **9**(d), **12**(c), **21**(h), **23**(b) (c) (d), **24**(b) (c) (d), **27**(c), **41**(a), **43** (d), **104**(a) *252, 253, 255, 258, 264, 265, 267, 268, 270, 271, 274, 277, 279, 281*

752 In Time of Death **12**(b), **25**(e), **59** (e) (f) *369, 447, 461, 497, 498, 510, 511, 512*

753 The First Explosion of the Atomic

Bomb 804 **45**(a), **46**(a) (b) *130, 155, 490, 500, 520, 522, 523*

754 Creation in Reverse **45**(c) (d) (e), **49**(c), **52**(a) *124, 132, 268, 311, 315, 441, 490, 500*

755 An Atomic Experiment 808 **47**(a), **54**(a), **62**(d) *118, 122, 145, 155, 268, 490, 500*

756 No Man is an Island **58**(f), **61**(d), **64**(c), **82**(e), **83**(b) *272, 273, 281, 294, 518*

757 Thoughts on Remembrance Sunday 809 **8**(a) (b) (c) (e) (f) *192, 206, 265, 266, 268, 520, 522, 523, 570*

758 And Death Shall Have No Dominion **58**(a) (b) (c) (d), **59**(d) (e), **60** (a) (b), **84**(f) (g) *117, 302, 303, 304, 515, 516, 517, 518*

759 The Young and the Dead **2**(a) (b) (c) (e), **57**(b), **59**(e) *149, 302, 303, 304, 510, 511, 515, 516, 517*

760 Life after Death **61**(a) (c) (e), **62** (a) (b) (e) *168, 189, 190, 195, 197, 198, 200, 201*

761 Doin' the Right Thing **31**(d), **102** (b), **106**(b) *160, 161, 162, 163, 168, 169, 183, 193*

762 Legend **24**(a) (b) (c), **37**(a), **38** (d), **97**(b) *200, 201, 215, 240, 382, 383, 384, 385*

763 Daedalus and Icarus 3(a) *145, 219, 456, 490, 535*

764 A Cool Square comes to the Rescue **61**(d), **105**(a) (b) *192, 198, 215, 217, 481*

765 Coping with Grandpa **11**(b), **12**(c), **31**(b) (d) *254, 259, 261, 269, 281, 517, 519*

766 The Emperor's New Clothes (1–3) **35**(a) (b) (c) (d) (e) (f) (g) *203, 210, 396, 397, 403, 411*

767 King Midas **1**(c) (d) (e), **14**(c) (d) (e) (f), **36**(d) *203, 204, 411, 412, 439, 441, 572*

768 The Sadhu and the Snake (1–3) **1** (c) (d), **3** (d) (e), **13** (a) (b) (c) (d) (e) *255, 263, 269, 273, 281, 388, 389, 390*

769 Chopsticks **6**(c) (d) (e), **21**(i) (k) *263, 273, 372, 496*

770 Circe **46**(c) (d), **49**(c), **70**(a) *141, 155, 163, 168, 169, 183, 190, 201*

771 Throwin' a Party for Junior **68**(a), **70**(c), **98**(b) (c), **99**(a) *148, 172, 184, 189, 194, 200, 205*

772 A Fable for Tomorrow **91**(a) (b), **92**(a) (b) (c), **99**(b), **101**(c) *130, 155, 268, 441, 520, 521, 522, 536*

773 Love and Hate 657 **66**(b), **67**(a), **68**(d) *255, 258, 259, 262, 266, 277, 281, 456, 533*

774 God and our Neighbour 703 **11**(b), **13**(a) (b) (c), **102**(a) *379, 388, 419, 421, 436, 568, 584*

775 Attitudes to Children: A Contrast 714 **47**(b) (c) (e), **63**(d) *149, 193, 197, 380, 389, 419, 421, 521*

776 How to be First: A Contrast 717 **82** (e) (f), **84**(c), **98**(a), **99**(e) *193, 281, 421, 505, 515, 532*

777 Unhappiness 723 (1–4) **25**(a) (d), **37**(b) (f), **66**(b) (c) (d) (e), **67**(b) (c) (e), **71**(a) *192, 208, 215, 294*

778 Trusting God 651, 748 **5**(e), **15**(c), **19**(e) (f), **21**(b) *444, 448, 465, 466, 469, 474*

779 Your Father 704 **8**(f), **31**(a) (c) (d) *147, 148, 259, 260, 261*

780 Rules 744 **20**(e) (f), **21**(b) (c) (e) *171, 187, 191, 198, 240, 242*

781 Excuses 707 **20**(b), **34**(c) *396, 397, 432, 433, 435*

782 Superiority 689, 690 **3**(c) (d) (f) *165, 183, 398, 399, 400, 401, 416*

783 Praise 622, 631, 641 **61**(e), **87**(e) *122, 289, 311*

784 What Artists Believe 633, 662 **45**(c) **49**(e), **85**(a) *116, 117, 121, 124, 130*

785 Art and Religion 672 **14**(d), **63**(a) (b) *120, 130, 373, 466, 471*

786 Fragrant Gardens for the Blind 685, 687 **87**(g) *124, 128, 373, 471, 505*

787 A Blind Gardener 686 **61**(c), **62**(e) *124, 128, 373, 505*

788 Humility 693, 696 **3**(d) (e), **65**(c) *398, 399, 400, 401*

789 Learn to Know Yourself 737 **12**(a) *196, 198, 202, 409*

790 Ignorance of Self 728 (11–13) **86** (d) *192, 195, 202, 409*

791 Self-Knowledge 728 (11–13) **86** (d) *190, 194, 210*

792 Peace 697 **61**(b), **66**(d), **67**(c) *168, 170, 175, 192, 197, 265*

793 God's Service 663 **41**(a) (c) *129, 387, 484, 486, 487*

794 God in His Creation 633, 668, 681 **45**(c), **85**(a) *116, 117, 121, 124, 130, 132*

795 Detachment 706 **8**(e), **9**(a), **73**(g) *279, 281, 427, 432, 464*

796 Charity and Self-Seeking 667 **14**(a) *263, 388, 389, 390, 419, 420, 421, 436*

797 God and Profit 627 **63**(a) (b) (d) *481, 482, 539*

798 Jacob 621 **73**(k), **102**(c) *381, 430, 444, 470, 472, 474, 486*

799 Art 622 **61**(a), **62**(b) (e) *309, 310, 311, 312, 313*

800 Religions 628 **22**(a) (d) *301, 302, 303, 304*

801 How we know God 651 **19**(c) (e) *444, 447, 448, 465, 466, 469*

802 The Instinct for Worship 650 **26**(a) *116, 117, 119, 122, 410*

803 Wisdom 646 **35**(c), **87**(b) (c) *395, 409, 450, 451, 456*

804 War 710, 753 **32**(e) (f) *490, 500, 520, 522, 523*

805 Slander 734 **43**(f) *374, 376, 377, 378*

806 Wrong-Doing 750, 756 **4**(g) *272, 273, 281, 294*

807 Politics and Religion 754 **52**(a) *267, 268, 311, 441, 490*

808 Man's Greatness 755 **47**(a), **62**(d) *175, 192, 193, 195, 198*

809 Human Nature 754, 757 **8**(a) (f) *265, 266, 267, 269*

810 The Word 641 **17**(a) (e) *117, 136, 210, 286, 351, 357, 372*

811 Grumbling 716, 717 **98**(a) *193, 198, 281, 419, 421, 429*

812 Self 721 **102**(f), **103**(d) *189, 198, 253, 263, 268, 281, 386, 580*

813 Love: The Subtlest Force 674 **61**(d) **63**(d) *192, 194, 198, 410, 584*

814 Self-Restraint and Sacrifice 673 **14** (c) (d) (e) *189, 190, 194, 195, 197, 199, 201, 203*

815 Sacrifice and Joy 617, 678 **7**(d) *125, 133, 380, 443, 609*

816 Trouble 618 **5**(d), **21**(a) *210, 263, 286, 459, 474, 566, 577*

817 A Valiant Spirit 725 **22**(d) *379, 418, 427, 428, 430*

818 Love: The Humblest Force 615, 616 **19**(d), **21**(k) *192, 194, 198, 410, 584*

819 Man and Religion 612 **22**(a) (c) (d) *299, 300, 301, 476, 479*

820 A Definition of God 616 **92**(b) (c) *463, 464, 469, 470, 472*

821 Religion and Morality 675, 680 **32** (c), **33**(e), **35**(c) *449, 450, 454, 456, 457, 459*

822 Justice and Sympathy 713, 726 **13** (a) (b) *193, 196, 200, 419, 494, 496 517, 519, 521*

823 Sorry no Coloured: and a Comment 729 **7**(f), **63**(d) *252, 253, 265, 281, 527*

824 No Coloured: and a Comment 735 **4** (g), **6**(d) *192, 198, 252, 253, 273, 527*

825 English Only: and a Comment 736 **9**(f), **12**(a), **13**(d) *252, 253, 265, 281, 527*

# Acknowledgements

The Publisher's thanks are due to the following copyright owners who have kindly given us permission to use their material:
African Universities Press for a poem by Wole Soyinka from *Reflections*, ed. Frances Ademola; George Allen & Unwin Ltd for extracts from Leslie Tizard's *Facing Life and Death* and for 'The Mahratta Ghats' from Alun Lewis' *Ha! Ha! Among the Trumpets*; The Alpine Journal for an extract from John Emery's *The Runcible Cat* (Nov. 1961); Angus & Robertson (U.K.) Ltd for a poem by Judith Wright; Jim Bates for five poems; Thomas Blackburn for his poem 'Hospital for Defectives'; Chris Blackwell for his poem *Generation' Sin*; The Bodley Head for extracts from G. K. Chesterton's *Orthodoxy* and E. R. Braithwaite's *To Sir, with Love*; Jonathan Cape Ltd and New Directions Publishing Corporation for Denise Levertov's poem 'Solitude' from *The Jacob's Ladder*; The Cambridge University Press and the Episcopal Church in Scotland for extracts from the Litany in *An Order of Holy Communion*; the text of the 1662 *Book of Common Prayer* is Crown Copyright and the extracts used herein are reproduced by permission; the Catholic Truth Society for prayers from *Prayer Book for Catholic Seafarers, Apostleship of the Sea*; the Central Board of Finance of the Church of England for prayers from the *Prayer Book as Proposed in 1928* printed with the permission of the holders of the copyright; the Church of England Council for the Deaf for extracts from the Rev. T. H. Sutcliffe's *Soundless Worship*; Christian Education Movement for a prayer from *World of Strange Contrasts* and *An Act of Worship for the London Festival*; the Synod of the Church of South India for prayers from *The Book of Common Worship of the Church of South India*; William Collins Sons & Co. Ltd for poems from Carl Burke's *God is for Real, Man*, an extract from Ernest Gordon's *Miracle on the River Kwai* and for extracts from Yevgery Yevtushenko's *A Precocious Autobiography*; Dacre Press, A. & C. Black Ltd for extracts from Dom Gregory Dix's *The Shape of the Liturgy*; Darton, Longman & Todd Ltd for 'Gentle Christ' from Ewan Hooper and Ernest Marvin's *A Man Dies* and an extract from David Cox's *What Christians Believe*; J. M. Dent & Sons Ltd for an extract from *The Mirror of Perfection*, trans. Robert Steele (Everyman's Library Text), and the poems 'In the Beginning', 'The Force that Through the Green Fuse' and 'And Death shall have no Dominions' from Dylan Thomas's *Collected Poems*; The Dolmen Press Ltd for 'Carol' from Thomas Kinsella's *Down-Stream*; the Publications Committee of the Episcopal Church in Scotland for a prayer from the *Scottish Book of Common Prayer*; the Epworth Press for a prayer from R. E. Davies's *Praying Together* and for extracts from David Head's *The Stammerer's Tongue*; Essex Music Ltd for Sydney Carter's song 'Standing in the Rain'; Evans Brothers Ltd for an extract from Alan Burgess's *The Small Woman*; Faber & Faber Ltd for an extract from T. S. Eliot's *Murder in the Cathedral*, 'The Killing' from Edwin Muir's *Selected Poems*, 'Jesus and His Mother' from Thom Gunn's *The Sense of Movement*, for an extract from Helen Thomas's *As it Was and World without End*, for 'i thank you god for this most amazing' from e. e. cummings *Selected Poems 1923–1958*, for five verses from 'Bread and the Stars' from Vernon Watkin's *Cypress and Acacia*, for 'I think continually of those who were truly Great' from Stephen Spender's *Collected Poems*, for 'Say this City has Ten Million Souls' from W. H. Auden's *Collected Shorter Poems 1927–1957* and for extracts from Stuart Jackman's *The Davidson Affair*; John Farquharson Ltd for an extract from James Baldwin's *The Fire Next Time*; Galliard Ltd and the author for 'I am the Man' from The Rev. Peter Allen's *Feed Us Now* and Sydney Carter's songs 'Lord of the Dance', 'The Devil Wore a Crucifix' and 'When I needed a Neighbour'—© 1965 Sydney Carter. Assigned 1968; M. H. Gill & Sons Ltd, Dublin for extracts from Michel Quoist's *Prayers for Life*; The Grail (England) for extracts from *The*

*Psalms: A New Translation*; Victor Gollancz Ltd for a poem from Barbara Green's and Victor Gollancz's *God of a Hundred Names* and an extract from Robert Jungk's *Brighter than a Thousand Suns*; Hamish Hamilton Ltd and Marie Rodell, Literary Trustee, for an extract from Rachel Carson's *Silent Spring*; Harold Ober Associates Inc. for a poem by Langston Hughes; Harper & Row Inc. for a poem from Countee Cullen's *On These I Stand*; George G. Harrap & Co. Ltd for extracts from *Man of Everest*, Tenzing's Autobiography as told to J. Ramsey Ullman; Wm Heinemann & Co. Ltd for extracts from Malcolm Boyd's *Are You Running with me, Jesus?*, Morris West's *Children of the Sun*, Wilfred Noyce's *They Survived*, Antoine de Saint-Exupery's *Wind, Sand and Stars*, Richard Church's *Over the Bridge*, Eve Curie's *Madame Curie*; and R. K. Narayan's *An Astrologer's Day*; Hodder & Stoughton Ltd for extracts from Joy Davidman's *Smoke on the Mountain*, Colette Richard's *Climbing Blind*, Sir Edmund Hillary from *The Ascent of Everest* by Sir John Hunt, based on the original dispatches to *The Times* from Brig. Sir John Hunt and other members of the Everest Expedition, Sir Edmund Hillary's *School-house in the Clouds* and for a poem from G. A. Studdert Kennedy's *The Unutterable Beauty*; Mrs Willa Muir and the Hogarth Press for extracts from Edwin Muir's *An Autobiography*; Rupert Hart-Davis Ltd for poems from R. S. Thomas's *Pieta*; The Rev. R. S. Ingamells, Bishop's Youth Chaplain, Norwich for extracts; Longmans Green & Co. Ltd for prayers from *An Anthology of Prayers*, compiled by A. S. T. Fisher, G. C. Binyon for a prayer from *Prayers for the City of God*, for a poem from Patricia Beer's *Loss of the Magyar* and an extract from Pierre d'Harcourt's *The Real Enemy*; Lutterworth Press for prayers from Beryl Bye's *Prayers at Breakfast*; Mac-Gibbon & Kee Ltd for Aldous Huxley's Introduction to Danilo Dolci's *To Feed the Hungry*; Macmillan & Co. Ltd and the Trustees of the Tagore Estate for extracts from Rabindranath Tagore's *Collected Poems and Plays* and the Trustees of the Hardy Estate for 'The Oxen' from *The Collected Poems of Thomas Hardy*; Marshall, Morgan & Scott Ltd and Bernard Geis Associates of New York for an extract from the Rev. David Wilkerson's *The Cross and the Switchblade*; the Methodist Publishing House for a prayer from the *Methodist Covenant Service;* Valentine Mitchell & Co. Ltd and Mr Otto Frank for extracts from *The Diary of Anne Frank;* Otto Nathan, Trustee to the Estate of Albert Einstein for extracts from Einstein's *Mein Weltbild*; *The Observer* for extracts from Colin Cross's 'Man Against the Sea' (28 May 1967), Laurence Dobie's 'Dying without God' (12 March 1967) and Paul Jennings's 'Facing up to Affliction'; Oxford University Press for prayers from *Prayers for Every Day*, ed. Vicars Bell, from *Daily Prayer*, ed. Milner-White and Briggs, John Baillie's *A Diary of Private Prayer*, 'Easter Hymn to St Mary Magdalen' and 'Whitsunday 1948' from Katherine Watson's *The Source and Other Poems* and for extracts from Simone Weil's *Selected Essays* and *Seventy Letters*; Penguin Books Ltd for 'A Day in the Quarry' from Miroslav Holub's *Selected Poems*, poems from Yevgeny Yevtushenko's *Selected Poems* and for extracts from Peter Laurie's *Drugs*, Mary M. Innes's *Metamorphoses of Ovid*, Tolstoy's *Resurrection*, trans. Rosemary Edmonds and Carson McCullers's *The Heart is a Lonely Hunter*; Pilgrim Publications, Sale, Cheshire for extracts from *Benedictus, Benidicatur*; Putnam & Co. for an extract from Roger Bannister's *First Four Minutes*; Random House Inc. Alfred A. Knopf Inc. for extracts from Kahlil Gilbran's *The Prophet*; Routledge & Kegan Paul Ltd for an extract from Simone Weil's *Waiting on God*; Martin Secker & Warburg Ltd. for an extract from Dennis Gabor's *Inventing the Future*; Sneed & Ward Inc. for a poem from Caryll Houselander's *The Flowering Tree*; S.C.M. Press Ltd for prayers from *Epilogues and Prayers*, ed. Barclay, *Contemporary Prayers for Public Worship*, ed. Caryl Micklem, *A Book of Prayers for Schools* and *A Devotional Diary*; the Society of Authors and the literary representative of the Estate of the late John Masefield for an extract from John Masefield's *The Trial of Jesus*; the Society of St Francis and Brother William for 'Can it be True?' from *Songs of a Sinner*; Sphere Books for an extract from Martha Gellhorn's *The Face of War*; S.P.C.K. for prayers from *Alternative Services* (Second Series); *An Order for Holy Communion* and an extract from Austin Farrer's *Lord, I Believe*; Sally Trench and 'The Listener' for an extract from an article (9 May 1968); Mrs N. le P. Warner for extracts from William Temple's *Daily Readings*; A. P. Watt & Son Ltd and the Executors of H. G. Wells for an extract from *The Outline of History*; The World's Work (1913) Ltd for extracts from Billy Graham's *Peace with God*.